PRAISE FOR *THE TRANSLUCENT REVOLUTION*

"Arjuna has given us the most comprehensive, elegant, and vital guide to the current stage of human transformation that I have read since Marilyn Ferguson's *The Aquarian Conspiracy*. It is must reading for all of us working toward a more positive future."

— Barbara Marx Hubbard, author, speaker, president of The Foundation for Conscious Evolution

"*The Translucent Revolution* is a brilliant and timely missive from an author who is deeply in touch with the pulse and essence of our evolution and our awakening. At a time when nothing but bad news seems to be the tenor of the day, this beautiful message emerges — uplifting, inspiring, and revitalizing the reader with a new seeing of the radical truth of our time. Clearly and precisely written, with eye-opening stories and examples, Ardagh leads the reader through a new map of our time and its possibilities and power. He draws on some of the great thinkers and mystics that we share this time in history with and explores distinctions that empower and further clarify who we are and the profound possibility of life. An excellent read and great piece of work."

— Lynne Twist, author of *The Soul of Money*

"*The Translucent Revolution* delivers a cumulative punch. It is a rare combination of reason, passion, and spiritual insight. After you put this book down you know that a great shift in consciousness is already underway and that the path to a sane, peaceful, and sustainable future has been seeded in our time. Arjuna Ardagh offers us substantial hope. At a time when the human story has been in a prolonged eclipse, he provides evidence to support a transformation of global society from the inside out."

— James O'Dea, president of the Institute of Noetic Sciences

"This is a brilliant book — really many books in one. I couldn't put it down. It is chock full of fascinating information, valuable insights, useful techniques and great wisdom. I would highly recommend this to anyone on a spiritual path. It is both a powerful mirror to our common experiences and a handy guidebook for the part of the journey we are all currently on."

— Jack Canfield, co-creator of the *Chicken Soup for the Soul*® series,
author of *The Success Principles*

"Translucent Arjuna has penned a luminous contribution to the individual and collective awakening of us all. I heartily recommend this book to anyone seeking inner knowledge, self-realization, and enlightenment."

— Lama Surya Das, author of *Awakening the Buddha Within*,
founder of the Dzogchen Center

"*The Translucent Revolution* is going to have a timely impact on the national conversation, picking up where Paul Ray's description of the "Cultural Creatives" leaves off. One of the distinguishing characteristics of Cultural Creatives is that they tend to feel that they're alone, and that society's dominant institutions not only do not reflect, but are at variance to their most precious values. *The Translucent Revolution* may simultaneously confirm this perception and stimulate the Cultural Creatives to finally begin connecting with others who share their values, get organized, and work together to create the world they want. It's certainly about time, don't you think?"

— Eric Utne, founder of *Utne* magazine,
editor of *Cosmo Doogood's Urban Almanac*

"Not since Marilyn Ferguson's *The Aquarian Conspiracy* has there been such a rich collection of views covering so many dimensions of the unfolding new paradigm on conscious awakening. A most valuable resource for personal and social evolution."

— Peter Russell, author of *From Science to God* and *The Global Brain*

"Engaging, enlightening, and even entertaining, *The Translucent Revolution* is a powerful handbook for the soul. With great clarity and deep heart, Arjuna offers the reader a rich feast of possibility and everyday practices for humanity's greatest quest."

— Mary Manin Morrissey, author of *Building Your Field of Dreams*,
founder of the Living Enrichment Center

"Arjuna Ardagh has created an insightful historical document and a festive celebration of inspiration. Ardagh has connected what at first may appear as unrelated ideas and activities into a coherent whole that explains the contemporary phenomenon of the translucent revolution. He frames his perspectives clearly and shows how they are manifest in the lives of accessible people. Readers will realize that the transformation of themselves and their world is within their grasp. I recommend this book to anyone who wants to live a more daring and authentic life."

— Joseph L. Subbiondo,
president of the California Institute of Integral Studies

"Compelling, compassionate, and clear, *The Translucent Revolution* is a comprehensive exploration of one of the most important and hopeful movements of our time. Arjuna takes us on a journey to the very essence of transformation and healing, and in so doing shines a light through a timeless truth: What we are looking for is what is looking."

— Gay and Kathlyn Hendricks, authors of *Conscious Living* and
Attracting Genuine Love, founders of The Hendricks Institute

the
TRANSLUCENT
REVOLUTION

ALSO BY ARJUNA ARDAGH

How About Now?
The Last Laugh (a novel)
Relaxing into Clear Seeing: Interactive Tools in the Service of Self-Awakening
Living Essence Tapes series (audiocassette collection)

the
TRANSLUCENT
REVOLUTION

How People Just Like You
Are WAKING UP and
CHANGING the World

ARJUNA ARDAGH

New World Library
Novato, California

New World Library
14 Pamaron Way
Novato, California 94949

Cover photograph by Idana Bluem
Text design and typography by Tona Pearce Myers

Library of Congress Cataloging-in-Publication Data
Ardagh, Arjuna.
 The translucent revolution : how people just like you are waking up and changing the world
/ Arjuna Ardagh.— 1st ed.
     p.   cm.
Includes bibliographical references and index.
ISBN 1-57731-468-9 (pbk. : alk. paper)
1. Spiritual life. 2. Self-actualization (Psychology)—Religious aspects. 3. Social service.
4. Consciousness. 5. Self. 6. Conduct of life. I. Title.
BL624.A72 2005
204'.4—dc22   2005002752

First printing, June 2005
ISBN 1-57731-468-9
ISBN-13 978-1-57731-468-4

 Printed in Canada on 100% postconsumer waste recycled paper

A proud member of the Green Press Initiative

Distributed to the trade by Publishers Group West

10   9   8   7   6   5   4   3   2

For my sons, Abhi and Shuba,
and for all the children of this earth,
for they inherit both the fruits of our foolishness
as well as those of our awakening

CONTENTS

Part Three. Collective Translucence

FOREWORD

by Ken Wilber

It's a rather extraordinary, even historical, time we live in, and not just for the perils but the promise. The perils I'm sure you've heard plenty of. This is a book about the promise, or certainly one of the brightest of them: the chance to awaken, to radically awaken, to who and what you really are, beneath the everyday surface-chattering mind and the chronic self-contraction that hobble a brighter tomorrow. By the end of reading this book you will have, I believe, an undeniable sense of this greater awareness — in yourself, in society, in the world at large.

The reason this particular promise is so extraordinary lies in the history of the last three decades, the history of what has come to be known as "the human potential movement." Starting in the sixties, there was an extraordinary explosion of interest in Eastern religions, meditation, encounter groups, psychedelics, awareness training, est, yoga, New Age this and that, you name it. Some of it was good, some bad, some silly. And, believe me, we all dipped into the silly; I even chronicled it in *Boomeritis*. But out of that extraordinary experimental period — which produced, on the more serious side, both Humanistic Psychology and Transpersonal Psychology — we learned at least three important things about human growth and potentials.

One: There are many different *states of consciousness*. Ordinary states, altered states, stoned states, meditative states, hypnotic states, dream states, shamanic states, formless states, nondual states, hypnogogic states, entrained states, peak experiences, flow states, awakened states — and what all of that taught us was that "there are more things in heaven and earth than are dreamt of in your philosophy." Different states of consciousness disclose very different worlds, and an exploration of those many worlds of reality began.

Since most states of consciousness and peak experiences are variations on the three or four natural states of waking, dreaming, deep formless sleep, and unity, they were often grouped into those four general categories and given the names of *gross* (waking), *subtle* (dreaming), *causal* (formless), and *nondual* (unity) states. This book particularly explores variations on a unity state or an awakened state of consciousness — an awakening or peak experience and its dramatic impact on people's lives, including people like you, as the subtitle has it.

But one thing was certain among those who investigated these issues seriously: the type of world that you perceive depends in large measure on the state of consciousness you are in. Different states not only perceive different worlds, they bring them forth, they co-create them, they have a hand in their very texture. The subject does not just perceive the object, it helps create it. But then, we really knew that since Kant and even before, but never had it been so palpably demonstrated to so many people in so short a time. Serious writers and researchers henceforth could never pretend that there was simply one world lying around and waiting to be perceived. No, my friend, the world that is perceived is a co-creation of your consciousness. Change your consciousness and you change your world.

Two: In addition to *states* of consciousness, there are *stages* of consciousness. What's the difference? States are *temporary*, stages are *permanent*. Okay, but what's a stage? Stages are the way that evolution catapults over chaos and into increasing spheres of organization and inclusion. A simple, typical example: atoms to molecules to cells to organisms. Each of those is a stage, and each stage transcends and includes its predecessor, so that evolution is indeed a series of nested spheres or *holons* — wholes that are parts of larger wholes, indefinitely it seems. And thus there is a directionality built into evolution, from atoms to molecules to cells: you never find molecules occurring before atoms, or cells occurring before molecules. There are no known exceptions to this anywhere in the universe, and so "stages" and "evolution" and "growth" appear to be virtually synonymous.

Examples of stages in human growth are too numerous to catalog here. There are stages of psychosexual development, linguistic development, self-development, embryology, physiology, neuroanatomy, and...well, the list is endless. But they are all variations on sequences like letters, words, sentences, paragraphs. Each stage in that sequence again transcends and includes its predecessors in a development that is envelopment; there is thus greater and greater wholeness and inclusion in each stage; and hence, as with natural evolution, there is a directionality inherent in the sequence — you never have words before letters or sentences before words, and there are no known exceptions in any human culture.

What does that have to do with human potentials? Just as it was discovered that there are higher states, it was discovered that there are *higher stages of human development*, stages that went considerably beyond the conventional stages of development thought possible by orthodox psychologists. These higher stages are inherent potentials of all human beings, although not everybody lives up to them.

Abraham Maslow was one of the first great investigators of these higher stages of human potentials, and he found that in addition to the typical, normal stages that humans possess — physiological needs, safety needs, belongingness needs, and self-esteem needs — there are higher stages of self-actualization and self-transcendence needs. He called the latter *being needs*, in contrast to the former *deficiency needs*, because the latter came out of an awareness of superabundance, the former, feelings of lack and deficiency. As with all true stages, they emerged in an order that could not be reversed, and each built upon and included its predecessor.

Let me give one famous example, the stage conception of Carol Gilligan. In her book *In a Different Voice* (and in subsequent works), Gilligan outlined four major stages of female moral development, which she called *selfish, care, universal care*, and *integrated*. Other words for those stages might be *egocentric* — I care only for myself; *ethnocentric* — I care for my tribe, my country, my nation; *worldcentric* — I care for all human beings, regardless of race, color, sex, or creed; and *kosmocentric* — where I integrate the masculine and feminine in myself, and, I would add, extend care to all sentient beings without exception. Like all stages, the move from egocentric to ethnocentric to worldcentric to kosmocentric is a sequential movement of increasing consciousness, care, and envelopment. As with every other stage sequence we have looked at, nature indeed builds holons upon holons upon holons...a series of ever-expanding wholeness, consciousness, care, and embrace.

We just didn't know the embrace could go all the way to infinity. But that is exactly what the human potential movement discovered: in the farther reaches of human nature, in the realms of the self-transcendence needs, in the deepest reaches of your very own Self and your ever-present I AMness, people reported being one with a Ground of Being, one with Spirit, one with infinity, a radiant riot of the all-encompassing, call it what you will....

And not just as a passing state, but as a permanent trait — a permanent stage of competence acquisition. Not that you always live up to it, but that you always have access to it (which is what makes this an awakened stage and not just an awakened state). This is just like language acquisition or any other stage competence: once you learn language, it means you have permanent access to it, not that you are always talking.

Just as there are many ways to classify states, there are many ways to classify stages. Some researchers used three stages, some used five, others used seven or more. And many different names and terms were also used as researchers looked at different aspects of various stages. Theorists in this book who have presented or utilized stage conceptions include David Deida, Duane Elgin, H.A. Almaas, Jean Houston, Fred Kofman, Jennifer Garcia, Andrew Cohen, Sofia Diaz, Frances Vaughan, and many others.

But a few very important points: in the modern conception, stages are very fluid and flowing affairs, not stacked on top of each other but enveloping and embracing and flowing into each other. They are often called *waves of consciousness* instead of stages of consciousness to emphasize that important discovery. Another important discovery is that there seems to be no highest stage or wave, it just keeps going and going, holon upon holon in an ever-receding rainbow of wholeness, with no end point, no omega point, only an ever-expanding horizon of consciousness and care, reaching to infinity but never resting in it.

Three: The third major significant item that researchers learned is how states and stages relate to each other. Neither states nor stages alone can account for the evidence. If you look only at the stage conceptions, for example, it appears that you can only have a spiritual experience if you climb through Maslow's stages all the way to the highest, transpersonal, self-transcendence stage, and then you get the prize. But we all know people — often including ourselves — who have had spiritual experiences or peak experiences and might not be at the top of the pyramid of growth!

But many early theorists mistakenly concluded that therefore there are no stages of growth, so they championed what amounted to nothing but states. Yet it soon became obvious that states alone won't work, because those imply that all you have to do is have some earth-shaking awakening experiences and you will be spiritual, but researchers soon found that virtually anybody can have those peak awakening experiences, even people at the ethnocentric stages, and all it did was make them more ethnocentric. Not good.

But that was the third major discovery, the relation of states and stages: namely, *you can have a profound altered state experience at virtually any stage you are at.* For simplicity's sake, let's use Carol Gilligan's four stages (egocentric, ethnocentric, worldcentric, kosmocentric), and the four major states (gross, subtle, causal, nondual). You can have one of those state experiences at each of those stages. That gives us sixteen types of experiential possibilities, and research found instances of all of them.

For example, if you are at an ethnocentric stage of development and you have a unity-state peak experience of being one with everything or one with a ground of being, you might interpret that as an experience of oneness with Jesus and conclude that nobody can be saved unless they accept Jesus as their personal savior (hence the "ethnocentric" nature of the interpretation — you must belong to this one group in order to be saved). But if you are at an egocentric stage and have the same experience, you might believe that you yourself are Jesus Christ. And if you are at a kosmocentric or integral stage and have that nondual peak experience, you will likely conclude that you and all sentient beings without exception are one with spirit in the timeless here and now.

See how that grid of possibilities works? You can be at virtually any stage of consciousness and have a peak experience of virtually any state of consciousness — and just as important, you will interpret the state according to the stage. That grid is now called the Wilber-Combs Matrix after the two astonishingly bright fellows who independently stumbled upon it. (For stages of development, see *Integral Psychology*, which gives charts of over one hundred models East and West; for the Wilber-Combs Matrix, see *The Eye of Spirit*.)

Now, let me try and bring all this together. I earlier pointed out that, in many cases, if people had strong awakening experiences or other strong peak experiences, it often tended to reinforce the stage they were at. For example, I mentioned that somebody at an ethnocentric stage can have an awakening experience and it just makes them more ethnocentric. We all know examples of reborn Christians who have had very powerful state experiences; they glow, they are radiant, they are translucent, and they are fascists. This is because they are still at an ethnocentric stage, and, bless them, think that Jesus is the one and only way.

But research also found a riveting fact: the more you are dunked into altered or nonordinary or meditative states, the more quickly you actually move through any stage sequence that was tested. In other words, if you take up meditation, for example, which *repeatedly* exposes you to awakened states, and then you are given, say, the Loevinger test — a very famous and well-documented test of developmental stages — you will not skip those stages (there have been no examples found of skipped stages, for the same reason that you cannot go from letters to sentences and skip words). *But you will move through those stages at a profoundly accelerated rate.* It's not uncommon to find that the percentage of the population at Loevinger's two highest stages (which are versions of integral), which normally is about 5 percent, goes to nearly 40 percent after four years of meditation. No other technique — not psychotherapy, not breath work, not body work, not Jungian analysis, not psychoanalysis, not Gestalt, not anything — has ever proven such an accelerated rate of development. And, in fact, these kinds of findings have become the basis of integral practice and training (www.integralinstitute.org).

So what does that mean? Very simply, the more you are dunked, or simply nudged, into awakened states, the more translucent you will become. And the book you now hold in your hands is a book about that simple but profound equation.

This is a book about the translucent revolution, a revolution that began in the sixties but has matured into an understanding embodied in the three factors I mentioned, and a book that can indeed change you, and change the world, if seen in the light of those factors. This book does not deal with stages of consciousness, which might seem a deficiency, given the book's claims. But I think that, although the criticism is valid, it is beside the point for what this book is trying to do. Worrying about which stage you might be at in this or that developmental line is not the point. If you choose to grow at all, you must begin to open yourself to wider experiences, deeper truths, higher realizations; and allow yourself — or push yourself, or simply nudge yourself — into wider states of consciousness and attitudes and perspectives and experiences.

What is so richly generous about this book is that each chapter not only describes a different aspect or trait of the translucent revolution and how that directly relates to your own life, it gives a wonderful series of experiential exercises — labeled "nudges" — that can help move you into a more expanded state or attitude, and therefore the cumulative effect of doing these exercises is that, no matter what wave you are at, this might indeed help your own growth and evolution into higher and wider and deeper waves, with each wave becoming not only more whole but more translucent.

Translucent to what? Well, my friend, please read this book and find out, this book of wonder and relish, radiance and release, and you might find your very own self becoming more and more translucent, even as you read. Whereupon, dimly worn on the horizon, shimmering in mists and memories of a Self realized but not yet confessed, find your answer in a release and recognition deeply your own yet shared by all. In that ever-realized, ever-receding infinity, you might seize the secret of all three historical factors rolled into one, that you can indeed begin to change the world by changing your deepest consciousness, so that the translucent revolution will reach ignition in the only place it could possibly ever begin: with the one and only Spirit who is reading this page — right here, right now, right *you* — but a you that goes out of you and into infinity, with a wink wink, nudge nudge, if you get my evolutionary drift, with waves and streams, and waking and dreams, rushing to the ever-present ocean of I AMness.

INTRODUCTION

From Islands to Archipelago

Robert had it all: the beach house in Malibu, the latest SUV, designer clothes, the right connections. He also had a small drinking problem, and a few personal difficulties to resolve at home. He had made his money in California real estate, and when the market crashed in the late eighties, so did Robert. He went from a net worth of millions to bankruptcy. He lost the house, many of his friends, and his confidence. By 1992 he was thinking about killing himself.

Late one evening, he was out taking a walk. He stopped and stood motionless, his mood blacker than the night. He had a thought, a simple thought. "I am finished," his mind announced.

He still has trouble explaining what happened next.

"I was overcome by a sense of relief," he reports. "A sudden feeling of inexpressible freedom. I even began to laugh out loud. My body was filled with happiness, as if I was suddenly getting a joke I'd been missing. For the first time I was feeling really good for no reason at all. I was totally here, in this moment. I could feel the trees around me, and hear the sounds without having to listen to thoughts telling me things needed to be different in some way. Everything was being experienced, but the 'me' was gone."

He went home and made love with his wife for the first time in seven months.

Later, Robert described his experience to a friend, a student of Eastern philosophies and meditation practices. Robert's epiphany, it seemed, had an obscure Eastern name. But his friend warned him it would pass, that he had tasted a fleeting glimpse of a state only great yogis could attain.

"It didn't pass, though," Robert says today. "I still have ups and downs, of course. Things still come up with my wife. My back still aches when it rains. But this mysterious sense of well-being I found that night, this feeling of lightness for no reason, has stayed with me for more than ten years. I couldn't get rid of it if I tried. In fact, it only seems to grow deeper and deeper. It is not happening to me, it is who I am."

A similar thing happened to Mary, while she was working the early shift at a vegetable-canning factory. Stephan was driving on the freeway, while Jacquelyn's awakening came in a hospital, after she gave birth to her third child. Michael went through a similar shift serving an eighty-seven-month prison sentence in a cell with thirty-two other inmates, and Douglas was hiking in the Himalayas. Some have come to this awakening through contact with a teacher, some from entering the depths of despair and coming out the other side. Some have woken up after years of meditation. For others this awakening has come out of the blue, for no apparent reason at all.

For me, the shift happened in 1991, at six in the morning, in a hotel room in India.

For more than two decades I had been "seeking." Even as a child, I intuitively felt there was more to life than what I saw around me. Growing up in London in the early sixties, I felt restriction and compromise in my mother, my father, my schoolteachers, and my extended family. They seemed to be surviving at life, rather than living it with zest. I knew there was something more than this.

Out of this longing, for what I could not name, I learned meditation at age fourteen. Over the next twenty years, I became an extremist spiritual seeker. I explored many techniques of meditation, radical therapy, and communal living. I did EST, yoga, primal scream therapy, tantra workshops, tai chi, long meditation retreats. You name it, I dove right in. I even ate tofu. Once.

I'd heard of a little-known teacher in northern India named H. W. L. Poonja. In 1991 I finally succumbed to a tremendous inner pull to visit him. He lived in a modest house on the outskirts of Lucknow. Within a second of entering the room, meeting his eyes, I knew the game was up. He meant business. Rather than teaching me this or that technique, he simply asked me, "Who is the one trying to become free? Who are you really?"

It took me a few days to catch on. I was a tough case. But finally, early one morning, I woke up in my hotel room and I tried to find *me*. For real. For the first time.

There was nothing there.

Where there should be an "I," a solid thing, there was only open space, absolutely at peace, always and eternally free. This was not a change in my condition, but rather a realization of what has always been true. More than illuminated with sudden insight, I was face-to-face with a lifelong, embarrassing oversight. I burst out laughing, right there in the hotel room, and did not stop for twenty minutes. What was seen in that moment has never since been overlooked.

I stayed with Poonjaji for about a year. One day he asked me to go back to the West to be a teacher.

"You must be joking," I replied.

"Yes," he laughed, "the Truth is a great joke, you must go and share it with your friends."

Back in America, it started with me and a few friends meeting in a living room, and before long dozens of people were showing up, five nights a week. Most of the people who attended these gatherings had a glimpse, at least, of awakening in their first or second meeting, similar to what had happened to me in Lucknow. They came back again and again because the realization was not stable and receded in their day-to-day life. They assumed I could help.

Sitting in a room, meditating with people they did not know, or going on a retreat, they would feel a deep sense of oneness. When they returned home to their troubled teenager, they found only separation. In the stillness of meditation everything was clearly perfect, unfolding as it should. That clarity was shattered the moment they opened a letter from the IRS. Work, family, busy schedules, relationships: all seemed to sabotage simplicity. These people longed to embody their awakening more deeply. Although the realization was of oneness, their habits were still loyal to separation. The realization was of limitlessness, but their thoughts were still full of fear and limitation.

Months of teaching turned into years. I traveled to other parts of the United States, and then in Europe. The situation was the same everywhere. The realization was incredibly easy; *living it* was the challenge.

When I took a good look at my relationship with my own family, with my friends, and with the earth, I had to admit I also saw a schism between the depth of realization and the quality of my life. I had fallen into the "guru" role out of a randomly bestowed gift of eloquence, a divine joke. Both the certainty of a reality deeper than the mind, and the longing to live it in every possible way, for real, was everywhere in the room when I was teaching, on both sides of the teacher-student dance.

I was fortunate to have many deep and honest friends who also played the role of "spiritual teacher." One was passing through a painful divorce, facing separation from his children. Another, deeply loved by her students, confided that she was lonely and often wondered why it was so hard to find the same depth of love in her personal life. Many struggled with financial issues. The list went on. These teachers were respected, successful, and of immense service to many people. Yet, like their students, they were challenged by the gap between the teaching and its embodiment in their daily lives.

So here we were, whether we wore a hat marked "teacher" or "student." The challenge was not so much in tasting enlightenment, but in living it. Faced with this conundrum, most of us turn for help to maps, models, and teachings, often from other peoples, other cultures, and other times. The majority of these maps were created by men and oriented to people who had decided to renounce the affairs of the world. Some of these teachings had been whispered in the desert, others were inscribed in caves by lamplight. Some had been chanted in India, others passed by word of mouth in Jerusalem. Despite their timeless beauty, seldom did they take into account the dramatic changes of lifestyle, the accelerated speed at which we now live.

When the reality of our day-to-day lives does not fit the map of choice, we often feel that something is wrong with us, that something is missing.

But we did not have these maps or concepts when we were born. We did not have them when we first felt the inner longing. The maps are all borrowed, all learned. Once we follow them, they become absolutes against which we measure our experience in this moment. The map says an "enlightened" person is free of the world; you reluctantly remember eyeing your neighbor's fancy new Porsche with relish — you just failed the test. The map tells you an enlightened person never gets caught up in feelings, especially "negative" ones; you remember the irritation you felt when someone took your parking space — failed again. The map tells you that a liberated person is beyond the desires of the flesh, and, well, let's face it, you're failing all day long.

As helpful as these maps and concepts can be, many of us have found that they simply do not fit the actuality of our reality, as it is. Jane, a single mother of two small boys, was looking for guidance from teachings given in India twenty-five hundred years ago. Mark, confronted by his sexual appetite and the wayward lifestyle of a musician on the road, turned to precepts originally given to celibate monks. And Jack, trying to satisfy both shareholders and employees in his role as CEO of a large company, sought inspiration from a yogi who had renounced worldly goods.

As time went by, my casual inquiry with a few friends turned into a full-blown investigation. I began to seek out the leading authorities on spiritual life in our time — people like Eckhart Tolle, Ram Dass, Byron Katie, and Jean Houston — to take a fresh look at our condition together, free from all maps and vantage points. I captured all these dialogues on tape.

The majority of our inherited maps point to some ultimate state of attainment or arrival, call it enlightenment, nirvana, liberation, or being born again. And the majority of us, as map readers, have ideas about what all this should look like in practice. I became much more interested in what people were actually experiencing in their lives. What maps were they following? What journey did they feel they were on? Had they reached a significant destination described in any of these maps? Do the variety of maps we refer to even agree about destinations? Are we, as some have suggested, "halfway up the mountain?" Or is it possible that the maps we have been using actually belong to a terrain and a time very different from the one we are now exploring? Maybe we are not climbing a mountain at all; maybe we are exploring a meadow or a forest. Which parts of the old maps turn out to be timeless truths? And what is just the bathwater we can throw out, as we cradle new-born awakening in this moment?

These are the questions I brought to the interviews. The 170 dialogues fill almost 250 cassette tapes; the transcripts comprise more than a million words. By asking the interviewees what they have experienced with their own students, readers, and extended circle of friends, I have also had indirect access to the experiences of millions of people in the United States and Europe. In addition, over the years, I have been able to survey more than thirteen thousand people in workshops, conferences, and festivals in many parts of the world. Finally, with the help of sociologists like Paul Ray and Duane Elgin, I have studied numerous polls and bodies of research that suggest a radical change in collective consciousness. I left the jury out during this long period of research, preferring to let our current condition speak for itself.

This book is the result. I have made some interesting discoveries, some of which I could have predicted, many of which have surprised me. For example, I had assumed that the current wave of awakening was occurring primarily among those influenced by specific Eastern teachings. How wrong could I be? The more interviews I conducted, the more I found descriptions of the same shift, and the same view, expressed in Twelve-Step recovery groups, in Unity churches, in the martial arts community, and among those interested in mindful parenting. When I pitched the book to my editor, I wondered if she would relate. It turns out that not only had many of the teachers at Spirit Rock, the Buddhist center she visits, been affected by such awakenings, but that her therapist had as well. Even her hairdresser. When Anders Ferguson, a business consultant, told me that he had found such shifts rampant among the top executives at Unilever, I was forced to fully relinquish the idea that any one group had an exclusive here.

I have discovered countless little islands of individuals and communities who are relating to their spiritual life in a totally new way. Many think, as I did, that they are the only ones doing this and don't yet see the vibrant, substantial archipelago created by all these little islands. By paying visits to so many of them, I have discovered that this phenomenon is reflected in a greater and greater proportion of the earth's population.

The people described in this book have been transformed in a way that does not neatly fit the maps and models we have inherited. Nor do they appear to be on a trajectory toward anything described by the old maps. Rather than renouncing the world, they are involved, active, and participating. Rather than aspiring to celibacy, they delight in sex more than ever. Rather than conforming to the ways that have been handed down through patriarchy, they embody a radical feminization of the spiritual life. And rather than being holy, pious, or "spiritual" in any external way, their most easily distinguishable quality is a wild sense of humor about themselves and their lives. They are honest, deep, remarkably wise, and at the same time remarkably human and humble about their weaknesses. They are mostly "shtick-free."

We either need new maps, or no maps at all. And we need a new vocabulary. These people are not "seekers"; they are more interested in the present moment than any future state. They are not "followers"; their spirituality is more grounded in direct experience than in imitation or belief. And they laugh out loud if you call them "enlightened." Rather than claiming attainment, they seem to have stepped off the hamster wheel of needing to attain anything at all.

I call them "translucents." They have been affected so deeply by a moment of radical awakening that their relationship to who they are and what this life is about has been permanently transformed. The process is evolutionary and endless rather than aimed at a fixed point or result. This book explores translucence, and the possibilities it opens. You may already know what I am talking about. Translucents recognize each other, sometimes without needing to say a word. If this sounds new or strange to you, I suspect you will be much more translucent after reading what is reported here.

In this book we will discover what occurs in a moment of radical awakening. We will explore how easy it can be to provoke such an opening, either alone or by sitting with a friend for a few minutes, in absolute allegiance to what is real in this moment. We will find that a glimpse of radical awakening can be the portal into a different way of living day to day: a translucent life. We will investigate the impact of translucence on our feelings, our thoughts and actions, our relating, our sexuality, our parenting, our work, and the way we see our world. Together we will unearth some of the common spiritual myths about these areas of our lives, many inherited from the old maps. We will discover how people like you and me are transforming these arenas of ordinary life, making every moment an ongoing spiritual practice, with no prescribed goal.

In this book, I present what has emerged as the prevailing translucent view, based on three thousand pages of transcripts from the interviews, as well as surveys of people with whom I have worked. Most were remarkably concordant. Not everything in this book, of course, represents the viewpoint of everyone I interviewed. The overwhelming majority of those interviewed, however, were extraordinarily nondogmatic, humorous, and similar in viewpoint.

These interviews have deeply influenced the book in a number of ways. First, collectively they have shaped it throughout. The result is more an orchestral symphony than a solo performance. These voices have managed to play in almost perfect harmony, without a conductor in sight. I have acted as the recording engineer and have done my best to represent the points at which the overwhelming majority of my interviewees converge. Second, I often include excerpts from the interviews in the text. None of these interviews has been previously published. Of course, the excerpts presented in these pages represent a minute fraction of the enormity of wisdom I received from remarkable people, and I am grateful beyond words to everyone who has given so generously of their time. Wherever I use material drawn from a source other than the interviews, I have added a note, referencing the source. You will find other quotations in sidebars throughout the text. These are also taken verbatim from the interviews.

Finally, this book offers practical tools to help you honestly address how fully you are incorporating translucence into the mundane procession of daily duty. Some of these are designed for you to try out while you are reading the book. They occur primarily in the first two parts of the book and are labeled "Try It Yourself." If possible, put the book down when you get to one of these and taste the strawberry rather than just reading about it.

Other tools are offered to creatively "nudge" your life into an art form. These "Nudges," as we will call them, can be practiced alone or with a friend. They occur at the end of every chapter in parts 2 and 3 of the book. Most take fewer than ten minutes. Some are very easy and yield immediate results; others take more time to integrate. They include dissolving separation in relationship, fully opening your body to infinity in sex, transforming the workplace into a spiritual practice, and being an agent of radical awakening in society, as a "spiritual activist."

When we are willing to take a fresh look, not only at our experiences but also at the teachings against which we measure them, we can feel quite disoriented. We no longer have true north. So let's start with some very basic questions. As human beings, why do we engage in spiritual activity at all? And what is common to all of us, despite the differences of our spiritual backgrounds and beliefs?

Let's begin there.

PART ONE

WHAT IS TRANSLUCENCE?

CHAPTER ONE

IAGO AND YOUR PURE HEART

For hundreds of years, science has operated on some basic assumptions about the physical universe. A causes B. An object cannot be in two places at the same time. Time moves forward, never backward. Indisputable, right? But in the last few decades, quantum physics has thrown everything we thought we knew into the melting pot and invited us to look with fresh eyes. In the same way, to understand the translucent revolution, we first need to review some of the most basic assumptions we bring to being human. In this chapter we will get back to basics: Human Life 101. What do we all have in common? Why do we, unlike penguins or dogs, have a dimension of life we call "spiritual"? What causes us to seek for something more?

Melissa met John when she was nineteen. Right away, she knew. Sure, they had both been in relationships before; they had both tasted the thrill of new beginnings as well as the pain of unhappy endings. She came from a broken home, as did many of her friends. Her father was an alcoholic and left her mother with the three kids when they were still quite small. Melissa knew the smell of trouble between people. But still, she knew. "We are meant to be together, there is a destiny," she said before the wedding. "We can make it, I know we can. I mean, human beings can do anything when they love each other. As long as John and I are always honest with each other, we're going to make it through the valleys as well as the peaks."

Melissa and John could live on your street. What happens when I tell you the story of their beginning? Perhaps you feel cynical. You have heard that kind of optimism before; you know where it leads. But I wonder if you also recognize the certainty Melissa was feeling? Such confidence offers us a peephole through which we can peer into a deeper dimension: the way we really are, the way everyone really is, the way life could really be, if we weren't all so...

Neal had only been out of business school for a few years when the offer of a lifetime came his way: a start-up Internet company helping other small businesses make the best use of cyberspace. "This is great," he said. "I've got a winning team here, an opportunity to help the small guy, to get some really cool products out there, stuff that usually gets overlooked. The best part is, I just can't fail to make money. We are promoting organic foods, environmentally friendly cleaning agents, solar power. These are the trends of the future, every one a winner. I've got a five-year plan. By the time I'm thirty I'm going to be retired."

I have talked to many people who have started up new businesses. Most assumed they would be fair and ethical and treat their employees well, that the business would not just be a way to make money but a way to make a unique contribution to the world. And that it would succeed. Everybody has vision. We all have an intuitive sense of our real potential. We often feel it when we initiate anything new, before cynicism sets in. A relationship, a business, having a child, moving into a new house — each opens a vista of possibility, of turning over a new leaf. We all have an intuitive feeling about who we are, what our life could become, and what this planet could be.

OUR NATURAL VISION

Vision is vital. It is the fuel that motivates action. It gives meaning to our lives, the aspiration to reach beyond our limits. Vision tells us where to put our energy, allows us to push through unforeseen obstacles, and, when a group of people work together, it is the cohesive force that keeps them motivated and connected.

> There is an inescapable sense of our original being in us, however much it gets battered by experience and repetitive conditioning. The original sense is that I'm good, I'm me, and within that me there is the source of my health and well-being and vitality.
>
> — James O'Dea

Vision also seems to be innate. My nine-year-old son used to have two rabbits. They had never spent any time among other rabbits; they were still babies when they left their mother. We built them a fenced enclosure in our yard so that they could hop around all day on their own. Their very first day in the enclosure, they started to make burrows. No one showed them how; burrowing was hardwired into their DNA. Our cat knows how to chase birds without an instructional video. Pigs roll in dirt; dogs sniff everything. And human beings...they have an innate capacity to sense their own, and life's, potential, without any outside help. We are born with a sense of wonder and awe that is untouched by the limitations of the constructed world. The capacity to rest in this innocence is what makes childhood a time of wonder, for many the only time of wonder that they ever know. Although unaware of the stresses and disappointments of the adult world, this vision of our true heart is full of wisdom. It knows something about what is ultimately real.

This wisdom of the heart is worth investigating. If we examine the assumptions we make when embarking on anything new — a romantic relationship, a business venture, even a spiritual practice — they can be very telling. These assumptions reveal something simple that the heart never forgets, even if the mind no longer dares to believe. This vision *feels* clearer, more authentic, even if it is constantly sabotaged by forces we never anticipate. If we pay close attention to how we feel and act when we are initiating something new, we can discover a great deal about our natural state, and, indeed, about the natural state of life.

TRY IT YOURSELF

Remembering Our Natural Vision

Let's try an experiment before we go any further. Cast your mind back to a specific time when you began something new. It could be entering a new relationship, buying a new house, or starting a career. Try to recall the vision you had of how things would unfold. How did you imagine you would meet each situation? How did you anticipate being received? Close your eyes for just a few minutes and remember.

Good. If you have a pen and paper handy, write down some notes about these assumptions. You will discover something valuable about your heart.

In my experience of working with thousands of people, many initially bump up against an ingrained habit of cynicism and disappointment. "It won't work out," they think, or, "I don't have what it takes." I ask them to feel a little deeper, to the original vision *before* the voice of doubt kicks in. It might be just a picture, or a feeling. If life has been hard on you, you might have to cast your mind back to how you felt when you were younger. The basic assumptions we all make, about ourselves and about how life will treat us, are always similar.

This innocent vision, the kind we live as children and later pull back into our secret lives, emphasizes play, laughter, connection with the body, physical pleasure, and the spontaneous and uncensored expression of life. In this state we know nothing of pressure, stress, or achieving goals within an imposed framework. We are naturally trusting.

Let me share with you what participants in seminars have reported when I asked them the same question. You can see if their answers are similar to yours.

QUALITIES OF NATURAL VISION

Happiness. Whenever we make plans, we assume happiness to be the starting and resting point of our actions. Don't we always expect our time to be relaxed, infused with happiness?

Contentment. Although we may desire things we could get in the future, aren't our dreams of that future always desire-free? You are sitting on a beach, watching the sunset, hearing the waves with that special someone; you can smell the sea air. Do you imagine your mind as being distracted with desires for something else? In our imaginings, we are content.

Being fully present. None of our fantasies, whether of the perfect date, quality time with our children, or an effective business presentation, includes time spent worrying about other things. We plan to be fully present, to feel alive, empowered, and capable of anything.

Harmony. In our imagination, we anticipate being attuned to others. Arguments come as a surprise and ruin our desire to meet in an atmosphere of love. Since harmony and conflict exist more or less equally in life, why should we constantly anticipate the former, and feel so surprised by the latter?

Fulfillment. We expect any new experience to bring us fulfillment, to feel whole. We don't expect dissatisfaction. We naturally anticipate feeling complete before, during, and after the activity.

Success. None of us plans on failure. We imagine the actions we take will bring us the results we want. Like Melissa and Neal, we believe we will be the exceptions, the ones who make it.

Ease. In our original vision we do not anticipate having to make a lot of effort. Each time I sit down at my laptop, I expect the words to flow like honey. It is always a surprise, even after all these years, when they don't.

Honesty. When we connect with our innocent, open heart, we don't plan to lie. As one seminar participant in Germany said, "When I feel into it, I would say honesty is who I am in my essence, more than something I do or say."

Other qualities of original vision include being centered, loving, patient, and generous and acting with integrity and social responsibility.

The Crash

Melissa and John split up, after two and a half years of arguing incessantly about unimportant issues. They were unable to tell each other the truth about either their love or their sorrow and felt their relationship was out of control. Melissa was left to take care of the two babies, while John had trouble making much of a contribution.

More than half of the marriages formed in the United States end in divorce within the first five years. Even though we all know this, each new beginning brings a new wave of hope and optimism.

Neal discovered he could not trust his employees. After many months of working seven days a week, twelve hours a day, his tendencies to control and humiliate the people working for him were shocking, even to him. His family sunk more than $100,000 into his dream before the dream finally collapsed.

> Everybody has some sort of deep knowing or deep intuition. All it takes is one moment of connection with somebody to know that they're wrestling with the same questions as I, in one way or another. The same "why are we here, what is this place where we are?"
>
> — Amy McCarrel

Three hundred thousand new businesses were formed in the United States in 2003. Eighty percent of these start-ups fail within the first two years. We can imagine that very few of their founders assumed they would be part of the unfortunate 80 percent. Why does our vision, which knows only happy endings and simple solutions, rarely lead to what we had imagined? When vision does take flight, why is it so often destined for a crash landing?

I asked the same seminar participants, who reported the qualities of original and innocent vision, what happened once their plans began to take form in the real world. Sarah's family reunion, anticipated as a joyful occasion, erupted into withheld resentments and then into a standoff. Paul envisioned he would be confident, amusing, and relaxed on his first date; instead he felt contracted and withdrawn. As a new mother, Amanda expected to be patient, calm, and gentle. By the time her child was walking, her impatience and anger took her by surprise.

Natural vision is invariably sabotaged by an unforeseen element, which affects us both internally and externally. It influences the way we parent, the way we treat our loved ones and each other, the way we do our work each day. And it influences the way others treat us. We never expect or invite it, yet every aspect of our lives exists in its shadow. And although we find evidence of its effects, this force in our lives is essentially invisible and hence never anticipated or understood. We do our best to keep this "shadow self" hidden from the world, assuming our dark secrets are ours alone. What is this mysterious element in human nature that stalks us and inevitably sabotages us?

THE IAGO FACTOR

In Shakespeare's play *Othello*, the protagonist and his young Venetian wife are deeply in love. Othello is a noble and simple-hearted soldier who trusts those around him. Desdemona is devoted to her husband and hangs on his every word. It is Iago, Othello's advisor and apparent friend, who plays one character against another, creating an atmosphere of separation and distrust. He whispers doubts into Othello's ear, inciting in him a violent jealousy that ultimately leads to senseless tragedy.

We are all Othellos at heart — open, trusting, wanting to see the best in each other — and we are all seduced and driven to insane action by our own invisible Iagos. Our insidious Iago is a state of mind; he can't be seen, he lives in the shadows. Yet his influence can be found everywhere. Iago whispers to us both from within and through other people as the voice of collective conditioning. Most of us live with a painful sense of separation from others, a sense of something missing, and a pervasive experience of limitation, fear, and desire. As a result we engage in a whirlwind of activity to avoid the objects of our fear and to obtain the objects of our craving. This trance of problem-based living, although widely regarded as normal, fuels an endless saga of struggle. It seeps through the cracks of our noblest aspirations, manifesting as disease, conflict, and failure. Globally it is expressed as war, as economic and environmental madness.

We cannot see or measure the Iago factor directly; we only know it by its effects. It is like the raccoons that occasionally visit our kitchen during the night. I have never actually seen raccoons in the kitchen. How do I know they visit us? I find that the cat food has been eaten, the garbage has been overturned, and there are muddy paw prints all over the floor.

QUALITIES OF THE IAGO TRANCE

Like our natural vision, the Iago state possesses numerous inherent qualities:

Sense of lack. The very basis of the Iago trance is a pervasive and unde-fined sense that something is missing. Enough is never enough; we always want more or better. We are never spiritual enough, skinny enough, smart enough, or hip enough. We filter everything through this sense of lack. In the ultimate suburban nightmare, we are driven to keep up with infinitely recurring Joneses.

Sense of separation. Looking to the external world to fulfill our per-ceived lack keeps us focused on a me-oriented reality, reinforcing alienation and separation. The Iago trance is characterized by this twenty-four-hour absorption in "me," while we are actually sepa-rated from our own true selves.

Addiction. Both the feeling of lack and the craving to fill this void are so strong in us that as soon as we sense, even faintly, that some-thing external may "do it" for us, we latch onto it and become addicted. In this way, Iago can lead us to an addiction to work, sex, food, drink, drugs, the Internet, or even to spiritual highs.

Fear. As soon as desire and addiction take over our lives, we are gripped by nonspecific fear. We decide our craving will be satisfied by money; we are gripped by the fear of poverty. We believe the right relationship will alleviate our gnawing lack; immediately, loneliness becomes a terrifying fate.

Suspicion. Nonspecific fear makes us suspicious. When deeply in Iago's trance state, we trust no one completely, not even family members.

Strategic living. We carefully plan for the worst eventualities. Some-thing bad could happen at any moment. Iago whips our thoughts into a whirlwind of emergency responses. We live in a permanent state of alert.

Anxiety. The notion that something is wrong, that we should be doing something more to be complete, creates a constant sense of worry. It's as though we are continually late for an appointment with something we cannot remember.

Hostile competition. Iago creates a feeling of hostile competition, as opposed to co-creation. When there is not enough, we must fight others who are trying to get it too. Our success, even our survival, rests in their defeat.

Other qualities of the Iago state include self-doubt, self-sabotage, disappointment, and meaninglessness.

Because we are faced with the impossible task of successfully competing against the rest of a (hostile) universe, the Iago factor creates in us a feeling of "I can't because ___" and then fills in the blank. Doubt becomes a self-fulfilling prophecy. We are sure we do not have it in us to find happiness, and we prove this to be true. Iago then diverts us from our natural vision, whispering justifications for destructive and reactive behaviors. From our trance state, even the most pleasurable experiences ultimately leave us craving more. We keep pinning our fulfillment on external things. But nothing outside us stays put. Every flower we grab onto eventually withers, the baby grows up and leaves home, the relationship ends. We come to expect disappointment. Sooner or later, we succumb to the resignation that nothing will ever do it for us. We become apathetic and mired in the meaninglessness of life.

And so we move on. Any life steeped in a sense of perceived lack, caught in the cycle of desire and fear, is a life of constant activity and change. We seek a different partner because our present relationship is lacking something we cannot even remember or describe. We change jobs or cars. We move. We are haunted by a constant sense of being in the wrong place at the wrong time. This Iago-based reality destroys any possibility of peace. The anxiety of unspecified problems and the need for urgent action creates all kinds of contractions and tensions in the body and is at the root of a great many physical and mental diseases.

Iago is the dominant trance state of our planet. It influences our relationships, our sexuality, our parenting, and our attempts to relax. It permeates corporate business, international politics, and our economic system. Yet we make decisions and plans as though the Iago factor did not exist, and we are surprised when it rears its ugly head. Cheating, lying, misunderstandings, warfare, environmental degradation all feel unnatural; we know that life should not be like this. We have a sense, deep down, that our natural state is loving and courageous and that life is benevolent. We instinctively expect things to work out, and they keep going off track.

THE TENSION BETWEEN VISION AND SABOTAGE

We all live in this tension between our original innocent vision and the cautious, strategic mind-set of Iago. At times, the Iago trance is very strong. Then we have no energy. We feel depressed. We cannot take any action with confidence, and our minds spin with self-defeating thoughts. At other times, we return to our natural vision, at least fleetingly, and to freedom from Iago's whisper. While making love, when we're on a roll of success, or as a result of spiritual practice, we return to the optimism and creativity of our original vision.

> We get trapped and configured in patterns of consumption, patterns of social organization, of education and value systems that don't seem to be feeding that sense of our original being. We fight ourselves, repeating other people's games and being fed their appetites and their amusement.
>
> — James O'Dea

Look around you. All of us, rich or poor, married or single, anonymous or famous, find ourselves at every moment somewhere between being able to feel life's potential and feeling defeated by its harsh reality.

Natural vision is strongest in childhood and continues for many of us into our early twenties. As we grow older, and, in society's terms, "wiser," these innate assumptions of natural goodness and trust are gradually eroded. Our parents and mentors encourage us to become more realistic, more down-to-earth, and finally we succumb. We come to expect Iago in our plans, and we cease to dream. We discover the safety of cynicism and call it "growing up." We look back on our earlier idealism and sense of vision as shallow and naive and even become angry with ourselves for having been so stupid. We accept the widespread belief that idealism is a symptom of youth and inexperience, and cynicism the mark of experience. The price we pay for this "maturing" is that we give up our passion and energy. Soon Iago's whisper calls the shots. We develop psychosomatic diseases, low self-esteem, and depression and rarely dare to feel that alive again for more than brief periods.

We long to return to optimism but do not dare, lest we crash. Our lives become a tension between the attempt to recover vision and the attempt to protect ourselves from its seductive allure. Caught in Iago's grip, nothing works; there are no good recipes. All the best advice in the world, all the best self-help courses, are undermined by our unconscious assumptions. When free of Iago, even for just moments, everything works and we discover that we need no help at all. We develop a love-hate relationship with our innate sense of vision. We try to protect ourselves from being naive and taking new risks. Yet we hold onto our longing in private and develop a secret life. The middle-aged divorcée may shun the advances of admirers but read romance novels in the small hours. The failed business entrepreneur may be cautious in investing and making contracts, yet watch *The Apprentice* on television.

Those who find ways to stay in touch with original vision become our artists, our innovators, our teachers. Those who lose vision become their halfhearted followers and critics. The degree to which this visionary sense is expressed is what differentiates the innovator from the imitator, and, eventually, the truly successful from the frustrated. But whether we succeed or fail in living from inspired vision, we all share a deep longing for, and love of, a life lived with passion and purpose.

> I came to a clear internal realization that there was *nothing* I could do as a separated self that would *ever* fulfill me.
>
> — Barbara Marx Hubbard

THE WAY OUT OF THE MAZE

Every culture, at every time, has offered ways to resolve this tension, answers to the questions poking out from under the thick blanket of cynicism: What if we could live without fear and desire? What if we could take the greed and trembling of our minds less seriously? What if we could deeply feel what is around us with gratitude, in a relaxed and open experience of fullness?

Throughout time Iago has been given many names, from Satan to the Axis of Evil. He is capitalism to the communist, and communism to the capitalist. He is called the mind, ego, Maya, and ignorance. There are as many solutions for eliminating Iago as there are customers to buy them. Politicians tell us that the source of the problem is the enemy out there, and if we can only exterminate them with large enough bombs, then we can relax. We try to improve our lives: "I married the wrong person, took the wrong job, bought the wrong stocks." Then Iago is your wife, your boss, your stockbroker, all in league.

We can try to eliminate Iago through imposing willpower, trying hard to think positive, and by "just doing it." Then Iago is negative thoughts. Some psychotherapists recognize Iago's voice as the inevitable result of childhood traumas. Then Iago is your mother or father. If we can revisit and heal the past, then we can be happy now. Often the last outpost of our battle with this mysterious saboteur is the quest for enlightenment — Iago as ignorance of the eternal "Truth." And so we become followers, taking out a mortgage on this moment to pay for assured deliverance later. All these alternatives more or less fail. Like trying to run away from our own shadow, the actions we take to get rid of Iago are all motivated by a basic assumption, that there is a problem to be solved.

> Human beings are driven by a core wound — this kind of madness that something's missing. The more conscious they get, the more desperate that becomes, and it eventuates in a quest for transcendence. We need that part of our nature desperately.
>
> — Saniel Bonder

There is a way out of the maze. It is absurdly simple.

Given the basic assumptions of the mind, most of us could never even imagine it. If you are asleep, dreaming of a confrontation with an armed intruder, you might consider fighting, pleading, running away, phoning the police, or hiding. But perhaps you would not think of the only solution that would work: to wake up and find yourself safe in bed.

Melissa and Neal have never met. But I know them both. I interviewed them, and countless others, to research this book. Like so many other people in the last few decades, they have experienced a radical awakening from Iago's trance. They both know how to return to the innocent state where action and vision are one.

CHAPTER TWO

RADICAL AWAKENING

---

*S*teve *started to practice Zen meditation when he was nineteen. He loved to sit in silence. Although he had many big openings, a voice would always say, "This isn't it, keep going." He was newly married, very happy in every area of his life. One night, getting ready for bed, he said to himself, "I'm ready." He didn't even know what that meant. He went to sleep.*

"I woke up in the morning and sat to meditate. I heard the sound of a bird outside. The question spontaneously arose, 'Who hears that sound?' It wasn't a question of my mind. It was as if something questioned itself. I'd never heard such a question. It just spoke itself. 'Who hears that sound?'

"As soon as the question spoke itself, everything turned upside down and inside out. I was the bird, I was the hearing, and I was the sound. I was all just one thing. All of a sudden there was no more reason to sit, of course. I hopped up. 'I wonder if I am also the stove?' I asked myself. So I walked out into the living room and I looked at the stove. 'I'll be damned, I'm the stove, too!' I realized. And so it went. Like a child, very innocent. I didn't feel, 'Wow, I've arrived, I've got it, I'm enlightened.' None of that was in my mind. It was just the recognition.

"I opened the bedroom door. Annie was sleeping. And it was the same.

'There I am, I am sleeping.' And then there was the experience of love. I am that, too. I am that love. It was just a childlike investigation of 'I am every-thing,' but in a very innocent way. In no way spiritual, and in no way holy. In no way hierarchical, just very, very humbling.

"About a half an hour later, there was a further waking up, even out of that oneness. There was an awareness of . . . who knows what? There is some-thing, or nothing, that exists when even an experience of oneness disappeared. Something that remains ever awake."

Over the last twelve years, I have spoken to thousands of people who have had similar shifts of consciousness. These moments have changed who they know themselves to be and the nature of the world around them. While some are notable teachers and writers, the majority are ordinary people leading everyday lives. These breakthrough moments may or may not lead to a sustained transformation, but their increased frequency is remarkable.

We will call such a shift in awareness a "radical awakening." It is the moment when you taste reality outside the limiting confines of the mind, when you know yourself to be limitless, much bigger than, yet containing, the body, beyond birth and death, eternally free. Despite the activity of thought and feeling, you know yourself to be the silence experiencing that movement. It is the moment when you can intuit the real potential of life, free from the incessant mental machinery of complaint and ambition. A radical awakening often releases a tidal wave of creativity and generosity of spirit, a natural impulse to serve and contribute. In these moments, we know that love is who we are, not something we sometimes feel.

Having such an acute glimpse of free-dom from the mind is a huge moment. We realize that almost all our suffering is caused by our addiction to untested beliefs. We can, at least temporarily, let go of our preoccupation with fear and desire and have direct contact with what is real, what is present. A radical awakening rips the veil of our preoccupation with a personal life,

I am a continuum of consciousness. The local self disappears utterly; it is a move from foreground to background. I am in psyche instead of the other way, not an encapsulated bag of skin dragging around a dreary little ego, but a symbiotic organism of environment within fields within fields within fields of life. "Jean" is an imagination piece that is butted out of psyche.

— Jean Houston

often so much that we acquire ongoing access to reality as peaceful and infinite, even in the midst of external noise.

Stephan was driving on the freeway when the veil lifted:

Suddenly everything shifted. I was this vast expanse of space. "Stephan" was in this space, infinitely expanded. Energy was rushing through the body. I had never had powerful energy experiences before. It was a feeling of tremendous empowerment. Everything since then has been contained in that awakening. That initial moment was like a seed. Everything else has grown from that. In the last twelve years it has been like I've been catching up to that awakening and fully experiencing it. There is just this present moment with nobody here. Now it is no longer an experience; it just is, ordinary.

> Who I am is unchangeable. It remains the same, no matter what the emotional currents or feelings. Openness and warmth are the core, at the bottom. I lean to that instead of toward the personality or manifestation of that.
>
> — Marlena Lyons

QUESTIONING SEPARATION

The essence of Iago's trance is the feeling of separation, a preoccupation with I, me, mine. This unquestioned assumption of separateness lies at the root of our ability to respond to life's challenges. We each believe we are one small person in a big scary universe, alone and lacking. To survive we feel we need to protect what little stuff we feel we have, to get ahead, to create security, and to make sure that no one takes advantage of us. This belief in "me," as separate from "you," is so basic that no one questions it. But if we don't investigate this core belief, the rest of our life becomes grounded on an unexamined premise. We are so frantic while evacuating the building that we never check to see if the fire in the basement actually exists.

Many people recognize this and try to free themselves of the Iago trance. But before we can deal with anything that disturbs our peace of mind, we must first know if our troubles are real or imaginary. We deal with plenty of challenges every day that are absolutely real, that require action. The car has a flat tire; it needs changing. You find a lump under your armpit; it needs a doctor's diagnosis. Real problems exist. Avoiding them ushers us into the dark and winding corridors of denial. No amount of visualization will eliminate the IRS if you've been summoned for an audit. If you've run out of milk, you'll have to take a trip to the store or eat your cereal dry.

But we also preoccupy ourselves every day with imaginary problems: *What if I run out of money? What if my lover leaves me? Look at the time! What if I get caught in traffic... I might be late for work... I might get fired... What then?* These thoughts do not require action, they require the snap of a finger to awaken us from the dream they create. To struggle incessantly with a completely nonexistent problem is to enter the world of insanity. Most of the fears that drive us again and again into the battlefield of doing or changing have no basis in reality. Yet we live this way, lunging at ghosts that only exist in our mind's eye. Like Othello, we listen to our inner Iago's whispered taunts, and jealously avenge wrongs that have never occurred in the first place. We panic about our finances, fearing a tax audit that has not been scheduled. We wage and re-wage arguments with our parents or our boss in our heads, alone at night. We expend enormous amounts of energy playing out various potentially harmful scenarios that do not exist.

> I am a no-thing-ness. I don't have to think, and am fully in the present moment, doing and being what comes next... a peaceful feeling, the no-thing-ness, nothing... nothing preoccupying my mind, just being in the moment.
>
> — Jacquelyn Small

Knowing when to act and when to snap out of a dream defines human maturity. Real problems require real action; imaginary ones call us to wake up from our delusions. Once we have recognized how much the Iago trance dominates us, we can free ourselves from the trance of separation and suffering. But before we can answer this call to action, we must inquire more deeply, to determine if our problem is real or imaginary. To do this we need to find the core identity, the separate "me" at the center of the Iago universe.

TRY IT YOURSELF
Who Is Here?

Right now, sitting where you are, reading these words, take a few moments to close your eyes and feel your body. Settle yourself... relax ... come fully into this moment.

Can you see the print on this page? It is seen, right? But seen by whom? In this very moment, outside memory or concept or images, who is seeing? Shift your attention for just a moment from the words on the page back to yourself. Perhaps you find thoughts and feelings. Shift your attention again from the thoughts and feelings, which are also experiences that are com-

> I am an energy field of phenomena: breath, sensations, thoughts, without any strong reference point.
>
> — Joseph Goldstein

ing and going, back to yourself. What do you find when you look for the real thing, what you have called "me"? Do you find anything? Is there something there with substance, with form and edges?

Pause for a moment and listen to the sounds around you. I can hear the hum of my computer; I can hear the tap-tap of the keys as I type. I can faintly hear the sound of the wood crackling in the stove next door. If I listen hard, I can even hear the sound of air moving in my nostrils as I breathe.

What can you hear? Listen.

Now, again shift the attention from the sounds here in this moment to you, to the one hearing them. Is that making any sound? Pay attention to yourself; find out what that is like, even deeper than thought and movement.

Feel your body. Can you feel any sensations? Can you feel your lower back? Can you let go and relax your belly, and feel the sensations there? Can you feel your feet just now? Can you feel your neck, the inside of your mouth? Can you feel the air passing as you breathe?

Who feels all that? You say, "My body, my belly, my feet." So you know you are experiencing the body's kaleidoscope of changes. Who are you, the one who has a relationship to the body and its sensations? Is that itself an object with substance? Is that a part of the swirling of birth and dying? Try to find out for real, in a way that satisfies you more than spiritual ideas, more than anything you have ever read or thought or heard or understood. Try to find out what is really true about you, deeper than thinking.

Keep asking this question again and again: "Who am I really?"

If you reach an answer like, "I am the soul," or " I am the higher self," that's fine. But then ask yourself, "What was that?" It was a thought, wasn't it? Maybe a spiritual thought, but still a thought. A thought that comes and goes. Unreliable. Arguable. We can keep inquiring more deeply, to find out who is aware of all these thoughts. Give yourself the gift of some relaxed and focused consideration of this question before you read on.

When I inquire in this way, I find that what is really meeting this moment, hearing sounds, seeing movement, and feeling currents of sensation is formless empty space, pregnant with infinite possibility. There is a mysterious presence, indefinable, with the capacity to embrace everything, just exactly as it is, but which in itself is nothing, just pure context, with no content. This presence contains the body but still exists, with or without the body. In this recognition, just here, just now, there are no problems and never have been. Disorienting and confusing as it may be, this realization brings a sense of peace, wonder, tremendous energy, and a feeling of love with no specific object.

> I don't know who I am. I don't know what existence is. I don't know what consciousness is. What I find is emptiness, and the emptiness is not devoid of anything. Not wanting anything. There is no It. There is totality, and totality alone, and what that totality is in its core and in its very expression, I do not know. I simply do not have any answers at all.
>
> — ShantiMayi

I have made this inquiry of thousands of people. At the start of each interview I asked: "When you close your eyes and try to find yourself, here in this moment, who or what do you discover yourself to be?" Listen now to a few of the responses I got, from a cross section of contemporary writers and teachers:

"Emptiness, space, awareness, that which knows but doesn't have a name or form, openness, joy," says Jack Kornfield.

"I find peace and spaciousness, a vast holding, surrender," says Aneeta Makena.

"Just the openness of consciousness that we know and feel as all kinds of love, limitless in every possible appearance," says David Deida.

"An immense vast space, an openness," says Gay Hendricks.

"A space that feels like it has rivers of love and color dancing," says his wife, Kathlyn Hendricks.

Throughout the book you will find many more of the answers I received to this question.

Along with hundreds of writers and teachers, I've checked with dentists, hairdressers, housewives, and hoboes. I've asked politicians, drug dealers, and my tax consultant. I regularly ask whoever is sitting next to me on the plane. All over the world, from every imaginable background and system of belief, people report the trance of separation being broken. For the majority, this radical awakening has occurred within the last fifteen years.

DOORWAYS TO THE REAL

In most cases, this view of being vast, universal, and nonseparate results from a specific realization, a dramatic break with the past habits of the mind, and the stepping into a brave new world. This kind of radical awakening can come in a variety of ways. Just about anything can be a doorway out of Iago's world, into the real world of "what is."

When Things Fall Apart

For many, the Iago trance is dissolved through the intense pain of living in separation. Suffering from anxiety, isolation, and distrust becomes so all-consuming that many may reach a critical point where the only choices left are suicide or waking up from the nightmare of a hostile universe. This climax of suffering may come as a one-time descent or as a sequence of visits, each one ripping us more forcefully from our clinging to our self-created hell. Following is Eckhart Tolle's experience, as he recounted it to me. It is typical of dozens of accounts that I have heard:

> The realization of stillness is the essence of who I am. Everything arises out of that stillness, and the whole teaching comes out of that. It knows where it's going; I don't know where it's going. It manifests in many ways, sometimes it is just there as this stillness in which perception happens, and other times words come out and there is the undercurrent of stillness.
>
> — Eckhart Tolle

I was very frequently depressed, very anxious, and deeply unhappy. I would often wake up in the middle of the night. In my late twenties, I was living alone in London. One night, I woke up with the thought in my head, "I can't live with myself any longer. I can't live any longer with the burden of being alive." That sentence became the trigger, because it led to the question: "Are there two here?" Then: "Am I one or two? Who is the self that I can't live with and who am I, the one who cannot tolerate this?" I didn't have an answer; there was just a stunned silence. Then it felt like being drawn into some void, with great fear. "Resist nothing." I heard that as the last thought that came into my mind, like coming out from the body, from the chest. "Resist nothing." Then it was like disappearing into some void.

The next morning I woke up, and the first thing I noticed was that everything was intensely lovely, the sound of birds, the objects, all were beautiful and alive. I thought that this state might leave me again. But it didn't leave. I got used to it, so it's not remarkable anymore. Life itself is remarkable.

Byron Katie had a very similar radical awakening in the attic of a halfway house. One morning she woke up and saw a cockroach crawling over her foot. In that moment, reality radically shifted. She was instantaneously free of suffering, and realized that she was beyond identification.

> Who I am is a very peaceful place that has a quality of love that I feel radiating out from me, a place of centered awareness.
>
> — Jack Canfield

Michael was serving an eight-year sentence, living in a jail cell with thirty-two other inmates, when he experienced a similar deep shift in awareness. His only link to his wife was the telephone, but his weekly call was frequently impossible because of the threats of violence from his cellmates. Most of his few possessions, even his sneakers, had been stolen. He was absolutely isolated and filled with despair. He had nowhere left to fall. But the depth of his despair proved to be fertile soil. One line in a book provoked his shift: "You are consciousness."

He began to feel uncontrolled love for the guards and fellow inmates. He felt blessed by his situation. This is how he speaks of his life today: "Now, my life is a constant state of contentment. It's interrupted a thousand times a day, but none of these interruptions shake the foundation of that contentment."

These experiences represent those of countless others who have broken the addiction to personal drama simply because the story itself has crash-landed.

The Role of a Teacher

An awakening can occur spontaneously when we are in the presence of someone who is already awake. The perfume of silence is infectious. Catherine Ingram shared the profound experience she had during her first encounter with H. W. L. Poonja, while conducting a magazine interview:

> I'm a prayer being prayed, and I'm a prayer being lived and it's a prayer of existence, of now, of connection, communion, of compassion . . . it's not conceptual at all, sometimes it's like a deep emptiness that's like a giant heart, just a big, big heart.
>
> — Richard Moss

I fell into such silence in the interview that he would have to remind me to ask the next question. He would say something, and I would realize that there was just nothing else to be said, my mind would stop thinking. All motion of mind that had me seeking for something better fell away at that moment. He embodied such a radiant, magnificent wholeness; he was so clearly not seeking anything. He modeled a possibility of really resting in the center of one's own being without the idea that there was anything more to get, to do, or to become.

Ingram has gone on to become an influential teacher in her own right, as have many of those I interviewed. Christopher Titmus has been leading meditation retreats for more than thirty years, so he is familiar with the other side of the teacher-student dynamic. He feels that his role as teacher is almost that of a bystander who creates an environment where awakening can come from within the student. "I would feel I was being too conceited if I thought I was doing something of importance. In the collective conditions of everyone being there together, something can happen. The teacher is not central to that."

Many teachers would concur. So many people are waking up naturally in the course of their daily lives; they simply need someone to validate what has already occurred.

The Fruit of Practice

For some, this shift, from being limited to a personal story to recognizing spaciousness, can happen as the gradual fruit of a daily practice such as meditation or tai chi.

Mary gave up her position teaching at the University of Oregon to pursue spiritual practice full-time. She traveled to India and entered into extensive meditation with her teacher, who gave her the name ShantiMayi. She thought she would remain in India, but after many months of practice her teacher sent her home with $40 in her pocket and told her to return in six months. She found a temporary job in a vegetable-canning factory, working eight hours a day, seven days a week, for $5.35 an hour.

> I find emptiness oftentimes shining through the colors of love, like a light shining through colored glass taking on colors of love.
>
> — Deva Premal

One day I was sent to a room at the back of the factory. I was completely alone, scrubbing huge pots and pans. Then one moment swept me into a wave of silence, and I became completely still like a rock. It was so minute, so delicate. From that little needle popping the bubble, I stood looking deeply into a place where I was not, where nothing was, and nothing was not. There was no me; there was no not me. I was standing in a yellow rain suit with a pair of boots and a hard hat on, and rubber gloves. It was very simple and very deep. This lasted for about an hour and a half. I looked at the clock as soon as a sense of time returned. After all, I was at work!

There has never been a time that it hasn't deepened, and there has never been a time that it left. My teacher knew it when I came to see him. Without speaking, he knew that this had happened.

Her awakening followed many years of deep and diligent practice. Today ShantiMayi travels the world, guiding others into the same wakefulness.

George Leonard describes an awakening after several years of practicing aikido: "Everything stopped; I was suspended out of time. There were no thoughts, no decisions needed. The body knew exactly what to do: it was a perfect fall, like poetry."

The Last Straw

Some people report that a simple phrase or even a word in a book precipitated a shift in awareness. Alice was walking near her church when she remembered Jesus' saying: "I and the Father are one." In that moment there was only that oneness everywhere. Like the crow that lands on a branch and causes the coconut to fall, these phrases, which do not have the same effect on everyone who hears them, can tip some of us from one reality into another.

Eckhart Tolle's book *The Power of Now* has sold more than two million copies. Tolle tells me that many people have written him saying that simply reading a passage in the book had led them to recognize the deeper nature of things: "This means that the experience is already happening in them; otherwise they wouldn't recognize it. I am amazed how many people without any previous spiritual knowledge, training, or practice, realize the truth and are open to it. The only reason can be that that which the book points to is already happening in them. That's a wonderful thing."

> I am everything, quite simply. Awake and alive, with no location; I am everywhere and everything. I am an alive and awake expanse expressing itself as everything.
>
> — Stephan Bodian

Extreme Experience

For some, a heightened sensory experience snaps them out of the Iago trance. Saniel Bonder, author of *Waking Down*, shifted from mind to presence while making love. Douglas Harding was hiking in the Himalayas when all thought stopped and he saw that the vast sky above his head was the same as the vast sky behind his eyes. Ram Dass told me of his first awakening to his natural state: "I had the first experience of who I was, of who I am, under psychedelics. It was as if I had been just introduced to home. A home in my body, a home in my true self."

Falling off a Log

There are, in fact, myriad windows to the real. As more and more people experience this kind of awakening outside the mind, it is becoming increasingly easier for others. As more individuals awaken, it affects the collective. As the collective shifts, even more people wake up, in a growing snowball of realization. Some of the stories shared here are quite dramatic, while many accounts are subtler, just like falling off a log.

Lama Surya Das, an American-born teacher of Tibetan Buddhism, sees awakening happening through many portals: "It might be that one realizes these things simply through observing the impermanence of all conditioned things and the transient, dissatisfactory nature of things, through one's own investigation, introspection, reflection, inquiry, and so forth. It might come through being moved to compassion by feeling the suffering of others, or even having your own heart broken open in some way."

> I know myself to be nothing. Consciousness without distinguishing marks. It is a mystery how it can appear to be compressed into a little life and a little body and the experiences of daily life. I close my eyes, and suddenly what is there has nothing to do with the little story I call me.
>
> — Gay Luce

Tony came to a weekend seminar in Santa Fe. He struck me as being extraordinarily relaxed, and he grinned most of the time. On the first morning, we talked about awakening, and I guided the group into a self-inquiry exercise. Afterward we talked about our experience. "It has been like this for a few years now," said Tony, still grinning. "I didn't know it had a name. Seems quite normal to me." There are many people today, like Tony, who have slipped into the stillness of their natural state with hardly a splash or a ripple. And some, like Christopher Titmus, have never lost that wakefulness; they have known it all their lives. In this case, a teacher or a gathering simply provides validation: "I don't have any recollection of going from one state to another, no shift from ego to emptiness. I can't report on that kind of night-and-day change of consciousness that others have reported. I can't recall feeling unfree. I have no recollection of it being different than what it is. This has certainly saved me from having to do a lot of practice!"

SELF-INQUIRY

Most of the above reports of radical awakening happened on their own, without any conscious intention. Some of these people have since become teachers, guiding others to the same realization. They have become the inspiration to countless others, demonstrating that awakening can also be provoked through intelligently questioning the assumptions of the mind, through looking for the "I." As we have seen, some of the stories can be quite dramatic. When we provoke a radical awakening through conscious inquiry, it is usually much more gentle and ordinary.

In 1991, when I was in India, Poonjaji asked me a simple question: "Who is the one trying to become free?" I sat with that question for six days, passing through all kinds of fluctuations, until things became simple and clear. A year later, when I started to teach, in the first few weeks a few people had similar awakenings. Last year my wife and I guided numerous groups in this kind of inquiry. Everywhere we went, we found either that people had already had an awakening of this kind, or that the whole group would shift into the recognition of being limitless in less than half an hour. The doors of the temple are wide open.

Self-inquiry is simple. It does not require you to do anything, change anything, think anything, or understand anything. It only asks you to pay careful attention to what is true and real.

I have two sons. When they were about four, they both went through a phase of having nightmares. I would go into the room and switch on the light. Two small eyes blinked at me from the corner.

"What's the problem?" I'd ask.

"Daddy, there's a monster in the room," a timid voice would reply. Now, I had more than one choice of how to respond. I could

> The awakening is happening in many, many people. They may still get drawn back into identification with mind, but increasingly they find that Presence is there. Sometimes, when I switch on the TV, I realize it's not yet happening to everybody. Otherwise, because of the work I do, I often think it's happening to everybody.
>
> — Eckhart Tolle

tell my frightened boy that it was not true, there was no monster, go back to sleep. That response is the equivalent of reading a book that says, "We're all one, there is no problem, just be with what is." Fine ideas, but they don't help much when you're feeling scared. I could also have offered to feed the monster cookies, talk with the monster, negotiate. That approach is like some kinds of psychotherapy. Treat the problem as real, then fix it on its own terms. But the only real solution I ever found with my munchkins was to have a good look. Under the bed, in the closet, behind the curtains, we undertook an exhaustive search.

Eventually my son would let out a deep sigh, smile at me, and fall back

> I am nothing and everything.
> Conceptual mind can't understand it,
> but experience holds it to be true.
>
> — Adyashanti

to sleep. The problem was not solved, but dissolved. It was never real in the first place, but it took investigation to make that a reality.

TRY IT YOURSELF
Self-Inquiry

It is best to do this exercise with a friend. One of you will "hold space," while the other will use the inquiry. Sit opposite your friend. Look into your partner's left eye. There's no need to stare, just don't look around the room. This keeps you present.

Partner A, ask Partner B: "Who is experiencing this moment?"

Partner B, try to find yourself, deeper than thoughts, feelings, and body sensations. Try to describe the real you to your friend. To do this you will have to stay right now, right here. Try to find yourself in this moment now, deeper than memory. Try to find the one who is hearing and seeing, and describe that to your friend. Try to describe who or what is meeting this moment.

Keep going for at least five minutes.

Partner A, if your friend falls silent, keep asking the same question. Do not speak in any other way. Partner B, even if you feel like being quiet, continue the attempt to describe yourself in this moment.

Then switch roles. You can switch back and forth in this way many times — there is no end to the deepening. You may get stuck, get caught in thoughts and memories. You may get bored. Many people quickly drop back into their real nature: free, limitless, and out of time and mind.

This is not an intellectual experience. It is not something to get right, and then stop. You may fail miserably at being able to talk about it. Most of us do, but it's a glorious failure. As with Rumi's poetry, in our attempt to describe the indescribable, the perfume of our real nature is released into the room. Indeed, we may well find ourselves intoxicated by this presence. Enjoy, there is no hangover.

ONE DIAMOND, MANY FACETS

Most of the above reports emphasize the relaxing of the "I-Me-Mine" reference point and the realization of limitless space as our true nature. But that is actually only one facet of the diamond of radical awakening. People describe an awakening shift in multiple ways.

"I could see through the activity of the mind, it became transparent."

In a moment of radical awakening, we see there is no problem in this moment now, and that there never has been. We create a problem-oriented universe with our need to protect the thought of "me."

> I find a huge endless force that is both alive and still; it permeates everything and is everything at the same time.
>
> — Susanna Perrett

"Only the present moment is real, there is nothing else."

We discover that there is no such thing as past or future; we need thought to create them. You have no childhood unless you think of it. Next Christmas does not exist, except in thought. All that can really be known for real, without thinking, is this moment. Many people I interviewed reported a highly accentuated, vivid perception of the immediate environment. Colors are brighter. Everything is more beautiful. When there is nothing to compare it to, this moment is perfect.

"I felt indescribably happy for no reason at all."

Trapped in Iago, we feel a general sense of lack, and we suffer without knowing exactly why. We can have plenty of everything and still feel depressed. In a moment of radical awakening, we experience just the opposite. Whatever the circumstances — lost job, dinged car, even a bellyache — we can't shake off this unreasonable happiness.

"There is an extraordinary sense of peace, pulling me down into myself and into the present moment."

As soon as we divert attention from the emergencies created by thought, we are bathed in peace. This stillness has always been here, waiting for us to stop waging war with reality.

"I looked into my friend's eyes, and I felt like I was looking into my own eyes. The face was not my face, but the consciousness looking back at me was my own."

Many, many people have reported this dimension of awakening. You relax back into yourself, and there is only space, only presence. You look into the eyes of your beloved, and you see infinity, you see God. As the attention dances between the vast presence behind your own eyes and the vastness looking back at you from the beloved's eyes, you know for sure that you are seeing yourself. Everything is meeting everything.

"I feel overwhelmed with tremendous love and compassion for everyone and everything."

In a radical awakening, all our habitual defenses relax and we feel others, and our environment, with no separation. In this moment, we discover what the word *love* really means.

"I experienced a surge of tremendous blissful energy through my whole body. I thought I would burst with the explosive ecstasy."

"For the first time in my life I feel totally free of fear."

"I laughed and laughed and laughed. I could laugh at myself, I could laugh at anything and everything I had been taking so seriously."

> There does seem to be a sense of this happening to a lot of people. I think that they're discovering that the prison door was never locked. I don't quite know what it is that made them get up and push it, and see it swinging open and discover that all the prison guards had disappeared. There is a sense of having been a prisoner to one's delusions and of finally realizing that the snake is just a rope.
>
> — Bishop Richard Holloway

If any or all of these statements sound familiar to you, you probably know firsthand what we mean by a radical awakening. But before we get too excited, ready to hang a certificate of Supreme Enlightenment on the wall, let's put things in perspective.

AN EPIDEMIC OF SANITY

As recently as the 1980s, the awakening shifts described above were quite rare. Today such experiences of "poking through" the fabric of our normal trance state of desire, fear, and self-preoccupation are becoming increasingly common, especially during the last decade of the twentieth century.

After his awakening, Stephen Grey received the name Adyashanti from his teacher. He tells me that when he started to teach a few years ago, perhaps one in twenty of his students had such an awakening. Today he estimates that more than 60 percent of his students do. In her early days of teaching, over a decade ago, Catherine Ingram reports that many people came in a spirit of seeking, of needing something. On a recent visit to New York, this is what she found: "There are still a few people who ask questions, but there are many who just sit there in silence. Some come up to me afterward and tell me they are just there to celebrate, to be in the ambience. I definitely get the sense that the majority in the room is just there to enjoy what is now their experience."

Christopher Titmus has been a prominent Buddhist teacher in the West for thirty years: "An exponential growth, a quantum leap is happening, both in the numbers of people involved and in the depth of their awakenings. The snowball is getting bigger." Whether it's Eckhart Tolle or Byron Katie, Jean Houston or Andrew Cohen, again and again I hear from teachers and writers from around the world that the veil is getting thinner all the time. More and more people are tasting awakening, and those awakenings are going deeper and becoming more sustained. What was considered a peak mystical experience a few years ago is today the basic platform of sanity from which our exploration begins.

As the number and depth of radical awakenings continue to grow, what we do with such a breakthrough in consciousness becomes far more important than the awakening itself. Will a glimpse of our real nature become a memory in a scrapbook, or the foundation of how we treat our friends, how we put our kids to bed, how we drive to work or scramble an egg?

> The resolution is not always what we thought, not a big burst of enlightenment. It can be much more mundane, but equally profound.
>
> — Catherine Ingram

Can an awakening to the timeless transform how we live in time?

CHAPTER THREE

LIVING IT

When Gay Hendricks was twenty-four, he weighed three hundred pounds, smoked two or three packs of cigarettes a day, and was drowning in a terrible marriage. One day, while ice-skating in New England, he slipped on the ice and smacked his head. He hadn't hit the ice hard enough to lose consciousness, but hard enough to break the Iago trance for a moment.

"I knocked myself into an altered state of consciousness where I had that feeling of open space. From that place, I could see my feelings, I could see where my muscles had tightened up around those feelings, and I could see that all that tightening was in resistance to sensations that I didn't want to let myself feel. As I came out of that altered state of consciousness, which I think lasted maybe two minutes, I began to come back into awareness of my body. I could feel my personality assemble itself again.

"I can remember feeling the heartbreak: 'Oh, my God, I'm going to come back into the same old person.' The last thought I had before my personality snapped into place again was, 'Okay, whatever it takes, I'm going to find a way to live from that space.' That was my last little commitment, and then all of a sudden, Boom! I was in my body again. Back to the same body *that wanted a cigarette and had to grapple with my horrible marriage and everything.*

"I couldn't live that way any longer, because I had to find the way to be in that space again. I spent years finding out how to live there, through meditation and many other practices. Once I had that space again, the next thing was to find out if I could maintain it in relationship."

Millions of people have now had an awakening glimpse into their real nature. The experience may not be stable, but it can never be overlooked again. It is not the access that challenges us now, but the actualization of it in our daily lives. David Deida, the prolific writer and teacher, calls such a glimpse a "poking through." To Deida, these moments are fleeting, almost inconsequential in and of themselves. "I think it's far more important what people do, given the 'poke through.' How, given a glimpse, they dedicate their occupation, their attention. Otherwise, that glimpse is fleeting and useless."

Without this essential, pivotal awakening there can be no real depth to life. We live preoccupied with hallucinations. After suffering the endless slings and arrows of outrageous fortune, it's a relief to know a dimension of reality where nothing is happening, where we know ourselves to be essential peace, where we are connected with everything, a state where love rules supreme. If our disposition and destiny are reclusive, then a glimpse is often enough. We can retire to the sanctity of our hermitage and enjoy the view. If, on the other hand, our calling is to participate fully in the swirling dramas of daily life, our task is more daunting.

> Realization has no value until it's lived. That's how it is born into the world.
>
> — Byron Katie

THE IMPACT OF AWAKENING

The moment of awakening may be the end of seeking, but it is the beginning of a sane life. Saniel Bonder emphasizes "waking down" more than "waking up" and stresses that our realization has its real relevance in how we live: "You really need to have realized the absolute immutable unimaginable awesome magnificence — just to be able to make your way through the day.

Once awakening is not viewed as a fetishism of escape, then its value in life becomes more and more evident."

An amazing number of people in ordinary contexts have been blasted open in this way. Good, we can stop the torture of feeling "he's got it and I haven't." We can stop giving our divinity away to someone else. But it is still only a glimpse and has changed five minutes later, or even within a nanosecond. Now begins the much more difficult work of living and embodying our own realization. A radical awakening can affect our day-to-day life in several ways. We may experience just one of these responses, or several together.

Business as Usual

For some, the poking through into deeper reality quickly disappears, crushed underfoot by the incessant march of daily life. Kids, carpool, shopping, bills, fixing the hole in the roof — who's got time for the timeless? Within days, the glimpse is erased from the hard drive.

The Lord Spoke to Me!

Others integrate radical awakening into a personal belief system or theology. Sandy was singing in the choir at church one Sunday, when suddenly everything changed. She could still hear the voices, she could see the other mouths moving, yet all became silent, as though a television had been switched off that she had not even noticed was on. "The sounds were made of silence," she told me. "I could feel the perfection of it all, as though a hand was stroking me and telling me it is all perfect. There was such sweet, sweet peace." This feeling of benevolence, coupled with the fact that it had happened in church, led Sandy to believe that she had received a message from Jesus. She interpreted her

> There is no truer expression of the natural state than you. But it's so much easier to recognize it elsewhere.
>
> — Robert Rabbin

experience as something "out there" instead of what is already here. In this way, simple reality, outside of mind, can be interpreted as a message from God or a prophet, a past-life memory, or even a visit to some higher sphere or heaven.

Many years later, when Sandy met others who had had similar awakenings from the mind, her need to mold her experience to her belief system softened.

The Reentry High

A radical awakening is often accompanied by strong emotional or physical symptoms. We may experience overwhelming feelings of bliss, rushes of energy up the spine, or waves of fresh understanding and insight. When these physiological, emotional, and mental states disappear again, we may feel that we have "lost" the awakening.

Take a fish out of the water and put it on a rock, then put the fish back into the water. I'm sure that the fish will experience ecstasy beyond belief and will probably have a deep and religious experience of oneness with the cosmic wetness. But come back the next day and things will be normal again. It was the reentry into the water that promoted those happy fishy feelings, not the water itself.

In a moment of radical awakening, we simply know reality, nothing more. But we can get attached to the emotions, body sensations, or insights that accompany the awakening. When they pass, as they inevitably will, we chase after them and once again seek for something we believe is missing. Renewed seeking for another high of reentry then follows our awakening.

> We call it a glimpse of reality. Of course one comes down. The clouds again obscure the sun. But now you know why it's light during the day. You can start your day without seeing the sun every minute. You know it's there whether you see it or not. The glimpse is not the end of the path as some people might think, but just the beginning.
>
> — Lama Surya Das

Total Supreme Enlightenment

Some claim that the moment of radical awakening causes *all* old symptoms of personal identity to dissolve completely. There's no more desire, no more fear, no more getting pissed off when someone nabs your parking place. No more of Iago's whisper. Gone. Poof! The divine light, and nothing else, shines through every orifice of the body. Most of the people who make such claims are men. After all, it's the hypermasculine curse to want to be totally finished and complete with the inconveniences of incarnation. So many men long to swoop down someday onto an aircraft carrier and proudly announce, "Mission accomplished."

"The clearer you get," says Isaac Shapiro, "the more you believe your own bullshit." When we see teachers surrounded only by adoring students, when these teachers no longer have a peer group to offer honest and supportive feedback, not about their enlightenment, but about their humanity, we are often watching an accident waiting to happen. The more grandiose the claims made about ultimate enlightenment, the more sordid the scandals we often hear about later, from disgruntled devotees and former spouses. Let's leave the jury out on such absolute transformations.

> It's not chosen; for example, I didn't choose to wake up, it chose me, and from that point on I've exercised my awareness in trying to separate the real from the unreal.
>
> — Richard Moss

Initiation into Endless Evolution

The fifth impact of radical awakening is the most interesting. What has been seen and known in a snap of the fingers leaves a strong enough mark that it can never be overlooked again. Have you ever come across those images that jump off the page if you look at them cross-eyed? At first glance, you see a bunch of squiggly lines and nothing else. Then, if you step back a little and look beyond the lines to an imaginary point a few feet beyond the flat surface, a dragon or a ballerina magically appears as a hologram. After you've seen the 3-D image just once, you can easily find it again when you look for it.

In the same way, when the awakening is strong enough, it leaves an imprint on the body and psyche. You are left with a deep knowing of the perfection of things, even when they are going wrong. You realize that everything is interconnected, even when you are caught in conflict, that who you are is actually much bigger than the person you have taken yourself to be. The game is up on Iago.

At the same time, you have the humility, the honesty, and humor to cop to the habits of this human monkey. You recognize that it is still predisposed toward craving ice cream, wanting more of this and less of that. It has addictions to particular pleasures, and it also has its favorite miseries. The

There is progression beyond the notion of the seeking, to having had experiences of oneness and unity that are transforming. A vast number of people know that this is no longer an infatuation. We've been at it for thirty-plus years, almost forty years in many cases. It's no longer just the next fad. This is the way we've chosen to live our lives.

— Jon Kabat-Zinn

awakening initiates a gradual metamorphosis, which is both evolutionary and endless. A spontaneous generosity of spirit, an impulse to serve, and a willingness to transform living into art gradually replace the normal relationship to life marked by fear and acquisition. You develop an amused, playful attitude to the only raw materials available: the strange habits of the bundle of thoughts you call "me."

This dual state of being both limitless and limited, of being both out of time and within it, reveals an evolutionary impulse, inherent in life itself — the impulse for the realization to continuously marinate the personal and to become ever more embodied.

We will call this endless process of evolution and transformation "translucence."

BECOMING TRANSLUCENT

Webster's dictionary defines *translucent* as "letting light pass through, but not transparent." A transparent object, like a clean sheet of glass, is almost invisible. You see everything through a transparent object as if it were not there at all. An opaque object, on the other hand, blocks light completely. A translucent object allows light to pass through, but diffusely, while maintaining its form and texture. Objects on the other side cannot be clearly distinguished. A crystal is translucent. So is a sculpture of frosted glass — if the sun were to shine on it from behind, you would see the light passing through the sculpture, and it would appear to be glowing from the inside.

Translucent people also appear to glow from the inside. They have access to their deepest nature as peaceful, limitless, free, unchanging, and at the same time they remain fully involved in the events of their personal lives. Thoughts, fears, and desires still come and go; life is still characterized by temporary trials, misfortunes, and stress. But the personal story is no longer opaque: it is now capable of reflecting something deeper, more luminous and abiding, that can shine through it.

Contemporary translucents defy many of the spiritual concepts we have inherited from religious traditions. The thousands of people I have spoken to in researching this book are not recluses. They play vigorously in their relationships with others, their work, their creativity, and their political and environmental causes, but they play to play more than to win. Translucents display an above-average generosity of spirit. Giving to other people and to the environment replaces Iago's habits, based in lack, desire, and need. Above all, translucents have a humorous and often irreverent relationship to their personal life, beliefs, and identity.

Translucents do not fit established pigeonholes. They generally don't follow one particular teacher, teaching, or group, although many have in their past. They are not "spiritual" in any way that can be obviously recognized through lifestyle choices. As a group they display as wide a variety of occupations, appearances, and educational and cultural backgrounds as humanity itself. They generally don't identify themselves as "enlightened" or as having attained anything, and they are also not trying to *become* enlightened. They are not overly materialistic or spiritually cynical. Translucents are not uniformly vegetarians, political liberals, religious zealots, new age hippies, or self-improvement junkies. And they don't all wear Birkenstocks.

The word *translucent* refers to the degree of embodiment of a realization, not to what has been realized. Hence it is a relative term, like *interesting, inspiring, boring,* or *idiotic.*

> One can have a great degree of realization, very authentic, very deep, but not actually be or express that realization in one's humanness. You can have great realization but a rotten embodiment. The realization is asking for a human response, to take up residency within my humanity. I don't think we ever feel really complete until our humanity has embodied our awakening.
>
> — Adyashanti

These words are relative because not everyone agrees on their meaning. You might find opera inspiring, whereas someone else might be put to sleep by it. Relative terms also have no finite end. You can be "quite boring," "rather boring," "really boring," even "extremely boring," but however boring you may be, you can always outdo yourself the next day. There is no such thing as "ultimately boring." Relative terms shift, from day to day or hour to hour. You might be really boring on Monday but more interesting on Tuesday.

Absolute words, to the contrary, are black and white, like an on-off switch. *French, married,* and *dead* are examples. "He's quite French" sounds a little strange, doesn't it? So does "I am married on Mondays, Wednesdays, and Fridays but single the other days." And what about, "The doctor says she's dead, but Frank doesn't agree. I feel I need to get to know her better before making a judgment." *Enlightenment* has generally been used as an absolute word. Even though people don't agree on what it means or to whom it applies, those who talk about enlightenment claim it is a defined condition, and one is either enlightened or not. (Usually a man is telling you *he* is and *you* are not, so you'd better do what he tells you.)

Translucence is subtler; it is relative. One can always become more translucent, one may waver in the degree of translucence, and the people I feel to be most translucent may differ from your top ten.

> We are not influencing realization — that profound, wide-open experience, wise and free of conditions, without any parameters, any borders, or any knowledge — but bringing that into life. It is through our uncontrived openness that we experience real love, clear insight, gentle kindness, and genuine creativity. Realization is not a process. The process is how it plays itself out in life.
>
> — ShantiMayi

SOME TRANSLUCENTS, UP CLOSE AND PERSONAL

Over the last thirteen years, I have talked to thousands of people in researching this book. I'd like to introduce you to a few of them. Bill works both as a drywall installer and as an artist. He plays in a rock band, drinks beer, and plays softball with the guys. He has had several relationships over the last few years, some of which ended a bit "stickily." He freely admits to being abrasive and insensitive from time to time and to occasionally having a wildly inappropriate sense of humor.

Cynthia lives with her husband and teenage son. She is a retired nurse. She shops at Costco, attends the local Unity church, and loves her garden. She suffers from arthritis, which gets worse in the fall and winter. Her son thinks of her as conservative. She laughs and puts up no argument. She was raised a Catholic and sees many of her personality traits as reflecting those roots.

Tom is the senior risk evaluator for one of the largest insurance underwriters in the country. He owns real estate and invests, conservatively, on Wall Street. His wife and close friends call him a reserved and retiring man.

Ewa raises her two sons, by two different fathers, in Stockholm. She works as a massage therapist and has a hard time making ends meet. She loves to kayak, swim, and play the flute. She is an environmental activist and participates in running the local Waldorf school.

All these people have had radical awakenings, powerful enough that their lives have changed as a result. They have all read, and can relate to, the descriptions of awakening in the previous chapter. Although they are as different from each other as people can be, they all display the qualities of emerging translucents we explore in this book. Below we will explore some of these common characteristics.

> In order for widespread embodiment to happen, it had to move to the West. Until recently you had people looking at the great cultural geniuses in India, basically compassionate people looking out and saying, "This is all unreal. I'll stand here, I'll radiate, I'll give you a teaching." It hasn't become embodied by great numbers yet, and until it does, it is irrelevant in some way. It's a promise of sorts, nothing more.
>
> — Saniel Bonder

Trans•lu•cent n. 1. an individual who has undergone a spiritual awakening deeply enough that it has permanently transformed their relationship to themselves and to reality, while allowing them to remain involved in ordinary life in a process which is evolutionary and endless. 2. an individual with a glowing appearance, as though light were passing through. adj. an individual or object that exhibits translucence.

Trans•lu•cence n. 1. the quality or state of being translucent.

TEN CHARACTERISTICS OF TODAY'S TRANSLUCENTS

We need fresh language to talk about translucence. What few words we do have for such matters have been commandeered by organized religions and reduced to cardboard cutout concepts, devoid of any real life. The implications and context of this current swell of direct experience demand an entirely fresh look at the meaning of spirituality. A number of factors make this thorough reexamination necessary. We will visit them briefly here and then return to all of them, throughout the book, in much greater depth, and see how they play out in day-to-day life.

Living Outside Traditional Frameworks

Today translucents live for the most part outside the context of organized religion and hierarchy. They no longer need to have one teacher or teaching, but rather have many teachers or experience all of life as a teacher. Ram Dass speaks of no longer being a Buddhist but being a "generalist." Richard Holloway, the retired bishop of Edinburgh, has reevaluated his relationship to the Christian church since recognizing God to be everywhere, both behind the eyes and in front.

It's a potentiality toward the future, and an unprogrammed excitement about it. It's not being externally guided by some prepackaged program. It's a fresh discovery of the world, a fresh sense of wonder, like in childhood, like in Adam and Eve, but without the sense of the "fall." A fresh, anticipatory feeling to life.

— Bishop Richard Holloway

Cynthia, who has attended events with the Dalai Lama, Wayne Dyer, and Thomas Moore, told me: "I think I'm as much a Buddhist as a Christian, or maybe I'm just all of it and none of it. Right now I've got Eckhart Tolle, the Tao Te Ching, *Cosmopolitan*, and a thriller on my bedside table. They seem to be getting along just fine."

Looking Beyond Enlightenment

As mentioned above, there is an important distinction to be made between translucence and traditional understandings of "enlightenment." Very few of the people I have talked to would seriously label themselves as "enlightened." At the same time, the overwhelming majority said that they were no longer seeking a state of enlightenment, although many had done so previously. Most said they no longer had any idea what the word was supposed to mean. This is in sharp contrast to the atmosphere of spirituality that existed even fifteen years ago, when most spiritual people were still following a guru, trying to win the cosmic jackpot.

Musician and songwriter Peter Makena and his wife, Aneeta, exemplify this change. They were both disciples of the controversial Indian teacher Bhagwan Rajneesh in the 1970s. (He has been known simply as Osho since a few months before his death in 1991.) Now Peter is less sure what the "E" word means: " 'Enlightenment' used to have an elusive meaning, something like the

Holy Grail. It represented a final end point, in my idealistic and dreamer-like search, of what human potential could be. Today my sense of that potential is more of a finger pointing, a hint, a direction, with no final product."

I asked Peter and Aneeta what they would say if someone were to ask if they were enlightened. "I'd laugh," answered Aneeta. "I couldn't say enlightened or unenlightened, I just don't think like that." Yet both feel they are always learning and growing. They call it an endless exploration. Today's translucents have fallen in love with the present moment and the possibilities of living right now as a gift of love, as a work of art. They've lost interest in potential future states. Translucents have seen past the dangling carrot of future enlightenment. They live for now, and now, and now.

> It's much easier to have a spiritual experience than it is to live a spiritual life. It's the life that is more important than the experience.
>
> — Lama Surya Das

As we deepen in familiarity with our silent, limitless, real nature, and as we broaden our forays into the uncharted territories of living from here, the very notion of some final graduation becomes obsolete. The silence is neither enlightened nor unenlightened; it cannot undergo any change. And the monkeylike mind-body organism is simply a sophisticated animal, no more. It is always undergoing change, unenlightenable. Have you ever seen an enlightened penguin or a liberated flea?

An Endless Journey

Translucents speak of life as a "rivering," a process without end. Like a fountain that is always pouring forth, it is an endless and spontaneous *enlightening*, not a fixed state. Unlike the goal-oriented self-improvement industry that has dominated our culture for so long, this process is an endless unfolding of discovery and delight. There is no attempt to fix a problem or to achieve a final higher state. Translucence is more a direction than a destination. Like heading East, the process doesn't imply a specific point of arrival. It is a way of living life with art and humor, returning continuously to here, and here, and here, always steeped in the vastness of the view and blessing each moment with a gift of creative presence.

"At some point, I just stopped seeking," says Tom. "There was a turning point, when I was about forty. I saw that I was like a rat in a maze, always thinking freedom would come later, after one more retreat or workshop. I saw how absurd this was, and it dropped. It was after that, after I stopped seeking, that I could wake up to things as they really are."

> Our lives are like tiny little boxes within the infinite realms of consciousness, creativity, and expression. How far can we take it? How much can we love? How large is this, how applicable in life? I can't imagine that there's any limitation to that whatsoever.
>
> — ShantiMayi

Spiritual seeking may have a defining end; the process of embodiment, on the other hand, is endless. It is a relaxing, the allowing of more love, more presence, more creativity to flow. How can we ever say, "I have reached the outer limits of love?" or, "I now have discovered all that can be discovered of creativity, or humor, or compassion?" As we wake up, we see the very nature of things as they are: still in their essence and constantly undergoing modification in their appearance. Recognizing this may bring more relaxation, more love, or more humor to our humanness, but there can be no end point.

Andrew Cohen, the founder of the magazine *What Is Enlightenment?* points out that both individual awakenings and their embodiment are happening within a larger context, one that completely transcends individuality. He calls this "impersonal enlightenment":

> *We are part of the developmental process. The evolutionary context is something very different from the experiential recognition of the timeless. An individual human being begins to glimpse that he or she is literally part of this 14-billion-year process of development, right now, and that their own awakening to that fact is the universe becoming aware of itself. It's as significant and as important, if not more important from a certain point of view, as the experiential recognition of timelessness.*

Many of those I interviewed have come to the same conclusion; they realize that their own spiritual experience is only a tiny part of the larger context of collective awakening and evolution.

Transcending Self-Improvement

Translucents are always evolving, but they also display an extraordinary and often humorous acceptance of themselves just as they are. Bill talked of his little personality quirks as he might describe an eccentric relative, with fond-ness, humor, and just an edge of cautionary damage control.

> The space is always the same. What changes is that within the space, the habits of being involved in completely unworkable ways of living get seen. Those habits require energy, and when the energy is no longer caught up there is a sense of deepening. As you rest as That, it gets subtler. Deeper and deeper layers of unreality get seen through, and the sense of space gets so much deeper.
>
> — Isaac Shapiro

Translucents have canceled their sub-scription to the self-improvement industry; they no longer pin their sense of well-being, their connectedness and peace, on the process of fixing themselves. Yet they fully recognize the dysfunctional habits that hurt people and create separation, and they take a tremendous amount of energy from the simplicity of this moment, from being able to live fully and gift life. So they have no resistance to looking at these old habits, not as an attempt to improve the personal, but in service to moving beyond it and giving the realization space to breathe.

The Return of the Goddess

Whenever anyone has an awakening outside the mind, that which is realized is beyond conditioning. At the same time, the realization is always *expressed* through human form. For millennia, spirituality has been dominated by the masculine expression of realization. This masculine viewpoint emphasizes transcendence, annihilation of the ego, the dissolving of limits and, ultimately, all form. The male psyche leans toward the stark nihilism of celibacy, solitude, and asceticism. Religions founded by men and perpetuated by patriarchy (basically all of them) worship the written word as absolute and set unwaver-ing moral precepts.

Feminine spirituality, however, is much softer, drawn toward deep and embodied love, open acceptance, the celebration of all life as the dance of divin-ity. The feminine delights in color, sex, children, blood, dance, and music as the very expression and demonstration of divinity in flesh. Art, music, images, and sensations are just as sacred as words. The masculine energy in all of us, both men and women, is associated with the left side of the brain, which processes words, logic, concepts, and time. The feminine, in both men and women, is associated with the right side of the brain — with images, feelings, color, and now.

> The feminine principle is the eagerness to collaborate rather than compete, it is the eagerness to relate rather than stand out as an individual, it is the longing for harmony and community and caring and nurturing.
>
> — Lynne Twist

Translucents demonstrate a restoration of this imbalance. When the left and right hemispheres of the brain return to wholeness, words and images dance together. Our understanding and our feelings find one common flavor. Emptiness is expressed as form, form as emptiness. We are neither turbocharging through time nor lost in the soap opera of endless drama, but out of time altogether, in this present moment. Freedom from life and immersion in life are no longer seen as opposed to one another but rather as two aspects of a total incarnation.

We need new maps — less a linear journey from one point to another and more an illustrated guide to the endless delights of exploring new territory and enjoying the divinity of this moment in a human body.

Embracing Life and the Body

Until just a few years ago, the choices available to a spiritual aspirant were extreme. Either renounce the world, turning your back on sexuality, money, your family, work, and creativity, and find God and peace in the sanctity of solitude and silence, or immerse yourself in the marketplace, have sex and children, make money, pursue fame and power, but forget all about being free. Buddha's early life story epitomizes these extremes.

Today, the choice to be a recluse is no longer attractive or even particularly available. Opportunities to turn our backs on the world are rapidly decreasing. In the West, the life of a monk or a recluse is no longer woven into the fabric of established society, as it was in medieval Europe or as it still is in many Asian countries. More important, translucents no longer accept this dialectic as valid. Instead, they are incorporating translucence tangibly into their daily lives.

Translucents are not choosing between spirit and the world; we embrace

both or we have neither fully. Spirit is expressed as form, and form only works when
it is infused with spirit. The inner life is
incomplete without material life, like a
metal untested by fire. Material life is incomplete without spirit, like a cathedral
without an altar. To be successful in a rapidly changing world, you need to be at the

> Moving into the domain of wholeness means moving back into your body, but not as a story of me. Then we can be in an intimate relationship with the world, one that is reciprocal, and yet boundaryless.
>
> — Jon Kabat-Zinn

source of your experience, awake to who you really are. Translucents embrace
life, inclusive of feelings and sexuality, the shadow as well as the saintliness,
the failures as well as the triumphs.

Translucents are in their bodies, and care for the body as a sacred garden.
They practice yoga, martial arts. They play tennis, ski, and surf, for the
sheer joy of being embodied, not to achieve anything. Michael Murphy,
Gay Hendricks, and Brad Blanton play golf religiously. Sofia Diaz and Kathlyn
Hendricks love to dance as a sacred art form. And translucents are generally
both sexual and sensual; they experience the body as a doorway to the real.
Ewa kayaks and swims and goes to all the events at her kids' school. Since
her second divorce, she has dated several guys and recently moved in with her
boyfriend, Eric. Cynthia is the events coordinator at the Unity Church. The
experience that has most deepened her spirituality, and for which she is most
grateful, is the painful death of her sister. Bill plays softball, sings in a band,
and paints. Tom is up at five. He loves to walk by the lake before he goes to
work. Then he checks stock prices online. He's just going in for surgery as I
write this, which will limit his freedom a little. His solution: "I've decided to
spend the next couple of months writing a book." These people are not, by the
wildest stretch of the imagination, recluses. They are embracers of life.

Unresisting Experience

While translucents embrace all life, they are also aware of the deeply ingrained
habits that keep Iago's trance in place. Hence, a plethora of tools have developed, aimed not at self-improvement but at reversing our instinctive habits
that lead us to, as Byron Katie puts it, "argue with reality." "When you argue
with reality," she says, "you lose — but only 100 percent of the time."

Katie has developed The Work of Byron Katie, Hale Dwoskin teaches the

Sedona Method, A. H. Almaas originated the Diamond Heart Work, and we offer the Living Essence Training. Although different in technique, all these approaches have the same vision: to support letting go of control and to allow the intelligence inherent in all life to flow rather than helping *me* to get what I think will make *me* happy. Unlike many traditional practitioners of spiritual life, translucents are not interested in running away from anything or amputating any part of their experience. In fact, they have learned to walk toward what they have previously run away from.

> The practice is simply being with things as they actually are. We notice how ingrained our habits are: to want things to be a certain way, to grasp, or to cling. In that very moment we remember that we are bigger than that. That is a very powerful, humbling, and satisfying practice.
>
> — Jon Kabat-Zinn

Cynthia had a lifelong tendency to avoid anger: both her own and other people's:

> *I was always the peacekeeper in my family. When things got heated at home, I was the one with the soft voice, tears in my eyes and trembling jaw, trying to get us all back into one happy family. In the last few years I can see how this segregation of feelings into good and bad has not served anyone. It has created tension. When I got more distance from my ideas of how things should be, I realized that I was angry myself. And it all came out sideways. Passive-aggressive. I've had to learn to feel my anger. Not express it, necessarily, but really feel it. I was living in a prison defined by what I was unwilling to feel.*

The tendency to resist life, to become a pattern of interference, is so strong in all of us that it takes considerable awareness, honesty, and willingness to feel what is uncomfortable, to not resist it. This is the pivotal difference between contemporary translucents and traditional mystics. Translucents are awake to the unchanging dimension of themselves and reality and also willing to question and dissolve the unconscious assumptions of the mind.

Engaging in Translucent Practice

In some ways translucence is just another way to describe a human being's most natural state. This is how children live, with an open, playful, total involvement in life, free of concepts, glued to the present moment. But to sustain this way of living, awake to our unchanging nature but without resisting the natural flow of life, is to take a stand against a lifetime of habits. Translucents embrace spiritual practice not as a means to achieving a future goal but as a way to a more fully lived present moment, with open heart, open mind, and open body.

We face a mountain of habits at odds with our heart's deepest knowing. This schism can be profoundly frustrating and painful. We have no choice, those of us with feet of clay and hearts on fire, but to face habits as they arise, allowing them to be alchemized through honesty and courage. As we encounter our old ways, passed down through generations, we must use increasingly creative tools to crack the concrete of our routine life and to wiggle our love and clarity into the crack. Anything short of this leaves us compromised and restless.

We find ourselves walking a razor's edge. We have realized the ultimate truth in snapshots, that all is perfect as it is. Hopefully, we also have the humility to see that

> Realization is a boundless inability to come to any conclusion about anything in life, period. There's no judgment, no opinion, no conclusions that can be reached, no theory that has any sound basis. Life itself is the process, but the realization itself is not subject to any process whatsoever.
>
> — ShantiMayi

we all have habits of thought that are in constant rebellion with this lucent reality, this living in the now. If we lean too far in one direction, we fall into self-congratulation and delude ourselves that a glimpse of a restaurant will satisfy our hunger. If we lean too far in the other, we get lost in the masochism of endless self-improvement, always creating new and different character defects to tweak before we can relax. We set up house with the ghosts of our childhood and live in a war zone of our own imagination.

Right down the middle lies this edge. It requires of us a continual process of meeting with old pains and habits of demarcation, lingering only long enough to feel them deeply, and then returning as fully as we know how, to this, and this, and this, allowing love to flow through us. No one living a translucent life claims to be an expert at this, but many of us now would rather live clumsily in this way than successfully in self-deception. It is a glorious failure.

In the maturing beyond dogma and the rules of tradition, translucents have also grown beyond hierarchy. The traditional setting of one Enlightened One sitting on a raised podium, answering questions from deferential devotees, is being replaced by the sacred circle, where wisdom is everywhere in the room at the same time, where the meeting is eye to eye, heart to heart. Realizing the deepest truth of who we really are may occur on the meditation cushion or in a cave. To discover our potential to live as radiant love and humorous art requires involvement with other people. Through the alchemy of meeting with others in honesty and trust, we can take our inner wisdom for a test-drive and find out what happens when the rubber meets the road.

> You meet other translucent people, and you feel less alone. You start learning from each other. People start realizing that they have a mission and a purpose. Everything today is done in groups; it's not done by individuals anymore. The world has gotten too complicated for people to do much of anything alone.
>
> — Jacquelyn Small

Life as Art and Generosity

"I can feel the possibilities, more and more," says Bill. "I've had moments where it's really pouring through me, and then I just walk into a room, and I know people can feel it. They are touched by what has touched me; it's coming through me, not from me. Funny, you know, I don't think I even know what 'it' is. I can't describe it. But that is what my life has become about now: to allow this magical mystery to live through me as it wants to."

However much an awakening may have touched us, if we stay entrapped in the habits of separation, the gifts that love intends to give through us will never be given. Do you have a family? A husband or wife or kids? Perhaps you have nephews and nieces. Suppose you buy them all wonderful gifts, those things they most want in life, the latest, the greatest, the best. Then you store them in your closet, all wrapped up.

Imagine that all the gifts you have for your children, your wife, your parents — for everyone — are never given. This is human life. We may dole out a Lego set now and then, but the real gift of potent love remains mostly ungiven. In this recognition lies an urgency to move beyond habits of separation, to really inquire and discover what we are when we're not living in strategic fear. Who are you outside the game? When we see and question these habits, we will be able to give all these gifts, the ones with our children's names written on them, the ones with our spouse's name, and the ones with the planet's name too.

This is our work, the discipline required beyond an awakening: to take a stand against the habits of separation, to recognize them, to be honest about them, so that the current of real love can flow through them. Then our children and our spouses and the planet can receive the love of an open heart. Then our husband or wife can say to us, "I could die tomorrow, I have been so completely loved." Nothing has been held back. It might even be the husband or wife we have not yet met, and maybe will not meet until we let go of the old. Real love is urgent. It can only happen when we bring a sober relationship to the habits that keep us separate. There is work in it.

> The goal is to move from a self-centered interest in transformation and enlightenment to one that ultimately transcends it completely. To where one's interest is really no longer for one's own liberation but in becoming a catalyst for the evolution of consciousness itself.
>
> — Andrew Cohen

Translucents are willing to do this work, not for themselves, but for love itself.

Being in Good Company

Finally, the sheer number of contemporary translucents is noteworthy. When I spoke at a Texas church, I described what I meant by translucence. Then I asked, "How many people here know what I am talking about, from direct experience, rather than from reading about it?" All but one person raised their hands. This is a church in Texas we are talking about, not an ashram in the Bay Area. In Sweden, I spoke to eight hundred people at the No Mind Festival (the name itself indicates something interesting blowing in the wind) and asked the same question. Again, almost all of them raised their hands. And this is a recent occurrence. More than 95 percent of those who have talked about awakening and its embodiment for this book described a shift that has happened since 1990. At the time of writing, that means we are witnessing a shift in collective consciousness that is less than two decades old.

Translucents are lions, not sheep. They walk alone, although sometimes in each other's company. Thus, the number of people who have undergone such shifts is not easily measurable. They do not belong to an organized group; there is no membership list. In fact, many translucents have dropped out of organized religions and spiritual groups. There are really two reliable ways to estimate how big this collective awakening has become. The first is through surveys and research, conducted by sociologists who have a feeling for this level of reality. The second is by talking to the troops on the front line: teachers and writers who focus on these issues and have direct contact with the people who are in the process of shifting.

Paul Ray, one of the foremost sociologists researching changes in the collective consciousness, has broadly defined three groups within Western society: traditionals, moderns, and cultural creatives. The third group is distinguished from the first two by values such as environmental and social responsibility, placing quality of life above material success, an acceptance and deeper understanding of values of other cultures and of subcultures within our own. Ray has conducted enough surveys to be confident that this third group now comprises more than fifty million people in the United States, more than eighty million in Europe, and is rapidly growing.

> We need to evolve. Not the experience of oneness, but the expression of it, the embodiment. It is up to us to bring sanity, depth, wisdom, beauty, balance, and compassion into the world. It is screaming out for people of heart and conscience to come forward and take the world into themselves as their own body and bring the same healing that they did personally to the larger person of the world.
>
> — Robert Rabbin

Ray has now identified a core group within the cultural creatives. This core is the emerging spiritual group, those whose lives have been touched enough by a glimpse or sustained knowing of themselves as limitless to irreversibly affect their lives. "They live in significantly reduced egoic referencing," says Ray. "They have some degree of access to the divine or no-self." He estimates this group to be somewhere between one and two million people in the United States, although he cautions, "Big surveys are not going to catch this because you need in-depth interviews." Duane Elgin, another sociologist, has come to similar conclusions and is even more optimistic in his estimates. If researchers like Ray and Elgin are right, this is very significant and very good news. It is this shift, in these kinds of numbers, to which every spiritual tradition has aspired.

A second way to get a feel for the size of this collective shift is to ask the people who travel and teach and thereby meet those who are in the process of transformation. "I sense a huge movement with this," says Catherine Ingram. "I think it will keep growing. This is the perspective that all spiritual seeking eventually has to come to." Saniel Bonder agrees. He shared with me that almost all the people attending his retreats now are more interested in deepening and integrating than in seeking after something.

Isaac Shapiro, who travels internationally throughout the year and meets with groups of several hundred people at a time, tells us, "There are always new people showing up, and the crowd seems to go deeper and deeper. The new people who come may have no preparation or conceptual understanding, but what's gone before makes it easier for them."

Michael, who woke up in prison in chapter 2, now writes and teaches with the name Satyam Nadeen. He talks to groups in the hundreds, and feels that about 1 percent of the world is going through this shift: "There is some sort of evolution occurring. More people are raising their hands in the hall when I ask who has had similar experiences to mine. It has gone from about 10 percent to 80 percent over the last six years."

As a consequence of this acceleration, more and more people are willing to come out into the daylight and speak openly. God is unmasking herself in millions of forms. We can ask, "Will the real World Savior please stand up?" and the whole auditorium rises to its feet. As more and more people speak openly about these rips in the veil, about their direct experience of being everything and nothing, it allows more and more people to recognize that it has already happened to them too. It was already there, behind the eyes, just waiting to be celebrated. Eckhart Tolle, who has met with tens of thousands of people worldwide since the success of *The Power of Now*, concurs: "There are many who have never read a spiritual book. They have had the awakening, but they didn't quite recognize it yet. For them, they only need to hear one or two statements, and then they know, 'Oh, so that's what's happening.'"

> There is definitely a change in transformation, individually and collectively, among people who are doing spiritual work. The hope is that those small numbers of people are like yeast that can leaven the whole dough and raise the bread.
>
> — Lama Surya Das

The mouth of the funnel is getting wider all the time, and each shift today makes many more possible tomorrow.

ARE YOU A TRANSLUCENT?

If most of what has been described here sounds familiar to you, then you are already in the evolutionary process of embodying translucence. You are probably more a part of the solution on this tired earth than the problem.

You may think that because not every moment of your life is marked by awakening that you are not embodying translucence. Our life can be very translucent in one area and still quite opaque in another. Each moment can be influenced more by Iago's trance or by translucence. Some areas of our life may already be infused with a generosity of spirit, humor, and creativity. Others may still be tightly bound by fear. The way translucence breathes into life is different in every person. Translucents feel called on to reject nothing as a potential art form: health, money, sex, work, creativity. The areas that need nudging will be quite different for you than they are for me.

> Whatever aspect is manifesting to us in this moment, our tendency is to think that this is where it's at, more valid than that aspect over there. But the Truth manifests like a multifaceted jewel. Somebody else might have a totally different way, one that manifests their way.
>
> — Adyashanti

Richard Moss told me of the schism he feels between his life as a spiritual teacher on the road and his life at home with his wife: "My marriage is the deepest source of stress in my life and also fuel for learning. I've accessed the part of myself that opens into a domain of Being that's much deeper, and then my personal relationships reveal to me what I still don't know about myself. I ask myself, How can I have realized the oneness of things, and then experience the feeling of separation provoked by the difficult process of relationship with people?"

Would that every teacher and writer were that honest!

In fact, many people experience this kind of tension. There is an interesting relationship between translucence and the way we lead our daily lives. I call it symbiotic, which means that the two affect each other in a cooperative way. Radical awakening transforms life. Repeated glimpses beyond fear and limitation naturally relax the tight beliefs that keep us feeling separate, allowing us to be more playful, generous, and present. And the way we live, the degree of awareness and creativity we bring to the nitty-gritty of ordinary life, will allow translucence either to blossom or wither. We pay close attention to how we live, not for moral or convenient motivations, but in service to translucence itself.

This is the point of a translucent life. We are no longer willing to separate spiritual experience from the fabric of our day-to-day existence. Our most mundane circumstances are the very context in which realization lives and breathes. An unattended life segregates realization into a small box called "spirituality." A well-attended life can make a trip to the grocery store a sacred pilgrimage.

In parts 2 and 3 of this book we will explore this symbiotic relationship between translucence and daily life. We will get down into the trenches of mundane human experience: relationships, emotions, sex, parenting, work, aging, politics, all the stuff we might not expect to discuss in a spiritual book. In each of these areas, we will explore specific questions that will help us to understand translucence more graphically:

> This is not a place where you arrive. As long as you live, you can really stretch past surpassing whatever subtle limits you have created. Those limits get very subtle. Life is practice. There is no practice other than life itself. We are not seekers, we are people who explore our Self-nature and its extraordinary beauty in this endless endeavor. The practice is Love, opening one's mind and heart. Arrival is a fallacy.
>
> — ShantiMayi

1. What do *translucents*, the people who are probably living on your street, in your house, look like? We will hear many stories about what translucents are like as parents, what they are like at work, how they deal with their feelings, and how they treat their health.

2. What does our life look like in the *default state*? What habits, fears, and desires have we inherited from countless generations? What does Iago influence us to do when we move through our day like a somnambulist?

3. What are the spiritual *myths* we have inherited about these aspects of our lives?

4. How does radical awakening *naturally transform* these parts of our lives, all on its own?

5. What do recognized *experts* tell us about living translucently?

6. How can we *nudge* our lives in the direction of translucence?

Let's meet the modern mystic.

PART TWO

INDIVIDUAL TRANSLUCENCE

CHAPTER FOUR

MY CRAZY UNCLE

Translucent Identity

Josh was a peaceful man. *After years of meditation and spiritual study, he had trained himself always to turn the other cheek. He spoke in an even monotone and nodded slowly and empathetically to anything said to him. Anger and conflict were, to Josh, stains on the purity of life; his mission was to avoid them. After experiencing a radical awakening, he began to sense this spiritual and loving persona as a sham. He recognized that his aversion to conflict was motivated more by fear than by altruism.*

Josh volunteers for a community housing project. He gives one day a week to building affordable housing for the homeless. The dam broke one day when he was working with Eddie, a licensed contractor who was put in charge of all the other volunteers. Eddie loved to call Josh "the rookie" and make his work an object of ridicule to the other volunteers. In particular, Eddie loved to show up Josh to the women. Josh had been pushed around and humiliated all his life, and had taken it all with a smile, but this time he stood his ground. A lion woke up in his belly. "Listen, Eddie, either you stop bullying me and everyone else here, or you can finish the building on your own." Josh was amazed at the words that came from his lips and at the way they had come from his gut. Eddie didn't mess with Josh after that day. And Josh discovered himself to be more than a nice guy. He found a wholeness that could embrace both saint and demon.

A transformed sense of identity is at the very core of an awakening shift. This shift in who you take yourself to be changes everything else in your life. Feeling small, threatened, separate from other people, and lost in a chaotic universe gives us grounds to act competitively, even violently. Feeling vast, at peace, and connected with everything and everyone gives us a totally different way of doing things. It changes the way we drive to work, the way we parent, the way we make love, and the way we treat the earth we walk on. Living from fullness rather than desire transforms our life from a struggle to a blessing.

> Humans are preselected beings, fascinated by and brought into the swirl of conditioning to be self-centered on making money, having sex, scheming, jealousy, the whole human trip.
>
> — David Deida

When we are fully motivated by Iago's whisper, we become completely identified with this personality. We defend its beliefs and habits and feel offended if it is criticized. Any potential change to our bundle of traits feels like death. When I initially moved to America from England, I landed in Los Angeles. The first thing I did was to buy a used car — living without a car in LA is like surfing without a board. My not-so-new car needed some repair work, to put it mildly, so I went to a local auto parts store. The only building I had seen in England of comparable size was a cathedral.

The guy in line before me approached the counter. "Got me a dent," he announced, chewing gum. "Some idiot hit me and ran." How terrible! I wondered when he had been released from the hospital, after his ordeal. The clerk asked where the wounds had been inflicted. "Rear end, bud, left side. Pushed me right out of shape. Gonna need me some bodywork." I peeked at the man's left buttock. It looked fine to me. Of course, he was talking about his car. You knew that, and now I do. In Southern California, where a car is central to your life, what you drive becomes synonymous with who you are. So it is with our identity. Instead of a shifting, evolving art form, an offering to the world, our personality becomes who we are, a matter of life and death. As Ayurvedic teacher Atreya Smith once said to me, "This whole enlightenment thing has gotten really blown out of proportion. It all boils down to a simple case of mistaken identity."

HOW WE DEFINE OURSELVES

"Trailing clouds of glory do we come, from God who is our home," wrote William Wordsworth. As preverbal babies, we experience ourselves as limitlessness. At one with what we see and feel, we have no need to define ourselves. We are both nothing and everything. Then Iago imposes a sense of limitation, of something missing, which we can never quite put a finger on. We can spend an entire lifetime trying to find a satisfactory ending to the statement "I am..." It's as though we have amnesia and just remembering the answer will allow us to rest. We take on labels and defend them. We resist their opposites. Assigning these labels allows us to function in the world of separate beings, but none of them really removes the fact that we have a very vague sense of who we really are, deeper than these roles we play.

> There is so much that is conditioned in us when we're young, through our parents and through the culture, about growth, and God, and responsibilities and duties.
>
> — Richard Moss

Every label we adopt creates a polarity. As soon as we identify with being intelligent, we live in a universe that also contains stupidity. Being wealthy is a resistance to poverty, and power creates weakness. So a personality is not only a bundle of qualities with which we identify, it is equally a unique set of resisted traits. In creating a "spiritual" identity for himself, Josh had also resisted his power, authority, and darker energies. His personality was "spiritual" but not translucent; it was fragmented rather than whole.

TRY IT YOURSELF
Would You Still Exist?

You can do this exercise alone or with a friend. It can transform your relationship to your identity. Start by writing down every quality you identify with. If you are working with a friend, one partner can ask the other, "Who have you taken yourself to be?" Be exhaustive in your answer. Write everything: I'm a plumber, I'm Jewish, I'm someone who likes Italian cooking, I'm a gardener. Keep going until you cannot find any new answers to the question. It might take you an hour or more.

Then go back slowly through the list and ask yourself, "If I no longer identified myself as..." and add one of the words you've written, "would I still exist?"

For some of your answers, you'll get an immediate clear "yes." For example, if I were no longer a plumber, would I still exist? Yes, I could go into selling life insurance. Some may be a little stickier: "If I were no longer a father, would I still exist?" You might have to carefully remember your days before you had children and ask yourself if the core of who you are now and the core of who you were then is the same. You might have to imagine what it would be like if one day you woke up and found that your entire experience of parenting was just a dream. Disorienting as it might be, would you still be here?

Some answers will be even more difficult: "I am a man." It might take you several minutes of feeling deeper even than your gender identity to decide if you'd still exist without the gender you are used to. Some of your answers may be conceptual, like, "I am light" or "I am consciousness." When you ask, "Would I still exist?" you may feel that this answer points to something deeper than the other labels. You can change the question to, "Would I still exist without this thought, without this concept?"

> Even with people who seem to have their act together, others can take a look and see, "There, this piece is missing." We can see how they appear to be governed. Bringing a creative responsiveness to the situation doesn't end with awakening. Awakening actually makes it possible.
>
> — Saniel Bonder

Whether you do this exercise alone or with a friend, you will need some time for it to go deep. If it does, stop and feel your own presence when you have let go of *all* definitions. Are you still here? Can you still feel and see and hear? Take some time to relax into knowing the face you had before you were born.

Married to the Past

The personality we create in Iago's trance is a by-product of our sense of personal history. What makes you different from your friends, your partner, or your co-workers? Of course, we all have differently shaped bodies, which is convenient when you need to find someone you know in a shopping mall. But that is not all that differentiates us. We experience the world in different ways; we have different reactions, likes, and dislikes. We are all the products of conditioning and memory, of different personal histories. The more opaque we are in the way we experience each moment, the more we are caught in Iago's web, the more attached we are to that past. Iago could persuade us that we are helpless victims of childhood conditioning, mechanically acting out the ways we have been programmed to behave. Or we could cling to affirmations, to ideas of ourselves, in order to feel secure, to feel we are somebody in particular. Either way, as we age, still in Iago's grip, we cling to memories of the past as a way to preserve a sense of separate identity.

For most of us, this fabricated sense of "me," put together like a scrapbook, is no laughing matter. Our habits of defending identity, resisting change, or submitting to its iron grip run our lives. When any one of the roles we have adopted and called "me" is threatened, we feel the deepest despair we can know. When Robert's real estate dealings went wrong, he felt suicidal. Years earlier, as a student, he had very little money and was happy. But when his fortune was taken away, even though he knew life to be fine without it, he contemplated death as a better alternative to pennilessness. Losing his money seemed a fate worse than death.

When Sandra's children left home, she faced a period of depression she had never before known. She lost her appetite, her will to live. Although she had spent twenty-six reasonably happy years before becoming a mother, once that role was taken away from her, she suddenly did not know who she was and was plunged into devastating despair. This desire to kill oneself is most often linked to the removal of a central role. *I'm Bobby's mother... I'm Amy's boyfriend... I'm John's wife ... I'm the president of the bank... I'm the one who everyone turns to ... I'm the owner of this... the creator of that.* Take away our core definition, and we want to die.

> We have to redeem the unconsciousness hiding in all our roles, duties, and responsibilities. We must do that with each other. Every time we challenge deeply conditioned forms of identity, there is real pain, a real threat at some level to the sense of self, since none of us know ourselves outside of relationship.
>
> — Richard Moss

Cookie-cutter Spirituality

We acquire our identity in Iago's grip through imitation. Because we have no intrinsic sense of self when we are hypnotized by separation, we create one from what we see around us. After Josh had his moment on the building site, huge chunks of his identity broke away. He realized that his soft gaze, his empathetic nod of the head, his habit of deferring to others, were all qualities he thought he should display, all created from the cookie-cutter image of a spiritual man. He had borrowed every characteristic from a meditation teacher or from stereotypical behaviors displayed by spiritual groups. As soon as he took one step out of the box, the box disappeared. The following week he discovered a whole new way of being with his girlfriend, his friends, and even his meditation teacher.

> Most human beings are terrified of stepping into the unknown. We worship the real flowers, like Jesus or Buddha or Muhammad. They aren't followers. Their awakening translated into some kind of incredible human courage and willingness to flower in the way that they were meant to flower in this life.
>
> — Adyashanti

Our best solution when Iago is the only game in town is to increase the qualities we find desirable — usually the ones for which we get the most external approval — and to reject their opposites. To the degree we are successful at this, we feel we are becoming a better person, and we call this raising our self-esteem. But it never really works. Sometimes we may feel useless, sometimes like a great person, but either way, as long as we feel essentially separate, as long as we ignore any lingering knowledge of our deeper nature, ultimately we feel like a fraud. Forgotten echoes of our innocent natural vision tell us we could, and should, feel connected with everything, relaxed, expansive, at home.

SPIRITUAL MYTH #1: After a spiritual awakening, there is no more ego, and personality traits disappear completely. What remains is just a homogenous oneness with everything.

SPIRITUAL MYTH #2: Awake people are not identified with the personality and therefore have no interest in changing it.

A TRANSLUCENT IDENTITY

In contrast, translucents share a sense of humor about their personality, a distance from it. They can allow it to be as it is. Translucents display a willingness to be wrong, to let go and move on. Their perception of their identity is the way we might experience a crazy uncle who can be tolerated, enjoyed, even loved. There is no reason to change your mad uncle, but there is also no reason to defend him or apologize for him. If he disturbs the neighbors, a little damage control is simply intelligent.

Translucents have shifted their dominant sense of self from content to context. They know that who they *really* are is what remains when they relax any attempt to define themselves. It is like being the sky instead of a cloud, being the ocean instead of a wave. Self-esteem yields to esteem for the Great One Self, which knows no limits. The Big Self was never born, will never die, has no limitations, and is untouched by the swirling dramas of this world. It is appearing in disguise for a limited time only in your hometown, ladies and gentlemen, as a small person with a great many small problems and a very severe case of amnesia.

Lynne Twist is the author of *The Soul of Money*. I went to a book signing she gave in San Francisco. "I need you to know that I did not write this book," she began. People looked a little puzzled. "Oh, I signed the contract with the publisher, and I got an advance, and my name is on the cover. But what really wrote the book is the same source that has been my teacher in life." She went on to list some of the manifestations of this real teacher: as children in South America or Asia, as courageous people who have shown her firsthand the real meaning of wealth as something more than just money. "I feel blessed by so many gifts in this life, it would be a crime not to pass it on. But I cannot take credit for what is in the book. It came through me, not from me."

> Part of the myth is: "If you're awakened, you are a superperson, a resource for the ultimate truth on everything." Which is crap! More and more, people are seeing through this myth. This new realism can't be set aside; it will have its development in our culture.
>
> — Saniel Bonder

This is the translucent spirit speaking. Before an awakening shift, we linger in the default setting of low self-esteem. We feel ashamed of our smallness and fear. Then, if we come to our senses and wake up, we lose even that small amount of esteem we were holding onto for the sense of "me" and instead have total esteem for the real source of our gifts, which is everywhere all the time. This overflowing esteem, for the real author of our books and for all our other offerings, is gratitude. By remaining internally undefined, you become nothing, but at the same time potentially everything. So we feel quite comfortable to be both intelligent and stupid at the same time in a way that defies logic but that we experience subjectively as wholeness.

Isaac Shapiro exemplifies this fluidity. He has been traveling as a translucent teacher for more than twelve years in Europe, America, and Australia. Hundreds of people attend his retreats and look to him as a source of wisdom. He could have every excuse for solidifying an identity as a "showbiz guru." Goodness knows many have gone down that road.

> I'm always coming out of that place. That's what it's lived by; that's what lives. People say, "Oh, it's Katie," and I say, "Yes, who is that unmasked woman?" There's no reason to mask.
>
> — Byron Katie

When Isaac's marriage fell apart a few years ago, he made no attempt to hide his confusion or pain. I remember sitting with him in a small circle of friends in Amsterdam. The circle included some of his students. I watched closely as someone challenged him, pointing out his unattended personality habits that had contributed to the breakdown of his marriage. I saw in his eyes a vulnerability, a rawness, an absolute willingness to be wrong that was as total as his willingness to play spiritual teacher when that role was demanded. When translucents are faced with being the great enlightened teacher or with being the most unenlightened fool, they just don't know which to choose. Both roles look interesting — like two flavors of ice cream. So they take on what is real in that moment and die to the rest.

Self-acceptance

I first met Byron Katie many years ago, when she was still traveling the country in an RV. She would meet with a handful of people in one city, then drive on to another. It was clear that she had unvelcroed her attachment to her story completely. She would speak of herself in the third person, but with no trace of affectation. She obviously experienced Katie to be a delightful, interesting, and quirky creature. She enjoyed watching Katie and also knew herself to be so much more than Katie.

She told me of a time she was walking in the parking lot at the grocery store. Most of her stories took place in shopping malls or supermarkets

— she embodied the Mahabharata, relocated to suburban America. In this story, she saw a woman loading her groceries from her shopping cart into the back of the car. Poking out of the top of the last bag Katie saw a bunch of bananas.

"And honey," she said, "this Katie just knew, without any hesitation, that one of those bananas was destined to be eaten by her." Katie walked right over. Without saying a word to the woman, she smiled, took the banana, and ate it. Katie relayed this story with a twinkle in her eye, as if she were giggling about her eccentric grandmother. There was neither self-aggrandizement nor self-apology, but rather absolute humorous acceptance of her natural character. The climax of the story was that the woman who owned the banana in question did not bat an eye. She, too, mysteriously experienced the whole event as quite normal.

This story is, of course, somewhat unusual. Perhaps not something you should aim to imitate, this kind of event cannot be duplicated. What is exemplary here is not the circumstance, but the relaxed and amused way that Katie speaks of her own unique way of moving through this world.

> Each person comes prewired with predispositions. Mine is to kick ass when it's appropriate, and being surrendered to life means I still kick ass when it's appropriate. Till there comes a point when it's futile.
>
> — Satyam Nadeen

The thousands of people I have talked to have nothing in common except that their awakening has imbued them with a growing translucence. Translucents are relaxed, accepting, and amused by the personality. There is no attachment to changing it, getting rid of it, or indulging in it, but neither is there any resistance to change, if it happens. In this awareness of being undefined and beyond the personality, a luminous presence is liberated that has no content or opinions, that is still and silent and empty. This presence uses the personality, as the best raw material available, to play in this world.

Natural Character

As translucents continuously relax into being less defined internally, they become more vivid and unique externally. This differs radically from the personality contractions created by Iago's anxiety. Life chooses to express itself through you in a way that is quite effortless, spontaneous, and original — as

> We're human beings. We have preferences, we have desires, we have wants. As long as the awareness of the larger context is the primary focus of our lives, and the choices we make are an expression and reflection of that, then there's plenty of room for personal preferences. It has to do with the fundamental thrust of our attention, our action, and our choices.
>
> — Andrew Cohen

natural character. Eckhart Tolle is quiet, very modest, and loves to stay at home for long periods in his apartment in Vancouver. No one has told him to be like that. He is not imitating a role model. And he has no impulse to interfere with himself. It is his natural character. Byron Katie is constantly on the road, traveling from city to city, talking with people from dawn to dusk, always fresh.

"Don't you get tired with so much traveling?" I once asked her. She looked puzzled for a moment. "Hmm," she finally said. "Do I look tired, honey?" I had to admit she looked great.

Bill plays in the band and drinks beer, Cynthia cooks for her son and volunteers at her church, and Ewa plays her flute. They are following their natural character. We all have natural character, but when we are caught in the Iago trance, we are hypnotized into feeling there is a problem to fix, and so we modify ourselves. Hale Dwoskin calls this process "shoulding": "We are 'shoulding' on ourselves all the time. All that does is create resistance. It causes us to resist the flow, if it does not match our rights and wrongs, goods and bads, shoulds and shouldn'ts. As you let go, you should on yourself much less. You do what you do when you are doing it, and you don't do what you are not doing when you are not doing it."

Because translucents internally experience themselves as undefined, they can let natural character do its thing. With less identification, there is no motivation to change anything.

Spontaneous Forgiveness

With the willingness to be less defined comes a loosening of our grip on the past. The past is of little use when you have no case to defend. If the trial is dismissed as boring and irrelevant, you can send the witnesses home to get on with their lives and dump the bulging dossier of carefully crafted case notes into the trash. Translucents have a natural interest in forgiving and moving on. Forgiveness is no longer a moral virtue, or something we need to practice, but the effortless by-product of no longer needing to protect an identity with a story attached to it. The past is not healed; it simply ceases to be useful.

Sarah had memories of abuse as a child. She was never quite sure which of the events she remembered actually happened, but they certainly all seemed real. She saw a number of therapists over many years. She visited her family from time to time; she tried to sit down with her father to find out what had really happened. She joined a support group. This identity, as a survivor of abuse, was one of the first things she would tell you about herself. Some years ago, Sarah came to a gathering I offered. She had an awakening; she discovered reality without the filters of her mind.

Recently, I tentatively asked her again about her memories. I knew it was a sensitive subject. "I don't really know if that stuff happened or not," she laughed. "Maybe it did. I don't think about it anymore. It's not interesting. It doesn't feel like I healed the past." She stopped and looked surprised. "It's more like I don't really have a past. I'd need to think a lot to create one." Sarah has been to visit her father on several occasions since her shift but feels no need to talk about the past. They discuss sports results and gardening and have a good time. Sarah discovered forgiveness as a by-product of releasing a part of her identity. It was the death of a part of herself and, apparently, a great relief.

A survivor of abuse has every reason in the world to be angry, to have strong feelings. A translucent's forgiveness is neither a moral quality nor a cultivated virtue, but the natural and inevitable consequence of knowing oneself as something more than the past. When we disidentify with the story, there's no need to hold onto it with regret. We forgive as an act of allegiance to the present moment; it becomes choiceless.

> As you start to let go, you let go of your desire to change what has already happened. What's already happened is complete. That's a big step, because any time we want to change what has already happened, we re-create it over and over again in order to change it. So when that drops away, a lot of patterns drop too, because you no longer want to fix what's already happened.
>
> — Hale Dwoskin

Instead of clinging to our familiar identity, as we grow in translucence, we discover a thirst for death and rebirth while still alive. Many of us have experienced several different lives all in one lifetime. This is very different from the discontented moving on described in chapter 1 that disturbs us in the Iago trance. Translucents welcome this death of identity with a sense of play and adventure. David Deida describes the process like this: "Once I feel complete with something, it's over for me as a gift, and it drops, letting a new gift evolve. If I meet someone who could do what I can do better, I stand aside and let them do it, and develop a service that is missing in the world."

At one time Deida was considered one of the world's top neuroscientists. He worked at Ecole Polytechnique and the Pasteur Institute in Paris. When that career was complete, he knew it. Neuroscience held no more interest or attraction. He then co-invented a new form of calculus, publishing articles about it in mathematics journals. Then, when he knew that life was over, he moved to Hawaii and taught Hatha yoga for many years. In the mid-1990s he started to write about sex, relationship, and spirit, since he didn't see anyone else doing that in the way he wanted to see it done. "I'll be moving on from the whole sex/relationship/spirit thing," he says, "as soon as someone gets up to speed. The sooner the better, as far as I'm concerned."

Translucents enjoy creating and letting go of identities as much as Iago resists change.

INHERENT EVOLUTION

As we deepen in translucence, we discover another dimension of our relationship to identity. It begins with the absolute acceptance of things as they are, of all our strange quirks and addictions and banana nabbing. Once we recognize everything to be fine as it is, we can relax even more deeply. We can feel, within each moment, an evolutionary impulse to steer life in a more artful, loving, open way. This is not a personal doing fueled by Iago. It is a surrendering, a discovery of the urge inherent within life to endlessly expand its expression of the mystery in form.

This is a subtle movement. As long as there are traces of Iago, which can appear in all of us at any time, it can be hijacked by

> So many people are getting, "Hey, awakening on its own doesn't cut it. I've got to find out how to be a human being with this, how to live with other human beings." There is this further awakening going on. This is cutting-edge stuff. It takes us into some very sober looking back at where we came from.
>
> — Saniel Bonder

effort and discontent. But within a radical acceptance of our broken condition, a willingness to endure it eternally and to abandon futile efforts at improvement, our habits of identity begin to mend and to evolve, always toward their ultimate potential.

Life is not a static event. It is a river of endless evolution. Look over your shoulder a few billion years. Once there was just a bunch of atoms. Look at how they have evolved into trees and rivers and rocks and sentient beings — at how life has transformed into this unimaginable, miraculous sentient being with the capacity to be aware of its own source. Within this huge evolutionary process, the birth, awakening, relative translucence, and eventual death of any specific individual is a very small, fleeting event.

Andrew Cohen speaks eloquently about collective evolution: "In the urge to become, there is a directionality toward higher and higher levels of integration. When human beings awaken to this and begin to emotionally care, not only about themselves, but

> There is a very pernicious structure that says our quest is to experience the pure witnessing eternal transcendent reality, and we have to escape this nasty business around suffering. I call it "God's escape route," and I don't believe it. It seems to me to trivialize what the reciprocal beauty of the human endeavor is all about.
>
> — James O'Dea

also about this larger context, the largest context that there is, then their response becomes one with the God principle itself."

Cohen calls this recognition "impersonal enlightenment" and sees it as the next essential evolutionary stage of human life. In what he calls "premodern, traditional models of enlightenment" the goal was to just "get up and out of here":

> *Their concept of time was cyclical — the idea was that we are on a merry-go-round that is going around and around for eternity. They hadn't yet discovered the deep time developmental context that we're all a part of. This knowledge is relatively recent, only three hundred years old. The fact is, we're not on a merry-go-round; we are the product of fourteen billion years of evolutionary development. Human beings have only existed for about sixty thousand years, and only very, very recently have we awakened to the evolutionary context of our emergence. We are living in such an exciting time!*

The moment of radical awakening described in chapter 2 is a part of this developmental process. And the very recognition that we are in a collective developmental process is in itself another huge shift, one that transforms the individual as well as the collective process itself. Cohen continues: "You realize that part of what you are is an individual human being that has been born in a particular time in history. On a personal, emotional, psychological, and physical level, you have a personal history. From the larger perspective, you are actually part of a fourteen-billion-year process of development."

As human beings, we are predisposed to become exclusively focused on "my" life. It is all that most of us will ever think about. Even when we have developed a higher degree of translucence, there still often remains a natural and inevitable interest in "my" liberation, "my" enlightenment, "my" spiritual experience. This is natural and good; without that predisposition, no one would even have the interest to mature and evolve.

> The biological programming for selfishness is very, very strong. I have a profound respect for that urge. I feel it in myself, the profound arising of "me first." We are not the gentlest of creatures, even though gentleness is an aspect that lives in us. We're a huge range, from gentle to completely depraved, and I think that we can feel that range within each of us.
>
> — Catherine Ingram

When sperm are released during sex, every single spermatozoan is focused on reaching the egg and fertilizing it. Either one or none of them will be successful. The eventual outcome may be a human birth and the continuation of the evolutionary process. Out of the countless billions of sperm ejaculated out of a male body in one life, only a very few will realize their potential to become human beings. But in order for that to occur, it is vital that every little ambitious fella rush like crazy to reach that egg every time. Almost all will die and disappear. The impulse to reach the egg is, we could say, the micro-motive, human birth is the macro-motive, and the evolution and continuation of human life is the meta-motive that lies beyond both.

In the same way, however profound our awakening, however deeply lived our translucence, it is highly likely that in a few hundred years no one will remember how enlightened or unenlightened any of us was, or if we even existed at all. Our personal lives, our spiritual journey, is the micro-motive, while the evolution of life is the meta-motive. Each human story is like a tiny grain of sand in an hourglass, irrelevant and dispensable in itself, but an essential part of the bigger picture of evolution. Everything living is carried in this evolutionary current, and everything is, to some degree or other, causing that evolution to occur. Cohen asks:

> *Do the actions we take, the choices we make, express the fact that we know we are a part of this process? Does this process itself, at a certain point in evolutionary development, actually begin to depend upon my own conscious participation in it? At this point there is an imperative to begin to be responsible for the process itself through one's own incarnation in the biggest possible way, rather than living for oneself the way that most people do.*

As Cohen points out, awareness of the evolutionary context is quite recent in human development. It takes the very peaks of human maturity to grasp that ultimately your or my awakening, translucence, and eventual death are a tiny part of a much bigger and more important process. As long as we are preoccupied with our own identity, that very preoccupation will keep the idea of a separate me locked in place, the very core of the Iago trance, and will prevent genuine realization. As soon as we realize the bigger context of collective evolution, our attention shifts from "me" to that process itself, and our realization of the timeless and formless deepens.

> If I let go of the notion of my individuality, then it's endless. I suffer when others suffer. I learn from the mistakes other people make. I see myself as a midwife to an emergent consciousness. I stand at the gate reaching both ways. With the simplest relaxation, I can be in complete gratitude, and the next moment I can feel my heart break.
>
> — Richard Moss

Cohen sees that simply by pursuing this awareness of the collective evolutionary process, people pass through an enormous transformation. He calls it the "authentic self" awakening. Not only do people return to an awareness of their natural state, but they also realize that the way they live is actually very significant; it is evolution in action, here and here and here. There is no evolutionary process happening outside of how you and I live every moment: "When you truly, deeply, profoundly recognize that your human experience is not really a personal journey," says Cohen, "and it's not a personal drama, your relationship to it changes in a way that's very profound. The individual

is transformed and becomes a different person as a result. They have a profoundly different relationship to what it means to be a human being, living
in the world."

With this awareness, we return to paying attention to how we live, to how
we relate, to the things we say and the choices we make. We pay attention to
these things not to improve ourselves, not to fix a problem or achieve a goal,
but because the larger current of collective evolution demands it.

AWAKENING AND MENDING

To surrender to this demand, we must be willing to look at the "broken
zones" of our personality with honesty and courage. In the last decades, several new approaches have evolved that address this calling. These are not
paths to psychological healing. They are also not spiritual paths to enlightenment in the traditional sense. Rather, to some extent they all rest on a
degree of awakening to be effective. They are skillful means to bring wakefulness into full embodiment.

Until recently, spiritual teaching presented an either/or choice. It was
thought that if you were trying to fix, mend, heal, or release tension from
your personality, you were identified with it, in a state of delusion. Awakening, in the traditional view, meant that you had seen through the personality
as fictitious, and therefore you no longer
touched it. This view has resulted in many
people with some degree of genuine awakening but who also carry horrendous dysfunctional habits. They obstinately refuse
to look at them, because to do so would
display "identification."

One of the most effective and powerful
ways to address this schism is found in the
work of Saniel Bonder: "It's a particular
passion of mine to communicate the extent of the brokenness of the human
soul and psyche, and how gravely impaired we are by the degree to which even

> I'm not seeking anything. I'm done.
> There's nothing more to be sought.
> And yet . . . there is this ongoing
> process of clarification, or embodiment,
> or deepening, which could last a
> lifetime. I know myself to be limitless,
> timeless presence, yet this presence is
> transforming and purifying the vehicle.
>
> — Stephan Bodian

'awakened' people continue to be governed by all that." He describes his approach, Waking Down in Mutuality, as "not formally psychotherapeutic, but rather initiatory and mutually grounding." Bonder's work has three dimensions, all contained in its title.

The first is waking. He and his community help people to awaken through a variety of means, including self-inquiry. This awakening is not the end of spiritual life, as it's often thought to be in approaches that emphasize transcendence. Rather, it catalyzes an exploration of our potential to live with sanity.

As long as you're predominantly identified with personality, as long as you think "this is me," you can't really make any big shifts, says Bonder. That's like trying to make a major renovation to the hull of a boat you are sailing in — first you've got to get the hull out of the water. You can't do brain surgery on yourself. Similarly, you can't begin to deeply mend your psyche if you overwhelmingly feel and think you are the psyche. That would be brokenness trying to mend itself.

> Whatever it is that's awakening us is much more intelligent than who we become when we are awakened.
>
> — Richard Moss

Bonder sees awakening as the essential foundation for the evolutionary work that follows: "You can't do that work for real without the transcendental ground of being. Otherwise, it is one part of your split-off self engaging the other, but still to some degree fearing and fighting it." Without an awakening, we are able to accomplish only a relatively superficial mending of our human brokenness.

The second dimension is down: bringing the liberated spirit into embodiment in daily life, and integrating the broken zones:

When wakefulness comes forward and starts to wake down, to embody, to descend more fully into the psyche, there is a sacred marriage of two great dimensions of ourselves. We undergo a challenging exposure to our issues, traumas, broken zones. When we fall into them, these dimensions of our identity feel radically discontinuous with our ordinary sense of who we are. We start reacting in ways that others may find quite disproportionate to the actual realities of the present moment.

I don't see anything wrong with hate or greed or sadness or joy. I don't see anything "negative" about anything that is. That which is human is me, and I'm not separate from anything that is human. Humanity is a part of all that is, and all parts of humanity are included there. And so all parts must be embraced.

— Jett Psaris

Bonder sees these broken zones as relatively untouched by a radical awakening. When we discover a deeper, unconditioned dimension to ourselves, we identify less with these old habits; we may feel they are essentially unimportant, but they continue nevertheless. He believes that most traditional spiritual approaches have tended either to ignore these broken zones or even to exacerbate them: "Under the guise of attracting people into ego-death and ego-transcendence, the teaching styles of many teachers have practically pulverized people in their broken zones. It takes an Olympic gymnast of a psyche and spirit to somehow leap over those gaps, collect enough energy and attention, and crystallize the awakening. Consequently, only a few in any generation pull it off."

Bonder feels that traditional spiritual approaches often hole up in awakeness, shying clear of the much more difficult, messy work of evolutionary embodiment. We know ourselves to be limitless and free, untouched by birth and death. "Good," they might say, "let's close the book on how we live and treat other people." In this way, the evolutionary aspect described by Cohen is more or less stopped dead in its tracks. Bonder feels that in order to bring forth the real evolutionary potential of awakening, we must return to how we live and heal, or make ourselves whole, from an awakened perspective.

The third dimension is mutuality, doing this work with others of like mind, catalyzing further transformations together. Bonder sees mutuality as an essential context, one in which everyone is equally vulnerable, open, and willing to see where the evolutionary impulse can be given more room: "You can't hide out in the enlightened ivory tower of 'my realization is superior to yours,' or, 'I know you better than you know yourself,' or, 'I've got a superior insight, wow, isn't that amazing to you?' "

In real mutuality, the teacher is no longer one particular person in the room; the real teacher becomes the meeting itself, the highest evolutionary potential of the group, called forth by the gathering.

ABOUT NUDGING

In each of the remaining chapters of this book, you will find invitations to nudge the habits of the human monkey in the direction of translucence. Some of the earlier exercises labeled "Try It Yourself" were invitations to experiment now, as you are reading this book. Nudges, on the other hand, are recipes you can carry with you into your day-to-day life.

We need to really understand what we mean by nudging, or the process could actually become a way to decrease translucence. Nudging has its firm foundation in acceptance of things as they are. It is not a form of self-improvement, a way to achieve something that is missing, or to get rid of anything. Real nudging is also not a serious activity at all; it is more of an art form than a kind of psychotherapy. Feeling our personality to be essentially unfixable, we abandon any serious effort to improve it and instead recycle the parts to create art. Nudging is not for the "me" but rather a way to loosen and melt this sense of separate "me" so that inherent translucence can glow more brightly.

Most nudging is best done with co-conspirators. We take ourselves too seriously to be able to nudge well alone. It would be like tickling yourself or telling yourself a joke. When in doubt, nudge with a translucent friend or, better still, with a small group of budding translucents. In our house, it is our family, friends, students, co-workers, even our cat, rabbits, and pet rats who help nudge us back into translucence every day. We ask them to. By the time you are done reading this book you will have many nudging games to play. If you feel inspired, you might want to get together with others now and then and experiment with living outside the box. But *puhleeze* don't get too holy about it. We've all done that ad nauseam. Playing gutsy rock 'n' roll is just as appropriate for a gathering of translucents as chanting sacred mantras.

Your community of fellow translucents may suggest which specific nudging

> Practice means "making practical," so that your life is not divided between your spirituality and your mundane existence but is so intimately interwoven that there can't be a difference. With the wisdom that you have inside, how are you going to live an enlightened life? If we're walking through life with a mind split by negativity, our experience is nothing more than a fragmented drama. It certainly isn't an entry into deep realization.
>
> — ShantiMayi

practices could bring deeper translucence. Nudging practices must always be done in an atmosphere of respect, humor, and mutual consent. As soon as someone is humiliated, pressured, or rationalized into a nudging practice, rigidity will be hardened rather than melted, and a backlash will probably be created. Above all, nudging is not something that we "do," but more something we play with. The nudging practices in this book should be like catalysts. They are little provocations to help the Iago habits relax their grip, just enough so that the force of translucence has a chance to sprout through the cracked soil of crusty habit and help dance us free of ourselves.

NUDGING IDENTITY TOWARD TRANSLUCENCE

NUDGE

Exaggerate

The glue keeping the trance of separation in place, keeping us bound to the roles we play, is seriousness. We take the way that we live out our personality traits very seriously. We also seriously maintain that we are not glued to them. "What do you mean, I'm too serious? No, I'm really quite fun-loving! Argumentative? You must be thinking of somebody else."

You can do this exercise with the help of your friends. Feel into where you are most glued to the habits of identity. Instead of trying to deny, improve, or get rid of them, playfully exaggerate them with humor. For example, if you and your friends agree that you are identified with being right, amp it up even more. But do it with a loud British military accent while marching around the room. If you and your friends agree that you are identified with being controlling, stand on the table and tell everyone what to do, in a German accent. If you enjoy playing the victim, take a few minutes to make an art form out of it. Outdo Woody Allen. When we turn neurosis into art, it no longer binds us, and the deeper force of translucence shines through our habits and transforms them.

> We have an awakening. Good, now we can get on with it. Now we can start. As soon as we've got our realization there's a way that the teacher will try to knock you off balance, again and again. In fact, life is more than happy to do that for us. Life seems more than adept at knocking us off balance.
>
> — Adyashanti

NUDGE
Do the Opposite

Once you recognize a habit of identity, you can also play with doing the opposite. You can experiment with this for a few minutes, hours, or even for a day. Someone very outgoing and gregarious might be given the task of going out for dinner with friends and saying nothing, thus experimenting with the "frequency" of shyness. Or if you and your friends see that you fall into an automatic habit of following what other people want, you might be asked to get authoritative for a specific time. Play with reversing automatic habits just long enough to feel fluid with another way of doing the dance, then relax completely. The homeopathic medicine will do its work.

NUDGE
Exchanging Personalities

In our family, we often play this nudging game at dinner. We also love to share it at weekend translucent gatherings. Write each person's name on a piece of paper, and fold it up small. Put all the folded papers into a bowl or a cup. Pass it around, everyone taking a name. Now you have five minutes to become the person whose name you've picked. Let it come from inside, not imitating the accent or obvious mannerisms, but really deeply feeling what it is like to exchange identities for a few minutes. What does your body feel like? What kind of thoughts and desires and opinions do you slip into like a tight T-shirt? If you pick your own name, have fun making an art out of the person you usually think you are.

A few minutes of any of these nudges is long enough to shake things up a bit. Remember, we are not trying to change the personality, just to loosen its rigidity.

CHAPTER FIVE

INSPIRED CERTAINTY

Translucent Action

Greg Steltenpohl started his juice company, Odwalla, with a group of friends in Santa Cruz. The company was founded on the principles of service, equality among employees, and having a good time. Many years later, Odwalla had become one of the largest manufacturers of freshly squeezed juices in the United States. When a few people in Washington state suddenly got sick with E. coli, a rumor linked the outbreak to Odwalla's unpasteurized apple juice. There was an uproar at the company. Withdrawing all apple juice products from the distribution network would essentially wipe out Odwalla's shelf presence for several weeks. Allowing the juice to be sold ran the risk of further illness. There were meetings. Everybody had different opinions and advice. But Greg knew what to do. It was not a decision made with his head, but more a "knowing" from his belly, as if a decision had already been made and he simply had to be sensitive enough to get to it. Greg ordered all products containing apple juice to be removed from the market. Within a few weeks, Odwalla had developed a different system of flash pasteurization. It took three years for Odwalla to regain its market position, but within five years it had doubled its market share.

Most of us live our life as though our thoughts are both who we are and facts. But neither is true. Thoughts are just that — not facts, and not true. The good news is you have the ability to let go of any thought and thereby change both the way you feel and how you act in life.

— Hale Dwoskin

Translucents have fewer beliefs to protect; they are comfortable with not knowing what to do until they really *know*. They have less need to think and dramatically less need to be right. When we are acting translucently, our actions come from a different place within us. Instead of reflecting a system of belief, they are a direct response to the situation as it is.

TO DO OR NOT TO DO

Spurred on by Iago's whisper, the urgent question in every situation is "What am I going to do?" It eats into us like the spur on the boot of an aggressive rider. When we think about it, we rarely know what to do for sure. We develop multiple sets of beliefs to guide us in our ability to make decisions. Even a simple question like where to go for dinner releases a cacophony of colliding points of view: *We need to save money... I'm getting over-weight... I'm the kind of person who appreciates good food... You can't trust franchises... Chinese food is too greasy, it's bad for the heart.* The internal debate goes on and on. Whatever we decide, often we feel like we made the wrong choice.

In the Iago trance, we think and talk and take action based on preexisting sets of belief about what is right and wrong. Our behavior is predictable, and we almost always meet the present moment based on our past. Caught between conflicting beliefs, we have an inward experience of indecision: a turbulent, stressful, mentally active place. Meanwhile, externally, we are unable to take action: a stuck, frozen place. And since urgency and crisis fuel the Iago trance, we feel inadequate and ashamed of not knowing what to do. There seems to be no way out.

Here is your upset spouse, here are your hyperactive children, here are your bills, here is your not-quite-enough income, here is a mysterious pain in your chest, oops, it's shifted to your belly, here is your boss wanting more from you in less time, here is your roof needing repair, and here is your world, being driven over the cliff at breakneck speed by fundamentalist politicians. *What are you going to do?* We just don't know. We try to anticipate circumstances, to alleviate suffering for others and for ourselves, and to find happiness. But it's like playing roulette. There's just no way to know into which slot that silver ball is going to land.

At our foundation, we, like many others, have been working for a long time with the dynamics of belief, in our weekend seminars. We experience any contraction as a belief when we perceive it mentally, as an upset when we feel it emotionally, and as a tension in the body when we sense it physically. Underneath all these ways of experiencing, it is just a contracted energy state, like a radio wave. This is much easier, and simpler, to feel than to talk about. These frequencies

> When you question your stressful thoughts, the freedom that comes out of that graces the world for all of us.
>
> — Byron Katie

are contractions in consciousness itself, in who you are. Have you ever felt a tension within yourself, perhaps a lack of ease, and noticed it *before* it started to create thoughts, emotions, or tension in the body? This is what we mean by the frequency, the atmosphere, underlying and preceding belief.

The first step in nudging these contractions is to recognize and label them. Frank came to one of our weekend gatherings several years ago. When it was time to explore the ways in which we are immobilized in indecision, he volunteered. Recently divorced, he had just attended a conference associated with his job. He met Suzie there; they spent time talking till after the bar had closed and the band had gone home, mostly about their mutual profession. Suzie stirred up some deep currents in Frank. After the conference, he felt immobilized about contacting her. After all, they lived on opposite coasts; what future was there in it? Frank thought about nothing else for weeks.

I asked him to talk freely, while I wrote down every belief I heard. Here are some of the beliefs Frank expressed: *don't mix work and pleasure... I'm too pushy... she might be in a relationship... nothing works out the way I plan it... better live for today... it's too soon for me after the divorce.* Altogether, I noted more than forty such points of view in seven and a half minutes of Frank's talking.

TRY IT YOURSELF

Put Your Mind on Paper

Here is an exercise you can do to free up your own beliefs. You can practice this alone or with a translucent ally.

Think of a sticky issue in your life, one that requires taking action. Ideally, find a situation in which you truly don't know what to do, but one in which *not* doing seems to invite catastrophe. If you are alone, write down all the thoughts you have about your impending decision, and list them as one-line points of view, as I did with Frank. If you have a friend, you can go a little deeper. You can kick back, close your eyes, talk about your issue, and ask your friend to make a note whenever she or he hears you express a belief. You will probably come up with quite a list.

THE ANATOMY OF BELIEF

The word *belief* originates with the Old English word *leof*, which means "to hold dear." The Encarta *World English Dictionary* defines it as "acceptance by the mind that something is true or real, often underpinned by an emotional or spiritual sense of certainty." But we only develop beliefs about certain things. There are many aspects of our experience we never question. For example, we may have a belief about life on other planets, but not about the existence of the moon. We may have beliefs about our ability to earn a million dollars in ten years, but not about our ability to brush our teeth. We may believe in past lives, but we don't need to believe in yesterday. In other words, we hold beliefs about things that we don't know about from direct experience. Why? Because we are unwilling to stay in not knowing.

> Everyone wants to find a way to happiness. And the way to happiness is waking up to what really is true. Until we question what we believe, we're blind to it.
>
> — Byron Katie

We take for granted that it is normal to come to fixed conclusions. But it seems we are the only species that clings to concepts in this way. The very idea of a fundamentalist penguin, or of an atheist cat, is absurd, the stuff of Gary Larson's "Far Side." What dog sits around the house postulating whether or not the universe is expanding? No, only the human mind in the grip of Iago comes to conclusions, independent of direct experience.

We need belief because we feel cut off from a deep connection to what is real. Animals, small children, and translucent people do not need to believe anything, because they are loyal to what is. Sometimes people ask, "Do you believe in God?" But what difference does a mental conclusion make? Either we feel God all around us and within us, and our heart is open to the Great Spirit creating and connecting all things — or we don't. Believing in what we do not feel creates a plastic, mental world with no nourishment or depth to it. We only need faith when we insist on closing our hearts.

Animals do, of course, learn from their environment. Our cat has learned how to use the cat door, an entirely conditioned response based on direct experience. And small children are the same. But Iago-hypnotized human beings develop many beliefs *despite* their learning, beliefs that may even contradict their direct experience. Let's look again at Frank's list from above: *No one likes me once they get to know me* and *she probably found me boring.* I asked Frank to reflect on the truth of some of his statements. As it turns out, the only person he could remember who had said she didn't like him was his former wife. And even she had adored him without wavering for thirteen years, until she fell for another man with a bigger car and bank balance and "staying power." As for Suzie, she had gone to embarrassing lengths, with the help of a few margaritas, to make sure Frank knew how fascinating she found him. Like Frank, we hold onto beliefs that defy the evidence of our immediate environment because of the imprints made on us by the past. Let's take a closer look at how this happens.

> When one is still in a very fundamental way absorbed in and deluded by the fears and desires of their own ego, there is a vague sense of the larger context out there, but mainly individuals are absorbed in this very subjective experience.
>
> — Andrew Cohen

Jean Piaget, the French developmental psychologist, discovered that newborns do not experience themselves and their environment as separate. Piaget confirmed this through close observation of how infants move. He saw that when a newborn grabs a rattle, for example, and pulls it toward her body, she is surprised when the rattle meets a solid form. He concluded that very young babies experience themselves as space. After six months or so, this

changes, and their body movement anticipates that they have a form. It takes
a few years for a child to lock into the idea of "me" as a separate identity
from the environment and to begin to negotiate exchange. Many people
retain this feeling of being space, later in their life, as a "cellular memory."

Human beings, then, come into the world with a sense of wholeness, a
sense of oneness, of nonseparation. Small children don't have any beliefs
about anything. Is your two-year-old a Christian or a Buddhist or a Hare
Krishna? Only if you decide to call her one. Does your three-year-old discuss
the presidential debates or side with political parties? Many different mechanisms cause us to adopt positions. We may imitate the beliefs of our immediate family or culture, or we may develop a belief system as a reaction
against them. But the beliefs that run deepest in us, and that are most hardwired into our bodies, we have assimilated by learning to cut off different
movements of energy within our psyches.

> The world appears to be suffering and
> imbalanced only when you think it is.
> Without a story, everyone is perfectly
> happy and has everything they want.
> Question what you think and stop your
> own suffering. That's what's important.
>
> — Byron Katie

You are very small. Your brother takes
your ball, and you feel angry. You are about
to strike out at him, and your mother yells,
"Stop!" That energy of anger gets locked
into your body. It becomes something we
no longer feel free to experience. We create
resistance to it. If this happens repeatedly,
with anger, for example, it hardens into a
belief that it is not okay to be angry. We
develop a docile personality with an angry shadow, just as Josh from the previous chapter did. As we get older, we polarize everything in this way. We
start to say *this is acceptable* and *that's unacceptable*. We inhibit the natural flow of
energy in our lives and make unconscious choices between what to include as
part of our personality and what to push down into the shadow.

So we develop our deepest points of view about ourselves and about life
in general by resisting specific aspects of our experience. As soon as we have
to say no to something, we develop a point of view. As soon as we say *black*
but not *white, intelligent* and not *stupid, good* and not *evil,* or *harmonious* and not
angry, we've split our otherwise undivided universe into this and not that and
chosen one over the other. Instead of recognizing that things are whole, we
cut off a part of our original integrity by preferring one thing to another.

Like cutting a melon in two, we choose to keep one half and push the other half away.

Do You Really Need That Thought?

We hold many of our beliefs to be sacred simply as compensation for this kind of fragmentation. *I am a kind and tolerant person.* Why would one need that thought? Many people are good, benevolent, and kind without ever needing to define themselves that way. We hold a strong belief when we struggle to keep its opposite hidden from ourselves as well as from other people. Who needs to repeat the thought, *Money is flowing easily into my life?* Who needs to tell people, *I am very open and loving and friendly?* Who needs to say, *You can trust me?* As Queen Gertrude says to Hamlet, "The lady doth protest too much, methinks." Belief differs from simple reality. Every belief has an opposite, with which it is in constant struggle. Reality has no opposite. It just is.

Soon after my wife, Chameli, moved here from Norway, we were listening to the news on the car radio. "We are a good and just people," a pumped-up politician declared. Chameli laughed out loud. She often does. "I just can't imagine in my wildest dreams the prime minister of Norway standing up with a straight face and saying, 'We are a good and just people,' " she said. "Not because Norwegians are evil, but just because it is such an absurd and meaningless statement. Americans or Norwegians, people are people, the world over." Why would our political leaders need to keep telling us how good we are? Some suggest it is to compensate for the unilateral bombing of civilians in other countries by the tens of thousands, rampant imperialism, and escalating greed and consumerism at others' expense. Who knows? Often people need strong beliefs to mask their opposite. Otherwise, things speak for themselves.

> It all comes down to the mind free of clinging. That for me is an understanding of freedom.
>
> — Joseph Goldstein

Only when we are willing to be both good and not good and everything in between does our feeling of being separate relax and the goodness of all life begin to flow through us. Effortful goodness is morality; effortless goodness is translucent. As we will discover, the way to dissolve a belief is to stop resisting both sides of the polarity. When the internal fighting stops, there is no longer any need for belief.

Byron Katie is masterful at unraveling the mind:

> We continue to condition ourselves away from ourselves. We continue to condition ourselves as separate, and needy beings. We continue to condition our societies as divided and dependent on faulty systems. This shows me that even though humans are potentially extremely bright, we're not so bright!
>
> — ShantiMayi

As long as we're at war with our own minds, we're at war with the world and with the whole human race. Because as long as we want to get rid of our thoughts, anyone that we meet is likely to become an enemy. There is only one mind, and people are going to tell us what we haven't dealt with yet in our own thinking. "You're fat. You're stupid. You're not good enough." If you are an enemy to your own mind, other people have to become enemies too, sooner or later. Until you understand, until you can love the thoughts that appear in your mind, then you can't love the rest of us. You work with the projector — the mind — not the projected world. I can't really love you until I question the mind that thinks it sees you outside itself.

The Principle of the Thing

So it is that a great deal of what we believe is simply resistance and is carried from the past. Instead of seeing and feeling your wife before you, in her vulnerability and her love for you, you filter this moment through the past; you think and act in response to your mother and every other woman who has crossed your path. Our actions cannot possibly be pure and appropriate responses if we use this kind of filter. We are reacting instead of responding; and that reaction is not even to what is here, but to something from the past. And as we have seen, some of our beliefs actually defy our experience rather than reflect it. Having developed a complex system of beliefs, we become more interested in defending them than in knowing what is true. The actuality of life becomes secondary to the "principle of the thing."

As we discovered in the last chapter, this idea of dissolving belief is extremely threatening until we know ourselves to be something bigger than the mind. If we are trapped in the mind, thinking we are the mind, to dissolve belief seems like a form of suicide; you are dissolving what you think you are. The Iago culture sanctifies individual self-expression as being more important than anything else, calling it freedom. Everything we do or say becomes an attempt to strengthen what we perceive to be true, even when reality doesn't match our beliefs. Our actions spring from a sense of what should and shouldn't be, and we become predictable response machines.

What are some of the outcomes of believing our thoughts and using them to define who we are? The first is indecision. We remain caught between conflicting points of view until the situation has changed so completely that these points of view are no longer relevant. For Frank, this dynamic translates into weighing the options for so long that Suzie eventually sends him an invitation to her wedding. To someone else.

The second option could be called weak action. In this case, we finally make a decision, because we feel we have to, but our decision carries with it tremendous doubt and built-in sabotage. Frank makes his phone call, but with all his qualifications and reservations still at play. In an almost inaudible whimper he tells Suzie all the reasons why he needs to be alone, then hangs up, kicking himself. When we don't attend to our conflicting points of view, our action has no energy, no dynamism. Restraint is built into the action's very core, because it sprang from a tension between opposing points of view.

> Are we divided inside? If we are divided inside, there's no way in hell or heaven that tomorrow we're not going to have a divided world. It doesn't matter if we've got the best intentions in the universe; what really matters is the state from which we act.
>
> — Adyashanti

The third option is as good as it gets in Iago's world. As Lady Macbeth advises, you "screw your courage to the sticking place" and, well, just do it. This involves using a will of iron, resolutely forcing all our energy into one rigid way of seeing things, obliterating all opposing points of view. In our Iago world we respect an iron will, thinking it demonstrates integrity.

Unfortunately, when we rigidly keep to one position, we are not really feeling every aspect of a situation or taking every factor into account. Even if we act with great dynamism and confidence, unforeseen elements may later cause us regret. In this option, Frank might take a course in self-assertion and call Suzie with flawless confidence. He might persuade her to come visit him, or even to move, but later discover all kinds of unexpected dynamics and wish he had given himself more time to heal from his divorce.

It is impossible, with our minds, to anticipate every aspect of a situation. When we act on principle, unforeseen elements will always take us by surprise.

And so we live in righteous regret, feeling that although we did the right thing, we were sabotaged by reality. Again.

Fundamentalism: Very Mental and Not Much Fun

Fundamentalism, of any sort, is the most solidified expression of Iago-based living. We take all the ambiguity out of life, leaving a very strict and rigid belief system, a morality, which allows us to take resolute and strong action. There is no room for doubt in the fundamentalist mind. In order to keep going, we need to reidentify, more and more forcefully, with our beliefs and so become increasingly more self-righteous. This is all very mental, and not much fun. When things don't work as planned, either you end up feeling like an idiot, or you become even more rigid and unbending in allegiance to your fundamentalism.

> The contractive mind either wants to change the past, or to control the future. It *believes* in the past and the future. As long as we are living in the contractive mind, we think that we are responsible for our actions and therefore we need to control life, we need to have it go our way.
>
> — Hale Dwoskin

We can drown in many kinds of fundamentalism. Religious fundamentalism leads to thinking that my God of universal love and compassion is better than yours (and if you don't agree, I'll kill you). Economic fundamentalism means my theory about how to handle the flow of money is better than yours, even if the majority of people stay poor. The end always justifies the means. There are fundamentalist positions about race, sex, food, relationships, the environment, and spirituality. Yet no fundamentalism can ever truly succeed, not because it is better or worse than a different position, but because it is limited.

The collective shift into translucence we are witnessing represents the death throes of the fundamentalist mind, the evolution from *Homo sapiens* to *Homo illuminatis*. When we see someone acting in a rigid, fundamentalist way, from a translucent perspective it is obvious that he will at some point crash and feel embarrassed. Every rigid belief system is destined for such a crash landing, because it is in conflict with reality. While historically we have respected leaders who demonstrated an unbending will and a consistent set of beliefs, this model is becoming increasingly obsolete. The translucent alternative to fundamentalism is an effortless capacity to surrender to the deeper current connecting all life.

SPIRITUAL MYTH #3: Awake people have no sense of a separate doer. Therefore they do not initiate action, but sit quietly doing nothing and wait for things to happen by themselves.

TRANSLUCENT ACTION

In a moment of radical awakening, the mental commentary stops. When mental activity solidifies again, as it does for most people, the mind often offers up these questions: *How will things get done if there is no me to do them? If there is no desire, what will get me out of bed in the morning? Who is going to pay the bills? Who will look after the kids? How can I make things happen?* Not only are these fears unnecessary, they are in fact unfounded. As translucents live more in the fullness of natural presence, they report that things happen with more spontaneity and natural ease than ever before.

> I have a similar relationship to thought as I do to the world . . . it's not my home. I can engage and find them useful to help me find my alignment, otherwise they are just present, floating around, but they don't trouble me.
>
> — Aneeta Makena

Questioning the Mind

In the moment of awakening, for the first time you know yourself to be something other than just the mind. You experience the activities of thought as events at which you are a spectator, rather than the fabric of who you are. In Iago's trance, we often mistake our thoughts for reality. If you have a jealous fantasy (a mental event), you feel as though you have actually been betrayed rather than watching a point of view arise, pass, and dissolve again. The same thing happens when we get lost in a good film. When we are living translucently, we still have thoughts, and we are also aware of their being thoughts. But for the first time, we can question belief without it threatening our identity.

As soon as we are able to recognize thought as a passing event, we become unglued from it. We can then question its reliability. However translucent we may have become, this process of letting go of a personal reference point always feels like a small death, but it always brings with it a rebirth. Thought and action can occur in completely new ways, as direct and innocent responses to the present moment, unclouded by the undigested past. Translucents still take action, but as a pure response to each moment, free from indecision, beliefs, or agenda. In a highly translucent moment, we know nothing with the mind but are able to act without hesitation, in inspired certainty. This certainty does not come from rigid belief, as it might for a righteous fundamentalist, but from an open and innocent capacity to respond to life, moment to moment.

> We are all in a life stream, flowing exactly in the right direction at the right speed toward whatever is most appropriate. When we are reactively driven, we are furiously paddling against the flow, trying to grip onto whatever imagined solid objects we see. When we are intuitively driven, we're relaxing into the flow, and it can just carry us to where we need to be.
>
> — Hale Dwoskin

Adyashanti told me a story that dramatically illustrates this process. His mother began to show symptoms of an undiagnosable illness: heart palpitations, strange sensations in her head. She would often think she was dying. This went on for months. No doctor could help her. One day he got a call from his father:

> He said, "You'd better get over here. Your mother is convinced that she's dying, and she wants to see you." So I got in the car, and I drove over. There she was on the bed, terrified, and thinking she was dying. "I just feel like I'm slipping away," she said. "I'm slipping into this blackness, and as soon as I slip in there I'm going to die." I had no idea what to do....
>
> For some reason, out of nowhere, I got up on the bed, and I was straddling her body, right about where her waist is. I took one of her hands and said, "Well, Mom, if you're going to die, let's die right now. You know where it's black? Let's go there together right now." I can't explain the intensity that was there. It wasn't like I was thinking, "This isn't real; she's not going to die." I really didn't know, but I grabbed her hand. She was so frightened that she was willing to go. I entered the space she was in, and I could see why she

was experiencing it as death; it was just this utter blackness. We dove in there
together. I didn't know if I was helping to lead my mother to her last few
heartbeats, I was just following what was happening. I was moved by it. She
went into the void, and the perception of the one who could die disappeared.
I opened my eyes, she opened her eyes, we could feel it, and that was it. It
was gone.

Adyashanti's actions came without his needing to think at all. He told
me that he deeply loves his mother; he loves to be around her. Had she really
died, he would have been in deep grief. He did not want her to die. But all
the same he told me he had the feeling "If you are going to die, we will die
right now together, because that is what is happening." While not every invitation to act without thought is so dramatic, these are the moments when the
rubber meets the road, when we find out
how free we have really become of old
beliefs and habits.

Satyam Nadeen runs three retreat centers, one in Costa Rica, one in Mexico, and
a new facility in Georgia. His centers
employ hundreds of people in three countries and accommodate thousands of guests
every month. Millions of dollars pass

> It's love lived. You meet the fear and
> the pain that are the effects of untrue
> thoughts. You question the thoughts,
> and you realize what's true. Then it
> lives as that one, that new identity,
> which is always kinder.
>
> — Byron Katie

through his business every year: "All day long, people come to me needing
decisions to be made. I don't make those decisions from thinking; I can't.
There is no way for me to have access to all the factors involved. I have to
relax and wait for the right response to come. And almost invariably, it is the
right thing."

When we act outside the mind, we experience almost no indecision or
complex mental processing. When translucents are presented with a new situation, a spontaneous, unresisted response arises that is not questioned.
When we can see the world without the filter of belief, it becomes perfectly
obvious what to do in each moment. Since we are not resisting anything, life
itself keeps asking us to play, to dance beyond our habits. To resist this playful invitation would itself be to cling to a point of view.

We know what to do, not from weighing pros and cons, or making lists

You go into action, but you don't get lost in the energy, and then you return to that immediately. Wonderful. And I often experience it when one has to hurry. Some people think you can't hurry in that state, move fast and still have that stillness there, but that's not true. The body is moving fast and might even be running to catch a train, and yet you're not trying to reach a projection out there, but simply enjoying the energy movement.

— Eckhart Tolle

or asking people, but from an open clarity, where there is no belief for or against anything. There is just quietness and a capacity to respond spontaneously to the present moment. Life is doing itself through you, and there is no need to interfere.

Translucents are always in an ongoing evolutionary process. After a radical awakening, all the usual trappings of a personal life can continue. There are, however, two notable exceptions. Almost all translucents report that they no longer have any experience of either boredom or indecision. Adyashanti explains:

Liberation is when there is no longer interior human conflict going on inside, subtle or overt. When conflict has ceased, a huge part of your human way of experiencing life is over with, and it is never going to come back. You literally cannot walk around with conflict inside. That doesn't mean that you've arrived, in the sense that you are the whole divine, absolute, total expression of God. It just means that that conflict has ceased.

This is not to suggest that life is always safe and secure. Many people report that they only know what to do, with inspired certainty, at the eleventh hour, and until that point the temptation to take impetuous action remains. When the mental processes of indecision have subsided, there is room for a real sense of integrity. Lynne Twist calls this process taking a stand rather than a position:

A position is usually for or against something; it calls up opposition and creates a dialogue that is adversarial. It creates fragmented pieces, because somebody takes this position, and then somebody takes that position. If you take a stand, like Martin Luther King, or Gandhi, or Mother Teresa, that's a different domain of life. You access a portal, a domain of "stand-taking," that gives you access to true power, tapping into the real truth and destiny of the human family. I take a stand. I don't necessarily say that what I stand for is true or false, or right or wrong, or that I'm accurate and that others are inaccurate. I stand for these things, and I know from standing in this place of possibility and power I can navigate myself and the people that I have the privilege of interacting with more successfully and more gracefully through the world we live in.

Unresisting Experience

To increase the translucence of our thoughts and actions, we do not change our beliefs, but we recognize and abandon them as unnecessary. When we are still caught in Iago's web, the best we can do is exchange one belief for another. This is the world of self-improvement: think and grow rich, attract the perfect mate, visualize success. The problem with changing our beliefs in this way is that they all exist as polarities. The more we try to believe, *I am in perfect health*, the more we deepen our resistance to sickness and solidify it as a part of our universe. The more we say, *Everything will be all right*, the harder we push against impending disaster, and the harder it pushes back at us, not as an event, but as a threat. The way to be free of Iago's tyranny is not by changing your mind, but by relaxing into inspired certainty. Translucent nudging means first recognizing a belief for what it is: an unnecessary mental overlay on top of simple reality. It is the ability to welcome not knowing as a more mature state than living in opinions, and to return again and again to what is real in this moment. By feeling into the resisted frequencies that underlie all beliefs, we dissolve them.

> A mind unquestioned is the world of suffering. It's that simple. If a thought is stressful, and we question it, it's gone, until the mind finally understands itself. And that's when the laughter begins. The mind begins to pull its own thread and unravel everything it believes. And what's left is always kinder. I love that. And finally the only thing that's left, if anything, is gratitude.
>
> — Byron Katie

A number of very powerful translucent methodologies have become popular in the last ten years, all of which are less about self-improvement than about not resisting our experience. Byron Katie's The Work is a notable example. "Who would you be without your story?" she asks us. Her work involves writing down our beliefs about how things should be. The Work involves four questions and a "turnaround." The four questions, which we can bring to every belief, are: *Is it true? Can you absolutely know that it's true? How do you react when you believe that thought? Who would you be without the thought?*

The "turnaround" allows us to take our beliefs about "out there" and see that they are actually powerful insights into living freedom "in here." Katie gives this example: *"Paul should understand me,* a typical thought for the Iago mind. She teaches us that we can turn it around like this: *Paul shouldn't understand me.* (Isn't that reality sometimes?) *I should understand me.* (It's my job, not his.) *I should understand Paul.* (Can I understand that he doesn't understand me?)" Each of the turnarounds gives a powerful insight into a more translucent life, allowing us to let reality be as it is.

> I saw that no thought is true. Before the thought, there was nothing. With the thought, there's an effect: sadness, for example, or fear or anger. The whole world is an effect of believing our thoughts. All four questions and the turnaround were already present in the first instant when I woke up on the floor of that halfway house in 1986.
>
> — Byron Katie

In the 1970s Lester Levenson developed the Sedona Method, a cognitive, visceral technique that uses a series of questions to redirect your focus from the content of your belief to what you're feeling in this moment, and at the same time shows you how to tap your natural ability to simply let it go. Hale Dwoskin, president of Sedona Training Associates, has condensed the method into a book and a series of CDs, which make it very simple to learn.

Like many other translucent approaches, the Sedona Method does not require us to know where a belief comes from or to understand anything about it. Dwoskin explains that the graceful simplicity of the method is in seeing that we can simply let go of mental contractions, without any effort, like unclenching a fist, or breathing a sigh.

> *When we identify patterns, initially there is a release, a big letting go. But when most people see a pattern, they turn it into a new meditation; they go looking for the pattern everywhere. Because we are infinitely creative, they get really good at finding it! Seeing the pattern, a point of liberation when you first see it, loops you back into limitation because you then become an expert on that particular pattern, and you simply reinforce it the more you see it. The mind says, "Oh I understand, I have this particular pattern, so I need to look for this pattern," and in the looking, it regrows it. Rather than looking for the*

pattern, which is the tendency of the mind, look for where it isn't. We're so busy looking from pattern to pattern, from sensation to sensation, picture to picture, sound to sound, we miss the emptiness, the space, the openness — the beingness that surrounds and interpenetrates these.

Dwoskin speaks on behalf of a growing plethora of translucent tools, which do not aim to change our thoughts and beliefs but to dissolve them, allowing us to respond to reality fresh in each moment. At our foundation, we have a playful means to dissolve belief, which we call the Living Essence Work. It encourages us to feel into and dissolve the energetic contractions underlying belief. The steps are laid out in the nudging section at the end of the chapter.

> It is such a relief for people to realize that they don't have to work it out, don't have to adopt a position toward whatever is happening at this moment, a mental position, a perspective, and identify with that.
>
> — Eckhart Tolle

Let's get back to Frank, waiting patiently for us. Once we had written a catalog of the beliefs he held about his call to Suzie, we set about dismantling them all, the "negative" beliefs (those that seem to interfere with him getting what he wants) as well as the "positive" ones (those that seem to help him with his agenda).

Some of his beliefs melted when I simply asked him if they were true.

"Do you know for sure that she found you boring?"

"No."

"Would everyone agree that it is too soon after your divorce to meet another woman?"

"You mean everyone? Everyone who knows me?"

"Everyone in the world."

"Well, no, not everyone would agree."

It was also easy for him to let go of some of his positions, once he simply discovered that he had that choice.

"When you think the thought *I might grow old and die alone,* could you, just could you, let go of that thought?"

A sigh. "Yes."

Gone.

But some of his points of view were stickier. They had a "charge," and he

> What's so beautiful about realization is that mind is no longer doing war with itself because it doesn't believe what it thinks. Mind has found an effortless way back home. It's a great joy to watch that happen.
>
> — Byron Katie

could not let go of them at will. I could ask if they were true, I could ask if he could let them go, but he still felt a contraction in his body, in his spirit. So we went a little deeper, and, just like clenching a fist very tightly so that we can then fully relax it, we discovered the core of each of these contractions and then let them go. Altogether this process took more than an hour, with others in the seminar not only silently cheerleading but feeling and dissolving the same contractions in themselves, until we ran out of beliefs.

When we were done, I asked him: "Are you going to call Suzie?" Frank grinned at me, giggled like a five-year-old, and shrugged. When the room laughed, he looked perky, like he was ready to go play now.

"Is it too soon after your divorce?"

Same response, same giggle. None of the thoughts seemed real anymore.

Frank phoned me several days later. He'd made the call. But his was not the fireworks testimony we might expect from a "Ten Steps to the Perfect You" approach. Frank and Suzie had a good talk. He told her a lot about the tension he had been experiencing. Apparently, she knew just what he was talking about. To finish the story, Frank finally did fly to the East Coast to visit Suzie for the weekend. It was on the drive from the airport to her house that they realized there was no chemistry. They both felt relieved. But Frank did meet Suzie's lifelong best friend on that trip and married her seven months later.

This story is typical of translucent practice. Generally, it is not a means to get what you thought you wanted. Letting go may bring as many deflations as victories. Instead, it is a way to relax our grasping, and to allow the process of life itself to give you all the gifts under the tree with your name on them. Almost invariably, the outcome of this kind of practice is not what we had in mind at all but, in retrospect, much better. Translucents discover that they must give up their agenda to be really blessed.

Eckhart Tolle discovered the magic of this mysterious benevolence a few weeks after his awakening. He was living in a one-room "bed-sitter" in north London, sharing a bathroom with eight other people, cooking all his food on a single gas ring. "The external situation," he told me, "wasn't very good." One day he walked into the graduate office of the University of London. He had no direction for his life at that point. The secretary handed him an application for a position at Cambridge. "You don't seem to know what to do," she said. "You might as well apply there." He filled in the form and forgot about it:

> They offered me a scholarship, so a few months later I ended up in extremely beautiful surroundings. I had this nice set of rooms, one overlooking the ancient courtyard, one overlooking Kings Parade. I also noticed a strange thing. Things came to me after the awakening, even little things. A thought came, "It would be nice to have a plant," and then the next day somebody gave me a plant. I thought, "I need a bookcase for my books," and two days later I talked to a man who mentioned a carpenter who makes bookcases. "Oh, I need one," I said. Ten days later the bookcase was there.

In researching this book, I was flooded with stories like this. At the beginning we may fear what will happen if we give up control. It feels as though we need our beliefs to avoid being left out in the cold. It takes time and practice. We let go of our agenda just a little bit, and life surprises us, as though a benevolent uncle or aunt were watching out for us. We trust a little more, let go a little more, and the blessings increase. In this way the mind is deconstructed piece by piece, contraction by contraction. Here is Byron Katie:

> I take on more and more; there's much more action because of less doership — the action seems to be running. Things are happening at a level I never could have imagined or tried to bring about. They happen, I deal with them, and the scope is getting enormous. It's very interesting, though, very, very interesting experiencing "isness" from this perspective.
>
> — Satyam Nadeen

> When you question what you believe, it only leaves the happy dream, the happy ending. It's kind and loving. Some people are under the illusion that a quiet mind is a mind that doesn't think. In one way, that's true. As soon as thought seems to appear, it is already gone. By the time you think it, there's only a thought left that says you thought it, and that thought is gone too. Everyone has a quiet mind. They're seeking what they already have. No one even thinks.

Intuition

The effect of this kind of translucent practice is cumulative. At first, we take small steps. We are willing to use nudging tools to dissolve the mind much like my nine-year-old takes his cough medicine: under duress, as a leap of faith, and with a scowl. But once we notice the magic a few times, that a whole world of delight awaits us beyond the small plans of me and my dreams, we look forward to letting go of our positions, like removing soggy shoes. We fall into a completely different way of taking action, bypassing the complex task of balancing opposite points of view. We intuitively know what to do.

> It's a movement of life itself. It doesn't have an agenda; it has no promise at the end of it. It's just happening. You don't really know why. It often flies in the face of what you would normally have done, that's my experience of it. And when that movement is allowed, then your life moves in that way. It's uncomplicated. You don't have to think about it, basically. Someone will ask me to go someplace, and inside I get a yes.
>
> — Isaac Shapiro

Translucents find out what they need to do by doing it. As Hale Dwoskin describes it, thought and understanding come after the event, not as the cause:

> *It appears in life that our thoughts either put us into action or prevent us from acting, but actually neither is true. Actions happen and thoughts happen about them after it, and because of that, sometimes we'll act on thoughts, and sometimes we won't, but it's really not in our conscious control. Sometimes we'll think a thought and we'll act on it, sometimes we'll think a thought and we won't act on it, and sometimes we won't think at all and we'll act, which is actually most of the time!*

The Iago worldview often dismisses intuition as unreliable and irrational. Terrified of making mistakes, we consequently feel decisions derived from carefully thought-out positions are more reliable, while we see intuitive choices as flaky and unscientific. Ironically, as long as our urgent need to fix a problem remains intact, intuition is indeed unreliable. The competing voices of conflicting beliefs, like those of the thirty thousand professional lobbyists in Washington, D.C., make it impossible to distinguish direct knowing from a particularly persuasive belief. Intuition is completely reliable, but only when it comes from a quiet mind, a mind well weeded of unconscious points of view.

Satyam Nadeen describes how intuition almost invariably allows for circumstances that he didn't know about consciously. Recently, he found himself making a decision to postpone an event at one of his retreat centers. He didn't know why, but he could feel what to do. Only later did he find out that one of the presenters had to be in the hospital on the original date. Greg Steltenpohl made the intuitive decision to withdraw all the Odwalla juice products from the shelves. Many other translucents report that they find themselves taking action not knowing why. The "why" is provided after the event.

You will feel the undeniable power of intuitive knowing in the arena of your life where you feel and live the deepest translucence. Ewa feels most translucent as a mother, and her intuition about her children is faultless. For Bill, his greatest translucence is in his art. He paints as though the brush is being moved from paint to canvas, while he is a marionette. Many, me included, feel most translucent when acting as a teacher of or spokesperson for the translucent view.

> As you unwind belief systems you simply feel more present, so you can show up for what's happening in the moment. You can either act or not act, but it is more intuitively based as opposed to being based in reaction, based on memory.
>
> — Hale Dwoskin

Two or three years ago, while we were teaching our Living Essence Training in Nevada City, a woman asked me a very esoteric question. She was concerned with how to live a "spiritual" life, which for her included lots of meditation, retreats, and even a visit to India. I paused before responding. At first, nothing came. Twenty or thirty seconds passed as we all sat and waited for the fax to arrive in my brain. Then an image of Ram Dass appeared. Many years ago his father had become very sick, and Ram Dass abandoned his more obvious "spiritual" life to return to Connecticut to care for his father. He became a full-time live-in nurse. Ram Dass discovered this experience to be a deepening of his inner life rather than a distraction from it.

"Life is a school," he said, "but we keep trying to avoid the curriculum."

As I told the woman this story, I felt I was listening to myself speak. My lips were moving, and I was listening, wondering why I was going into so much detail about Ram Dass's father. It seemed to have nothing to do with her question. She listened, then she started to cry. Not a whimper, but full sobbing.

"Thank you," she finally said. "That was exactly what I needed to hear."

During the break, she approached me. "How did you know that I am living with my father and nursing him as he dies? Did your office manager tell you?" I had to admit that I didn't know. The story I told her had appeared out of the willingness to sit back in the saddle and wait until the mind had settled, wait until the silence spoke instead of the "me." When we wait like this, speaking and action come from our intuition, a deeper place than cognitive thought, a dimension of us that is connected to everything else.

> There is a time when I feel I'm moved; I actually don't have a choice. I could say I resist it, but it would be so foolish. At this stage in my life, I don't have a choice to say no when the spirit is calling. I have learned to trust that this is what makes my life rich and full and even if it moves me into the total unknown, I don't really have a choice to say no.
>
> — Peter Makena

This is not a rare occurrence. It is the very fabric of how real translucent teaching happens. Ram Dass says, "My name is RAM. It is an acronym for Rent a Mouth. People hire me to tell them what they already know." The role of a translucent teacher is to relax and allow a deeper part of the questioner to tell her what she already knows but cannot hear. This is the deepest role of a teacher: not to deliver a precooked set of dictates and theories but to be used by the Great Knowing. Whether we are leading a seminar, running a business, raising children, creating art, or cutting hair, wherever we are most translucent we will know the magic of acting now and understanding later.

How can we know the difference between action guided by intuition and action driven by belief? Iago is sneaky and loves to imitate translucence. Contractions and intuition arise from the same source, and subjectively an intuitive action and a reactive one will feel the same to us. The only way to know the difference is to let go. When we let go of a belief arising from a contraction, we will return to the natural state, and the need for action will be gone. Whatever we were concerned about will seem absurd. When we try to let go of an intuitive response, any contraction around it will dissolve, but the impulse to speak or take action will be even stronger and clearer. Every time we let go in this way, we become more and more intuitive and less and less reactive.

Relax and Wait

The key to accessing a deeper source of thought and action is the willingness to relax and wait. In Iago's trance, "I don't know" is to be avoided at all
costs. Translucent action requires the wisdom of "I don't know" as its firm
foundation. Through practice, we come to recognize that the thought
machine is unreliable. Based in a distorted view of the past, resisting all kinds
of unmet contractions in the body, and out of touch with the immediate
environment, thought is never able to deliver the goods in a way that will satisfy all the factors involved. Knowing this, as the core of translucent practice,
we learn to relax the first impulse to react. We relax, and we wait. We relax
into not knowing. We relax into feeling the disturbance in the body. We
relax into feeling the environment as if it were an extension of our own body.
We soften into the acceptance of the unreliable nature of the mind, and we
surrender.

Indecision is not a problem if we can
rest at its center. Allow yourself to stay in
the middle of the mental tension, with all
its conflicting points of view, and feel them
all. Give yourself permission to not know;
feel the inevitable reality that you actually
don't yet know what to do or say. Stay with
all that and wait, then see what happens.
Relax back from the whole thought process,
and just wait for the current flowing

> That state is very dynamic, and the
> ability to respond to the need of the
> moment is wonderful. To realize that
> spontaneous action happens out of that
> state, if it's required. If it's not required,
> it doesn't happen. Sometimes it's a
> rested state. When it's at rest it
> appears almost passive, and suddenly
> it gets transformed to dynamic.
>
> — Eckhart Tolle

through all of life to move through you too. Then, whatever you say and
whatever you do is going to be connected with what everybody else is saying
and doing. This is true surrender.

THE GREAT RESPONSIBILITY

True surrender means to sit present in the middle of all of it: the demands
and beliefs and fears of everyone involved, as well as your own thoughts and
feelings swirling around the inevitability that sooner or later something will
happen anyway. Surrender means to accept and not resist the impulse that

will eventually arise from within you, like it did for Adyashanti when his mother thought she was on her deathbed. Surrender is an act of great creative responsibility. Everyone has known it, in moments of freedom from the mind.

In the aftermath of September 11, one of the greatest alarm clocks ever to wake us from our collective sleep of "consume and complain," thousands of people stepped out of their little boxes of should and shouldn't and fear-based living and did what had to be done. Firefighters rushed into a building that was on the verge of collapse. Strangers helped each other. Politicians suddenly began to cooperate. A crisis such as this draws people out of familiar patterns of separation. We recognize pure response, unfiltered by thought, as heroism.

Many translucents speak of realizing there is no individual doer. Life is in a dance with itself, responding to itself continuously through me, through you, through everything. Freedom from the mind is the only way to act with real responsibility, the ability to *respond* to life as it is, unclouded by a mind carrying its past on its shoulders. Translucents respond to each situation as it is: fresh and new, unencumbered by conclusions reached in the mind.

You surrender your position, give up needing to know, relax into not knowing, and allow action to happen spontaneously from there. And we discover that in this surrender, everyone is better served than by working things out in the mind. Every time you find your intuitive, spontaneous responses connect up with everything else, your trust in the process of life itself deepens. It becomes an evolutionary, symbiotic process. Trust fuels even deeper surrender in the next situation that arises, and surrender increases trust in the wisdom of not knowing. Now you have the foundation to trust your mind a little less and to trust that intuitive relaxing back a little more. Byron Katie lives a life that is outwardly dynamic and active, although it requires very little effort or decision:

> And that's the possibility of living in alignment with Now. The focus of the entire spiritual practice becomes the present moment and whatever arises in that. That is all. The only question that remains is: Am I in alignment with the form that this moment takes? Already there is stillness in the background when you welcome this moment as it is.
>
> — Eckhart Tolle

I love where I am, wherever that is. When people invite me, it shows me the way of it, so I follow that. There's nothing else to do. When those invitations stop, I stop traveling. I just continue doing what I do, wherever I am, which is what I'm doing all the time anyway. It doesn't have a motive. It's lived fully, and I love the way it lives me. The truth is no respecter of what we think it should be. In my experience, it's only kind. It really is. Even if it's crawling in pain, with blood running out of its mouth, screaming at the top of its lungs, if it doesn't believe what it thinks, it's free.

Liquid Belief

As we deepen our practice of relaxing, waiting, and not knowing, we start to experience our points of view as if they were a variety of costumes. We dress ourselves up for play, like a child putting on a cowboy hat or a nurse's outfit. And then we take the costume off again.

Most translucents share this fluid relationship to belief. They pick up and discard points of view, knowing them for what they are, just fleeting opinions that we can ride like a bus, and then get off when we need to. Through practice, we do not lose all beliefs; we simply melt them from solid to liquid states. We dissolve the stuckness

> I think "no-doer" has become a catch-phrase that people use to absolve themselves of accountability. Sure there's no doer, and this no-doer happens to be showing up as you. But in this moment, as long as there is any sense of separation, any sense of a doer, then you can "do" the surrender to what is.
>
> — Stephan Bodian

around belief so we can embrace contradiction. Translucent living means living in paradox, while remaining at ease. To the dominant Iago trance, this fluidity appears flaky and lacking in integrity. The old model respects leaders with iron wills and concrete mind-sets.

In ancient times in China, the Shao Lin monks would debate in the courtyard. Whenever one monk had debated a point to perfection, like reaching checkmate in chess, he would slap his thigh and make a loud shout, *Ha!* The joy was not in being right, but in debating the truth from every angle, playing in the waves — loving the great mystery of life. Recently I have seen this sport revived. Every year in Sweden, there is a gathering of more than a thousand people, called the No Mind Festival. Translucent teachers from all over the world travel there: ShantiMayi, Byron Katie, Brad Blanton, Deva Premal, and Miten: it is quite a feast! They give talks and workshops for the participants. In Sweden in the summer it remains daylight till one in the morning, and the sun rises again at four. I have had so many lively debates there, into the small hours, as we travel together into the uncharted territories of collective awakening. No one needs to have the final say on anything; it is a dialogue, an investigation, where conclusions are adopted and discarded like Kleenex.

> The perception of my life changed. I had always lived as if I was an individual, my body and my ego. The person I thought I was. Suddenly I saw that I was a cog in a wheel in a much larger system. I was part of a dharma team that was an evolutionary direction towards the One. And I had tasted the One. That was the team I had, and I saw myself, I saw my acts, either they were dharmic or they were adharmic. Which gave me new criteria for my acts.
>
> — Ram Dass

The word *integrity* comes from the Latin *integritas*, which means to be whole. The word *entire* has the same roots. Over time integrity has come to mean a rigid adherence to a moral or philosophical code, but there is nothing whole about this if it rules out one entire end of a spectrum of possibility. Translucents know that real integrity means the capacity to *embrace* all the different dimensions of a situation. To have real integrity you need to embrace paradox and to live with all of it simultaneously, to be so flexible you can respond to the river of life in its constant change instead of crashing on the rocks.

To live with this kind of integrity is a challenge. However much translucent practice we may have under our belt, it is always possible for Iago to kidnap us again, to impersonate real surrender and integrity. Saying "I trust my intuition" can in itself become just another form of fundamentalism. "I have let go of all points of view" can become the most rigid point of view of all. And an attempt to surrender and let go can solidify into a very stubborn and stuck place. A belief system imitating translucence is not translucent at all. So you cannot "do" not knowing, you cannot "do" surrender, you cannot "do" living outside of belief.

Real integrity is an art form, not a rigid science. Once we set our first toe in the water of dissolving the mind, it is time to let go even more. The fruit of dissolving belief gives us the trust to dissolve even more. So the only way to act from inspired certainty is not by "doing," but by "dissolving" the old and resting in not knowing. This takes practice, repeatedly nudging the old habits of being right back into the wisdom of not knowing.

NUDGING BELIEF INTO
TRANSLUCENCE

There are many ways to dissolve belief through translucent practice. Sometimes one will work well, sometimes another.

NUDGE

Is It True?

Whenever you notice yourself holding onto a belief out of habit, ask yourself if it is really true. Would you rather be right, or free from rigid mental limits? Find out where you are a fundamentalist, holding onto beliefs out of old habit, and ask yourself if they are reliable or worth defending. For most of what we hold true, we could just as easily believe the opposite and it would be just as valid. *There's not enough . . . there's plenty . . . you can't trust people . . . everyone is trustworthy, deep down.* All opinion. Just in the moment between the inception of the thought and the solidification of the thought, get into the habit of stopping, pausing, taking a breath, and asking yourself, *"Is it true?"*

> So what is the practice? The practice is constantly surrendering to the mystery. Constantly diving in, letting go of all your ideas and concepts and moving into the not knowing, living in the mystery, surrendering to the unknown.
>
> — Stephan Bodian

You could also ask yourself, "Would everyone agree with this thought?" I mean everyone on the planet. If there are even abstentions, then it is an opinion.

Or ask yourself, "Is it possible to disagree with this thought?" If it is, then it is a belief and not reality. And this simple observation can be enough to let it go. *Paris is in France.* Hard to disagree with this, as long as we understand what it means. *You can't trust the French.* Not everyone would agree. At the very least, the French wouldn't.

This, then, is the first level of practice. Get in the habit of challenging your beliefs by asking, "Is this true? Would everybody agree? Is it possible to disagree?"

NUDGE
Get Support

It is not easy to question your own mind. It's often better to get support from the people in your life who would rather see you free than righteous. You can ask your partner, friends, and family to question belief with you. Ask them, "Any time you hear me expounding a belief unconsciously, just ask me, 'Is it true?' or, 'Do you absolutely know that's true?' " The more you do that together, the more distrust you'll have in your own mind and the more trust you'll have in the intrinsic benevolence of life.

> You really get progress when people with different belief systems recognize in a concerted way, in a mutual respectful way, that whatever differences there may be in their systems, they point towards the same ideal of oneness.
>
> — Stephen Post

NUDGE
Letting Go

Once we recognize that limiting beliefs are only thoughts, and not real, we can ask a very simple question. "Could you, just could you, let it go?" This is the question at the core of the Sedona Method. Ask, then wait and see what happens. Don't *try* to let the belief go, just ask if you could. Hale Dwoskin reports that when we bring this question to most of our beliefs, we find ourselves just taking a gentle sigh, and something relaxes deep inside of us. The idea is to just playfully toss the ball in the air a few times, to see what life might be like without that thought.

For example, you are driving to work, you are late. You still need to drop your child off at day care and make three calls on your cell phone, and just look at the bumper-to-bumper traffic. *There's not enough time.* Just feel that thought cutting into your gut like a knife. Now ask yourself, *Could I let that thought go?* Just could I? Could I sit in this traffic, on my way to day care, and on to work, and let the *not enough time* thought go? It is the recognition that you can live without the thought that brings freedom from the mind, more than any intention to do anything about it. Whenever I ask this question, and just consider the possibility of letting go, I find myself taking a nice, spontaneous deep breath and a sigh. Sit in the possibility of letting go; you may discover that it is already gone!

Try it today and see what happens.

> One way to describe it is getting beyond being governed and actually bringing a creative responsiveness to the situation. It establishes each individual in a fundamental confidence and integrity that is not otherwise available to us.
>
> — Saniel Bonder

NUDGE
Unresisting

You will need to practice this nudge with a friend. One of you dissolves the belief as the other guides.

1. Find a stuck belief and put it into a simple sentence. For example: *There is not enough time.*

2. Feel where there is a contraction in the body when you say the thought out loud. Put your hand over that place in the body. Feel the atmosphere, the frequency, as deeply as you can.

3. Call out a number from one to ten, designating the strength of the frequency, with ten being strongest.

4. Now do everything you can to increase the intensity, not just the contraction in the body, but the frequency underneath it. Keep calling out a number, so your guide knows how you are doing.

5. Keep amplifying this frequency until it cannot be any stronger. This step should take about two minutes. Take it to the uppermost limit and call out a ten.

6. Relax completely and let go. Ask yourself the question, "Who am I?" Dive into that question completely, as we did in chapter 2.

7. Feel under your hand again to see if any charge remains.

8. If so, go back to step four and repeat the process.

9. Once there is no more charge in your body, try saying the statement from step one again: *There is not enough time.* Then say its opposite: *There is plenty of time.*

You will know you have fully liberated the belief if both the thought and its opposite appear to be meaningless, just sounds. Then you can rest in not knowing. Then you can live from inspired certainty.

CHAPTER SIX

DROPPING THE DRAMA

Translucent Feeling

race and Mario had lived together for more than twenty years. They
had worked together, traveled to different countries, and studied with
the same teachers. So when Grace returned home after three weeks of treatment for her skin condition, she instantly knew something had changed.

"I'd thought everything was clear between us. But from the way he was
behaving, I knew that something was not right. Finally he told me. He had
found a younger woman.

"My first impulse was to leave, to move to another area where I had
good friends. I felt betrayed. Unseen. Unheard. Clear communication was
so important to us. Why hadn't he talked to me? Why hadn't he told me how
difficult it was for him, with my skin, and with having less sex between us?

"Mario told me he had wanted to protect me: I was already going
through so much. As we kept talking, we saw that we had both been dishon-
est. So I stayed. This was my home after all, and anyway, my habit was
always to run away. And he continued to see his younger girlfriend.

"At the beginning, I felt so alone, so abandoned, as a child, as a woman,
as a friend and ally in our spiritual work. I felt it through my whole body.

I would cry, a deep wailing, as I entered the sense of being abandoned. Feelings came, and I let myself fall into them.

"I had to make time, it was so important. I might be out shopping, and then I would feel it, the loneliness, the sense of abandonment. I would come home and just sit down and give the feelings some space. They would pass after some time, after feeling into them and letting them be, and then I could get up and do what I needed to do. I took a lot of time, just allowing, allowing the many different feelings to come and go.

Translucents embrace feelings as they arise. As internal boundaries dissolve, they make room for all feelings, both the ones they once labeled positive and those they have banished as negative. As translucents learn to remain open, human, and vulnerable, they have a richer and more varied emotional life, while remaining spacious and connected with themselves. The capacity to remain present with whatever arises, instead of resisting feelings as potentially overwhelming, becomes a direct and powerful gateway into a deeper love.

> Tears are always like a breaking. When tears fall it is a rain of grace. It means that something has actually touched the truth of your heart, has actually cracked and caused some rain.
>
> — Sofia Diaz

BEHIND A LOCKED DOOR

Iago thrives on emotional chaos. We are afraid of our strong emotions, and often regret words and actions prompted by them. Then we suffer, not necessarily from the feelings themselves, but from our resistance and the shame associated with them. Caught in Iago's trance state, we feel limited, separate, and afraid. Like Stuart Little in New York City, we sense that everything else is bigger than us, that everything is potentially threatening. Not only do we feel small and powerless relative to external things, but our inner life feels overwhelming too. Hence almost everyone is terrified to feel without restraint. Feelings seem like tidal waves, and we are a tiny boat. Any feeling released from its stranglehold of control has the potential to shipwreck us. We may then believe that the spiritual solution lies in overcoming feelings or in making them go away.

We constantly resist not only our grief, but also our wild passion and sexuality, our anger, even our exuberance and joy, repressing their free expression. Big feelings overwhelm us. They can easily upset the fragile equilibrium of our lives. We keep a lid on ourselves, till we periodically explode. We don't realize that any deep feeling, pleasurable or painful, can be a wave we surf home into ourselves, into love.

The habit of repression is so deeply ingrained that what we think of as a feeling is most often the conflict between an original feeling and our resistance to it, the result of which is tension. In our Iago-saturated culture, only small children play and laugh with abandon, scream with frustration, cry fully and deeply, and then play again. The rest of us associate anger with a tight jaw, and excitement with a flutter in the chest. Even our laughter is often accompanied by restraint, if not embarrassment. Isaac Shapiro explains: "Memories get touched, and in an instant the whole defense system kicks in. Then you've not only got the pain, but you've got the movement away from it, the defense, which hurts more than the actual pain. Then it gets projected onto the present moment. We try to solve it now; we resist what seems to be happening in this moment, even though it is really secondary."

Repressed feelings usually lead to a well-adjusted mask, but with a distorted face behind it. When we resist our anger we become superficially sweet but passively aggressive. When we shut down our grief, we shut down all of life, becoming gray and stooped. We cease to look people in the eye. When we repress sexuality, we change a healthy means of sharing love and translucence in the body into a dark and secret perversion. Here we are not expounding the benefits of irresponsible free expression and venting, but the restoration of our capacity to feel in a way that returns us deeply to ourselves, with an open heart and nothing to hide.

Let me clarify what I mean when I say "feelings." The words *feeling* and *emotion* are often considered synonymous, to be used interchangeably. But they have quite different roots. *Feeling* comes from the Old English word *fellen*, the physical capacity to experience something as it is. Feeling is one of the five senses, along with sight, hearing, smell, and

> Imagine having the experience of an angry moment without the interior conflict powering the emotional event. It's not that you lay down and become a piece of Wonder Bread, but you totally embody your humanity to such an extent that the reactivity goes away.
>
> — Adyashanti

taste. And it is deeply associated with being present and in touch with the sensations in the body. *Emotion* comes from an Old French word, *emouvoir*, to stir up, to create agitation. Emotion, then, creates a movement within consciousness.

Feeling is passive, a capacity to experience, while emotion is mobile and leads to action and expression. Feelings happen in the present moment and are all flavors of our natural state. If we remain open in the middle of them, they can lead us home to peace, to a love that has no cause. Emotions usually become velcroed to a story in time, and then lead us into whirlwinds of drama. By assuming that every internal flavor has an outside cause, the purity, power, and mystery of feeling are lost. They become dramatized into emotional drama: feeling acting in a soap opera. In order for our emotions to be a gift to those around us, they must be freed from the imprints of memories; they must become pure response to the now. Says Eckhart Tolle: "Emotions arise and flow into the mind structures of the conceptualized me, with its insufficiency, its not-enough story, its sense of lack, its great need to add more to me, its sense of threat and its identity threatened by other me's. Emotion empowers the mind to conceptualize itself, and it becomes a habit, so that every feeling becomes a self-referenced emotion as me, and me, and me."

> Feeling is actually as simple as feel the texture of what you're sitting on. Feel what's behind you, feel me from your heart, feel the color green around you, feel the texture of the telephone.
>
> — Sofia Diaz

We can be very emotional without feeling deeply at all. And we can feel things powerfully, to their very core, without becoming lost in emotion. In fact, over time translucents develop a much greater capacity to feel, and in the process become less emotionally reactive.

The Price of Not Feeling

Sofia Diaz is a yoga teacher in Boulder, Colorado, who has become a mentor to thousands of people, primarily women, in their capacity to feel. She sees feeling as neglected in our culture, subjugated by the masculine emphasis on rational thought and cause and effect:

> *The body of the lineages of Western civilization is barbaric, retarded in feeling sensitivity, because it hasn't been emphasized. It takes practicing it, for real.*

How much of our nervous system is devoted to the eyes and the thought process? Conception is confused with perception. You can practice some technique, and in actuality there isn't an effect descending into your perception. Nothing is changing, because there is an incapacity to feel. If you feel the trees from your belly, it's an entirely different universe than if you think about feeling the trees. The more you practice, the more an entire realm of perception reveals itself, one that seemed like it didn't exist before. It actually does exist; it's just like an atrophied limb that needs to be practiced.

We pay a high price when we avoid feelings as they arise. They then become "sticky," instead of passing through us. Several distinct outcomes may occur. First, we create habitual tension in the body and literally cut off the free flow of sensation. In order not to feel anger in the belly, we clench the solar plexus and block feeling, blood flow, and energy. To avoid feeling fear, we contract the pectoral muscles and collapse the chest. Over time these unconscious attempts to block feeling in the body often lead to postural imbalance and stress-related illness.

> Everything is always washing into my heart. And I have the choice in any moment to open to it or to close to it, to resist it or to allow it, to protect myself from it or to open to it and let whatever response comes just be.
>
> — Amy McCarrel

A second outcome of avoiding feelings, particularly the ones we view as negative or threatening, is to become rational. We develop strategies to control or stop the feelings. We ask, "Why am I feeling this?" then seek for an answer beginning with "Because": *I am angry because you . . .* or *They made me feel sad when they . . .* And so we get caught in an endless cycle of cause and effect.

The third outcome of not wanting to feel is venting. Sometimes this happens immediately (particularly if you have some Italian blood in you), and sometimes it brews for a while before boiling over — after a few hours, days, or even several years if you're British by birth, like me. When the lid finally blows on the pressure cooker, there follows a lot of noise and a lot of mess to clean up afterward. You can even cause some permanent damage.

Venting is a rebellion against the tension created between feeling and its repression. We compensate for having resisted our initial response with a volatile mixture of emotion and willfulness: *Angry? You're damn right I'm angry, and you are going to sit right there and listen to why!* Exploding is actually just another way to try to have control over feeling and avoid being overwhelmed. You think you're managing the feeling by deciding "I'm going to be angry." In fact, you are not feeling a feeling, but *doing* emotion. We create melodrama. Rather than experiencing feeling as a wave, made of who we are, passing through, we restrict our sense of self and become the wave itself. Instead of *feeling* anger or sadness, we say, "I am angry," "I am sad." This expression of, and movement in, who we are has temporarily taken over our identity.

> I require the strength of the absolute in order to let humanness rest in my lap. I feel so honored to be living both at the same time, and they're not two, just one radical embodiment of human and divine. The full spectrum of wonder and ouch, which is really living.
>
> — Pamela Wilson

In the Iago trance, the only choice we think we have is either to repress our feelings or to be taken over by them and become reactive. Either way we are still caught. We are still run by emotional states disconnected from the world around us, and we are still unable to give our deeper gifts.

SPIRITUAL MYTH #4: People who are awake do not have feelings, particularly "negative" ones like anger, fear, jealousy, or greed. Instead, they are always calm, in an unchanging state, feeling an unbroken oneness with everything.

SPIRITUAL MYTH #5: You have to choose between feelings and presence. When you have feelings, you have lost who you are.

FROM BOAT TO OCEAN

As translucence deepens, our range of feeling, as well as our capacity to feel deeply, expands. We learn that it is possible to welcome grief, anger, even the depths of despair as waves, made of who we really are, and so as portals into a bigger love. Then feelings are more liquid, moving, flowing, and transforming continuously into one another, without the rigidity or charge of emotional drama. Feelings can exist as pure energy, without a story. Translucents have less resistance to feelings and embrace and welcome them as they arise. They discover how to feel into each one fully, to be complete with each experience rather than living in postponement. To the same degree that you have completely felt what's left from the past, you can be total and present to meet life as it is in this moment. Here is Hale Dwoskin, who teaches the Sedona Method: "If you are willing to welcome what you are experiencing in the moment, and at the same time choose to let go of the past responsibly, your emotional life gets richer and richer, and at the same time there is less and less attachment and aversion to what is arising within you. You experience everything more fully, but you are neither using it as a license to suppress and deny emotions nor as a license to express it."

Translucents can access the limitless dimension of themselves with ease. At the same time, unlike our stereotypes of spiritual people, they make no attempt to renounce life. A translucent, then, bridges the mystic and the enthusiastic participant, for when a translucent experiences feelings, even very painful ones, it is within the context of some connection to limitlessness.

> When I resist in any way, I am really stepping out of spaciousness. When I rest in whatever is arising, without resistance, whether it is an opaque emotion or not, then I am not outside of that spaciousness.
>
> — Aneeta Makena

To a small boat, waves can be threatening. They could be devastating; they could be the end of that little boat. But what kind of a wave can threaten the ocean itself? To the ocean, even a tsunami is just an event happening within it; it could never wipe the ocean out, it is in fact made of the ocean. As we awaken to being the ocean itself, our entire relationship to feeling is transformed. You no longer create fresh resistance to feeling, because it no longer appears to threaten your identity. You can even invite old feelings, which have been banished, locked away in the cellar like rabid dogs, back into the sunshine, to be welcomed, felt, and liberated.

Pain still hurts. That does not change. We may have turned to spirituality to try to stop pain from hurting — the giddy goal of enlightenment as the cosmic emotional anesthetic. When Grace faced her feelings of abandonment, she had already passed through many portals of radical awakening, and she had many years of translucent practice behind her. She had enough presence and openness to feel them completely:

In the beginning it was a strong sense of being abandoned, as if I was letting lifetimes of neglect keep coming up, and coming up, and coming up. I would just let all these feelings be there, and I would experience them — you know, "Oh, I feel so alone, I feel so abandoned, I live here in this country, there's nobody, I don't have any family, I feel so unconnected." I just let these feelings come up, and I'd feel them, and then they'd pass.

There were different levels of feeling abandoned, from the child, from the woman, from the warrior. I would just go into the state of feeling really abandoned, and feel it. I felt it, and then it was gone. It didn't affect me anymore because I really went deeper, into a deeper self. And then from that deeper self I could continue to live. I could continue to do whatever I needed to do.

That which arises, allow to arise. The danger is to find it to be interesting. So if you follow it, sentimentalize it, exaggerate it, expand on it, or identify with it, you're adding something to it. The longer and more fully we can meet an experience, the more dynamism begins to take over — the unfolding is organic.

— Jett Psaris

Grace still deeply felt her betrayal, her loneliness, her sense of abandonment, and they hurt as much, or maybe even more, than they would have without her translucence. The connection with her limitless dimension did not take away the hurt. But it did enable her to fully feel it. With internal spaciousness, feelings happen *within* you rather than *to* you.

THE GENIUS OF THE FEMININE

The feminine in all of us intuitively knows how to feel. People with more feminine energy (usually, but not always, women), whether translucent or not, have a much greater intuitive capacity to feel than people with more masculine energy. Amy McCarrel also works with women to cultivate feminine translucence:

A woman's heart is a genius of the moment. If you look around a room of people, women's hearts are particularly sensitive in this way, constantly feeling what's mean in the room, what's closed in the room, what feels good in her body when somebody speaks, the sound of the voice, how relaxed it is, what they're saying, or if it's coming from a place of mental tension. It's happening all the time.

The world is metered by my heart. The way somebody walks down the street: I'm safe, I can relax, or I need to protect myself. Just metering constantly what feels true, a truth meter. Woman can always know, feel, when a man's words are correct. It's truly one of the most profound gifts of the feminine, the genius of the heart, her inability to not feel. Everything is washing through. It's coming in constantly, coming in, coming in, coming in. If something coming at it is less than true, it hits the heart and it hurts. If something comes at the heart that's true, it washes through, and it opens. Whether I'm completely conscious or not in any given moment doesn't alter the heart's receptivity.

This feminine gift, of being able to feel everything in the body, can become contracted if we are caught in the Iago trance, and then it turns into melodrama. Consequently, the feminine in all of us is always afraid to be too much, to feel too much.

It is also quite possible to have deep awakening, to be resting deeply in spaciousness, and to still be very shut down in one's capacity to feel. A traditional masculine spiritual path can be very strong on wakefulness, but very weak on emotional embodiment; masculine-based spirituality has illustrated this for thousands of years. As a result, in most spiritual teachings, the advice has been to remain still, like a Buddha statue, to watch feelings pass, not to touch them. In a masculine approach, deeply feeling grief or anger would simply be a symptom of spiritual immaturity. Hypermasculine spirituality cannot help you to free up feeling, or to feel more deeply, because generally it has been founded by men who are themselves emotionally crippled.

> The return of the goddess brings wholeness back into spirituality. She reminds us that there is no separation to be found anywhere; feelings are part of life, part of this. It is just not possible to divide between consciousness and the manifestation of consciousness as feeling.
>
> — Chameli Ardagh

Translucent feeling is the combination of a real awakening to your luminous essence as limitless and a restoration of respect for the feminine dimension in all of us, which knows how to feel. Translucent feminine people are awake to their own natural presence and are also alive and healthy in their emotional body. They know how to feel. My wife, Chameli Ardagh, guides women in the art of translucent feeling:

> Even confusion, or identification, is honored as a guest. Nothing is as it appears to be, it's all the self playing with itself in all these myriad of disguises. I'm just going to bow a deep bow and say come here, come rest, show me your true nature.
>
> — Pamela Wilson

Traditional teachings warn you that it is in feelings that you get lost, where you get distracted, where you get distorted. A translucent woman would see that and say, "Whoa, so where do I get lost? Let's go there, because that is where I need to practice." It is the openness of awakening that brings love to anything that occurs. The presence is love itself. But of course, in order to stay present with really strong things that occur in life, it needs the practice of a real embodiment of that openness. That is in the body. It has to be a real thing; it cannot be an aloof dimension in another place. It is right here.

The translucent revolution is not simply about more people having glimpses of awakening to their transcendental nature; it is about the unrestricted embodiment of that awakening in every aspect of our humanness, especially in our capacity to deeply feel and to be real with what we are feeling. And that requires the balance of both masculine and feminine energies. In the last few decades we have seen an explosion of women emerging as spiritual teachers: people like Byron Katie, Catherine Ingram, Jean Houston, and Sherry Anderson, who remind us that feeling this realm is just as divine as transcending it. Pamela Wilson is one of those emerging voices of the goddess:

> *There is a difference in the feminine invitation to rest as one's true nature. It is about being kind inside, including the arising emotions and contractions and the senses rather than meditating them away. It is gorgeous, because there is always a balance of the fiercer masculine aspect, and the warm feminine voice of "this too, this too, this too." I find that sitting inside myself, just allowing everything to come to rest, to invite it all in as an honored guest works really exquisitely for me. I notice more and more, when I sit with my friends, that it is a lovely balance to have the cool inquiry of "to whom does this come?"*

and the warm invitation for anything to arise, to come to rest, to give it clarity and kindness.

This capacity of feminine translucence in welcoming feeling home into the ocean of loving presence brings three precious miracles.

The First Miracle: Everything Changes

Translucents enter into an evolutionary process of feeling more and more, while becoming less and less reactive. They can feel without a story, without justifications. Usually, we need to say: "I am angry because of what so-and-so did." Most of our energy then goes into changing so-and-so and very little into what we feel. It is very, very rare for anyone to be willing to feel without a logical cause:

"How are you doing?"

"I'm so mad I could kill with my bare hands."

"My God, why?"

"No reason, it's just a wave passing through. Feels great, actually. I love it!"

Translucents can be with feeling as a vibration, just as one might listen to a piece of music. If we are deeply honest, we have no clue about why we are feeling what we feel. *Is it really the parking space? Or was it that funny remark in the elevator last week, or the promotion last January? Perhaps I am actually angry with my father.* More likely, that extra glass of cheap wine last night is the culprit. Most of our stories are inaccurate, and in the final count there is no one reason for any specific feeling. The more stirred up you become, the more complicated things get and the more you are pulled into reactive behavior and disconnected from your depth.

When we feel without a story, our feelings become less distinct, more a part of one another. They defy labeling. Let's look at an example. You are on a first date. You feel a quickening in your heartbeat, a tightening in your belly. Label it fear, and you have the beginnings of one story: *I might get rejected. I know I'll say something stupid.* Label the same feeling excitement, and spin a different

> The moment you learn to welcome even suffering, a very rapid transformation happens. It can sometimes be instant; when you totally welcome the pain, it turns around. One could do it with fear: fear arising, fear without the story, and all of a sudden what once was fear is intense aliveness.
>
> — Eckhart Tolle

story: *Maybe he's the one.* But if you leave the sensation undefined, and just feel it as a mystery, you discover that fear and excitement are a hairbreadth apart, separated only by a different explanation. They easily change into one another.

Try this the next time you feel afraid. Ask yourself if you *know*, for sure, that what you're feeling is fear. Could it equally be labeled excitement? Can you leave it without any label at all? The same is true of grief and gratitude. The next time you feel deep grief, see if it is possible, just for a moment, to feel it more deeply while thinking less about why. Then look around at anything, a flower, a color, a bird, and see if your tears are only of regret or also of thanks. Fear and excitement, grief and gratitude, anger and power, sadness and vulnerability: they are all separated from one another when we make them into an emotional drama but one when we feel them as pure energy. Chameli talks about how our feelings shift:

Stay alert to changes. Be aware that your feelings might change any moment. When you say "yes," but not just to make it go away, you will very soon discover that it is changing all the time. The story, the explanation, keeps it going on a track that would otherwise change very quickly. When you are present with feelings, they are just waves arising and changing into something else. Just to be in that flow brings you into the present, which can be very light, or may become anger, or change into sadness, and then change into laughter. It changes so quickly. The Big Love is right here, all the time, it is the medium in which all the waves are moving. It is always right here. If we are not following the addiction to a story, feelings change quickly.

> If something is coming at my heart that is painful and I open to it, my response may look like grief or rage or *no*, but the response is open, in the moment, to serve that person, so they can feel what they're doing, and the way that they're not loving.
>
> — Amy McCarrel

The more we become emotionally reactive, the more complicated things get, and the more we are disconnected from depth, and from the present moment. The more deeply we can feel, the more at peace we become and the simpler outer situations become. We can really give the gift of pure response to the situation instead of reacting to it. We can express what we are feeling, in tune with the present moment. We are no longer carrying any resistance. Now grief or anger or overwhelming affection can all be gifts to enhance the world, to bring to it more color, more aliveness. Feelings become a form of honest gifting, a generosity of spirit.

The Second Miracle: Emotional Alchemy

Feelings are our children. Some are well behaved: clean, polite, socially acceptable. Others are little terrors, our Dennis the Menaces. So we pamper the children we like, feed them, dress them well, pose them by the fireplace for the neighbors to see. The ones we don't like we banish to the backyard, with no nourishment and underdressed. In the snow. From time to time, we see them peering in through the frosty windows, hungry, the beginnings of malicious intent in their eyes. All sorts of strange things can happen. A

> It's scary as all hell to make our self be known, the parts that are unlovable, the parts that we don't love, that no one else will love, that are just too messy, that are unworthy. Yet we're dying inside to be completely loved and received and forgiven.
>
> — Jennifer Garcia

few may break through a window and climb right back in. Or we might open the door to let a pleasant, happy feeling out to play and an unwelcome ruffian or two darts in uninvited. Our banished feelings may make horrible noises in the night and fill our dreams. And they will certainly sabotage our every attempt to look good to the neighbors.

This is true, no matter whom you go to war with. The harder you push your enemies away, the more barbed wire fences you build, the more they will concoct devilish schemes to disrupt your cozy life.

As we relax more into who we really are, into the natural state, and we no longer feel so threatened by our feelings, slowly we begin to invite our rejected children back inside. This process happens gradually, as you open the door to your banished offspring, one by one. Invite Grief inside, and sooner or later you are sitting down to dinner with Anger. Watching Arnold movies. Enjoying yourselves. "Listen, I'm sorry," you say. "This was a misunderstanding. I realize now that you are my child. I gave birth to you. Come on inside, sit by the fire, and have something to eat. And look, your bed is right over here. You can stay here." At first these banished children will look at you bleary-eyed, not quite believing what's going on. They may even be a tad pissed off. Burning holes in the couch. Insulting people on the phone. They need reassurance. "I don't just mean for the night, I mean you can stay forever," we might say to our anger. "I am sorry I pushed you away, and I'm really sorry that my father did before me, and my grandfather before that. I'm sorry my entire culture has made you feel that you don't belong. But you are welcome now. Come on in."

As soon as we welcome our banished, delinquent children back inside, they are transformed. This is a lesson I have learned with my own children. Often when I am on the phone, one of my sons decides he wants me to get him something to eat or to play a game with him. If I push him away, he becomes more and more demanding. But if I draw him close to me, often his apparent need disappears. His real longing is for attention, and once it is fulfilled, the fulfillment eclipses all else. And so it is with feelings. When we feel them as they arise, and draw them close to us when they need our attention, then their agenda of upset and cause and effect disappears. Translucents welcome this process because they know themselves as something bigger than, and deeper than, any particular feeling. Feelings arise, they are embraced, they pass again, and we are free again to be empty and spacious, and to be available to life and connected with the world.

By welcoming feelings, we can transform them. Anger, when brought home and embraced, fed a good meal and given clean clothes, becomes authority, power, and strength. Sexual desire, when all charges have been dropped and the fingers of moral accusation have stopped wagging, becomes our basic life energy, our *shakti*. Having a friendly attitude to grief lets us uncover our innermost depth. Fear reveals excitement and energy, judgment reveals discrimination, and boredom uncovers our desire for depth and meaning. By consciously dropping the story and returning to pure feeling, translucents discover the great secret: *there is no such thing as negative energy.* Even the most unwelcome emotional currents, which have faced lifetime imprisonment, which seemed capable of destroying us and other people, are transformed into divine qualities when they are embraced and given as gifts. Everything that arises within you in this atmosphere of welcoming is just another facet of the

> One day fear arose, and there was curiosity. I heard the teacher within say, Fear is welcome here. I finally see that everything just wants to come home. For me the great play now is undressing all the identification.
>
> — Pamela Wilson

natural state. Translucents discover that feeling itself is always a gift to be given, for it comes from the source of life.

Let's look at anger as an example. At first we may be a little hesitant to let our anger out of the cage. What might happen? But this is because we are confusing feeling with reactivity. When anger is thrown onto another person without first being deeply felt, it can have disastrous consequences. But we experiment, a little at a time, with feeling our anger. We breathe deeply into the belly and allow it to be just as it is. Once we feel its raw, savage beauty, we feel a deeper connection to the earth; the body opens and comes to life. We can feel our anger again and again, each time more deeply. The more we allow it, the deeper anger takes us into ourselves. Now it can be given as a gift to others, the gift of authority, of waking up, of integrity, the voice of righteous indignation in the face of social injustice. When anger is felt and given, free of resistance, it can be received by others as a blessing.

The teacher Michael Barnett lives in community with his friends and students in Freiberg, Germany:

> It starts in the body: a really deep openness, surrender, and relaxation. It's a complete relaxation at every level. It shows in the body; it shows through the body. It's radiated so others can see it; it glows.
>
> — Jennifer Garcia

I'm conscious when I'm getting pissed. There's no residue afterward. It's a very important thing. There's no soap opera. It happens, bam, and then it's finished, and then I'm back. I allow myself to get pissed. I don't lose my awareness; I let myself really flow with the energy of it, and then it becomes a gift for whomever I'm becoming pissed with. Almost all the time when I get pissed, the person feels completely enriched by it. I'm still in touch with them.

When we are willing to disengage feeling from whomever or whatever it was attached to, there is an immediate liberation. Instead of solidifying into emotional drama, feeling becomes a loving presence, with no cause. Without a story, there is nothing to defend, nothing to resist, and we are liberated from the addiction to niceness as an antidote to all we have repressed. Real Love can be ferocious, it can be deeply honest, it can gift in a hundred thousand flavors. It has been set free of the narrow confines of sentimentality, of being nice and sweet. When we feel fully now, and free ourselves of the shadows of the past, every feeling fully felt, without resistance and openly given, is an expression of love.

The Third Miracle: It's All Love

Once we discover the mystery of being present with feeling, our entire emotional life changes direction. If someone gets angry with you, you have no need to control things or change your immediate environment. There's a movement within you, and you feel it. There is no need to understand why you feel as you do, you simply feel. And in that feeling, you sink a little deeper into your body, into yourself. Staying with the momentary pain, you feel more connected with your own depth, with everything. Now the initial pain is gone, and you return even more deeply into this moment, into yourself, with resistance neither to the feeling nor to the external event. You may even feel genuinely grateful for this catalyst that brought you home. Instead of resisting feelings, and the circumstances that might have caused them, translucents welcome both. The cycle has been broken.

> To feel love, all you have to do is gaze at a flower or breathe the fresh air. Watch the river flow, or look up in the sky. Everyone can feel this kind of love. I tell people, when they feel constrictive pain, "Fill that gap. It is a gap between you and your Self. Fill it with love."
>
> — ShantiMayi

This willingness to allow feelings to shift and change into one another, to reveal their deeper dimensions, is the result of staying present in the body. As we stay present, we can experience not only the feeling that is passing but we can also feel our own presence — the medium in which all these waves of feeling are arising and falling again. That presence is love. Chameli says:

Love is the openness in which anger is arising. If you are present enough that you fully feel the anger, then anger brings you to love, not because it changes into love, but because it is made of love, it arises out of love, it moves in love, and it returns to love. Either we are lost in the feelings, and then presence is not there, then there is only the anger and nothing else, or we are bringing some conscious practice to feeling: the anger is there, and we are present with it. Presence and Love is the same thing. We can be fully present, as love, and we can also allow the anger to arise and to transform.

The real miracle of welcoming all feeling in this way is in allowing life to dance as it is. We see that feelings do not really matter, they are just a part of, an expression of, life. You enter into the true dimension of life, always coming and going; you no longer resist it or interfere. We move beyond what we are feeling, to being the ocean in which all feelings are moving, as waves. We know our real nature to be the context of all feeling, to be love itself. Anger, joy, enthusiasm, sadness, and grief may be feelings, but love is not a feeling, it is who you are. You can feel sentimental, you can feel sexual desire, you can feel sympathy or attraction, but you cannot *feel* the Big Love, the Real Love: you can only be it.

> This is not a neutered state. The more we are willing to be free with what is really true, with what we are really feeling, and to offer it freely, and be with it and not try to be free of it, the more we become like rainbows — much brighter, more creative, more colorful, more artistic, more crazy and perfect.
>
> — Jennifer Garcia

Let's return to Grace. Her process of transformation continued for many months. The outer circumstances changed and changed again, as they always do. She moved out after some time, got a place of her own. Mario finally begged her to come back to him. And by this time she was not sure. She felt good being alone now. But the miracle that unfolded for Grace was not in the details of her life, but in her return to herself:

I understood after a period of time that all this had to happen. It was the great wake-up call. I recognized that the real betrayal had nothing to do with Mario. I saw that I had betrayed myself, in that I hadn't lived my deeper self. I have come back to only wanting to have true freedom and connection to God. Even though it has been incredibly hard these years with my body, and with all the circumstances, it has brought me to myself, to this self that was always searching for God, that always wanted to be connected to that.

I can say, "Your will be done." I have found a tremendous gratitude for life, for trust in existence. As long as there is life, there will always be emotions and stuff that keeps coming, but it's no longer such a big thing. Before, I didn't want to face it. Now I find the courage every time to let whatever is coming up to be there and not to be afraid.

If there is anything I would like to give to people, it is to say that you will not die for letting feelings come up, because you will fall into that which is so great, and that which is so great will carry you. I have come back to myself.

THE BIG PAIN

Feminine translucent practice is not always easy. As we start to say yes, everything that we have pushed away will return to be embraced. However deeply we may have been touched by an awakening, however committed we may be to living life from the depth of realization, to really feel without defense demands great courage. Almost all translucents describe this practice as a work in progress. To really live without a story, without why and because, to really live in vulnerable, naked communion with each feeling that arises, is to live in an unbroken river of mystery. It is to die to each moment as you are born to the next. This does not always feel good. It does not even mostly feel good. Most of what we have repressed was painful, so the practice of returning to feeling instead of running with emotion requires facing discomfort. But do not be disheartened. Just to live with this as your vision and to fail again and again is in itself fulfilling. It is a much richer life than to succeed in denying feeling. It is a glorious failure. The reward is not pleasure, but depth, real connection with our world and ourselves.

> When the guest comes to your door, whether he be angry or sad or despondent or in despair, the opportunity is there to host him. Invite him in, ask him to have some tea, have him sit down. He will know if he's hosted exactly how long to stay and exactly when to leave. Invite him in.
>
> — Lynne Twist

With practice, all our most resisted, dark feelings become pathways into the Big Love. A translucent person knows the magic when grief, for example, comes to visit. Unresisted grief will take you down through itself into something much deeper. Since this process is not generally pleasurable, it therefore only becomes really interesting once we discover a dimension to ourselves beyond pleasure and pain. Pain is inevitable in life; suffering is optional. When we let go of clinging to feeling good and avoiding pain, we pass down through them both into our deeper heart, and the net result is that we are ejected into the Big Love. Always.

Marlena Lyons and Jett Psaris, who co-authored *Undefended Love*, teach men and women how to feel with courage. Marlena reflected with me:

Let it pierce you, and if it disturbs you let it disturb you. If it tortures you let it torture you, because that's what the awakening is. There is a misconception of awakening as always bliss. Ultimately that is where we end up, but . awakening stirs up whatever is within you so that it can find its path to its ultimate unfolding. Let it disturb you, let it pierce you, and find out what within you is having difficulty with the present moment.

Translucent practice allows us to respond to new situations differently. When your lover doesn't call, when you get less appreciation than you wanted, when someone behaves rudely or with anger, instead of reacting emotionally, you know how to feel more deeply, how to surf the feeling home into the Big Love. And then, as news of this cease-fire reaches the far-off corners of your kingdom, old feelings, long ago banished, begin to show their faces again. They return home because they are family and know they must be reunited for the kingdom to be whole again. Old feelings return to be met, without any obvious external stimulation. In other words, stuff comes up.

> God is dyslexic. And because of that, negative things are bound to happen. So my philosophy is that life is like photography: use the negative to develop.
>
> — Steve Bhaerman
> (Swami Beyondananda)

It might come up when you are quiet and alone, or in meditation, or in nature. You might feel overwhelmed with feeling, for no apparent reason at all. Walking through the woods in the early morning, hearing the sounds of the birds, feeling the contact of your feet with the ground, you see a squirrel running up a tree, and...what is this unbearable grief? Old pain, banished long ago as too overwhelming, stuffed down into the tissues of the long-suffering body, returns to be transformed through soft presence. It has emerged from what Eckhart Tolle calls "the Pain Body." And who even knows its full history? It may not even be pain from your lifetime. This body you call "mine" was formed from the bodies of your mother and father. You inherited their noses and eyes, their DNA and their gifts, and their buried pain too. The inheritance may even be cultural. The sudden wave of anger you feel when you see poverty, the guilt you feel arising out of nowhere when you hear of a child abused, these may have nothing to do with the small story you call "my" past.

We may reach a point when our relationship to feeling is almost entirely friendly, where our habit to repress or dramatize has almost entirely disappeared. We are still operating a human vehicle, however; we are still part of the collective human race. All over this planet there is injustice, needless cruelty, unchecked greed, wanton acts of violence and destruction. Every day we can see on our TVs, and then feel in our hearts, the results of military attacks on civilians and of terrorist bombings. The victims are all somebody's mother or father or brother or sister or child. As you become more translucent, as the awakening deepens, not only to the impersonal and transcendental but also to the very human dimension, you feel all this too. Feeling is feeling. And as you feel your own present and past pain more responsibly, you also feel that everything on this earth is, in a certain way, happening to you. ShantiMayi has made this capacity to open more and more deeply to feeling all humanity, all living beings, the primary focus of her work in the world:

> The world is in such trepidation now. We are one being; we are one living life force. Some of the depressions that people get don't belong to them personally. Our world is very, very difficult right now. Even people who are well balanced may feel fear; it's just the condition of life these days. The people who are most open get a lot of that.
>
> — ShantiMayi

> *Sometimes it frightens people, that they will feel the pain of everyone. But this pain is quite different from personal pain, because it dissolves the borders of the heart. It is this resonance where humans just feel love. That is all there is to it. It is the pain of real true love, rather than the pain of personal drama or personal disappointment. It's very sweet. It's very bittersweet. People don't mind feeling this, because they've felt it in themselves all the time. It's certainly not the same thing as personal pain. It is felt, and it is wonderful. It is deep and tearful and pushing all of your heart borders down, and very painful. It gives your awakening a deeper vista than personal pain, which always constricts your view. This pain is worth it. The pain of compassion is like the sun shining. Wherever you sense a border in your heart, that is where this pain comes from. Wherever there is even the most subtle separation, when compassion is flowing, you'll feel that as pain, as compassionate, heartfelt pain.*

The Dalai Lama calls this the capacity to bear the unbearable. When you feel this kind of pain, it does not mean you are just in a dark mood. It may be the result of opening yourself enough to feel the suffering all over this earth. It may be that your skin is getting less hard, the armor that separated my feelings from My feelings, the big Me that is connected to everything else. It is otherwise so easy to use spirituality as an escape, a way to avoid feeling any of that. Translucents report that the more they can be here as love and compassion, the greater becomes their capacity to feel the suffering of humanity in an undefended way. You can experience great emotional pain, deeper, richer, and much more profoundly than when you were trapped in your own little story.

> It's a constant practice of maintaining a depth of openness, a willingness to completely feel whatever you're feeling all the way through, but not be attached to it. To feel it and confess it; to realize both that whatever feeling is coming up is absolutely true, and also that that is not, fundamentally or absolutely, who you are.
>
> — Jennifer Garcia

NUDGING FEELINGS INTO TRANSLUCENCE

Practicing with your emotions and feelings is very challenging. When you become emotional, the very problem is that you have become caught up in the story of cause and effect. To practice your way out of this trance by yourself is next to impossible. If you feel Iago's grip most strongly with powerful emotions, it will be easiest to nudge them with support from your friends. Or you may benefit from the help of a translucent psychotherapist, of which there are a growing number.

Ask others to remind you to move through these steps:

NUDGE

Let Go of the Story

Whenever you feel emotionally stirred up, stop. Listen to the story your thoughts are telling you about why you feel upset. An emotional upset is always a meeting of an external event and a contraction in the body. Focusing on the event will make you more upset. Staying with the body, and holding the cause as harmless, will help you to move deeper.

Do you know for sure *why* you feel as you do? When we take the time to inquire, we often find that a feeling or sensation actually preceded the upset rather than followed it. When we abandon the need to know why, we are free to feel with totality. Be open; without a story the feeling may change very quickly into something else.

NUDGE
Breathe into Your Body

Scan your whole body with your breath. Look for places with the most energy and contraction, and stay there with your breath. If you feel very emotionally charged, move your body, dance, stretch, even close the doors and windows and make wild sounds, to allow your energy to move. When you notice a stuck place somewhere in your body, a place that's contracted, linger there. Massage that place with your breath.

> Breath and movement are particularly important because they just happen to be very efficient ways through the black holes and into space again. Every time some emotion gets a grip on us, it always compromises the breathing. That's just a good place to notice.
>
> — Kathlyn Hendricks

NUDGE
Welcome What You Most Resist

If you remain with sensation in the body in this way, you will discover feelings you have been unwilling to feel. Stay there and whisper a quiet "yes" under your breath. Welcome your lost children home.

NUDGE
Distill Feeling to Its Essence

You might start with a tight place in your solar plexus, a place that feels willful, angry, and pushing. Your thoughts may be spinning with what you should have done. Say "yes" to this in the body; keep breathing into it until it reveals another dimension. Perhaps then you will feel you want to cry. Don't get caught in that either; don't make up a story about why you are sad. Keep going. Feel the sadness, breathe fully, massage it, knead it with your breath, keep saying "yes." Cry if you need to, just let it be free of cause. Say "yes," not to make it go away, and not to indulge it, but so it can invite you deeper into itself.

> There is not an end to the deepening and unfolding. One could almost say that the humanity of a human being is truly born now, as this consciousness arises. Yes, there is an end to the suffering. The end of suffering can be now. Suffering is self-identification with pain, and then for a while the pain will still be there, just pain, but no suffering entity.
>
> — Eckhart Tolle

Keep feeling into each wave until it opens into something else. Sadness may open into exquisite vulnerability and surrender, where you feel more open in your body and begin to discover more receptivity. You feel all life through your skin. Keep breathing, caressing that also with your breath, again not to make it go away, not to indulge it or take a ride on it, but just to stay present, kissing it. Pass through each feeling with a welcome embrace, until it opens; you may well fall into something mysterious, into a vast feeling of connection with everything.

NUDGE
Be Taken by the Big Love

When you have passed down through all the layers of feeling, you will come to a place of complete openness and vulnerability. Walk in nature, be with people, feel your body. Worship the divine through your skin. This is a sacred act of devotion.

At first, these kinds of translucent practices may not go as deep as we have described here. Just the first nudge, to question the cause and effect of the story, is great liberation. But if you can follow feeling all the way home into the Big Love a few times like this, it will reeducate the nervous system. And once you have this knowing in the body, that all feelings bring you home to the Big Love, it will happen all on its own.

CHAPTER SEVEN

OTHER-REALIZATION

Translucent Relating

As a child, Michael Barnett went on vacation every year with his family to Broadstairs, on the southeast coast of England. On the beach, there was always a Punch and Judy show, a small tent with an opening like a stage at the top. A puppeteer would hide inside the tent and control his puppets: Punch and Judy, a husband and wife who were constantly fighting.

One year, when Michael was about seven, he went to the beach with his brother, David, who was a few years older. The two boys got separated near the tent. Young Michael forgot about his brother as he wandered on his own, past all the other shows and entertainments. But eventually he returned to the Punch and Judy show, looking for David. This time he approached from the back.

"I saw a man kneeling in a box, his hands in the air. On one hand was Punch, and on the other was Judy. With my beloved Punch and Judy as gloves, he was creating the whole show, all by himself. I stopped, open-mouthed. I was absolutely shocked — it was like realizing that Santa Claus does not exist. I thought, 'My God, it's all a game! And what's more, Punch and Judy are the same person! From the front, they are fighting each other.

From the back, it is one man playing out a struggle, pretending a war between a man and a woman. What are they arguing about, why are they attacking each other? They are the same! Punch and Judy are the same person. This guy is both.'

"Of course I didn't interpret it then as I do now. This is the truth I have discovered, that we are all Punches and Judys... husbands and wives, brothers and sisters, fathers and sons, mothers and daughters — we are all playing Punch and Judy, ultimately. But every Punch-and-Judy in the world is the same person. When you argue with your lovers and your friends, you are all the same person."

We all have hundreds of relationships in our lives: with our parents, our children, our friends, and our co-workers. When we leave the privacy of the meditation cushion and the sweetness of our solitude, we discover in these myriad relationships both the greatest challenge to our awakening and also the greatest opportunity to deepen it. In this chapter we will address relating in a general way; in the next we will focus more specifically on sexual, intimate relationships.

ACROSS THE GREAT DIVIDE

Our normal habit of relating, influenced by Iago's whisper, is to feel everyone as separate, and therefore to act and speak strategically. As long as we are in the grip of Iago's assumptions, even when trying to be altruistic, we are still driven by the obsession with "me": How do I fulfill my needs, What am I feeling, How can I express my truth? It is, in fact, this underlying feeling of separation that causes us suffering in relationships, more than who said or did what to whom. From the vantage point of separation, we inevitably try to fit the other into our world and, without even trying, become unconsciously manipulative. The stakes are too high, the unmet needs and fears too great,

> Whenever you're being phony, Machiavellian, manipulating other people by withholding, creating a story, or indoctrinating people, you end up cheating yourself of contact with that other person. The reason for telling the truth is to have some authentic contact or intimate experience in your life.
>
> — Brad Blanton

to allow us to do otherwise. We then enter into unspoken agreements to support each other in a drama of need. "I'll go along with your story, if you'll go along with mine." A relationship based on mutual need is called codependent. We are both trying to fill a sense of lack that only exists in belief.

Tensions can run so high with this mutual dependency that we are willing either to lie or to avoid talking about important issues to keep the situation manageable. Sparing someone's feelings, maintaining harmony, and avoiding feeling foolish or needy or vulnerable become higher values than honesty, integrity, or innocence. Our relating becomes a way to reinforce Iago's grip, and even to strengthen it, rather than being in the service of love. Secrets and lies are what we have learned to live with. The sense of separation and otherness causes us to see the source of every problem and feeling of discomfort as external. If I don't feel good, it is because you made me feel that way. I need you to change to make things all right again. Iago-based relating is founded in blame, in holding the outside world responsible for how we feel.

When we relate to each other from a place of separation, we act as if the other person is on the far side of a deep canyon. We can shout and wave and find empathy in our feelings of isolation. So-called skillful communication means building a stable and well-constructed bridge between one side and another to effect transactions. But even then, the deep feeling of isolation has not been addressed.

> When we pretend, the price we pay is that we live a longing: to be seen, to have every corner of our being completely loved. Even the dark places that we feel are unlovable — the secret parts that never get light through them, can be honored, permeated, penetrated, dissolved.
>
> — Amy McCarrel

SPIRITUAL MYTH #6: Awakened people do not need anything from anyone. They do not have relationships, since they feel oneness with everything.

SPIRITUAL MYTH #7: It does not matter what you say or do. Once you are enlightened, every action, even lying or manipulating, is spontaneously for the good of all beings.

SPIRITUAL MYTH #8: After an awakening, there is only peace and harmony with everyone, with no need to do anything. Translucent relationships are always harmonious.

OTHER-REALIZATION

The secret Michael Barnett discovered on the beach in England is at the core of translucent relating. In the Iago trance, we appear to be separate entities, with independent sources of thought, affecting each other with our words and actions. With focused inquiry, we come to know who we really are: we recognize that what is really meeting this moment is limitless space, context more than content. We can call this recognition self-realization.

You can also look into the eyes of another and discover who is looking back at you. We need to look beyond the appearance of a face, a name, and an agenda and find out who is really there, behind those eyes, seeing you. When this inquiry extends to another person, we can call it Other-realization.

Kathlyn Hendricks never really lost the recognition of herself as limitless space as a child. She told me that it was deeply threatening to her family and that she tried to conceal it. When she met her husband, Gay, she experienced the meeting as "an invitation to take off the artificial veils so that I could directly experience my spaciousness again":

> We recognized infinity in each other in the first few seconds that we met. The experience of seeing the space in each other, and recognizing and affirming that in each other, was the ground of our relationship. We didn't come together out of personality, we really came together out of that space, and then all of the other layers got filled in. Feelings and different personality structures got altered from that first commitment, from that first recognition.

People come in touch with a new dimension of reality. It's a move from the personal to the universal. There are no defenses, just an immediate connection between people that flows. Whenever people who have connected on that level meet again, there is an enormous energy flow between them.

— Michael Barnett

The Hendricks' experience is not isolated. It is the flavor of every description of translucent relating: the capacity to see oneself in the other, as the other. This does not mean that I look into Chameli's eyes and see Arjuna Ardagh, the man with his thoughts and opinions and habits. That would be dementia. It means that I know myself to be that which is deeper than a man and his story. I know myself to be space, free and open and with an infinite capacity to love, and I recognize that the same mystery is looking back at me. The packaging may be a little different, but there I am, just the same. This is not a philosophical conclusion, but a direct perception. You look into the eyes of another from the wakefulness in yourself, and their eyes become windows rather than objects. They become "mirrors" is another way that people often phrase it. You see your own infinity looking back at you from behind the window, and, just like Punch and Judy, you realize that even in conflict you are still in relationship with the one Self.

This recognition makes every kind of interaction potentially intimate, even humorous, not because of the content, but because of the context in which it occurs. After this happens enough times, we get used to it. We relax into knowing that we are a wave, rather than a solid entity. When we pause long enough to look deeply into and through another wave, we are no longer surprised to find the same ocean there, looking back at us. Translucent relating is like sitting down on our side of the canyon with our most beloved friend and enjoying a picnic together, looking at the view. There is no gulf to be crossed. Eckhart Tolle puts it like this:

> The one thing that is most responsible for the gift we experience with each other is that we both individually abide within ourselves, within a place of peace and spaciousness. We hold this as the most important aspect of our own selves, and we bring the value of that to our togetherness.
>
> — Aneeta Makena

The essence of every human interaction that takes place is the freedom of still-ness. You meet another human being through that. That often enables one to not get entangled in the game of thoughts and emotions that may be there in the other person as you meet them. It seems that when you are relating from still-ness, you can touch the stillness in the other person, without a prior intention. It just happens, and that's often how transformation takes place. This is "heal-ing" in a wider sense.

TRY IT YOURSELF
Who Is Looking Back at Me?

This is an exercise you cannot do alone. Self-realization can happen in your cave, but for Other-realization, you'll have to poke your head out-side. Try this now, if you have a friend handy.

Sit opposite each other, so your knees are almost, but not quite, touching. Decide who is A and who is B. Partner A, ask Partner B: "Who is experiencing this moment?" Keep asking your partner this question, maintaining soft eye contact.

Partner B, try to find yourself. You may pass through many layers of answers, as you did in previous chapters. Keep coming back to this moment, and try to find the thing you call "me." Try to describe to your partner who you really are, beyond concepts or images.

Partner A, once you can feel that your partner has dropped deeper than the surface mind (you'll feel a much deeper sense of connection once you do), switch the question to: "Whom are you meeting here?"

Partner B, really pay attention to who, or what, is looking back at you. Look into one of your partner's eyes; look through the eye, to the luminous awake presence that is seeing you. What is that? How big is it? How does that feel?

Partner A, keep switching between asking your partner to ask themselves the question "Who am I?" and asking the question "Who am I meeting here?" Ask your partner: "What is the difference between the one behind your own eyes and the one who is looking back at you?"

When you feel ready, switch roles and do the exercise again.

> In deep communion with other individuals, there is a quality in which the love and ecstasy are so intensified that everything dissolves into that. It is not a different oneness than awakening, because the oneness is already established, but it's a tremendous intensification.
>
> — Saniel Bonder

This is not a mental process, although it may begin as one. You need to really look; you need to really want to know for real. This inquiry leads to Other-realization, to the knowing that "I am you, I am meeting myself." There is no separation anywhere, except in our thinking. Many who have taken the time to inquire like this say that they would call this deep recognition "seeing God."

THE CURRENT

Chameli and I have guided thousands of people into this kind of inquiry over many years. The response is almost always the same, no matter where we go or what kinds of people we work with. Whenever anyone is open to really connecting with another person from this willingness to look deeply, he finds that he is meeting himself, the same no-thing, the same infinity. Often people look a little startled at first, as though their partner has just turned into a stoat. There is a look of amazed disbelief. But it quickly relaxes, because although our minds may have gotten lost in separation, the heart has never forgotten oneness. "Myself," they often whisper, "I am looking at myself." It is true, not poetry or mystical exaggeration, but a truth that can be verified whenever we pay attention to this moment.

After the endless bruising of Punch and Judy, this realization comes as a tremendous relief. In the Iago trance, when everything is only about separation and lack, the personality is nothing more than a desire machine. Cut off from connection to our real source, we have nothing to give when we feel separate, and our entire relationship to the world is based on addressing assumed deficiency. But when being meets being, it brings a palpable sense of no separation at all. You are me, we are one. No more imaginary needs, no drama, nothing happening.

But there is even more to explore. After basking in nonseparation for some time, we also realize that luminous presence longs to play in human life. Somewhere between the stark separation of personalities at dangerous play and the homogenous goo of Oneness lies what we can call the Current. The Current is a warmed-up flow of Being, expressing itself through a unique human form. No longer completely nonseparate, we recognize the unique beauty of the other as an expression of life. But we also remain connected enough with our source that we no longer foster a sense of isolation. This Current of alive presence is the domain of real love. It needs nothing, for it is marinated in infinity. It gives everything, because there is just enough sense of the other as unique, mysterious, and different in flavor to draw forth a flow of generous devotion. This realm between Being and personality is where life finds its real fulfillment, in the embodiment of real love.

The Current only gives; it needs nothing from the other, for it is

> It has to always reflect back in the person's heart that they love, no matter what. No matter what. This is the quality that cannot be negated in relationship for any purpose, for any reason. When you get that, things start falling into place.
>
> — ShantiMayi

connected to its own fullness. In giving all from within itself, it comes to know its own potential. Relating from this Current of deeper love is the opposite of our Iago habits. Instead of meeting the other to get love, you meet to express and share the love that you are. In one of our many dialogues, ShantiMayi put it like this:

> *What you want, you have to be; you cannot get anything from another person. If you want love, you have to love. If you want respect, you have to respect. If you want dignity, you have to dignify. We know this with our children. It's not so much others loving you back that's so rewarding, as it is to have them to love. When a person reaches inside themselves, and ceases to need, and exudes and expresses love, then relationship goes on by itself. It's like the river flowing, or like the trees dropping their leaves and picking up the flowers in the spring. Everything is going on quite harmoniously when there is no demand made on another to fulfill you. When you see the other person as an opportunity to really love, to really express what's in your heart, every action is nothing but the opportunity to really dig deep in your own heart. Then this relationship is very divine. It's very simple.*

An underlying feeling of inner richness and fullness is the base of where we meet and from where we love each other. We don't have a relationship, we are two individuals who are supportive in letting each other be and showering each other with the best, highest blessing.

— Peter Makena

The shift from personality-based relating to meeting in Being happens through a moment of awakening. The shift from Being to the awakening of the Current happens through innocent play and natural curiosity. When we meet in this Current, each human being becomes fascinating, relevant. There are gifts that can flow only from that person; love seeks to express itself uniquely in each human form. Love has never been expressed in that way before, and may never again. We slowly develop a natural curiosity about the Other. I want to know what it is like to be you when I am less obsessed with my small story. Like someone recovering from depression or grief, we become more interested in the world beyond us as the burden of our own suffering passes.

I have had several wonderful meetings with Gay and Kathlyn Hendricks. They have been married for more than twenty years, but being with them often reminds me of being with a couple newly in love. They are genuinely fascinated with each other. When one speaks, the other sits with bated breath, not wanting to miss a single word. I love to be around them, because the power of the Current is so strong. Listen to Kathlyn talk to us about her marriage, and also to her husband in an aside:

> *When a person's body is really open to space, the unique expression of that person is so magnificent, so awesome to me. That's where I get most of my sense of what the divine really is: when people allow themselves to be space in form.*
>
> *Gay, you are right out at the edges of yourself! You are expressing who you are. Space is coming through your body without holding back or trying to control it — your flow, your willingness to be authentic, to allow space and your body to dance together in a way that I think of as simply play.*
>
> *It's entertaining, and it's what we do.*
>
> *That's what the universe is doing, I think, putting space into form so that play can happen. I want to tell you, I have the most fun that I ever imagined possible with Gay on a day-to-day basis.*
>
> *Gay, just the play that happens out of spontaneous space coming through your body and my body and how we play with that, it's just the most fun! I never knew that that kind of fun was available.*

In this meeting, of Being come fully alive and embodied as the Current, there is absolutely no desire to change the other person, but instead an intense fascination with them, in the deepest possible way. Adyashanti talked about this, both with his wife and with his friends and students:

> It's a predisposition to be interested in what is so with another person, to get down to fundamental, base-level curiosity about what's really going on.
>
> — Brad Blanton

> *Sometimes somebody really wants me to do something, or really doesn't like the way I am or what I said. We all know what that's like. When I experience it, there's nothing in me that wants them to change, and that has a profound effect on how we relate. It is what makes everything possible. The mind has its own idea of what that means, what the implications are. The human implications of*

allowing everybody to be just as they are, not wanting them to change, is actually the opposite of the way the mind thinks. It's more passionate. If I'm in relationship, and I sense that my beloved, or my friend, is not really expressing the deepest thing in them, there is a curiosity: Is this what you really want? Are you living the life that you really want? Are you relating to me as you want? There's nothing in me that wants to change you, but I do want to have this discussion because I'm really curious.

This open curiosity is the essence of translucent relating. I had great difficulty choosing what to include while writing this chapter, because I had literally hundreds of examples of translucents I had interviewed who were passionately in love with love, delighted to discover the simple magic of paying attention to another without an agenda and the many new pathways that open up as a result.

RELATIONSHIP AS A PRACTICE

As with every other area of our lives, there is a symbiotic relationship between the depth of our translucence and the way we view otherness. Translucence naturally shifts our habits of relating, without our doing anything about it. We have less to defend as we come to know ourselves as bigger than our own story, and our relating naturally becomes less strategic. As we see the other as myself, even if only in snapshots, we find that compassion occurs effortlessly. We develop more humor about the idiosyncrasies of our personality. We have less investment in laboriously working things out, and a greater willingness to breathe a sigh and return to innocence. The need to change others relaxes, since we are less tied to them as a source of our well-being. All these things can happen more or less spontaneously as by-products of waking up.

At the same time, the attention we bring to our habits of relating can

> When we start telling truth, we discover that who we are is a being who notices rather than a personality who thinks. Our essential self, each one of us, is as a noticing being, moment to moment to moment. Then there's no particular reason to lie because you have nothing to defend.
>
> — Brad Blanton

deepen and stabilize our expression of translucence. We can always bring more skillful means, more as an art form than as self-improvement, to our relating. We can become more aware of, and tell the truth about, the old habits that have created separation. These old habits run deep, and they will not necessarily die on their own. Our social environment reinforces them. When we are willing to put awakening into the fire of relationship, it will reveal all old habits and allow them to be released. Says Gay Hendricks:

> *I think therein lies the difficulty, as well as the awesome beauty, of relationships. The universe is attempting to meet itself in play. When one person meets another, as that space links up with that space again, it pushes to the surface all the little places where we've withdrawn from space. Whether it's being physically beaten, or starved to death, or criticized, or in beating others, those are the places where we've withdrawn and crystallized into mass, and then that has to come to the surface.*

The many translucents I interviewed about relating are deeply committed to bringing more awareness, more humor, more practice to every meeting, every day. But this practice is not in the service of making the relationship better; it is in the service of deepening translucence itself. Relationship becomes the most effective tool, better than yoga and meditation and every self-help seminar rolled into one, to free us of all that is not love. Jett Psaris elaborates:

> *One can use relationship to develop one's full humanity. At some point, our seed begins to vibrate, our essence wants to unfold, and if our defenses don't give way, then our potential remains unrealized and untuned. The motivation begins to shift. There is nothing else that I know of that can as reliably, as methodically, bring us to the places where we are unfolding, and the places where we are trapped in our defense system. So it becomes a path, an awakening to our humanity, to what it is to be fully human: not just spacious but also*

For those of us who have had some degree of realization and then attempt to live it with another person, it's actually not that romantic. Now we are going to transform, in the alchemy of our relationship, this deep conditioning that is both personal and collective.

— Richard Moss

contracted. To embrace that humanity wholeheartedly, we become vehicles for love and consciousness and for evolution itself.

This willingness to recognize old habits is no longer merely in the service of improving a specific relationship; it becomes a spiritual discipline that affects our whole life. The old addiction to needing something from another, or needing the other to change, is no longer the primary force driving us. Rather, we can use our relationships, all of them, from those with our parents and children to those with lovers and co-workers, as a practice to deepen the actualization of latent love. Relationship is not an end in itself. If it were, the limits of our vision would cause us to suffer. By noticing the way we answer a question from our young child, or the way we greet our beloved when we first open our eyes in the morning, we are paying attention to the way we relate to all of existence, at the level where it is most tangible and real.

We can use relationship as a skillful means to awaken the Current, to allow the Current to flow through the old habits, and in this way to allow more love to ooze into this parched world. If love is not given away, if relationship is not a discipline radically affecting our meetings with everyone, it has all been wasted.

> This is the requirement for relationship as celebration: that I get wholeheartedly, whole body, whole mind, whole me committed to relationship as a path.
>
> — Kathlyn Hendricks

The unequivocal commitment to meeting in shared translucence will naturally lead us into a cycle of alternating rapid expansion, as we embrace greater space and contraction, as we feel and release habits of nonlove. Kathlyn Hendricks calls this "carving space":

When these barriers would come, it was really carving more space. We would see over and over again in our relationship, and in thousands of other people's lives, that the capacity for having the blood and neurology run that much energy was limited. We top out the thermostat, then have some very typical personal themes that look like they are real, but are simply expressions of our own limited capacity. Now we put a lot of our attention on what will allow us to increase our capacity so that we can experience more co-creation in space and less time in the gunk. We put most of our emphasis on that, and only now and then on the story. We're not very interested in the story, and do our best to get other people unfascinated with the story. We're more interested in what is happening at the edge of our own spaciousness, especially when coming into contact with someone we really love. What happens to the energy between us is very interesting.

When we enter into relating with the commitment to continuously deepen translucence, we need to know how to be with these periods exposing the story, without getting lost in them. Below we will discuss four potent means of bringing more translucence to our relating.

Making Agreements

Translucent relating begins with clear and unequivocal agreements about why we are meeting and how we might dedicate our relating to the deepening of translucence. We may enter into such agreements as friends, as lovers, or even as a community. We need to make sure that we are all on the same page before we enter into relating as a translucent practice.

> Make agreements consciously. Select the agreements you want to make, keep the agreements that you make, and know how to change agreements if they're not working. You will discover that keeping agreements creates more spaciousness, rather than seeing them as an authority issue.
>
> — Kathlyn Hendricks

When meeting with both couples and individuals in retreats Chameli and I lead to amplify translucent relating, we suggest that agreement can be made in four stages:

1. Take some time alone, if possible, a few days. Stay with the question, "Why am I alive?" Discover what is most important to you, what you most deeply value. For example, you might discover that you are alive to express and share love, to remain open, no matter what.

2. Find out where you are naturally committed. For example, you might discover in stage one that intimacy is important to you, and now in stage two, you realize that you are committed to honesty or to listening. We discover where we need to "take a stand," in order to have a fighting chance to live what we most value.

3. Discover how you sabotage your commitment. These are the old habits, which a translucent relationship will uncover and eventually dissolve. For example, you might be committed to honesty but find you easily sabotage your commitment by censoring, because you are afraid people will not like you. When you have explored these three questions alone, you can bring them to your beloved, to your family, or even to a group of friends. Take your time to share everything you discovered, and to listen to others' discoveries too.

4. Now it is possible to make clear agreements in any relationship, agreements that serve what you most deeply value, that allow you to honor where you are naturally committed, and that can liberate the ways we all sabotage ourselves.

Honesty

The most powerful gift we can bring to our relating is the conscious practice of honesty. Under Iago's spell, telling the truth evokes many conflicting reactions. We may try to be honest to protect an image of being a morally superior person; to prevent the other from leaving us; to avoid guilt, fear of punishment, and other uncomfortable feelings; or to conform to a learned moral framework. We may also avoid being honest in an attempt to look good, to protect the other from hurt feelings, or to rebel against moral conditioning.

> Honesty is just being completely present, and describing that. Honesty is describing; it doesn't have any adjectives. You can talk about what's going on in your mind and report it as a thought you're having, without doing a sales pitch for it.
>
> — Brad Blanton

We can also adopt honesty as a discipline to deepen presence, to expose and evaporate everything we carry within us that interferes with love. It can be a spiritual discipline, rather than something done in service to separation. Honesty is not just a moral principle. When we avoid the truth, we are cut off from ourselves. If you lie to another, you've also created a wall between you and yourself. We split infinity into two, and divide our own intrinsic wholeness. Brad Blanton, who has been a clinical psychologist for more than thirty years, came to translucence through the rigorous and sustained practice of radical honesty. Blanton describes honesty as being completely present and describing your experience just as it is: "You can take the whole awareness continuum and divide it into three parts. Notice what is going on right now outside of you in the world, what is going on within the confines of your own skin, and what is going through the mind right now, and that's all there is. Noticing and reporting what is here is honesty...just saying it right out as though you didn't know any better." Blanton thinks of honesty as a spiritual practice more than as a moral virtue:

> We know meditation develops your capacity to be present. It becomes more complicated with eyes open, and even more challenging when it involves feelings and interactions with other people. Radical honesty is simply the predisposition for meditation that involves interactions with other people. Honesty and intimacy are really the same thing. When you're honest, the boundaries between yourself and the other break down, and you experience more oneness or more of a mutual beingness.

Entering into mutual agreements with your partner, friends, and community to end withholding and deception may be more challenging than first meets the eye. But it is worth the price we have to pay. The old habit that creates most separation, and that pulls attention back most forcibly into Iago's grip, is the tendency to withhold. Says Blanton:

> The biggest rationalization for lying is "I don't want to hurt anyone's feelings," the second is "I don't want to offend anybody," and the third is "I don't want to make a fool of myself." I recommend that you do all three. But stay present with people and let them stay with you until you feel your way through it and get clear. I recommend that you hurt people's feelings till they get over having their feelings hurt, and offend people but stay with them; don't do a drive-by. Make a fool of yourself, be a fool in life, be embarrassed, ashamed, whatever emotion comes up, do it out loud, and if you're scared, feel your way through it and go on to the next limit.

> Relationship is like a dance floor. Anytime you don't tell the truth it's like putting a gob of well-chewed bubble gum on the floor. Your foot sticks to it, and you can't quite participate in the dance until you handle that. Then you are free to look for a bigger space to dance in, and new ways to dance together.
>
> — Gay Hendricks

While researching this book, I was hard put to find anyone who had added honesty to their awakening and later regretted it. Practicing honesty as a translucent discipline is not just a disposition; it involves cultivating very specific skills, which in many ways run counter to our habits. Kathlyn Hendricks gives her definition of being honest:

> *It is to describe what is going on in any given moment in a way that doesn't blame anybody. It's a whole set of skills: being able to pay attention, to notice what is actually occurring, and then to describe what is occurring in a way that matches the experience. And the act of doing that is tremendously enlivening. It literally will flush out and create a burst of aliveness; it flushes out any old grit, either physical or emotional. It is very, very powerful, but it is also a skill that people can learn and can develop. They don't have to either know it or not know it; they can literally develop it.*

> I love every moment I look and there's Peter. I just love that he arises in my world again and again. I delight and enjoy and feel showered upon by his presence in my world. I love him!!
>
> — Aneeta Makena

Following is an exercise you can do with your intimate partner, or with anyone interested in deeper intimacy, for practicing moment-to-moment honesty.

TRY IT YOURSELF

Here-Nowing

Sit opposite one another. Breathe. Maintain soft eye contact.

Partner A, you will only listen. No interrupting, no commentary, no reaction at all.

Partner B, you will tell the truth about this moment by describing body sensations, feelings, sounds you hear, things you see. When you notice a thought or a judgment, you can include it but label it as what it is. "Now I'm having a thought that I am boring." "Now I am having a judgment that you have a terrible haircut."

Keep coming back to now, and tell the truth about it. Be careful of words and phrases like "why," "because," "you made me feel." None of them is true right now; they are all interpretations of experience, not the real deal.

After five minutes, switch roles. When you are both done, find out if you still feel any separation remaining between you. If you do, take another five minutes each.

During this exercise, you are both practicing skills that are at the core of translucent relating. One of you is learning to tell the truth about what is real in this moment, free of explanations, history, and blame. The other is practicing an equally valuable skill: the capacity to be still and to listen, free of defense, free of giving advice or evaluating. Chameli and I practice this simple exercise almost every day. It only takes ten minutes. We have found that both these skills carry over quite effortlessly into the rest of our day and marinate everything else we do in greater transparency and deeper listening. Marc Allen described this capacity to just listen as the single most important element in keeping his marriage clean and as an expression of the eternal:

> You discover another dimension of being, a deeper intimacy, more laughter, more fun, and also more trouble. The trade-off of more trouble for more presence is a very good deal; it's the best bargain in the spiritual warehouse.
>
> — Brad Blanton

My wife is Brazilian. She tells her friends, "Marc won't fight with me." When someone is upset with you, just shut up and listen. Our first reaction is to deny or defend, but instead we can always just listen and take it all in. The universe is in your face telling you something. There's something for you to get there. The argument dissolves when you don't defend; "I'm listening to you." I think if you understand this you can live in harmony with absolutely anybody.

Calling Back Judgment

Iago's habit is to externalize everything. If we have not fully accepted the anger or hurt or rigidity we carry within our own hearts, we seek it out in others and blame or judge the qualities we see. Says Kathlyn Hendricks: "You scan the field, and your inner self calls forth or casts out a lasso to the one person who can reflect to you that thing you couldn't see or be with in any other way. The relationship will be successful if both people are willing to learn."

All relationships provide opportunities to feel and then call back judgment. Iago's influence leads us to externalize everything, to project our disowned ghosts somewhere "out there." We judge someone else as fat or lazy or rigid or cold or closed when we do not want to see those tendencies in ourselves. In this way we create divisions between you and me, between us and them. We also fragment ourselves by creating buffer zones between the personality, celebrated as who I choose to be, and the shadow, denied as what I keep hidden. In the last several years thousands of people have come to a deeper resting with themselves through The Work of Byron Katie, who teaches us to write down our judgments: "She is arrogant," "He should be more sensitive," "I need her to listen to me," and then to turn them around: "I am arrogant when I think I know what is best for another person," "I should be more sensitive when I'm thinking about John," "I need to listen to myself when I am busy trying to change other people." This simple work has been an effective journey home for many.

> It's very difficult to see ourselves clearly on our own. In a relationship all the things we get upset about are the things we're not accepting in ourselves. The other person is a mirror
>
> — Paul Lowe

You can also call back judgment very simply with three words: "Just like me." It really does not matter if you make judgments, as long as they are inclusive rather than rejecting. Tell your friends that they are lazy or stupid, and you risk losing the friendship. Tell them, "You are so lazy, just like me," and you may invite empathy. As we call back judgment, we are calling back the fragmented parts of the psyche we have evicted. Now laziness no longer needs to wait outside the back door in the cold; it has been welcomed back into the fold and can curl up by the fire and sleep. Anger, despair, excitement, fear, grief, greed, and stupidity — all can be brought home and integrated as parts of our wholeness. As we deepen this process, we become more invisible; we include everything, and so the boundaries between what I am and what life itself is become less distinct.

Marlena Lyons makes this capacity to call everything back a central part of the work she does with people:

It's easy to fall in love with that which you love in your partner and in yourself, but it's that which is most difficult that we need to learn to love.

That's the biggest difference. With truly successful relationship, we are able to relate to those areas in ourselves and in the other that are difficult for us, not only those that are wonderful and lovely and awake. You can fall in love with everybody, and from that place, everybody is luminous and open and loving. It's when I meet the rejecting face, or the one that seems to not be open to me, that I say, "Ah! What is that?" That's where the work begins.

This is not to say that it is impossible to see things that are true about another person or to offer feedback or even criticism. When we have called back our judgments, our feedback is free of "othering" — making it all about another rather than ourselves — and only then can it be received.

> Life is not just a gift given, but something we continuously invest in by sharing our appreciation for what we know, and not holding the other responsible; by realizing that our judgment is our own and has nothing to do with the other person.
>
> — Aneeta Makena

To offer this kind of support, we are called on to embrace a paradox. Only when we fully accept another as she is, abandoning the desire to change her, can we actually offer support for her deeper flowering. We learn to feel through the surface appearance into the deeper heart, which is already free. We love beyond the customary limits, into this deeper wild heart, and call it forth. Anything less than that is enabling mediocrity. We all possess a natural curiosity to know the heart's deepest calling, to know if it is indeed willing to live within limitation, or if it longs for greater freedom. Adyashanti elaborates:

If awakening is taken out of the rarefied atmosphere of "my realization" and applied to "my life," it actually becomes a way to carry the uniqueness of that person into their human life. That is where we feel drawn: to the passion, the aliveness of that. But most humans are terrified, because it means stepping out into the unknown, beyond our boundaries. We are all like flowers, growing out of the same soil, but unique in our appearance. And just like flowers, we can remain as buds or open as blossoms. It takes incredible human courage to flower in the way that we were meant to; it means taking a stand against habits that are not only personal, but also collective.

Appreciation

The last skillful means that we can bring to our relating is the conscious practice of devotion and appreciation. Here, our relating fulfills its original intent, as a celebration of Being meeting itself. Recognition of our own intrinsic nature certainly initiates the capacity to see beauty, but a little appreciation practice adds the needed lubrication. Once we discover relationship as celebration, it is no longer a means to awakening but a dance that deepens that awakening through simply loving. For Gay Hendricks, appreciating his wife has become his most powerful catapult into a deeper resting in himself:

> *When I got into relationship with Kathlyn, my top goal in life was space and the creativity that was sparked off by my relationship with space. Relationship was the testing ground that would determine whether I was able to experience my spaciousness on a moment-by-moment basis. Then, as I realized that my top priority was actually my appreciation of Kathlyn, and my ongoing appreciation of the relationship itself, lo and behold, it became easier to maintain spaciousness all the time.*

It may require experimenting with the first three skillful means described above to discover real celebration of another. Eventually we lose interest in our defenses after running through them thousands of times, and we realize there is nothing left to defend. We are simply not interested in protecting ourselves anymore. At that point we find ourselves in a celebratory relationship. Kathlyn Hendricks sees the discovery of celebration as our evolutionary potential: "In a celebratory relationship, the purpose is to celebrate who the other person is, and their evolution into more of their spaciousness, more of their expression in the world, more of their creativity. Then there is the possibility of truly co-creating a whole new way of being, and a whole kind of presence and rippling out into the world that hasn't existed before."

We do not need to wait until we have let go of all our defenses, however, to begin exploring celebration. Kathlyn continues:

> We both hold a gratitude, not only for each other, but also for the gift of life. It's extraordinary, what we have. We have a sacred opportunity for love. We know how easily it can be gone, how easily it could not be as it is, and how precious and how fragile.
>
> — Peter Makena

To be able to generate appreciation, even in the midst of a painful, despairing place, is so powerful for people, because it lets them know, right now, "I can create a different kind of consciousness." The act of appreciating is being sensitive, aware of and experiencing another person as a work of art in process. We can leapfrog a lot of what could have been psychological work and go directly into celebration. In a state of appreciation, those other kinds of experiences, like reclaiming projection and taking responsibility, seem to dissolve. Appreciating organically brings forth authenticity, contribution, taking responsibility, wondering, and being curious.

TRY IT YOURSELF
Five Things I Love about You

We can practice appreciation as a skillful means right now. Find a friend, a lover, your sister, your mother, a colleague. Now sit them down, maintain eye contact, and tell them five things you appreciate about them. Then swap roles. Notice what happens within as you give and then receive appreciation. Try this when you have a small- or medium-size issue between you, and see if you can still remember it after doing this exercise.

NUDGING RELATING INTO TRANSLUCENCE

NUDGE
Agree to Be Truthful

With your intimate partner or a friend, agree to experiment with radical honesty for three weeks. Make an agreement not to withhold anything from each other, and to do the Here-Nowing practice as many times a day as you need to keep clear and up-to-date. After three weeks, stop to notice how it feels to be together. Notice what has happened to the sense of space when you are with each other.

NUDGE
Call Back Judgment

With your intimate partner or with any friend, agree to call back any evaluation you make of another person by adding the words *just like me*:

He is so arrogant — just like me.

The Dalai Lama is so wise — just like me.

You aren't really listening to me — just like me.

Try it for three weeks.

NUDGE

Practice Appreciation

Every day, sit down with your partner, or with anyone willing to receive, and tell him five things you appreciate: *I really appreciate the beautiful way you are dressed . . . I appreciate your smile . . . I appreciate that you cooked for us tonight.*

CHAPTER EIGHT

OVERFLOWING FULLNESS

Translucent Sex

Paul had been a seeker for as long as he could remember. He'd practiced meditation, yoga, and whatever else he could find for more than twenty years. When he attended a gathering with an American teacher of awakening, he had no expectations. He'd seen it all before. But that night his life changed. For the first time, he tried to find the one who was on a spiritual quest, and he knew himself as empty space, always free.

For Paul, it was such sweet relief. After that night, he wanted nothing more than to rest in the stillness of himself. He lost interest in watching movies, in reading, and even in having sex with Sandy, his wife. This newly found peace eclipsed all else. For Sandy, things did not seem as good. "I can't feel you anymore," she told him. "Where are you?" Paul did not care; his own silence was so much more real and peaceful than her drama — until, that is, she told him she wanted to leave. Then he began to pay attention. For the first time, he began to pay attention to his breath and to work with his body.

"It took practice to bring my awakening down into my body," Paul reflects. "I can see now that my whole spiritual trip was in a way a denial of the fact that I even had a body. But I had to be honest with myself *eventually. Even though I have a deep habit of wanting to escape, actually I love this place, I love my woman."*

Now Sandy has no complaints about her man. She tells him that he has become the lover she always wanted.

Out of the thousands of translucents I have spoken with in researching this book, virtually no one practiced or advocated celibacy, but almost all were interested in letting their sexuality become a vibrant expression of wakefulness. Translucents are in their bodies, open and sexual. Both through the impact of awakening, as well as through specific practices, sex is transformed from a desire-driven impulse for release and the alleviation of loneliness into an art form, a way of worshipping all life through the body.

> A moment of awakening won't radically change your sex life or allow you to enter into the world more fully and participate. It will allow a place of relief, of rest inside the body-mind. In my experience, if I just try to hold onto that in daily life, it can lead to a disconnect.
>
> — Sandford Perrett

BABY, I NEED YOU

When we bring our Iago trance state into the bedroom, sex is all about desire and need. Switch on the radio, any station, any time of day, and listen. You will likely hear lyrics like "I want you baby, I need you, I can't live without you." Our romantic movies, novels, and poetry all reflect the same unquenchable longing, driven from a sense of incompleteness, from the hope that the other will make us whole again.

The masculine energy in all of us, when it is drugged by Iago, feels an urgent pressure to do something, to fix a problem, and thus to break out of a feeling of constriction and limitation. Most men are unable to rest because there is always something to be done, some problem to be attended to. Many have a sense of wasting their lives, of having forgotten their true purpose. Instead life feels like a heavy burden. This constant anxiety creates tension, a bursting feeling that needs to be released. The masculine seeks out all kinds of ways to alleviate that tension, with drinking, watching television, sleeping, overeating, doing extreme sports: anything that provides either enough sensory

overload or enough dullness to at least temporarily alleviate the anxiety and
pressure. Sex is a great candidate for creating this kind of temporary release.
Having sex is one of the few times when you can feel life coursing through
you, when it feels good to be alive.

When a man sees a woman's soft breasts
or her thighs, an excitement, a fullness
of energy, is created in him. The anxiety of
Iago-based living does not allow that energy
to flow through the body as a natural dis-
persing openness, but instead becomes a
tension trapped in the genitals. Men rush
into sex with an insatiable hunger, turning it into a very quick operation.
With ejaculation and orgasm come a few precious seconds of freedom
from desire and pressure. Many men then fall into the blissful oblivion of
sleep.

> The secret of life is that every human
> being wants to be a great piano
> player. But I can't take credit for that;
> Sigmund Freud discovered it in 1905
> and called it pianist envy.
>
> — Steve Bhaerman
> (Swami Beyondananda)

When a woman is lost in the Iago trance, she also has learned to block
the free circulation of energy in her body. The pain of not being able to feel
and give the enormity of her love through her body causes her to shut down.
Many women carry tension in their vaginas left by superficial sexual interactions. Women generally enter sex as a way to return to love, but man's preoccupation with finding quick release often makes the meeting a brief one and
can leave her even more deeply stranded in the pain of separation. The train
leaves the station too quickly, just as she is unveiling her real offerings, and
she is left alone on the platform in her finery, jewels glistening in the rain,
still holding the ungiven gift of her Big Love.

For the feminine in all of us, it is the feeling of separation, the longing
to open fully and surrender, that initiates sexual attraction. The feminine in
all of us is a devotee and wants to be taken over by the divine. When a woman
can feel a man exude enough strength or focus of intention, be it physical,
emotional, or spiritual, she longs to be taken over by that. Man reminds her
of her longing to surrender to God.

The best we can strive for, while still caught in the Iago world, is more
pleasurable, powerful, longer, and deeper orgasms. Both men and women
have learned to tense up their bodies in ways to create intense pleasure, and
then to release that tension, for a man as ejaculation, for a woman as clitoral

orgasm. So each stays contained in their own body, rubbing boundaries with each other. Two people are separately having sex, together, in the same bed.

Margot Anand has been teaching conscious sex in the West for two decades and is the author of the classic *Art of Sexual Ecstasy* and the founder of the Sky Dancing Institute, which has helped thousands of people worldwide to discover a deeper dimension to sex. Here she explains the difference between release and expansion:

> Lovemaking eventually becomes a minefield that has to be walked through when you're in a daily life with someone. The minefield is full of obstacles and resistances: one is tired and one isn't, one wants it and one doesn't. There are so many difficult dimensions before the people can be in sync with each other.
>
> — Margot Anand

The average orgasm is ten seconds long, and the average frequency of sex among couples is twice a week. Twenty seconds a week, in fifty years of sexual activity, is about fourteen and a half hours of orgasm. For this, we devote how many thousands and thousands of hours thinking about sex, worrying about sex, daydreaming about sex, wishing for sex, planning for sex? The average time from entry to ejaculation is less than six minutes, which for a woman usually means extended stimulation without orgasm. In the "grunt" kind of sex, because the emphasis is on release, like sneezing, people are not looking for the expansion of that kind of circulation through the whole body. Even if they were looking for it, they couldn't have it, because they are so focused on the genital part. When the focus is on the genitals and the other channels have not been opened, you can only go to what I call the explosive orgasm of release, as opposed to the implosive orgasm of expansion.

Feeling such pleasure in the body is, of course, a good thing. And we've come a long way toward enjoying ourselves in bed. A hundred years ago, hypermasculine culture and religion would not even allow for the possibility of women having pleasure in sex at all. Lovemaking and masturbation for both men and women can help to open up tensions in the lower body, which can lead to deeper, more fulfilling orgasms. There are hundreds of books, seminars, and techniques, all of which have their own special tweak on the ultimate orgasm. In this chapter, however, we will explore the possibilities of taking sex beyond the limits of physical pleasure into a powerful means of expressing and deepening translucence itself.

SPIRITUAL MYTH #9: Sex is an event of the lower chakras. Awakened people have transcended sex. Sexual energy completely disappears with awakening.

SPIRITUAL MYTH #10: Awake people automatically have open and flowing sex, without the need for any practice.

STARTING FROM THE GOAL

The more translucently you are living, the more you enter into sex from the very place you were trying to reach. The goal becomes the place of departure. Instead of using sex to get to feelings of relief, spaciousness, well-being, and love, you can enter into sex from those same feelings. In this way, translucent sex becomes the very opposite of Iago-based sex. Rather than a means of getting something you are missing, it is a way to give that with which you are already over-flowing. Sex becomes an act of worship and generosity of spirit, an occasion of mutual giving — not just give and take, but give and give and give.

> We deepen into translucent sexuality by recognizing the emptiness of pleasure, and the pleasure of emptiness, by noticing the moments when conditioning takes over and relaxing deeply in those moments.
>
> — David Deida

Translucent sex invites, serves, and worships divinity in flesh, the awakened source fully giving to itself. When we dare to live our deepest realization in the body, sex becomes alive and passionate, in service to the fullness of consciousness and love rather than only to lust and need. Sexuality becomes a means for fullness to meet itself, to form a union bigger than any individual embodiment could ever be. The meeting of masculine and feminine essence becomes the endless dance of consciousness penetrating life, of love giving to and nurturing consciousness.

When we become sexual from our awakened translucence, we are meeting the other from fullness, rather than from need. We no longer feel tense, we feel open. We no longer feel separate, we feel loving. We no longer feel the urgent pressure of an unsolved problem, we feel present. But this is only the beginning of what is possible. A number of contemporary translucents, notably the prolific writer and teacher David Deida, have explored where, and with specific practices, sex can become a powerful means to deepen translucence and to move beyond the personal completely.

A Sexual Odyssey

Sandford and Susanna Perrett have deeply explored the full range of possibilities of translucent sex, specifically through Deida's work. Their journey reflects how embodied awakening can reveal a new dimension to making love. Like many of the people I interviewed, Sandford felt like a misfit in his childhood. "Even at school," he told me, "I felt there must be more." He channeled his dissatisfaction into seeking worldly accomplishment and money, first studying economics at university, then going into business. "I started to meditate just to be functional, but I still had the feeling that I did not fit in. Always the question 'What is this place?' That grew and grew, and I got more and more desperate to make money."

> I was celibate for fourteen years. Then I turned fifteen. Oh, boy!
>
> — Steve Bhaerman
> (Swami Beyondananda)

Sandford's sex life at that time mirrored his longing for success. "I wanted to be found sexy, I wanted to be loved, to be mothered. I wanted to prove to myself and to others I was a good lover." He had several relationships during this time, always looking for the most beautiful woman he could find: "I remember when I got on an airplane, I would walk up and down the aisle, looking for beautiful women, just to make sure I was not missing out. That's how my sexuality was. I wanted the most beautiful women; I wanted to be with them all. But in each relationship, after six months to a year, I would always come back to the feeling of 'Is this it?' "

Sandford eventually married a beautiful young medical student and acquired considerable real estate. But still the feeling gnawed at him from the inside. "It's just not it, it's not it." Then his marriage fell apart: "And that's when I came to feel, 'Unless something drastically shifts in one year, I'm going to shoot myself.' I just could not see the point of life. I said to myself, 'I'm going to do whatever it takes to find the shift.' "

Sandford threw himself into spiritual seeking. Just a few days before his deadline, while in India, he went through an awakening shift with the help of a young German teacher. Today he describes it like this: "I let the attention pull back inward, to rest in a null state, a point zero, and just to relax into that. It was incredibly relaxing and beautiful, because the whole seeking mechanism stopped. I saw that it was the disease of the mind, to be seeking for something to be different than it already is in this moment. That was such a profound gift."

> In the first stage, people use sex for selfish reasons. In the second stage, people share sexuality as a means of loving one another. In the third stage, people use sexuality to open one another to the very recognition of oneness.
>
> — David Deida

Sandford returned from this pivotal meeting to his life in Australia, and he soon began teaching. Within a year, he was traveling all over the world, conducting meetings with hundreds of people. But like almost all the people I have interviewed, he realized that a return to stillness could remain quite impotent unless it was embodied and lived in the world:

> *After some time, I noticed there was a disconnection from the world in the people who would come to me. The inward-turning, quiet, peaceful stillness was more and more of a disconnect. Myself and other people, we were giving up, giving up interest in worldly things. I could see that this gift alone doesn't allow you to enter into the world more fully and participate. And I could also see that sexuality would always break through the disconnect. Sexual desire is designed to pull you out into the world. I met with a lot of other men at that time. They might think their sexuality was great. They might feel less desire, and feel they had it under control. But then their partner would say, "No, he's not really here with me. He's totally withdrawn."*

Then Sandford met his wife, Susanna, who had already been researching and practicing more conscious ways of lovemaking, particularly the work of Barry Long. From the beginning she told him, "This is the only way I want to explore sex. Are you willing to go there with me?" It was in this agreement to explore consciously that they discovered Deida's work.

Deida offered them many exercises to help bring the awakening down into the body, including specific yoga postures, breathing exercises, and ways

> Sex, over time as the recognition stabilizes, has nothing to do with the motions of the various bodies of the individuals, and yet those motions continue. One has a choice to play out those motions, to whatever degree one wants to, or not.
>
> — David Deida

to circulate energy. As Sandford was able to flow energy through his whole body, he no longer felt the need to burst out in ejaculation; he was able to store the energy for greater fullness. Sandford was able to relax so deeply that he could send sexual energy up through his spine and down the front of his body:

I felt total vulnerability and much deeper connection than my mind was willing to experience. It was incredibly pleasurable and beautiful, but we would both resist it, because it took everything away. Over time, about six months to a year, we were more and more able to relax into that openness. As everything releases, it's incredibly obvious. You suddenly feel your consciousness feeling everything. It's as if the whole world is your body. It's shining from the inside, like a fourth dimension. Everything goes flat. There's no more experience of three dimensions, of "me" being in the middle of this big place. All of a sudden you are all of it; it's excruciatingly blissful, terrifyingly blissful.

Once he experienced this opening with Susanna during sex, Sandford found that it often continued into the rest of his life:

If you're there with other people, it's like some force of the living divinity is looking out through your eyes, it's looking out through the other person's eyes, and the living divinity can talk to itself and express itself and feel itself through both people. We are usually buzzing with thought, attention locked inside the body-mind. As that releases, everything goes flat, it accentuates the feeling of this place as like plastic, like one solid mass of plastic, that's painted all different colors and shapes. That plastic is really love. It is being breathed into, felt into, relaxed into. The excruciating ecstasy of the moment is felt more and more as love. Everything becomes more and more alive.

Susanna told me she had always had an intuition of what was possible, something much bigger than what she was experiencing: "I remember the first time I made love. It was beautiful. Then my boyfriend fell asleep. I was just crying and praying to God, 'I don't want this, I want something deeper.' This was not only true with sexuality, but with everything in life." As she grew older, she was always looking for more heart connection, more deepening. But she reports that she was losing contact with her lower body. She chose the heart, the higher dimensions, over the physical. Even though sex was still pleasurable, it was much more restricted and much more soft and gentle and sensitive:

With Sandford, for the first time I felt completely safe to explore fully. Through practice, my whole body has opened in a way that is totally full. We have made it possible to explore every domain of sexuality, without restrictions. We have lived out any fantasy or dream or longing and fully engaged the body in the sexual play. Through breathing together, looking in the eyes, sometimes just being there, talking to each other, praying, connecting in different ways, we discover the depth of conscious light, of real love in the midst of the full exploration of bodily sexuality. Now, it feels like we are both stretching our limits all the time. It gets more and more wild and crazy and free and open and sensual and sexual and pleasurable. And at the same time, it gets more pure, more divine, more spiritual and deep.

The first orgasm I ever had transposed me into a sense of total freedom and propelled me into the nature of who I am. Today I am in a paradoxical situation where sexuality is not all that important, yet when I make love, it is phenomenal. I am less attached to having sex; what matters more is the closeness of the heart.

— Margot Anand

MASCULINE AND FEMININE ENERGY

To understand the full implications of practicing with sex in this way, let's explore the central core of David Deida's work, which is a unique understanding of masculine and feminine essence. Deida calls awakening a "poke through," which he defines as "the realization that there is no separation of anything from anything at all; there is just one consciousness that shows itself as light." When we turn completely inward to our core, there is only this One, which Deida calls conscious light or luminous consciousness. For life to happen, the One divides itself into two principles: light and consciousness.

Everything that manifests, everything that arises, first as energy and then as matter, Deida calls light, the *feminine principle:* Shakti, the goddess, mother nature. That which remains still, always aware of energy and matter, is consciousness, the *masculine principle:* Shiva, godhead. All sex, all life, all creation, is the continuous penetration of light with consciousness.

Deida explains that each of us contains both polarities, both masculine and feminine essence: "Every human being tends to identify more with one or the other and so has a more masculine or feminine essence. If one identifies more with consciousness than light, then along with that identification goes a whole set of correlate activities that I call more masculine." Most, but not all, men have a more masculine essence, and most, but not all, women have a more feminine essence. A very few individuals may be evenly balanced, but that is very rare.

The most revolutionary aspect of Deida's gift has been the understanding that embodied awakening will express itself quite differently in different people, and specifically that it will have a very different flavor in masculine and feminine incarnations. Almost all religious traditions have implied that spiritual awakening means to transcend gender; they have advocated some sense of androgyny, which usually translated into everyone conforming to a masculine expression of awakening. Translucents represent a break from those traditions, because they accept and allow their humanness, as well as their transcendence. Says Deida:

> Any time realization is expressed at all, it is expressed through a vehicle of some kind. Even though all the momentum in the body may continue, one is more and more deeply lived by the obviousness of the recognition of unity.
>
> — David Deida

Human shapes are like trees, with knots, gnarls, and whorls of expression. When realization is expressed through a human, it is expressed through a specific human shape, much as the wind is given sound by the shape of a tree's branches and leaves. As light shines through each human shape, it creates a unique art, the style of which is implicit in the medium of offering. Although the light or consciousness expressed by the translucent is always spontaneous, the conditioning of the medium's shape creates each unique offering of love. As one becomes more translucent, one relaxes more and more as a spontaneous offering of love, consciousness and light to others. Each human, each individual body-mind, will display this offering in a unique way. The way is conditioned, but the offering doesn't have to merely reinforce the conditioning. The difference between somebody who is more or less realized isn't how much conditioning they have, but how much conditioning they reinforce, or how much conditioning is joyfully surrendered as the bright art of the unique offering itself.

A translucent man, with a masculine essence, will have a realization of undivided oneness, and a translucent woman, with a feminine essence, will have the same realization, but she will express it in a completely different way. In our collective shedding of millennia of hypermasculine role models, we are all relaxing into the recognition of both masculine and feminine expressions of awakening and living them more freely.

Masculine translucence expresses itself as penetrating focus. It is the part in every one that just witnesses and is simply aware of the swirling impressions of life, like a Buddha statue. It doesn't change or move but is constantly permeating everything. The masculine lives as total freedom in the midst of the shifting dance of form. It breaks through boundaries, remaining untouched in the center of the storm, empty, present, and conscious. The more translucent a masculine person becomes, the more he relaxes any attempt to distort his natural essence. He becomes more naturally masculine, not as a conditioned macho stereotype, but as that aspect of the original oneness that is conscious and empty and that pierces form with awareness. The masculine is the penetrating consciousness of the divine. Through him is offered the deepest gifts of clarity and unmoving presence.

> The world is my womb. The more deeply I relax into my body, the more it feels like I am being penetrated all the time by the Universe, and, at the same time, just completely full and juicy and alive. I can't help but move my arms and fingers and dance in this love affair.
>
> — Jennifer Garcia

When translucence expresses itself through the feminine, it has more of a quality of dancing light than of penetrating consciousness. The translucent feminine gives her gift as radiant love. The feminine in all of us is caring, endlessly forgiving, compassionate, and nurturing. She delights in color, texture, and expression. The more translucent a feminine person becomes, the more she relaxes any attempt to distort her natural essence. She becomes more naturally feminine, not as a Barbie look-alike, but as the aspect of original oneness that is radiantly loving and constantly surrendering. The feminine is the embracing love of the divine.

Getting Permission to Flow

Maria attended one of our retreats a few years ago. Now in her fifties, she has been practicing meditation, which she had learned from a well-known Indian guru, for more than thirty years. She had a very calm, empty, silent presence. She dressed in plain, very sensible clothes, and her gray hair was cut in a short, boyish style. After some days, she told us that her greatest difficulty and disappointment was that she still had strong emotions. She felt herself overwhelmed by grief or anger from time to time, which both she and her husband agreed was a sign of weakness, a lack of depth in her meditation practice.

Everything changed one morning when Chameli spoke to her. "Your feelings are beautiful, they are your gift to your husband and to all of us. They bring color and texture to man's world, which can so often be gray and burdensome. Over the next days, please show us all what you are feeling, not only with your words, but with the way you move, with your laughter and your tears." Maria was more than a little disoriented by this invitation, after so many years of practice and masculine discipline. But the transformation that followed was dramatic and inspiring. At first she experimented, a little clumsily, by expressing quite chaotic and painful feelings that had been locked in her body for decades under the mantle of masculine spirituality. But we all also witnessed her tears of joy and her immense tidal wave of love, which was big enough to drown the entire retreat many times over. On the last night we had a party. Everyone dressed up beautifully. One of the other women, a teacher of sacred Indian dance, helped Maria dress in flowing, colorful clothes. She was transformed.

> Every woman's very nature is to be a high priestess, to be an initiator. Only when a man knows how to give her pleasure will she be radiant, devoted, loving, satisfied, and able to be in the fullness of the whole relationship.
>
> — Margot Anand

Watching Maria dance that night was something I will never forget. She was in pure rapture, taken over by God. Tears streamed down her face, and she poured love into each person in the room, one after another. When I looked into her eyes, I saw *that* look; she was taken, transported, she was dancing in her heart with Mira and Mary and Sita. Since then, Maria has met often with other women to deepen her translucent feminine practices; she dances every day. The transformation of Maria from chrysalis to butterfly is ongoing.

For thousands of years, men have blazed almost all spiritual trails, so we only have models for masculine wakefulness. When feminine people long to live their awakening more deeply, they feel they have to watch, to be very present and empty. Some even shave their heads and *look* like men. So for most feminine translucent people, the invitation to relax into what is natural for them can be a huge relief. So many feminine people long to be invited to flow in an endless river of feeling, to confirm what their heart already knows, that all feeling is the kiss of the divine.

> Everything that can be felt through the body is a feminine practice, as a doorway to feel that deepest surrender. I mean everything — like feeling the texture of your skin, feeling the texture of the clothes that you're wearing, feeling the texture of the apple in your mouth.
>
> — Susanna Perrett

Polarizing and Merging

It is not only hypermasculine spiritual disciplines that cramp the awakened feminine spirit in this way; it is society as a whole. After the honeymoon period is over, many couples depolarize, becoming neutral, the same. It is one reason people get bored with each other and may eventually feel attracted outside of the relationship.

Before we've had any sort of radical awakening, our tendency to get rather than to give is lived out as much in sex as anywhere else. As discussed, man wants release and relief from the burden of his life; woman wants to feel loved. Both want to escape, for a few moments at least, into physical pleasure strong enough to override the dirge of lack created in the mind. Couples who undergo any degree of awakening, or even just adopt some basic meditation, yoga, or other practices, discover the realm of no-you-no-me and melt into a recognition of oneness. In this, little sense of gender remains, and sexual attraction can easily go down the drain.

You activate realization by giving it a physical dimension. It is almost like looking at yourself in the mirror. We are reenacting something that exists within: the play of the inner reflected in the outer, and the outer reflected in the inner. Ultimately, in the highest moment of it, which we all hope would be forever, there is no difference.

— Margot Anand

Translucent couples discover that they have a wide range of frequencies in which they can meet each other, from fully merged at one end of the spectrum, to fully polarized at the other. The dance of deeper love occurs between these two, always moving from one end of the spectrum to the other. At times of great merging, the beloved is closer even than your best friend, closer than family. You can look into your beloved's eyes and see your own eyes looking back at you, albeit in disguise. It is a strange feeling every time. We merge like this when we meditate together, when we are still and present, or when we are completely transparent and honest. Then we feel the most exquisite melting, safety, and relaxation, but little sexual polarity, no mysterious other to explore.

There are other times when translucent lovers polarize. It can happen intentionally, through time apart, or through specific practices. Polarization also occurs when either partner spends time with his or her own gender. Then they become mysterious strangers to each other again. Man may feel a renewed sense of mission, clarity, and expansive presence, ready to wrestle bears, save the world, and meditate for years in a cave. All at once. Woman softens into her huge heart. She delights in making her surroundings beautiful, she savors an infinite variety of textures of feeling, most of which man has no idea about and never will. When they meet in this polarized way, they can deeply gift each other. Each can bring forth offerings that the other feels is missing.

The great majority of people get stuck by favoring one end of this spectrum over the other. If you have the idea that you should stay merged all the time, you will feel safe, cozy, and familiar, but you will also get bored with each other. If you stay polarized for too long, you will feel attracted, fascinated, you will have passionate and wild sex in every corner of the house, the garage, and the car, but sooner or later you'll get lost in fighting and feel misunderstood. You will feel like your partner is a spy from another culture — very, very different from the one you are familiar with, and, well, let's face it, weird. For the overpolarized couple, all the mystery and great sex in the world cannot prevent the relationship from self-destructing in what is legally referred to as "irreconcilable differences."

THE BIG EVENT

All sex, in fact all life everywhere, is about the meeting of masculine and feminine energy, the meeting of consciousness and light. This does not mean that men always represent the masculine, or that women always hold feminine energy. It means that sexual union is always about a more conscious presence penetrating a more yielding, loving surrender. We have worked with translucent gay couples, male and female. With some, one partner holds more masculine energy, and the other holds more feminine. And in many cases, they alternate who is the leading, masculine polarity and who is the surrendering, feminine polarity. For any couple, these polarities can sometimes be reversed. This has less to do with physical position than with disposition. As soon as a man relaxes, waits, becomes soft and vulnerable and yielding, and as soon as a woman becomes more assertive, initiating, and penetrating with her presence, you have reversed polarities. This can be a great thing to practice intentionally, for a few minutes at a time, to experience more deeply the opposite sexual essence.

For a translucent couple that has learned both to polarize and merge, sex is transformed from a personal act of intensified pleasure into something of quite different proportions. Orgasm is a glorified sneeze compared to what is possible when we step out of the small box of physical pleasure.

> Sexuality can become art. It is no longer compelled by these conditioned bodies going through their trip. It is emanating spontaneously from openness to openness, playing as if it were touching another, knowing it is only recognizing itself.
>
> — David Deida

When partners are willing to practice with translucent sex, they both come to the sexual meeting from a physical fullness. The man has not only realized himself as empty consciousness, absolutely present and able to contain all movement, but he has also brought that realization down into the body. The woman has not only experienced the essence of love, but she has also practiced opening so much that she emanates that love itself, from her whole body. She becomes an embodiment of the divine feminine paradox: the supreme strength of absolute yielding, vulnerable surrender. This is not a matter of imitating or acting out certain qualities but of relaxing into your natural essence, which takes no doing or effort at all, only conscious practice.

A translucent couple is not meeting to get something from each other, or for themselves, although they will both be blessed. They are not meeting to get off on waves of physical pleasure, although their bodies will pass through those states as a result. They are not even meeting to love each other in a personal way, although they will know that love more fully than they could in any other way. They are not actually meeting as Hank and Loretta Higgins of 1032 Marigold Lane anymore, although that will be the point of departure. Sex is now being offered at the altar of translucence itself.

Translucent sexual union is what Deida calls "the human realm replication of the union of consciousness and light." This union can, and often does, occur *within* an individual. Tantric art shows us the union of Shiva and Shakti as the melting and merging of the inner man and inner woman. In hypermasculine traditions, this was as good as it got, finding this union of the inner masculine and feminine, then meeting the world without gender.

With translucent sexual practice, we consciously choose to embody the great union of consciousness and light. The more masculine person (usually, but not always, a man) embodies consciousness gifting through the body, and the more feminine person (usually, but not always, a woman) embodies light and love in the body. Both partners are allowing a gifting that is universal, rather than personal, to pass through them. When a man and a woman meet in this way, the two polarized offerings become a full circle, and there is a fusion of consciousness and light, of yin and yang, much greater than could ever occur within an individual. The masculine essence gifts the feminine so deeply with trustworthy conscious presence, through one partner's body, and the feminine essence gifts the masculine so deeply with love and light, through the other partner's body, that the boundaries of fullness meeting fullness finally break, and they pour into one another.

> You are aligning yourself with the way you actually are, at your deepest. This is just a matter of getting out of the egoic self-contraction and feeling more of whom you really are. For me, sex is the fastest way I know to do that.
>
> — Sandford Perrett

Without this full circle, a masculine person's disposition is to feel, "I want to get back to that nice peaceful emptiness; I don't want to deal with all this stuff of life. It's a burden, a hassle." Through the completion of the circle, through giving the gift completely to the feminine, he realizes that that "stuff" is not a problem at all; it is all made of consciousness anyway. He can surrender into life. He becomes uncollapsible, free in the midst of the swirling of form. No matter what, he can still fully give of himself. He is no longer afraid to open into life and finds the marriage of consciousness and form.

> There is immense joy and love, every shade in existence and then some. I feel like a storm, like the ocean, the waves, like a blade of grass, like a craggy rock. I want to fuck everything into my womb. A woman suffers not giving her love. To be truly satisfied, she must absolutely live in the depth of her love.
>
> — Jennifer Garcia

Woman is freed of her longing to be fully penetrated by God when she opens her heart way beyond the known and allows the Big Love to move through her. She realizes, in the undefended giving of everything, that her world of form is already fully penetrated by divine consciousness all the time, and always has been. She is no longer just Loretta Higgins; she has become Kumari, the Divine Goddess. She has become the feminine principle itself, opened in radiant undefended love. She allows herself to be completely penetrated and taken in a conscious act of surrender and devotion to the masculine principle, which is entering her and filling her with its consciousness. She is transported beyond her longing to be loved into being love itself.

Making Love All Day

Translucent sexual practice is just that. It is *practice* for the bigger relationship with all life. The energy that is created by moving sexual energy through the body becomes a gifting that extends far beyond your immediate partner. The channels are opened in translucent lovemaking, and they remain open when you go to a restaurant, or to the supermarket, or to work. This does not mean that you behave in a sexually suggestive way in aisle 13 of Kmart. It means that your whole body is open, so that Love Itself can give its gift through you. You use the sexual connection with each other not as an end in itself but as a catalyst to amplify the big gift of blessing to the whole of creation.

When a man can penetrate the swirling feelings of woman, not only with his genitals but with his whole body, with his whole self, he finds this perfectly reflected in his seemingly mundane relationship to the rest of his life. When he brings the gift of conscious presence to the feminine, he's not just gifting his woman, but through her he's gifting all life. To the degree that he can deeply touch and satisfy and be present with his woman, he can also touch and satisfy all of life through his work, his creativity, his art. When he holds back from giving everything to his partner, he inevitably holds back in the rest of his life, too. Sandford Perrett puts it beautifully:

> I can breathe that energy, that bliss, that beauty, down into my body and let it move around in my body and our bodies together. That is an awesome force that comes through in my life that can make me live, and give, and breathe, and support, and love people in a different way.
>
> — Susanna Perrett

Susanna is a condensed version of all of life. All life is a woman. That is what we call Mother Nature. When I am open, I am not recoiling to try to get back into emptiness, which is the unconscious masculine way. A more full way is to penetrate out into life, to feel like you are pressing emptiness, pressing consciousness, pressing presence into the world. Through that, you are able to steer life in a more open, artful, and loving way.

The same is true for the feminine. To the degree that woman allows the enormity of her feminine love to break down the dams and protective walls of normal living, to move through all the circuits of her body and to wash over her man, she will also be loving all life. This is how Susanna describes it:

It is not so difficult for many women to relax and enjoy pleasure, to open her body and give her heart and soul to a man. It is not difficult to have a deep feeling of connectedness. The main error women make is to restrict the whole thing to being personal, keeping it for themselves to feel better. For me the big practice is to really relax and open the body and let myself surrender to my man, to the moment, to God, in lovemaking, and to offer the lovemaking as a gift constantly. I am not making love for myself, for my own pleasure, not even for his sake, but for God's sake, for everyone's sake, as if the bed is an altar where you are offering yourself as a blessing. This is a huge thing. If I can open like this in lovemaking, beyond myself, beyond him, to all of life, then later in the day I can feel this love offering itself through me with strangers on the street, not as something I say or do, but as a disposition of generosity of spirit.

The musicians Deva Premal and Miten have discovered that performing together has become a form of lovemaking, just as intimate as in their bedroom. Mita explains:

Playing together in concert is as rich and as fulfilling as making love. It's an area of creativity I enter into with my beloved that I never had before. What happens is way beyond the music; it's like great sex, in that you're with your woman and you're feeling each other and you're sensitive to when it's not feeling good and when it is. I'm aware of everything that's happening in the room. I feel like I'm making love to this energy. I'm sensitive to it. I can feel how I can bring the energy out. We share this: I suddenly feel Premal taking over and I have to back off. This dance is a big part of our fun together and our awareness of who we are together and our respect for each other.

> Tantra is thoroughly misunderstood in this country. People think it is a panacea for sexual release and indulgence. They think it is only about sex. Sky Dancing Tantra is a unique path to enlightenment as embodied in the ecstatic heart and the ecstatic body.
>
> — Margot Anand

Ironically, you are not always the best person to know the depth of your translucent practice. Nor is your partner. In Iago-based sex, you mainly feel how much pleasure and release you experienced: "How was it for me?" With more sensitivity, you feel more how much pleasure you are giving to your partner: "How was it for you?" With translucent practice, it is the depth and quality of your entire life that demonstrates the depth of your practice. It is the feedback you get from your children, and your work. For Miten, it is the quality of the concert. It is your entire ability to live as a gift that will tell you how deep your practice is going.

SEX AS A PRACTICE

Using sex as a vehicle for embodied translucence is not for everyone. Many people scratch their heads in wonder or giggle in excited embarrassment at

the suggestion that sex could be about anything other than physical pleasure, or that we would even mention it in a "spiritual" book. To take sex
beyond the personal, beyond millennia of human habits, takes conscious
practice. We are hardwired to be addicted to pleasure, to contract down into
a small and personal agenda. To shift that in the circuitry of the body
requires commitment and time. While there are many ways to bring awakening into life, sex is one of the best, because it works through the body, as
the bridge between spirit and matter, between our inner and outer life. If
you know how to use sex, it is one of the fastest routes to embodiment.
Margot Anand was one of the first to pioneer this kind of exploration in
the West:

> *You begin to open up a channel to allow the orgasmic energy to move through*
> *your body, beyond the orgasmic explosion of release to an implosive orgasm of*
> *expansion of consciousness. You move from the genital orgasm to the belly, to*
> *the heart. You feel the energy circulating upward. Instead of having gravita-*
> *tion, you have levitation. You don't fall in love anymore; you arise in love. And*
> *then sexuality genitally, per se, takes on less importance, even though it was a*
> *stepping-stone. When you have an orgasm of*
> *the heart, an orgasm of surrender, where you*
> *become the other and the other becomes*
> *you, it's a tremendous heart opening. When you*
> *have an orgasm of the third eye, you are in*
> *total spaciousness and total peace with each other. It's very subtle, and move-*
> *ment in the genitals is less cared about. This is a wonderful art. It's a pas-*
> *sion. You have to devote a lot of time to this.*

> You use the pleasure as a doorway
> into a greater opening, into gifting all.
> — Sandford Perrett

Cultivating Masculine Translucent Sexuality

The luminous presence that is recognized in a moment of radical awakening
has no gender. The practices involved to bring greater translucence to sex,
however, are different for men and women, since their bodies are wired differently. In the nudging section at the end of the chapter we will go into more
specifics. If you would like to explore these practices in greater depth, it is
important that you seek out the guidance of a qualified teacher.

For a man, the practice required is primarily one of moving energy from the head of the penis and allowing it to flow through the rest of the body in a way that can eventually make ejaculation a conscious choice, and distinct from orgasm. We come from an infinitely long line of premature ejaculators. Our far distant ancestors were cavemen, hunting for food in dangerous conditions. Thog would put down his club, spread bearskins in the cave, light oil candles and incense from herbs, and lay naked with his woman for many hours, as they lost themselves in tantric union.

Ugg, on the other hand, was a missionary man. Not even bothering to take off his thick outer garments, he would lay his woman over a rock, club still in hand, and it was over in a couple of minutes, foreplay and all. Who do you suppose was more in danger of being killed by another tribe or a passing wild boar? Natural selection has favored the quickie, and so we have inherited Ugg's DNA, useful in the mouth of a cave but not so necessary for Hank and Loretta, who can lock their door and unplug the phone.

> In the Tao they say sexuality is connected to longevity. If you're squandering your sexual energy, you are squandering your life force. As you cultivate that energy, you not only live longer, you live healthier.
>
> — Lee Holden

To use sex as a translucent practice, a man needs to retrain his nervous system from releasing quickly, like Ugg, to recirculating the energy through the whole body. This is not very complicated to accomplish, but it means taking a stand against very, very deeply ingrained habits.

There are two significant rewards to inspire you. First, it does not take very long. Lee Holden has studied for many years with Mantak Chia, and teaches Taoist sexual practices in Santa Cruz, to retrain the way energy flows in the body. He reports that if a man practices specific energy redistribution techniques daily for twenty-one days, the channel or "microscopic orbit" will be open enough to really feel the benefit. Second, there comes a point, fairly quickly, when a man can restore choice over ejaculation. Holden says that once a man can remain aroused for twenty minutes in this way, stimulating himself and then redistributing the energy, he will be able to continue as long as he wants without ejaculation. It does not take very much practice or very long to reach the twenty-minute threshold.

Holden explains:

The sexual practice for men is to control ejaculation, not to necessarily stop it. It's not to never ejaculate, just to cultivate that energy. When you control your sexual energy, that fire stays within you and helps to open the heart center. When a man is able to control ejaculation, to redirect it internally and to cultivate his own energy, he's able to open his heart and stay emotionally involved and connected with his partner. They say that when a man loses too much sexual energy to his partner, he becomes indifferent emotionally. You see that in couples that have been together a long time; they sometimes develop this distance and this indifference toward each other.

> If I ejaculate, I lose energy and the interest in any sexual activity. The loss of desire to enter my woman is the same as the loss of desire to enter or penetrate life after that. I feel a lot less energy to come back into life and open life and have the energy to thrust into life.
>
> — Sandford Perrett

A man builds the capacity to bring presence, consciousness, and depth to his partner for extended periods of time. To the degree that he is able to remain sexually aroused without ejaculation, he will have the capacity to remain absolutely present and centered in the rest of his life, without "ejaculating" energy through being reactive or impulsive. This gets easier and easier over time. The longer a man practices without ejaculating, the more energy he accumulates, and this energy then opens the channels in the body even more.

Cultivating Feminine Translucent Sexuality

For a woman, the focus of the practice is to fully open her heart, and to connect the heart energy to her womb and ovaries. A woman cultivates the capacity to come to lovemaking free of the need to connect, but from a deep connection to herself, to all of life. As she awakens her heart energy through specific practices, she brings it down and awakens her vagina. Once her whole body is awake in this way, woman moves beyond sexual feelings only as physical pleasure, and transforms them into an act of worship, an offering to the world.

Holden explains that a man's genitals are yang: penetrating, charged, and quick to be aroused. His practice is to spread this energy throughout the whole body, and in this way to deepen translucence. A woman's vagina is yin: yielding, embracing, receiving. Her heart and emotional energy, on the other hand, are yang, while the man's are yin. Her practice is to bring this naturally open giving heart energy down into the body, and with it to awaken her vagina. At the genital level, the masculine yang energy is giving to and penetrating the feminine. At the heart level, the feminine yang energy is giving to and loving the masculine. Hence, a man will practice stimulating his genitals and spread that hot energy into the whole body, and a woman will practice by stimulating her heart and then spreading that hot energy down into the rest of her body.

When both partners are open and alive in this way, a loop of energy is created, in which the man is giving energy from his penis to the woman, and she is bringing it up to her heart and transforming it, giving it through her heart to the man, who is drawing it down into his penis and giving it back to her again. The energy gets amplified and begins to transcend physical or emotional pleasure: it becomes the human replication of the meeting of consciousness and light. Ultimately, both man and woman have their heart, genitals, and everything else involved, but they have different points of entry with the practices.

> The exact practice for women is deeper and deeper surrender into the body, and a deeper relaxation of all the areas where we may refuse to feel something, or dissociate, or allow anxiety, or a pulling up and out of the body, or a not trusting the complete love that we are. That is the gift: I am Love. My deepest desire is to completely be Love.
>
> — Jennifer Garcia

The Fruits of Sexual Practice

As a couple continues to practice, they can have sex much more frequently. Since they are both circulating the energy throughout the whole body, and the man is not ejaculating, many couples find it beneficial to make love several times a day for short periods. They may find that they have far fewer arguments and that their relationship stays simpler and clearer. Practicing in this way will not always be tied to desire, as sex usually is. Like any practice, it is something to do regularly to deepen and to open more and more. Sometimes you will want to practice more than anything in the world. Many times you won't. The superficial fruits of instant pleasure are eclipsed by the long-term rewards of a more profound relationship to everything. Sandford and Susanna Perrett have discovered that translucent sex is the most effective way to process difficult issues when they arise: "Things come up between us all the time; relationship is intense. When we feel stuck and separate and caught in misunderstanding, we can try to process it emotionally and talk it through. It takes hours, and usually doesn't work. Or we can enter sexual practice, and after fifteen minutes we can't remember what the conflict was about. It is like that every time."

NUDGING SEXUALITY INTO TRANSLUCENCE

While these practices are mostly very simple and easy to learn, they are also extremely powerful and need to be done precisely. What follows are very general guidelines, a preview. If you feel attracted to redirecting sexual energy in this way, you will definitely need more specific instructions. As Holden points out: "The practice is about balance. It is a very powerful practice, and one that was always guarded in secrecy because of its power. You have to have the right teacher to really delve deeply into the practice."

> Practice being alert in high states of presence, breathe together, and allow the boundaries between your and your partner's body to dissolve. Know that there is no more difference between the two, and then there will be a merging of the two energy fields.
>
> — Margot Anand

The Multi-Orgasmic Man, by Mantak Chia and Douglas Abrams Arava, is a great place to start for men, and Chia's *Healing Love through the Tao* (written with his wife) is a good primer for women. Margot Anand has written several good books that offer ideas for how to enter into sex with greater sacredness. And David Deida's books all offer a portal into the more translucent aspects of sex.

NUDGE

For a Man

The first step for a man is to open his body to allow energy to flow more easily. You can do this with yoga, with qi gong, or just by stretching and opening the whole body.

The next step is to begin to arouse and recirculate sexual energy. It is best to start this alone, before you practice with your partner. Begin with self-stimulation until you begin to feel the first waves of sexual energy, and then use breath and intention to draw that energy up through the spine and through the rest of the body. Once you get into the habit of practicing in this way, you can send the sexual energy up the spine, over the top of the head, and down the front of the body again.

Your penis will go through waves of being very charged with energy, as though you were close to ejaculating. As you move the energy with the breath, your penis will become almost without aroused energy again. Each time you move the energy in this way, your penis becomes less charged with energy, and the rest of the body becomes more energized.

Keep practicing until you can stay aroused without ejaculating for at least twenty minutes. Then you are ready to practice with your partner.

NUDGE
For a Woman

For the feminine, the practice is to open the heart, to use the heart energy to open the sexual energy, and then share the alchemy between those two energies with your partner. Although the genitals will become fully enlivened, the practice does not involve their direct stimulation, but the circulation of energy from the heart downward.

First, massage your breasts to stimulate and open the heart center. When you begin to feel a warming and concentration of energy in the heart, use the breath to practice drawing energy up from the ovaries to the heart. As this continues, feel the energy in the lower part of the body being continuously drawn up into the heart and flowing out of the heart, particularly from the breasts, as a blessing and a prayer.

> Sexual practice can be a prayer in which you don't get completely focused on release, but more on love, on sensuality, on holding each other, on communicating clearly, on all the parts that come before an orgasm can happen.
>
> — Margot Anand

As you continue drawing energy up into your chest and out through the breasts, feel your friends, your family. Expand your attention, feeling the whole world, the birth, the joys, the wars, the pain, all of it. Like a prayer, a meditation, you are giving yourself. It is as though you were saying with your body, with your breath, with your relaxation, "I am here, I am giving myself to you, to all of you." Once the heart is aflame with loving compassion, let it flow downward and awaken the vagina. Feel yourself welcoming all of life through your vagina, draw it all up into your heart, and keep pouring it out as a river of blessing. Feel as big as the universe and beyond, and just give everything away through your body.

NUDGE

For Both Together

Man: Sit comfortably on a pillow with your legs crossed.

Woman: Sit on top, straddling your partner with your legs.

Man: Hold your arms around your partner to support her back.

Looking into each other's eyes, breathe through the nose down into the belly. It is best if your bellies are touching. Find the same rhythm with the breath. If you want, you can start to rock your hips in movement with each other. Feel into each other as if wearing the other person's body.

> You want to cultivate rather than squander your energy; you want to use your energy with purpose rather than unconsciously. With dual cultivation the purpose is to enhance your own energy and to make a connection with your partner and to strengthen that bond between you and your partner.
>
> — Lee Holden

Man: As you enter your woman, feel your strength entering her as a gift. Fill her with your conscious presence. As soon as you start to feel a buildup of energy in your genitals, stop moving, breathe deeply, and have the intention to spread the concentrated energy throughout the rest of the body. If need be, tell your partner out loud when you need time to recirculate energy.

Woman: Feel the gift of your man's energy entering you, receive it in your womb, and draw it up into your heart. Give it back to him as love and nurturing through your breasts.

Keep focusing on this as an act of worship and giving. You will inevitably get caught in feelings of physical pleasure. There is no need to try to stop them, but do not get stuck there. You will also get caught in strong personal emotions. Allow them, but go deeper. Allow the gifting to pass through you, not from you. If you continue circulating the energy and allowing it to give through you, after some time your partner will become an invitation into something vast, something much bigger than the personal.

Man: As you keep giving to her with your body, you will start to feel that you are giving through her, to all women, to all of life.

Woman: As you pour love into your partner through your breasts and your heart, and keep opening your womb to receive more freely in undefended surrender, draw this up into your infinitely open heart, and you will feel through him to all men, to the divine source.

Unlike with sex that is only for physical pleasure and release, the need to reach orgasm may lessen in this kind of sexual meeting rather than grow. Instead of climaxing in an orgasm, keep circulating the energy until you come to a place of absolute fullness and stillness. Remain there without moving, and feel the great union, one you could never feel alone. This is the union of you and your partner, of masculine and feminine, of translucence with itself. When you know union in this way, you know why there is life.

CHAPTER NINE

BREAKING THE CHAIN

Translucent Parenting

For six months at a time, Vickie was essentially a single parent — her husband worked two jobs, and he would leave at six in the morning and not get home until midnight. "It was crazy," she recalls. "I was so exhausted." Of course Vickie adored her two children and wanted to be with them. At the same time, she hated the loss of freedom that seemed to come with parenting. Very early on, she told her husband, "When I put my last child on the plane to college, I'm going to do my spiritual practice. Then I'm going to India." All this changed one night, over a sink full of unwashed dishes.

Vickie had finally put her three-year-old and her seven-month-old to bed. She came out into the kitchen only to face several days' worth of dirty dishes — on top of holding down two jobs, her husband had just broken both his thumbs, and she'd been too exhausted herself to stay on top of things. She decided to first listen to a recording of Thomas Moore's Seed of the Soul. At that exact moment on the tape, Moore was talking about doing dishes as a spiritual practice.

Vickie had an epiphany. "I remember thinking, 'I have twenty-plus years of my children in my home, for sure. Obviously, this was my practice,

195

because this was hugely present in my life. And could I find a way to just feel good about 'doing the dishes'?"

How we parent either passes on the Iago trance to our children or breaks the chain of conditioning that has been passed on to us from previous generations. Without some form of translu-
cent practice, we parent by default, in the same way that we were parented. We pass on the Iago trance from parent to child in specific ways. We may train our children in the same strategies we lived with our-
selves. For example, we may feel a sense of lack, and try to alleviate our discomfort through acquiring more money: *If only I were a little richer, then I could relax.* To the degree that we are unsuccessful at fulfilling our dreams, and still believe in them, we require our children to live out our ambitions: *I never made it, but you can. I have high hopes for you....* Whether our ambition is for money, political power, social change, or spiritual or moral redemption, our frustrated goals become our ambitions for the next generation.

> We human beings tend to either do what was done to us, or we do the opposite as a knee-jerk reaction. We re-create our childhood, unless we make a very conscious effort to do it differently.
>
> — Vickie Falcone

Or we may fulfill our ambitions to some degree and realize too late that our goals were not the right ones: *Don't waste your life, don't make the same mistakes that I made.* Whether we end up rich and powerful, or we manage to drop out of society, we still feel Iago's thorn in our side. Either way, we try to make our children do things differently. Our ambitions for our children become the antidote to our own mistakes.

Put under this kind of pressure, a child will either obey or rebel, depending on her relationship with the parents, the influence of the rest of the family, and the child's personality: *I must get a good job and work hard, my parents know what's best for me* or *There is no way I'm going to do what those los-
ers tell me. What do they know? I'm going for dreadlocks and tattoos, and hey, pass that reefer, will ya?* Either way, in obedience or in reaction to parental influence, a child's life is conditioned by the parents' agenda, and the Iago trance is passed on from one generation to another. We call this bringing up a child.

IAGO'S HIDDEN AGENDAS

When we are caught in Iago, everything we do, consciously or not, is influenced by the need to solve a perceived problem and to alleviate lack. Even the desire to have children is laced with this feeling of trying to make something all right. We can bring all sorts of hidden agendas to parenting in this way. Some people feel lost, drifting from one activity to another to try to find meaning and purpose: *My life is chaotic; if I had a child it would force me to settle down. I guess then I would have to grow up.* The separation intrinsic to Iago may also cause us to feel a lack of enough love, and to have the notion that a baby would turn a gray life into Technicolor: *I see other women with babies, at the park, in stores. They look so happy, so full of love. I want to feel that kind of love, too.* Sometimes pregnancy seems a good way to save a marriage: *Greg and I have drifted so far apart. What do we have in common now? Maybe if we had a baby it would give us something to focus on together.* Of course in some cultures having a child, particularly a boy, has financial motivations: *I am getting older now, who will help me with the store, who will carry on the business? Praise God, let us have a boy-child to take care of us in our old age.* And sometimes babies happen "by accident," the unconscious force of biology at work.

> It is a form of violence, to not see a being for who he or she actually is. You think, "Oh, that's my son." But the lens, "my son," completely obliterates the multidimensions of that being. Maybe you only see your disappointments in that child, or your aspirations for that child, but that's not the child.
>
> — Jon Kabat-Zinn

As long as we have any agenda of shoulds — about what parenting should look like, about how a "well-brought-up" child should behave, and about how the whole experience should pan out so we can feel our needs are being met — Iago-based parenting begins with tension: *What if something goes wrong? What if little Johnny turns out to be ugly, or stupid, or defiant, or wants body piercing or a mohawk? What if he isn't like us?*

When we enter parenting with expectations like these, Johnny has become a potential disappointment or failure, a problem to fix, before he has even taken his first breath. Along with the obvious physical dependency of a child for milk and warmth and security, we now have created a second, more insidious dependency, that of the parent on the child for their well-being: *You must be like this, and like this, in order for us to be happy.* We manipulate our children to fit the mold, and call it "raising" a child. There is tremendous tension, frustration, and stress waiting to erupt should our agenda be thwarted.

Hence we often experience parenting as a power struggle. We have a model of how a child should be, what family life should look like, how a child should develop. Either we win the battle of wills, which requires some element of force, manipulation, or bribery, or we lose, and both our parenting and our children seem to be failures.

Disconnection

Vickie Falcone is the creator of the Positive Parenting Network and the author of *Buddha Never Raised Kids and Jesus Didn't Drive Carpool*. Falcone's book and approach reflect the budding translucent revolution. She teaches people how to parent translucently, from their deepest connection with their own wakefulness, and, from there, with their children. Falcone points out that when we parent with any kind of agenda, we pay the price of losing a real connection with our children in this moment, as living beings, as evolving mysteries. She describes seven distinct ways that we create disconnection with our children when we are run only by Iago:

> "Subtle attachment disorder" is my name for the pervasive, epidemic, and socially acceptable process of not connecting to our children.
>
> — Vickie Falcone

- *Physical absence.* Busyness is the bane of our lives. In many households, both adults work. Hence children suffer from a deficit of attention and physical presence from their parents.

- *Emotional distance.* Even if we are physically at home, we are often so wrapped up in activity that we go through the motions of cooking and physical care without being emotionally present for our children in a way that they can feel.

- *Force.* When children do not fit into our model of how things should be, we are driven to acts of "discipline" or even, in a sudden burst of anger, to hitting them, to get our way.

- *Manipulation.* Even when we do not resort to physical force, we may use bribery, threats to withdraw pleasurable activities, or isolation from the rest of the family, to force an agenda.

- *Permissiveness.* When we are caught up in our own needs and drama of lack, we may simply allow our children to do whatever they want, so they will give us space for ourselves. Surprisingly, when a child is allowed to stay up late, to watch limitless amounts of television and eat as much sugar as she wants, it may translate into a message that no one cares enough to set limits.

- *Being right.* Iago often drives parents to need to be right more than to connect in a deeper way. How many times, as parents, have we leapfrogged over the possibility of a heartfelt connection, of real dialogue, just to assert who is boss?

- *Worry, guilt, and fear.* We can also become overly involved in our children's lives. We worry about their health, their academic achievements, their social life; we worry if they have ADD or some new, as yet unnamed disease. We then pass on the recurring message that there is something wrong with them.

> There is a huge dichotomy between the magnificent acts of love that happen every day with people all over the planet, in the service of their children, and the opposite — not being able to make the best of the situation, not even if the rudimentary feelings are there. Because in some way or other, the sense of being overwhelmed by unwholesome emotions stands in the way of actually expressing love effectively.
>
> — Jon Kabat-Zinn

Falcone calls these seven familiar traps of parenting "The 7 Deadly Disconnects." They are all symptomatic of a lack of connection with ourselves, which manifests as a lack of ability to connect with our children. For Falcone, translucent parenting begins and ends with awakening to the deepest possible dimensions of yourself, and then bringing that depth to your children.

SPIRITUAL MYTH #11: Having children is a distraction to spiritual life. Like Buddha, Jesus, and all the great masters, you must choose between family life and spiritual freedom.

SPIRITUAL MYTH #12: After an awakening, all the negative influences from your family will dissolve through divine grace. You will spontaneously know how to be a perfect parent.

FREEDOM OR FAMILY?

We have inherited ideas that spirituality is about going within, meditating, freeing oneself from attachment. The chaos of family life can only be a distraction. In the Christian traditions, those really serious about God became monks, nuns, or priests. In India, Buddhist monks and Hindu *sadhus* renounce family life.

> My spiritual evolution placed a lot of importance on finding the guru. I was constantly going from place to place, guru to guru — can't find the guru, and then we gave birth to three gurus! It is amazing to relate to a baby as a divine teacher — everything that is not at peace within me is reflected immediately.
>
> — Barry Vissell

I too was influenced by this myth. In the early 1970s, like many young people, I turned to teachers and teachings from the East and learned to meditate. But after some years, I realized that I had all sorts of psychological quirks and contractions that were not being addressed by traditional teachings. In 1979 I traveled to Poona, India, where Bhagwan Rajneesh had a center that embraced alternative therapies and meditation. I plunged into the deep end, participating in every possible kind of bodywork, breath therapy, and group process available. Some were very radical. I spent two weeks in a cellar with twenty other explorers, doing primal therapy; with the help of mattresses, baseball bats, and tennis rackets, we released all the anger and frustration we had inherited from our family conditioning.

I thought I would never have children. I did not want to pass along to another generation the pain I had felt in my own family. I had a few friends with children. I saw how wrapped up they were in the duties of child rearing, and I decided that parenting could only be an immense distraction from my life's true purpose, which was to become enlightened.

All this changed in 1991, when my girlfriend and I first met my teacher, Poonjaji. After a few weeks, he suggested we marry — as far as he was concerned, it took far too much energy to be in a relationship that was not fully committed. We married, and within a few months, every time he saw us, he dropped small hints about babies. I think he knew how much resistance I had to fatherhood and loved to watch me squirm. In the spring of 1992, a few days after I left for a short visit to the States, my wife discovered she was pregnant.

For the first few months, I went through every imaginable reaction. I felt that my freedom was being flushed down the drain, that I was heading on a path to tremendous distraction from what was really important. I entered parenting reluctantly, to say the least. At the same time, we both wanted the birth to be a very "spiritual" experience. We planned a Lamaze water birth, complete with candles, soft music, and a special taped message from Poonjaji, to be played for our son the minute he was born. When my wife's water broke, the midwife came to do an examination. "Well, he's down in the canal, all right," she said, "but I feel a bit concerned. His head seems very, very small." I went into a panic, remembering a cartoon character from Popeye who had a head like a peanut. We rushed to the nearest ultrasound machine. It turned out the small head was, in fact, his knee, and he was wedged into the birth canal. We were told there was no possibility for a regular birth; he would have split in two if we had tried. Twenty minutes later, he arrived by cesarean section.

> Before I had children I was probably meditating five hours a day; my whole life was based around a spiritual path. When Rami was born, all the meditation and all the books and all the studying and everything I had been doing suddenly became real. I was always trying to go toward something; when she was born, suddenly I was there, in the space that I had been seeking.
>
> — Joyce Vissell

With his mother still under heavy anesthesia, my son was taken from the operating table and placed under a heat lamp in a plastic basin. There he was, very white, bloody, and totally terrified. He was screaming. It was all up to me. "I'm your daddy," I said by way of introduction, bending over the crib. Abhi looked up, and our eyes locked. He grabbed my outstretched little finger and stopped crying.

That was it. The entire internal monologue about *Is this the right thing?* and *What about my freedom?* switched off, like pulling the plug on a TV. All that was left was this very small creature, holding onto his daddy's finger for dear life.

For the first week I was left to look after our son as his mother recovered from the operation. It took him several days to catch on to what comes out of his mother's breast, so he began to get dehydrated. And he made a firm decision that he would only sleep if I carried him up and down the corridors of the hospital. Even after hours of somnambulistic walking, if I put him down in his crib, he would wake up and scream.

> How can you bring more translucence to parenting? By accepting what is, even the small things. This is what's happening, so I can either be upset about it or, as gratefully as I can, accept this is what is happening right now.
>
> — Vickie Falcone

We spent eight days in the hospital like this. I was completely sleep deprived. No meditation, no exercise, no time for myself. No time to even think about myself. Everything became distilled down to being fully present for this small, vulnerable creature. And in that week, instead of being distracted from spiritual life, I underwent an initiation into what has become my most powerful vehicle for living translucently: being a father. When we finally did go home, parenting became my primary activity. Abhi remained a sensitive child for the first few years. He had trouble going to sleep, so I'd often spend time in the evening driving him around in the car till he dropped off. He was also what is sometimes called a "fussy eater."

I have done some very extreme things in the name of living an awakened life. Besides those two weeks in the cellar, I've done long meditation retreats, sitting for ten or more hours a day, for ten days. I've participated in orchestrated environments to help break the trance of self-preoccupation: sometimes through sleep deprivation, physical endurance, or confrontation. But there is no question that the most powerful and effective way to deepen translucence, for me at least, has been as a parent. Nothing else demands such presence, such a need for abandonment of self-preoccupation again and again. And, unlike other methods, the parenting intensive does not end after a couple of weekends. It is ongoing, until further notice.

With the birth of my second son, Shuba, three years later, the practice only intensified. I am remarried now, and my sons spend half the time with us and half with their mother. The weeks when the boys are gone are down time, when I can rest and gather energy. When they are with us again the heat is on. Chameli and I get to find out if we just talk about embodied spirituality or if that talk is being lived out for real.

THE TRANSLUCENT POTENTIAL OF PARENTING

In the workshops that Chameli and I lead in Europe and the United States, we introduce people to the possibilities of translucent relationship. Sometimes we get quite carried away with the potential of it all. I remember one time when we were in Stockholm. The Swedes are very innocent people, grounded in reality. So there we were, waving our arms in the air, talking about growing beyond personal agendas...moving from lack and need into an overflow of generosity of spirit...feeling into others and life itself...responding with what we can give more than what we want. We stopped and looked at the ladies in the third row. Their brows were knitted; they looked lost and confused. It was all so removed from their daily experience. Then we spoke of the times when your child wakes you up at one in the morning with an earache. You don't feel like getting up, but you do anyway. The ladies looked up. They nodded their heads with enthusiasm. *Ja, ja,* they grinned. We had found common ground.

We have found that the easiest way to explain what we mean by translucence is to appeal to people's experience of parenting. Whether or not you think you have had a radical awakening, whether or not you define yourself as a spiritual person or just a regular slob, it is as a parent that you generally have the most vivid glimpses of your translucent potential.

> Of course you lose something: time alone, your house will never be as quiet. But what you gain is enormous. Someone from the outside can't see how much accelerated growth is going on inside parents. What you lose is infinitesimal compared to what you gain, and what you gain is for your whole life.
>
> — Joyce Vissell

Parenting is not a give-and-take relationship, at least not for the first several years. With your spouse or a friend you may be able to make exchanges: Look, you cook tonight, I'll do the dishes. Your turn to do the shopping. I

People who have never heard about dharma, or awakening, or any of that, care for their children in ways that a spiritual seeker might find incredibly tedious and overwhelming. Most people do it day in and day out, with no notion they are doing bodhisattva action, or no idea there is such a thing as bodhisattva.

— Jon Kabat-Zinn

paid for gas, how about you cover dinner? We do not have these conversations with a young child: If I make your breakfast and take you to kindergarten, I want you to cook tonight, okay? As a parent you give and give and give, without hope of return in kind. In all other areas of our life we have resistance to living that way. We are afraid we will get burned, used, taken advantage of. With our children there is no question about it. Ironically, people say they feel the most love in this relationship, the most opening of the heart, the most fulfillment. If we know how to ride it, parenting can become a powerful translucent practice, a perfect departure point for a similar relationship to all of life. Jon Kabat-Zinn talked about this when we spoke:

I consider mindful parenting to be as powerful a form of spiritual practice as any other. Every single thing that you hold onto is going to be challenged. This gives you the opportunity to either feel incredibly put upon and tied in knots, creating an adversarial relationship between you and your child, or to realize that you were given the gift of a live-in Zen master, guaranteed (as every good Zen master would do) to push absolutely every one of your buttons. Wherever you are holding on, parenting gives you incredible opportunities to look at what's most important in the present moment, and to respond, outside of thought, immediately. The more your awareness is infused with presence, the more it allows you to respond spontaneously to the continually shifting moves and moods of the Zen master, rather than trying to control them.

Parenting is not an easy practice. All kinds of challenges come up. It is a practice without a break that keeps calling on you for your deepest gifts. You are being challenged all the time to draw deeper into yourself and to find resources beyond the limits of "me" and personality. The key is to choose parenting as a practice you can fully embrace, to make it the center of a life of endlessly evolving translucence.

"I Don't Know"

When we bring more translucence to our parenting, we first become more aware of our old Iago-based ideas. Translucence means to wake up from the mirrors of the mind, to know who you are prior to thinking. We begin to question all the hardwired assumptions that have been passed down to us from our predecessors: what it means to be a good parent, our responsibilities as parents, our do's and don'ts, our shoulds and shouldn'ts. We may have become lost in maps, in an attempt to find guidance through the sometimes-rocky terrain of raising children. Our notions are either carbon copies of how we were parented, or rebellious reactions to it. When we try to free ourselves from both, we are just as likely to get lost again, in more maps and models on loan from our well-meaning friends and the endless array of how-to books.

To the degree that we can question these beliefs, we are able to begin parenting as a process of learning, rather than simply asserting that we know what is best, or at least faking it. At first our exploration may be very tentative, in sharp contrast to the way most of us have been raised, and the way we see some parenting around us. We fear losing control and never getting it back. But once we meet our children, even

> If you hold everything up to some external standard that you've put on some kind of a pedestal — I'm always supposed to be like this, or I'm not a mindful parent — then you're continually judging yourself and the situation. How could that possibly be either generous or mindful, or for that matter, accurate?
>
> — Jon Kabat-Zinn

for moments, in a place of "I don't know," of relinquished authority, we return to the realms of mystery and magic, where real connection becomes alive again.

Jon Kabat-Zinn and his wife, Myla, emphasize this magic in their work with mindful parenting. He reminds parents of the mysterious and miraculous dimensions of being human: "The questions are, 'Who are these people? How did this come about? Who am I, and what is my relationship to this other being?' All of this becomes alive again within the lens of awakening. You see deeply into the mystery of it all, as opposed to, 'Oh, yeah; we just had a baby,' which reduces it. It is an ordinary experience, but it is also extra-ordinary."

When I asked him if that means to take the time now and then to stop and smell the flowers, I loved his answer:

It's not just to smell the flowers, it's to realize that you just gave birth to a flower, a multidimensional flower. A flowering, because it's more a process of unfolding than it is a thing. You, too, are a flowering. You were once the same. You are both on a path between here and . . . who knows where? What is this all about, what is this path, this brief moment we call a lifetime? How does one nurture that unfolding in a little one, so that they can realize their full potential? At the same time you are moving along that trajectory yourself, so what is your full potential, and are you anywhere near even contemplating that question?

Whenever we release our need to be right about everything as parents, we are able to meet our children in a relationship of mutuality and respect. As parents, we can demonstrate an openness to learning and a surrender rather than demanding obedience from our children as an unquestioned right. We can certainly teach our children about the material world, about things that are not obvious or intuitive. An infant can't know that sticking a screwdriver into an electric socket is dangerous. A child does not know from experience that large amounts of sugar can corrode the teeth and wreak havoc with energy levels. The mutuality comes in the recognition that there are also many things our children can teach us, or at least remind us, things we have forgotten. For example, my children teach me a great deal about integrity, about keeping my word. They always notice when I say I'll do things and then I don't follow through. They point it out to me, not always logically, but it always makes the point.

> Our children have just as much to teach us as we have to teach them. There are certain things that they teach magnificently, like forgiveness. But then of course they need us to set limits and to have healthy boundaries to teach them the ways of living on the earth.
>
> — Barry Vissell

Connection

Translucent parenting begins not so much with your connection to your child, but with your connection to yourself. When we feel fully connected to who we are, deeper than concepts, we are also connected to reality as it is, and this allows us to really connect with our children as they are in this moment. Rather than trying to manage or control our children, or mold them to our expectations, we can feel them as living mysteries.

Connection is at the very core of Falcone's work with parents. More than half of her groundbreaking book is devoted to this topic. "The most basic human need is to feel connected to another human being," she says. "Every action that every infant, toddler, and child takes is directed toward meeting that need." She makes the revolutionary observation that the time you spend in deep connection with yourself, even for a few minutes, is the essential foundation for real connection with your children. Without this essential connection to ourselves, we have hired Iago as the babysitter, and of course he will, despite our best intentions, find a way to pass on the trance as it was passed on to us. As soon as we return to ourselves, which for many people only takes a few minutes of silence, being present with the body, or just breathing deeply, our parenting breaks the trance instead of perpetuating it. Translucent parenting, from this internal connection, allows you to feel your children's need to connect to themselves also.

> The first thing is to set your intention to connect. This sets my approach apart from so much other parenting work. The energy behind your action is just as important, if not more important, than what you actually do.
>
> — Vickie Falcone

Molly is in the kitchen, fixing dinner. She looks out the window and sees her little Johnny sitting under a tree, staring at the horizon.

"Johnny, what are you doing?"

"Nothing, Mom," he calls back.

"Well, you stop it this instant, young man," she shouts. I remember the same message when I was fourteen. I had learned to meditate and spent twenty minutes, morning and evening, sitting with my eyes closed. "Doing nothing will make you crazy," my mother told me one dinnertime.

Both my sons sometimes go to their rooms, even for hours at a time, and "do nothing." I can hear my nine-year-old talking to imaginary characters, sometimes acted out with small Lego men. My twelve-year-old may just stare at the ceiling or doodle on a pad, rehearsing apathy for his teenage years. Often I also hear a voice, an echo from my own childhood, prompting me to usher them into useful activity. I used to think that if they were not drawing, or talking, or doing *something*, they must have a problem. I now realize that they need time, everybody needs time, to just be with themselves. To do nothing and just feel their own interiority. If I value my connection with myself as the foundation of translucent life, I must also value the time they need to connect with themselves.

Peter Levine, a celebrated authority on recovery from trauma, points to the intuitive ways in which rabbits and other wild animals unwind and return to their natural state. When the danger from a predator has passed, they will twitch, dance, and jump, and then just vegetate, to release stress. Children know how to do this too, as long as we respect their need for space, and demonstrate this respect for internal connection in how we live.

> Our society puts efficiency over connection — and there's absolutely nothing efficient about connecting. Western parents are so stimulus driven: if the children are hungry, feed them; if they need you, that's when you go to them. It's a whole different way of thinking to anticipate and understand that your child always has the desire to connect and not to wait for a stimulus.
>
> — Vickie Falcone

From this connection to ourselves, and the respect we bring to our children's need for internal connection, a real meeting can happen. Falcone sees the depth of this real bonding as both the essence of translucent parenting and the potential antidote to many of the problems within families in a world out of balance. This depth of intimacy with your children may be unfamiliar. Even for parents who have known moments of radical awakening, and who may find other parts of their lives permeated with translucence, this means taking a stand against generations of aloof child-rearing habits. Falcone breaks down the elements of connection into seven steps:

1. Decide that connection is more important than any other agenda.

2. Approach your child in a friendly way, smile, and make it clear from your body language that you come in peace. This may be important if you are in the process of reversing a more authoritative style of meeting her.

3. Get down to your child's level, or bring her up to yours. This is a way of saying with your body, "What you have to say is important

to me. We may be different sizes, but we have equally valid things to say."

4. Make eye contact. This will allow you both to become more present and to feel each other.

5. Reach out and touch your child.

6. Give all your focused attention. Even a few seconds is long enough to be completely present and say, "I really want to hear all about your project as soon as I have finished cooking."

7. Let your communication be informing or questioning rather than commanding.

Translucent parents are giving birth to translucent children. This new generation, sometimes called Indigo children, is born with much greater inward connection and often has a no-nonsense, kick-ass intolerance of Iago mythologies. They do not do well with mandates. In many ways, these children recognize that they have a higher level of wakefulness, maturity, and connection than their parents. If you are parenting such children, high-level connecting is not just an option — it is all that works. These kinds of children are often labeled by educators and psychologists as "difficult," "spirited," or even as having ADD, a diagnosis that has become rampant in recent years. Jon Kabat-Zinn has deeply explored this phenomenon:

> Many children are completely touch-deprived; we live in a touch-phobic and touch-depriving society. Just hugging your child, with full awareness, is an extraordinary thing. Making eye contact, real listening, paying full attention, that is the richness of the universe.
>
> — Jon Kabat-Zinn

They say there is an epidemic of Attention Deficit Disorder among children and adults. The entire society has a deficit of attention, because we are not attending to the moment. People are really starved for a certain kind of presence, a certain kind of mutual regard, that in some way is embodied in the mother's gaze when she is nursing. That is accessible, virtually moment-by-moment, if you are willing to live inside it. Everybody is talking about it, but nobody is paying attention. Everybody wants a drug solution to it, to calm people down.

Meeting the Deeper Needs

Highly connected parenting may seem overwhelming, too much work for a busy parent, a luxury we need to postpone for later. By making parenting into a translucent practice, not only do we usher in more wakefulness, but our parenting also becomes much easier.

> The game is to keep giving children responsibility, but then keep being sensitive in each moment. It's a matter of really being there. It's always about unconditional presence. Every now and again they get overwhelmed; this is a very difficult dimension to be in, and they're closer to the source than we are.
>
> — Paul Lowe

Recently, while grocery shopping, I passed an aisle where a small child was screaming. She was refusing to walk, and her mother, who looked extremely stressed, was dragging her by the arm away from the freezer. A battle about ice cream was under way. Finally, the mother picked her daughter up by the arm. There she was, dangling in midair. Her screams became louder. Her embarrassed mother yelled at her daughter to be quiet and finally hit her. It didn't work too well. The child screamed even louder. I winced and moved on. We often see these kinds of battles, where parents are imposing discipline. It hurts. I am always reminded of how easily I have gone there myself as a dad.

A few minutes later, I was standing in line at the cash register, behind a woman with her young son. Chocolates and candies were on display by the counter. The young boy took a chocolate, nudged his mother, and looked up at her hopefully. I watched as his mother turned and looked, not *at* her son but right *into* her son with absolute attention and focus. Smiling, she reached out and touched the boy's hair. I was transfixed, energized by how much presence and love went into that look. If you tried to translate that look into words it would be: "I totally adore you, I am here for you no matter what you do, I care for you completely." The mother did not say a word. She didn't even need to shake her head. Her son just laughed and put back the chocolate.

Many parents, however translucent, think of their children's demands as a bottomless pit; that if they give in to their demands today, they will want even more tomorrow. In Falcone's experience, children's requests for things like sweets, television, more new plastic stuff are actually an attempt to fulfill what she sees as their most basic needs. She uses the acronym PHIL to represent them: children need to feel Powerful, Heard, Important, and Loved. What matters most in shifting to greater translucence in parenting is the ability to translate what the child is asking for into a call for their deepest needs to be met. Chocolate becomes irrelevant when a child gets the deep attention and connection he was really asking for. Once we recognize the hidden mechanics, the rest becomes simple. Once basic needs have been met, the demands for external things lessen, and power struggles often subside. This does not take time as much as presence and our willingness to shift into translucence.

BIG DA-DA, BIG MAMA

What is mother? Mama, Mummy? Stop and feel the words. What do they do to you? If there is any pain or recoiling from personal memories, feel even deeper. What is the deepest resonance of Mama? What is father...Daddy...Dad ...Da?

> It all comes down to what we most value. The thread that goes through it all is the love of being real, the love of love. With my kids, I keep finding places where I'm not fully showing up, and that is only revealed in the light of what I love. I'm getting more and more present with them, as they want and need me, rather than when I'm willing to give.
>
> — Isaac Shapiro

Recently, I was woken up at 3 A.M. by the Voice. "You are a father," it said. I knew this must be important, because it was exactly the same guy who told Kevin Costner to build a baseball field. But no further instructions came, just that. "You are a father. A father."

I sat up in bed and felt the word *father*. What does it mean? Of course the word can simply define a role. Father is the man who provides the sperm that fertilizes the egg, the man who drives the children to school, helps with homework, takes them to the game, and embarrasses them by cheering too loudly. I felt my own father, there in the silence of the night. He is old now; he may die soon. Of course he fulfilled a long list of obligations: material ones, financial ones. My father came to the hospital when I was sick, he gave me things, and he made sure I was well educated. How do you remember your father?

But there is more to father than all those roles and duties. I can also feel a paternal caring that came *through* my father, a quality of authority, presence, and strength that was often there *despite* his personality, not because of it. This quality of father is very big; it is not personal. It comes *through* the parent, not *from* him. This deeper dimension of "father," which I felt in my own father, is the same quality my children feel in me. Sure, I am a provider, a broker in the limited beliefs and opinions and traditions I would just love to palm off on my children, given half a chance. And...I am also something like an antenna for the real father, the Big Father energy that is absolutely trustworthy, protecting, and truthful in a way that individuals can only aspire toward.

When we are most caught in Iago, as we all sometimes are, small father and small mother are all we have to offer. Then we feel the obligation to raise our children according to our own values, to teach them to be just like us.

> Think about the grandparent or parent who looked into you and believed something about you that you may have hardly understood. "I see you, I know you, I see you, God in hiding, and I call you forth." You become larger; you're called into being by another's belief. What a power we have to call each other into being!
>
> — James O'Dea

Ironically, small mother and father have an exaggerated sense of their own mastery and wisdom. Translucent parenting means to see our utter incompetence as individuals to teach anyone anything useful at all. Don't follow me, I'm lost. Translucents have the wisdom to cease trusting their own minds, and so step aside, allowing space for Big Father, for Divine Mama.

We all know what Big Father feels like. Big Father has relaxed authority, power without force, firmness with absolute love. Big Father has no biased opinions but can feel deeply into what is best in each moment, and takes action decisively, like a samurai. Big Father can show wrath like thunder but is not lost in anger. Probably you have felt Big Father, at least at moments, in your own father, even if it was not there all the time. If you are religious and you pray, you may feel Big Father then. You may feel Big Father when you look into the sky or feel beyond your own small story. If you are a man and have children, you cannot be Big Father or do Big Father. You can only become translucent enough, become still enough, to allow Big Father to *do you.*

And we all know and love Divine Mama. She is soft, absolutely loving, forgiving, and playful. Her laugh is like a waterfall that gurgles deep in her belly. Her breasts are so soft and welcoming they can heal every pain and bruise we have ever known. She welcomes you, embraces you, adores you exactly as you are, and needs nothing from you. She does not *do* love, she *is* love itself, she is the ocean in which we can drown and be reborn. Have you ever seen how a woman is transformed when she is breast-feeding? If you are a woman and you have had children, you may feel that in your mothering you have had your most mystical experiences, that you have been taken over by love. Divine Mama will mother through you when you give up, and accept that this little personality would mess up looking after a mouse, let alone a human becoming. In the defeat of utter incompetence, you step aside and let Divine Mama do her thing.

> Any deep spiritual insight or practice has to be adequate to the enormity of the texture of real life unfolding, as opposed to living in a forest or in a monastery. And that is the beauty of the practice, exactly right there. You are being challenged, moment to moment, to rest in the fullness of your being, to be love, to be responsible, where you are responding to the needs of another, who is really helpless when very little, and requires your full attention.
>
> — Jon Kabat-Zinn

Whenever we drop our agenda as parents, whenever we are willing to not know, whenever we can show up and feel our children beyond the notions of "shoulds" we have inherited, when we can feel our children as autonomous human beings, we are breaking the chains of countless generations. We are setting a new tradition in motion, which will allow us to give our children space to discover their limitless nature and potential. Small mother and small father retire their habits of handing down the chains of restraint and limitation. Parenting becomes an act of translucent surrender to our core as Big Father and Divine Mama, the only dimension of us that knows how to amplify freedom from one generation to the next.

Stewardship

When we hand parenting back to Big Father and Divine Mama, we also release the idea that these children are "mine." We become stewards instead of autocrats. As we trust the dictates of the Iago mind less, we realize that our children have their own integrity, that they will make their own choices (whether we agree or not). They have their own destiny and trajectory to follow, both of which may have little to do with what we had in mind at the time of their conception. We may have to abandon our aspirations to be a "good" parent in order to be a translucent one.

Both my sons love to fight. It begins playfully, with wrestling and imitations of various heroes, but it often turns to anguish when one of them goes too far. Sometimes, when they are in mortal combat in the kitchen while I am cooking their dinner, it gets to be too much. "Stop fighting!" I command. I remember the day when my youngest son, only six at the time, turned to me with a confused and earnest expression. "But Daddy, we were born to fight!" He had no question in his mind about the purpose of his incarnation; it was his father who needed education.

As translucent parents we see the wholeness in our children. When we meet them in our own sense of wholeness, symptoms that might be interpreted as problematic through Iago's filter seem healthy and natural from clear seeing. Translucent parents speak of their children with gratitude, with admiration and appreciation, and with deep trust of their unique trajectory. When we see our children as whole, they will also see themselves as whole.

INTUITION

When translucent parents put to rest the arbitrary moral codes they have inherited from their family and culture, they are able to feel what will serve everyone best. There are a million and one things about the material world that children do not know. It is a parent's role to guide them, to inform them, and often to set limits that can ensure their well-being. Falcone's favorite piece of advice to parents is to not follow advice from parenting experts and how-to books. "Don't follow what I say," she cautions, "follow your intuition." There is no one-size-fits-all approach to parenting consciously, no model that can tell you, "Do this when they do this," and "Do that when they do something else." Translucence means to relax into the dimension of yourself where there is nothing carried in the mind, and to act from there. To leap before you look.

> Children need us to be adults, but if we're really adults, then we don't need to define arbitrary rules or standards that are then enforced in an insensitive way that fails to acknowledge the fact of who children are.
>
> — Jon Kabat-Zinn

If we feel deeply into the present moment, if we feel our children as they are and respond, sometimes we are called on to sit down, to relax, to talk things through. There are times when we are called on to listen to our children's justified complaints, to say, "You are right, I apologize for what I said and did, thank you for correcting me." And there are times when we are called on to become God on earth for a few minutes and to set absolute limits, because that is what our children are crying out for in that moment.

Vickie Falcone was home one evening with her seven-year-old daughter, who was run ragged from too many parties and playdates. Someone called and invited her to spend the night:

I love to say yes to my children, but I looked at her, and I could see she was not up for another sleepover. I said, "It seems like you're tired and I'd rather you be home." She argued with me, said, " It's not fair!" The very way she was arguing with me showed me that she was at the very end of her rope emotionally and physically. I heard her get back on the phone and watched her. She had a smile on her face as she said, "You know, I really can't sleep over tonight. I'm just too tired." I realized I had given her permission to say no. She needed me to do that, and she was not able to do it alone.

> There are times when I shout at my kids and it feels really clean, and there are times where I know I was off. And I'm able to make the distinction. And if I feel that there's someplace where I've been out of order, I go to them and say, "Look, I really am sorry." It is amazing how easily they forgive.
>
> — Isaac Shapiro

You might think the angriest or most violent youths are those who've been abused, and those are, too, but the most violent I meet are those who've been raised without limits. Children absolutely equate clear limits with being loved and cared for, with having their emotional needs met.

Natural Translucents

Children are naturally translucent, freshly arrived from and in touch with an inner spaciousness. It is very easy to connect with your child in a translucent way if you are connected with yourself. Many parents talk openly with their children about moments of awakening and involve their children in translucent practices. "I remember moments I've had with my children, both spoken and unspoken," Julia says, talking about her daughters. "We often look in each other's eyes, and hold the gaze, just naturally, for long enough that something is recognized between us, outside the game of 'I'm mommy and you're a child.'"

Once, while I was taking a bath with my sons when they were little, Abhi looked at me with big eyes. "Daddy, I am you, and you are me, right?" I nodded. "And I am Mommy too." Then he looked at his little brother, not quite one year old. "And I'm Shuba, too, and he is me." I nodded again. "I knew that," he said. He went back to his yellow duck. What we consider to be our most esoteric mystical experiences are intuitive and natural to children. They only need an environment in which their knowing is accepted.

> Even if you've had a glimpse of it, there is the risk that you cling to the glimpse, and you spend all of your time trying to get back to some idealized state. Meanwhile, it's right under your nose. The beauty of bringing awareness to parenting is that it can bring you immediately back into the dimension of things as they are, with a degree of openhearted acceptance.
>
> — Jon Kabat-Zinn

Rather than feeling that life as a parent and spiritual life are opposed to one another, it's a great idea to invite children to join in translucent practice. For example, when I meditate, I do so openly in the living room. Sometimes my boys come and sit with me. They come and go as they please. My oldest son has been "meditating" for years, even though he may not call it that. He has a Buddha statue in his room, and one of St. Francis, and he imitates what he sees around him. We chant mantras together on the way to school. Chameli and I use all kinds of practices with the children to deepen translucence together, and now it is often the boys who suggest, "Let's do some practice now."

NUDGING PARENTING INTO TRANSLUCENCE

Parenting is a challenging practice in which we can discover how deeply moments of awakening have permeated day-to-day life. Many spiritual teachers have discovered that it is easy to look enlightened to their students, it is even quite easy to look enlightened to oneself, but it is next to impossible to pull the wool over their kids' eyes. Children refuse to be fooled by any sort of claim to attainment. Bringing translucence to our parenting, even 10 percent of the time, is a huge gift to our children and to ourselves, one that transforms the quality of the relationship and the outcome of our children's lives.

Here are some suggestions for nudging parenting into translucence. Take them playfully.

> The more I did my practice, the more I would catch myself in the middle of saying something in the old, unconscious way. Then I would say, "This is not feeling good, I don't want to go forward with this. Give me a few minutes to think, to sort this out."
>
> — Vickie Falcone

NUDGE
Catalog Your Inheritance

Write down the concepts you carry from your family about parenting. Include what a father should be, a mother, a family. Write down any ideas you have inherited about how a child should be raised and what determines success or failure in parenting. It's worth taking the time to write down as many of these assumptions as you can. As soon as they are on paper, you can begin to see if they are true, if everyone would agree with them, if they actually support you or your children, and if they have been consciously chosen or are simply an inherited reaction.

Go back through the list to see which of these values you have preserved intact in your role as a parent, and which you have reacted against. Now make a fresh list of the concepts you have inherited from your peers, from books you have read, from classes you have taken. Look back over every idea you have carried from the past and discover how many are absolutely true. Would everyone agree with them? Do they serve you, your children, the relationship between you? What kind of a parent would you be if you let go of each of these ideas?

NUDGE
Connection

Practice Vickie Falcone's seven steps of connecting, at least for a while. You may be surprised, even if you consider yourself to be a conscious parent, how much difference it makes to pay attention to every detail of high-quality connection. A few minutes of absolute presence will last for many hours.

Practice with your children. Many of the other nudging suggestions in this book can be done with your children. Kids can be your most enthusiastic allies in living translucently.

NUDGE
Rotate the Boss

Every Saturday morning we clean the house. We start by sitting down together and listing all the jobs that need to be done. Then everyone gets to be the boss for half an hour. We always start with Shuba, our youngest. While he is boss, everyone must do what he says. He is the king. He will check if you are cleaning thoroughly, allocate the jobs, and tell you when you can move to a new one.

We started this game when he was seven. You might anticipate, as we did, that it would be chaos, that he would give crazy commands or not know what to do. But he turned out to be the most caring and careful supervisor of the family. I remember him coming into the bathroom while I was cleaning the toilet. "Do you have what you need?" he asked. "Are you clear about what to do? Let me know when you want to take a break." I pinched myself. Was I dreaming? When his half hour was up he resorted to his usual personality, complaining bitterly about having to work at all. I learned that we all rise to the occasion.

> My daughter has her own life. She belongs to nature. She comes from nature, and I'm just a support.
>
> — Christopher Titmus

Of course, we don't want to make this a daily practice. Kids need time to be kids. But giving everyone a chance to change their role in the family in this way, once a week, shakes up encrusted habits. Everyone, kids and adults, can experiment with other ways of doing things, gaining insight into what it's like to play another role in the family. When my child gets to be in charge of the family for half an hour, and I get to be the one ordered around, he can feel what it's like to be boss, and I can feel what it's like to have someone either bark an order at me or be considerate and patient. My son makes a much better boss than I do; I learn a lot from him about how to supervise others.

NUDGE

Assignments

This is another translucent game we sometimes play together. Everyone gets a turn. When it's your turn, everyone else considers what you could do, or not do, that week to bring more translucence to the family. Don't worry; kids understand what you mean by this as soon as you explain it to them. Just say, "Less thinking, less being right, and more aliveness, fun, and love." Everyone suggests an assignment, and then together you pick the best one. Everyone must agree, including the person who is going to do it.

Usually, an adult goes first. Everyone asks themselves, "What would make Dad a better dad, more loving, more fun to be around?" I have gotten assignments like, "No work after 6 P.M.," "No phoning except in the office," and "Take a walk in the forest every day." My wife gets assignments like, "Have a bubble bath every day," and "Dance for twenty minutes in the morning to loud music." Once my youngest son got "Every time you complain about something or ask for something, stop and say thank-you for five things in your life." After a day or two he started to love his practice, and so did we.

> Most parents are quietly doing the good work, day in and day out, unsung and unrecognized. To a large extent, I like to believe that people are doing the best they can. My work has to do with reminding people of the mysterious and miraculous dimensions of being human, the relationship between one generation and the next, and the huge mystery of having children in the first place.
>
> — Jon Kabat-Zinn

These kinds of translucent exercises and games are something we can easily share with our children. Then parenting, instead of being an obstacle to spirituality, becomes fertile ground in which our entire life grows in translucence.

CHAPTER TEN

THROUGH, NOT FROM

Translucent Art

S*teven Halpern takes the back roads when he drives the one and a half hours from his home in Marin County to Banquet Sound Studios in Santa Rosa, California. He has trained himself just to be present, to notice the beauty around him. "I'm just driving, sometimes in silence, sometimes listening to a tape of the work in progress. I'm just driving," he says. "There are no preoccupations. I'm in three-dimensional visual space, totally solitary. Listening is happening, hearing is happening. And very often, in that state, I hear music that has not yet been played. I hear it as if it were on the tape machine. I hear suggestions; I hear direction, maybe even some tonalities. I tend to remember it, and when I get to the studio, I can plug in and play the music I heard on the drive over.*

"When I reach the studio, I feel as though my fingers are being guided. I don't know what is going to happen, but things start happening on their own. I am not classically trained, but I play something I have never played before, sometimes intricate two-handed movements. I have had this experience many times, that a whole piece of music unfolds in this way.

"In 1969 'Spectrum Suite' came to me like that. When I first started hearing it, it was as though I tapped into an ongoing broadcast, like the old

radios with an analog tuner. You turn the dial, and suddenly you get new stations, suddenly it's clear."

Translucent painters, songwriters, filmmakers, and writers all describe the creative process similarly. They say that it comes through them, from an unknown source, when they are open, relaxed, and out of their own way. Their specific artistic gifts, playing a musical instrument, for example, or having a mastery over words, are picked up and used by something much bigger than individual expression. The resultant translucent art has the capacity to connect us back to ourselves, to the still center of things, without being overtly "spiritual." Often the most powerful and successful translucent art deals with the darkest and most difficult aspects of our humanity, but in a way that reveals inherent sacredness. Yet unlike the stereotypical "struggling artist" models, the translucent artists I have broken bread with for this book are neither struggling nor suffering. They display an infectious quality of gratitude, even of worship, which the majority of them associate with the creative process itself.

> I am a great believer in creativity. The art of living is the ultimate creative act. We are all practitioners of that, and we are all artists. We can start to learn how to be alive, not just by putting paint on a canvas in a painting, or writing a poem, or making a pot or a dance. But are we creating ourselves and our world every moment?
>
> — Lama Surya Das

LOOK AT ME!

The Iago trance is a contraction down from the capacity to feel openly into an intense preoccupation with "me" as a separate entity. There remains only the sense of "my" thoughts, "my" feelings, "my" fears, and "my" identity, and everything else shrivels in comparison. Iago-driven art is primarily a means of self-expression, a way for artists to assert their unique identity, to scream to the world, sometimes in as extreme a way as possible, "Look at me!" Born from feelings of inadequacy and separation, art becomes a stage on which to enact a compensation for unworthiness and shame, to squeeze out our most uncomfortable feelings and be free of them. The artist Alex Grey, one of a new breed of translucent or sacred artists, believes that twentieth-century art reflects this struggle between Iago and translucence: "By the early twentieth century, the Impressionists and other precursors to modern art had pretty much freed artists in all media from obligations to church or state, or to be beholden to anyone on the subject matter or manner in which art was made. The possibilities were becoming infinite, with no restrictions anymore on form or content."

Grey singled out Pablo Picasso as representative of this burgeoning obsession with invention:

I think of Picasso as an incarnation of the absolutely insatiable hunger for novelty. It is still driving the fashion world and art world today to a great degree. That voracious search for newness in his painting was mirrored in his relationships with people. Women came and went through Picasso's life with tremendous speed; the constant flow of muses inspired some of his greatest masterpieces. The relentless creation and destruction cycle in his work and affairs relates to the twentieth-century drive for invention. Twentieth-century inventions resulted in profound material changes for people throughout the world. The invention of the telephone, the lightbulb, all the things we take for granted at this point were being discovered in the early twentieth century. This capacity and human genius for innovation is exactly what Picasso exemplified. His fountain of creativity also became very much identified with the material world and its politics; it became associated with Marxism, with a materialist relationship to the world.

> A lot of what makes art great has to do with staying in the moment, so that what you do is fresh. Look at the tree, observe it or feel the tree inside and you're letting each line be felt. And as soon as you start to fill in the leaves mechanically, you've come up with something that flattens.
>
> — Dana Lynne Andersen

Grey's description of Picasso's creative invention could just as well be applied to Henry Miller, to Sartre or Camus, or to Schoenberg. As artists of all kinds were able to shake off traditional constrictions, their work became a frenzy of experimentation, more loyal to the actuality of human experience than to any specific dogma, tradition, or patron.

For some, this new freedom gave rise to a revived human conscience and the pursuit of social equality, often inspired both by the revolutionary writings of contemporary socialists and a disgust with the hypocrisy and often cruelty of monarchies and organized religion. Folk musicians like Woody Guthrie, the painter Diego Rivera, and novelist John Steinbeck all began to use their artistic expression as a political voice.

At the same time, other artists, some influenced by Sigmund Freud, explored the darker, more repressed aspects of the human psyche. Writers such as D. H. Lawrence and Virginia Woolf, surrealist painters including Salvador Dalí, composers like Gustav Mahler, and later songwriters such as Leonard Cohen and Bob Dylan used their art both to bare the wounds of the soul and as an attempt to heal them. But above all, twentieth-century art was all about transgressing boundaries and expectations of what was acceptable. "Artists weren't all that interested in referring to the same old sacred forms," Grey explains. "They wanted to invent new forms. Who cares if they are 'sacred' or not? What is sacred, anyway? We don't know."

> Everything in modern art is on a roll where if it's more outrageous, if it breaks the latest rules, if it pushes the boundary, if it's more on the edge, then that's where it is happening. Breaking the rules is just a game, having to be more outrageous. It has nothing to do with creativity.
>
> — Dana Lynne Andersen

If it was shocking, it was worth doing.

Having abandoned traditional reference points, twentieth-century artists began to express and expose themselves, warts and all. The whole process became agonizingly personal: the Iago-driven artist is plagued by self-doubt, caught between the compulsion for self-expression and feelings of boredom and disgust at their contracted world of self-preoccupation. We have the image of an artist as neurotic, self-important, minutely sensitive to the opinion of others, and plagued with self-doubt, a stereotype that, as far as we know, would not have applied either to Shakespeare or to Leonardo da Vinci. This struggle, between the push to express and create, and the inevitable self-doubt born of introspection, leaves the Iago-driven artist endlessly distracted, making cups of tea all day, tearing up manuscripts, fantasizing about what his audience is going to say. *Just like me.* Do you think this is boring? It's a little too theoretical, isn't it, going on a bit long, perhaps? *Who even gives a toss about your precious opinions about art anyway, Arjuna? Art? Hah! It's a joke. You know as much about art as you do about feelings, which you had the blatant arrogance to write about in chapter 6.* I know, I know. What are we going to do? I hate this book, I wish I'd never even... *Shut up! The readers, they're hearing all this! Pull yourself together, man.*

Now, where were we?

The endless quest for shock value led artists to place novelty above content, at any cost. Andy Warhol is the quintessential example of an artist transforming himself into a living art form, in this case a work of pop art. Elvis Presley, Allen Ginsberg, and later David Bowie and Madonna, although brilliant and talented people, all explored the possibilities of the persona of the artist becoming as important as their art. Fifteen minutes of fame equaled a meaningful life, and celebrity became the benchmark of successful art.

When an artist relies on the general public for approval, not to mention for physical survival, he becomes caught in the tension between novelty and imitation. On the one hand, the endless quest for novelty requires more and more shocking extremes of expression, such as Damien Hirst's butchered pig parts or his dead shark floating in formaldehyde in London's Tate Gallery. Ironically, the crusade for public approval can just as easily flip Iago-driven art the other way, into imitation and commercialism. Dana Lynne Andersen calls this "production mode." We repackage what has sold recently, hopefully with a new twist. Neither the obsession with novelty nor the blind imitation of last year's fad allows the artist to really be connected with her core, with a place that is always flowing with energy. Alex Grey comments: "Fashion, celebrity, materialism, and ego became primary values. You would simply need to work out a distinctive style to have the work be recognized as unique, to make a cultural statement of some kind. The artist had become a kind of charlatan."

> Ignorance has so many levels and ways to perpetuate itself, especially in art: blindness, catharsis, and repetition of habitual expression. Simply said, ignorance is the distortion of not seeing yourself as a manifestation of God.
>
> — Peter Makena

This fascination with celebrity, with the artist as a charlatan performer, was initially greeted with great suspicion. But it may have laid the foundation for the translucent art now emerging. Jackson Pollock was filmed in the 1950s entering an almost shamanic trance state when he painted. "That film brought people back to the tribal function art can have," says Grey. "To the authentic role great art can serve, to connect us with ourselves again." For the first time since art divorced itself from religion, the artist's state of consciousness was seen as a relevant factor in the creative process. Although Pollock was a lifelong alcoholic and suffered greatly, through his creative process he transcended his personal life. "When I am in my painting, I'm not aware of what I'm doing," said Pollock shortly before his death, at only forty-four. "I have no fears about making changes, because the painting has a life of its own. I try to let it come through. It is only when I lose contact with the painting that the result is a mess. Otherwise, there is pure harmony, an easy give-and-take, and the painting comes out well."

Two decades later, the Beatles explored psychedelic drugs and then meditation, and the cultural revolution of the 1960s threw us into a new understanding: the exploration of new forms in art tied to the exploration of expanded states of consciousness in the artist. In every medium, artists began exploring what can happen when they get out of their own way. Alex Grey has studied for years with a variety of Tibetan teachers; David Lynch, the filmmaker, has been practicing meditation for thirty years; Madonna has turned to the kabbalah; Leonard Cohen spent years in a Zen monastery. Contemporary translucent art rests in this capacity of the artist to be, in some way, a medium for something deeper and more universal than mere self-preoccupation.

> Mastery anywhere is to be aligned with That. It lives, acts, speaks through you. So these artists or sportsmen, in that field of activity, are able to enter that state. Maybe not in the rest of their lives, maybe the moment they turn away from that all the normal patterns come back, and they are as mad as anybody else. But it is wonderful to watch action being performed out of that state.
>
> — Eckhart Tolle

SPIRITUAL MYTH #13: Awakened people are naturally creative. Great art flows through them spontaneously, without any need for formal training or skills.

SPIRITUAL MYTH #14: Spiritually awake people would have no need to paint, write poetry, or make music; those are all just activities of the restless mind.

A DEEPER SOURCE

Translucent art does not come from the artist's personal identity, but rather through it. In this sense, all great art is, and always has been, translucent.

Vincent van Gogh suffered greatly, yet his paintings, like *Cornfields* or *Sunflowers*, are celebrated as masterpieces, not just for their content, but also for the mysterious energy that breathes through them.

Dana Lynne Andersen has been a painter for many years. The more her own wakefulness has deepened, the more translucence imbues her work. Now she teaches classes, for beginners as well as established artists, to discover how spiritual life and creativity can find common ground. I asked her what makes truly translucent art distinct from the mundane or the imitative. Like the many other artists and critics of whom I asked this question, initially she had a hard time being specific. When art is infused with spirit, it is more something that you feel in your essence than recognize with your mind:

> *The distinction lies primarily in the source of inspiration. . . . You can source your inspiration from what you see outside yourself. Then you reflect the outer world. You can source it from the subconscious, as Surrealism does. . . . Or, you can shift attention to the place where you think and experience things superconsciously. That means with more clarity, more ability to see the larger perspective, and yet to maintain discrimination. In Native American traditions they say the eagle can fly high and see the whole panorama, but it also sees the tiny mouse on the desert floor. So it's an expanded and clarified state of consciousness.*

Translucent art, created from that expanded dimension of the artist, has the capacity to awaken the same expanded dimension in anyone who experiences it. But generally it does not do so by focusing on obviously "spiritual" themes. Most translucent art embraces the whole spectrum of human experience, from the darkest to the most sublime, without making distinctions in the mind. It has less to do with content or form than with an invisible, yet unmistakable, felt quality of expanded consciousness. Translucent art embraces both light and dark, which sets it apart from another genre, known to cringing art critics the world over as N.A.M.

> I love being played. When this happens it's a gift. I am connected with the energy that is alive in all living things. It's palpable. It's recognizable, and it creates a wonderful, resonant circle with the audience. It doesn't get any better.
>
> — Peter Makena

Beyond Unicorns and Angels

New Age Mush is easy to spot, mainly because it offers very little variety. There are now literally hundreds of CDs available with titles like *Dolphin Rainbow Suite* or *Angelic Symphony*. The covers display the same narrow range of what's acceptable: soft pastel colors, a unicorn, dolphins, rainbows, throw in an angel or two, and that's it, you are an artist. Not long ago, with time to kill, I was sitting in a store that specializes in such heavenly offerings. I sipped celestial tea with organic almond milk, surrounded by crystals, angel cards, affirmations, a million kinds of smells to balance the chakras. Soothing music played in the background: soft choral harmonies, slow repetitious melodies created on synthesizers to sound like a choir of angels. Maybe the occasional tinkling bells, nothing too jarring. No messy body fluids here, please. One track gave way to another, with no perceptible change of mood. Finally, after more than an hour had passed, I went to pay for my tea. "This CD goes on a long time," I casually remarked to the celestial tea maiden. "Oh, no," she smiled serenely, "the machine is on auto shuffle. We have more than five hundred CDs loaded. It goes to a *different* CD at the end of each track." In my hour, which had seemed like six, I had probably heard music from a dozen different albums and artists, yet they all sounded exactly the same. I left the store in search of Guns N' Roses and a beer.

Art that tries to be spiritual attempts to draw us into the etheric realms, the higher chakras, while amputating the darker sides of life. We may feel soothed, we may feel calm and harmonious, but we rarely feel deeply connected when we choose one narrow band of living and reject the rest. And why would we want to do that? What is it that makes unicorns, dolphins, rainbows, and a soft chorus of angelic voices more attractive as the content of art than, say, despair or frustration or wild, crazy, up-all-night, dance-till-you-drop chutzpah? Or even murder? Why choose to censor reality?

> We've been conditioned to think of death as the darker side of life. I think it's just a part of life the same way birth is. And I think any real true sort of spiritual state has to acknowledge the presence of death.
>
> — Alan Ball

In contrast, translucent art, in fact all great art, does not choose, and that is what makes it great. It opens its arms wide enough to embrace the pus and puke of the underworld, and the harmony and glitter of the heavens, and finds no real difference between them. All one taste. All equally real. And all a dream. It is this willingness to surrender to the full spectrum of reality, in its small triumphs and its dismal defeats, that gives really great art its depth. The content is secondary to the willingness to include it all, no matter what.

New Age Mush remains superficial not because there is anything wrong with angels and dolphins, but because the choice to retreat into a soothing pink corner of the playground is often made out of weakness, a flinching from meeting life in relaxed openness. Art then becomes more a carrier of that closure itself than of the celestial world it has fixated on. Dividing the world into light and dark, into the welcomed and the resisted, creates suffering simply in the enactment of the split.

> If a work of art is created out of that state, it contains a fragrance of it. Perhaps that's why people love great art; it's the state out of which it came. Contemplation of great art can connect you with that state. Now this is becoming the new state of humankind on the planet. It's not just confined to one particular activity, but your whole life becomes That.
>
> — Eckhart Tolle

Art that truly welcomes the dark and sinister as freely as the celestial, and that neither fixates nor pulls back from either one, communicates that feeling of unconditional acceptance itself, the surrender to reality that brings us home to ourselves, yet again.

Leonard Cohen's Secret Life

During the years of researching this book, I asked literally thousands of people which contemporary artists "did it" for them: What could take them back to the mystery of their "original face," the one they had before they were conceived? Among musicians, the singers Deva Premal, Peter Makena, and Krishna Das were high on the list, as was the composer Philip Glass. But the highest praise, from Stockholm to San Francisco, was reserved for Leonard Cohen's 2001 CD *Ten New Songs*.

Cohen earned a reputation in the late 1960s and early 1970s as the quintessential representative of despair, creating albums suitable only to slit your wrists to. He is known for songs like *So Long Marianne* and *Famous Blue Raincoat*: all in various shades of blue. He did indeed suffer from depression for long periods. He tried to fight it with all the resources he could find: religion, drugs, art, drinking, women, and therapy. "My depression, so bleak and anguished, was just crucial, and I couldn't shake it; it wouldn't go away," he reflects. "I didn't know what it was. I was ashamed of it, because it would be there even when things were good, and I would be saying to myself, 'Really, what have you got to complain about?' But for people who suffer from acute clinical depression, it is quite irrelevant what the circumstances of your life are."[1]

Cohen has maintained what he calls a lifelong flirtation with spiritual practice. "Religion is my favorite hobby," he says. "It's deep and voluptuous — a pure delight. Nothing is comparable to the delight you get from this activity."[2] He has known Sasaki Roshi, a Zen teacher, for more than thirty years. In the mid 1990s, when his personal life seemed mired in chaos, Cohen made the bold decision to move to the Mount Baldy Zen monastery, near Los Angeles, and to become a Zen monk. For five years, he woke every morning at 2:30 A.M. and spent hours meditating, chanting, making beds, washing dishes, shoveling snow, and acting as personal secretary to his teacher.

> A lot of "me playing" has dropped away. I feel so present allowing the song to come through and being with it, aware and as expressive as I can be, putting my heart and soul into it, yet stepping out of the way.
>
> — Peter Makena

Cohen claims no great attainment from his stay at the Zen center. But at some point his depression mysteriously lifted and did not return. "Not curing the self, but releasing one's grip on it — that was the solution," he says now.[3] He feels that he was never a good disciple: "My discovery towards the end of my stay as a monk was that I had no religious skills. And after that came a deep relaxation and something that reminded me of peace. I didn't absolutely have to understand. Actually I couldn't understand."[4] Cohen's description of the process of letting go that he passed through is reminiscent of many of the translucents I have talked to: "The sheer fatigue of the effort required me to stop the effort," he says. "And then things started to change rather swiftly. But I don't know what it was."[5]

Cohen came down from the mountain, free of his quest to cure himself, with a sheaf of lyrics he had written there, and spent two years more or less completely dedicated to working on *Ten New Songs*, with a co-vocalist and sound engineer. The entire process happened in a relaxed but meticulous way, a process he describes as "a very peaceful, agreeable time."[6]

Ten New Songs transmits a mysterious magic. It is the quintessential translucent artwork: imbued with Cohen's extended periods of meditation at Mount Baldy, and his involuntary lifelong familiarity with the dark side of life as well as the light. Cohen is certified Mush-free. He himself acknowledges, "The whole album reflects the relaxed condition under which it was made."[7] After its release, he played the album for two Zen monks. When it was finished they were silent for some time. Then one of them said, "That was as good as two weeks of intensive meditation retreat." The other monk just kept his eyes closed.[8] All over the world, people say the same thing about these songs. They carry the fruits of Cohen's translucent practice; they transmit both wakefulness and the spirit of embracing everything without conditions. When Chameli and I do retreats, we often play just one of the songs at the start of a session. In minutes the room is transported, everyone is bathed in translucent magic. We have found no chant or mantra or classical masterpiece that can do the same trick as Cohen's new songs.

> If you're getting back to the source, you throw a little ingot of that into your work. In Tibet, there is a notion that certain blessed objects can implant a seed of liberation in the viewer. To me, that is the ultimate goal of art. If you can plant seeds that will catalyze a person's spiritual growth, what greater motivation or possibility could there be for a work of art?
>
> — Alex Grey

Cohen is discreet; his is a subtle intuition, which scents the lyrics with a featherlike delicacy. In "Love Itself," he uses the way that the sun, shining through the window, illuminates specks of dust in the room, as a metaphor for the glimpse of our true nature beyond the mind. The song is almost written in a code: some immediately recognize that it is about the mystery of who we really are; others hear it simply as a poem about dust and sunlight. One of his admirers, clearly in the first category, wrote to him, "Your music and words resonate with a place I call Home, your latest work even more deeply so." Cohen replied to her: "Home, Sweet Home. Roshi said you never lose your home. He also said that home is not an object. It is not fixed. Any perspective you have on your home is the distance you are from it. Being at home is the activity of not needing to look for a home, and not needing to abandon a home. The mirrors are clear, the shadows are past, the wandering heart is homeless at last."[9]

But Cohen does not use his discovery of home as a collapse into escapism; he knows that we are born and that we die in this realm of work

> For me nowadays, the experience of transcendence comes through modern poetry more than through the old scriptures. I'm more likely to find an epiphany in a modern novel than in an ancient scripture.
>
> — Bishop Richard Holloway

and desire, and that it cannot be avoided. It is this capacity to relish the limitless, and to embrace the limited, with its exquisite quivering delights as well as its crushing defeats that has made Cohen the spokesperson for the translucent perspective. The album is not so much spiritual as whole; it is honest and real.

O Crown of Light, O Darkened One,
I never thought we'd meet.
You kiss my lips, and then it's done:
I'm back on Boogie Street.[10]

Boogie Street is an actual street in Singapore: a place of commerce by day and prostitution by night. But in the album Cohen uses it to stand for this realm where we work, where we express desire, make mistakes, and find occasional blessings. "You cannot live in paradise," he quotes his teacher as saying, "because there are no restaurants or washrooms there. Boogie Street is the place of restaurants and washrooms."[11]

Ten New Songs has captured the hearts of so many people because it perfectly articulates the emerging translucent perspective: it is written from a heart that has been visited by love itself but that has also learned, through the roller-coaster ride of human chaos, not to flinch from any of it, neither the "little winning streak" nor the "invincible defeat."

Cohen's work has become translucent not because he has gained spiritual experience or understanding, but because he has stumbled on the knack of relaxing the grasping for either one. Every line reminds us of the grace that shines, not from us but through us, when we are willing to embrace everything in exquisite surrender. Much as Rumi wrote poems to the Beloved, many of Cohen's songs are written to the mystery itself, to That which lives through us when we get out of the way:

You kept me from believing
Until you let me know:

That I am not the one who loves
It's love that chooses me.
When hatred with his package comes,
You forbid delivery.[12]

Cohen talks of this love as impersonal. "It is not ours," he says. "We are the expression of love. Our birth is an expression of impersonal love. And our death is a return to that impersonal love.... It is not romantic. Nor possessive. It is a general love, in the sense that it is extended to all. It is absolute.... We are instruments of a will that is not our own. The intention and the purpose of that will, we cannot know."[13]

WHAT MAKES ART GREAT?

I posed the same question about movies to my captive translucents as I had about music. The nominations for the most translucent film went to *Waking Life*, *A Beautiful Mind*, the *Matrix* trilogy, *Life Is Beautiful*, *Powder*, and *American Beauty*. What is it about these films, or indeed about certain books or works of art, that brings us back to ourselves, that allows us to feel a bigger love than mere sentimentality? There are no unicorns or rainbows in these films, not even Hollywood happy endings. One is about disconnection in the suburbs and ends with the protagonist's murder. One is about a lifelong struggle with mental illness. And one devotes more than half of its plot to a concentration camp and also ends with the main character's meaningless death. But according to the many people I surveyed, these are nonetheless the top candidates for translucent cinema, these are the films that "take us there," that let us feel the divine all the way down to our little toes.

> Great art in its essence breaks you out of the normal constraints of ordinary awareness and gives you a full spectrum, an expanded universe.
>
> — Dana Lynne Andersen

How do we recognize the difference between mere excitement or entertainment and the real deal? What distinguishes a "good" movie, or song, or sculpture from one that has some mysterious additional ingredient that transforms it into a spiritual event? I took these questions to writers, filmmakers, critics, musicians, and the UPS delivery guy. There was a surprising convergence of conclusions.

Translucent art happens when three factors occur simultaneously. Each of these three elements can exist by themselves, and often do. When they come together, they create a magic that transports us beyond ourselves, and we enter the realm of sacred art.

The first, indispensable to the rest, is basic technical skill. Leonard Cohen spent years working on the lyrics for *Ten New Songs*. He's been writing novels and songs since before I was born. Alan Ball had already made his mark as a New York playwright and worked on several network sitcoms before writing the screenplay for *American Beauty*. Steven Halpern may hear melodies spontaneously while driving on the back roads in Marin, but he has decades of mileage on his Roland piano to help him download those melodies onto tape. Even the most inspired translucent artists need discipline and technique to transpose the gift from beyond themselves, down and through their medium. The artist may have to hang in there, through days and nights of not-quite-right, through Iago's discouraging whisper, till ah... the shoe fits perfectly.

The second factor, which may exist independently of the other two, is an artistic honesty, a relaxed willingness to face the full spectrum of human experience without flinching from any of it. The work then reflects the artist's integrity: allowing reality to be just as it is, which may require the courage to face and feel great pain. If we lean just a little too much into favoring the light, we are lost in the land of lightweight network soaps or "new age mush," which soothe us from the need to face reality, like a sedative. We may feel entertained, uplifted, but rarely whole. If we lean too far on the other side, we get lost in the dark side, the land of violence and destruction. Bloodbath movies, punk rock, or heavy metal music exude a destructive quality with which we can all sometimes find a resonance. They allow us to experience our own anger, our hatred, and because it is being acted out on such an extreme scale, we experience catharsis, we feel alive again. We may temporarily drain

> I commune with the muse, the same way I meditate. I just do it. And it is there for me. I keep a poetry notebook, and write, and I open myself, and I trust. Half the secret is that you have to master the craft enough that the art can happen by itself.
>
> — Lama Surya Das

the reservoir of resentment, but neither punk rock nor gratuitously violent movies generally allow us to feel deeply connected. Artistic honesty walks right down the middle of the tightrope, without leaning too far one way or the other. It discovers a humor and a stillness in the midst of the chaos of opposites.

The last, most mysterious ingredient of translucent art concerns the artist's state of consciousness: how translucent she can be when the art is flowing. This is where art itself becomes a translucent spiritual practice, as effective as meditation or yoga. As we have seen from great art throughout the ages, this quality has less to do with the artists' individual personalities in day-to-day life than it does with their capacity to get out of the way, to poke a hole in the usual contin-uum of daily preoccupations, allowing something deeper to have its way. This deeper quality infuses the content with an invisible flavor, a perfume. When this third

> The main thing is that you are in the game that you are doing, that you are playing. You can open yourself to let-ting it happen through you and not impede it, not get in the way, by not being a tyrant, or too much of an editor, interfering with the pure luminosity coursing through oneself.
>
> — Lama Surya Das

ingredient is added to the mix, we can feel it, independent of the content. We feel it while reading a poem, gazing at a painting, watching a show, or listen-ing to a symphony.

David Lynch brings decades of translucent practice to his filmmaking. His movies are frequently praised by translucents I interviewed. But they are a far cry from expressions of sweetness and light. *Twin Peaks* and *Mulholland Drive* both dance around murders, weaving in bizarre twists and characters. Many of us love Lynch's films, even his darker *Blue Velvet*, not because of a fascination with the twisted, but because of how the material is presented. We are not only experiencing the story but also receiving a transmission of the openness of consciousness that created the film. We are, for a period, see-ing the world as David Lynch sees it; in this case it expands our capacity to embrace the full spectrum from darkness to light, from the bizarre to the absurd, and to say yes to all of it.

We can feel it when all these ingredients come together. We have a vis-ceral response. Alex Grey shared with me a powerful experience he had when he first saw Michelangelo's *Last Judgment* in the Sistine Chapel in Rome:

I was watching it for two hours, and it felt like just a moment. I felt caught up in the swirls of flesh Michelangelo had laid down, these huge ripples of flesh, the convulsion of tumbling figures, and the tapestry that is the skin. Christ was the center, the hub, the divine light in the very middle of this swirl of flesh. He was at peace. Everyone else was agitated. The painting says to me, "Be the hub of reality, the heart which is the still small point around which the universe turns." Christ was that. Rather than being the damning judge whom we always fear, he was benign, like a Taoist master in a qi gong posture.

American Beauty: Translucent Cinema

Let's take a deeper look at *American Beauty*, written by Alan Ball, directed by Sam Mendes, and the winner of my contemporary translucent cinema poll. On its surface, the film addresses such common contemporary themes as meaninglessness, infidelity, ambition, and family dysfunction. But, as the movie poster urged before we even bought our tickets, "Look closer." Everything in this suburban movie may be familiar, but as with life, nothing is as it appears. I talked to the film's writer, Alan Ball:

We have this idea, especially in American society, that we know everything, and we're in control of everything. And we don't. There's so much we don't know, so much mystery and wonder in existence and being alive in the world. Children have that but it gets ironed out of us; it doesn't go away, it just goes to sleep. Those of us who are lucky enough to have a certain kind of experience can have that part of us reawaken. The legacy of the Judeo-Christian ethic in our country teaches us to deny all the parts of ourselves, the desires that don't fit into what is universally agreed upon as being good. That is what keeps us from being whole. The notion that the road to what the Christians would call salvation, and what the Buddhists call enlightenment, is a very clean road, a very straight and narrow road, may work for some people, but it hasn't worked for me.

> Spirituality for me is like feeling alive in the moment. I'm where I'm supposed to be, I'm what I'm supposed to be, I don't have to judge it, I just need to let the energy flow through me and try to be a positive force in the world.
>
> — Alan Ball

The film is about the awakening of Lester Burnham, a middle-aged man who has lost his passion. "It's the weirdest thing," he says early in the film, "I feel like I've been in a coma for about twenty years, and I'm just now waking up."[14] Says Ball: "He knows he needs to find his passion, and Angela (Lester's daughter's Lolita-like best friend) is the initial catalyst for that. But he thinks she is the goal, and she's really just the knock on the door. He needs to get back in touch with his spiritual connection to living."

The film evokes the Iago trance with visceral force and biting humor. We see ourselves and our own trance in every frame. We see ourselves in Caroline, Lester's wife, and her failing attempts to contain her life gone out of control. We see ourselves in Buddy King, the real estate magnate who projects "an image of success at all times," in Colonel Frank Fritz, the retired marine who embodies the values of the far right, and in his wife, whose state of total submission has left her in the realm of the walking dead.

> Absurdity is a very powerful tool of waking up. A good situation comedy is a wonderful Buddhist teaching, because it's a parody of suffering. The cause of suffering is attachment to outcome, attachment to income, attachment to the world being a certain way.
>
> — Steve Bhaerman
> (Swami Beyondananda)

Lester's awakening is catalyzed by meeting the colonel's son, Ricky Fritz. Ricky embodies translucence. "He's certainly the most evolved character," says Alan Ball. "You look at what he's grown up in, the environment of repression and brutality, and it's amazing. His ability to see the beauty in life is what kept him from just shutting down and becoming twisted and brutal. I think everybody has that ability, and we all make choices."[15]

Ricky is awake, conscious, watching, attuned to the present moment. His penetrating, unwavering eyes are invariably looking directly into the camera whenever he is on screen. Ricky's ability to see the world, to see the hidden beauty in things, is accentuated by his video camera, which is almost always zooming in on something. Ricky invites us to "look closer." He can see the beauty underneath the appearance of things. A conversation between Ricky and Lester's daughter, Jane, expresses the essence of the film's gift. Jane has asked him why he would capture a homeless woman, frozen to death, on video. "Because it was amazing," he replies. "When you see something like that, it's like God is looking right at you. If you are careful you can look right back."

"And what do you see?" asks Jane.

"Beauty," says Ricky.[16]

The "Beauty" celebrated by the film is the beauty Ricky sees every-where, the beauty Lester comes to discover, as his eyes are opened during the film, the beauty of a plastic bag dancing in the wind on an icy cold day. Ricky describes this moment of beauty as he shows Jane the image: "It's a minute away from snowing, there's this electricity in the air, you can almost hear it, and this bag was just danc-ing with me. Like a little kid begging me to play with it for fifteen minutes. That's the day I realized there was this entire life behind things and this incredibly benevo-lent force that wanted me to know there was no reason to be afraid. Ever. Video is a poor excuse, I know, but it helps me remember. I need to remember, I need to remember. Sometimes there's so much beauty in the world, I feel like I can't take it, and my heart is just going to cave in."[17] The scene in the film is based on a real incident in Ball's life:

> *American Beauty was a journey of rediscovery for me in the sense that I could be involved in a creative process where the work itself seemed to have a personality, seemed to have a soul, that was revealing itself to me.*
> — Alan Ball

> *I had an encounter with a plastic bag! And I didn't have a video camera, like Ricky does. I'm sure some people would look at that and go, "What a psycho!" But it was a very intense and very real moment. There's a Buddhist notion of the miraculous within the mundane, and I think we certainly live in a cul-ture that encourages us not to look for that. I do like, though, that Ricky says, "Video's a poor excuse, but it helps me remember." Because it's not the video he's focused on; it's the experience itself. He's very connected to the world around him.*

Ball is the youngest of four children. He was closest to his sister Anne. When he was thirteen, she was killed in a car accident on her twenty-second birthday, while driving him to a music lesson. "That brought me face-to-face with tremendous loss, and the impermanence of things," Ball says. "I struggled for years and years with how to cope with that — and, ultimately, I started developing an innate sense of detachment." Ball says he has never had a spiritual teacher. "I don't trust that," he says. "I need to make my own discoveries. It's always been that way." His practice is instinctive and home-grown. "Rather than just sitting silently in a room every day, or meditating, I try to get in touch with nature as much as I can." He walks his three dogs every day in the Hollywood Hills. He is brought back to himself by "living with creatures who don't have the self-obsessed conscious-ness that we have; they really seem to exist purely in the moment."

> A lot of my spiritual awakening has involved tragedy, has involved experimentation, with different experiences, sexual experiences, drug experiences. I have to be real honest and say that those experiences have contributed to my spirituality.
>
> — Alan Ball

He talks about his work as a "very spir-itual experience," which he distinguishes from anything having to do with religion. He wrote *American Beauty* during an eight-month period while he was working during the day on the television sitcom *Cybil*. He would get home at one in the morning and write for two hours before going to sleep. He described his process to me:

> *A movie or a television show is such a collaborative venture, and there are so many people involved, so many different hearts and minds and energies, that the thing takes on a life of its own. Part of my job is to step back and get out of its way. To step in when I feel like it's going astray, but to recognize where the show wants to take us, as opposed to what am I going to do with these chess pieces, these characters that I've created? I don't feel like I've created the characters. The show and the characters have a life of their own that is very real. Part of my job is to get out of their way and let them show me what they need to do.*

NOT FROM BUT THROUGH

In the 1970s Andy Desmond played with artists including Fleetwood Mac, Ry Cooder, and Lou Reed. He left his career at its peak. "Over the years, songwriting and playing music had become associated with pain, frustration, ambition, helplessness," Desmond says. "I was damaged by my years in the music business and ready to embrace a new set of values." He moved to a spiritual community in rural England and stopped playing completely for more than a year. During that time, he explored the meditation techniques of the Indian mystic Osho, an event Desmond now calls his initiation into a translucent life. He reemerged with the name Miten. He described to me the way his creativity happens now:

> When the songs started to come back, they came in a very natural way: small offerings of gratitude. I just wanted to say thank-you. They weren't loaded with the weight of ambition or heavy with the need for recognition, as in my past. Just very simple melodies, very simple chords, very simple words.... I'd collect a few lines that said something to me and I'd sing them. Songs live in a kind of ethereal world. There are many songs, and they live in the ether. If you're open you can call on them. Today, it feels that I'm not writing the songs — the songs are coming through me. When I'm walking, lines come to me. I have no musical upbringing, or poetic or language or literary background. It's a kind of maverick thing.... If no more songs come, fine. But I'm always open to miracles.

Miten's partner, Deva Premal, is an icon of translucent music to most of those I interviewed; every new CD she produces meets with critical acclaim. Despite standing ovations wherever she plays, she remains completely untouched by her success. When she was a young child, her father loved the Sanskrit sacred chant the *Gayatri Mantra*. He sang it to her every day as an infant and later taught her to sing it herself. This experience receded into the background, until she met Miten. At first, he encouraged her to join him in harmonies, and later to play keyboards. Premal was very shy at first and always took a backseat, but as she slowly gained in confidence, something began to take her over as she sang: "I don't feel that I'm creative. I don't feel I'm a singer; I don't feel I'm a musician. Something happens, but it has nothing to do with me. I don't practice. The singing changed by itself. Suddenly I could sing differently; suddenly I could sing better. Before I discovered the mantras, I could never sing alone. When I found the mantras I could sing alone. It's just what I can do."

> What I'm really good at is organizing! It's very easy for me. Music is a challenge, and I'm scared of it. Sometimes I hope if I keep myself busy, I won't have to play. I'll be too busy organizing.
>
> — Deva Premal

Despite their growing world renown, Premal and Miten could hardly take less credit for their gifts. Their humility is typical of many translucent artists I spoke to. Here is how the singer and songwriter Peter Makena put it: "Sometimes, I feel a niggling that needs to be written. I get absorbed, I get lost. I feel I am being used in a good way, my skills and ability to express song. The process is like a state of trance. I feel I am nearly leaving this world."

> There's a well, a source from within that wants to be expressed, that wants to share, that wants to participate. When I go with it, that's what has me, the flame of the creative force. After a while it has its own momentum, its own life.
>
> — Peter Makena

When Makena plays a live concert, the entire hall moves, as one organism, from the pin-drop silence between the songs (he asks his audience to show their appreciation in stillness rather than applause) to huge tidal waves, songs of gratitude and celebration in which everyone in the hall is an enthusiastic participant.

Stepping Aside

Translucent artists often describe specific techniques for getting out of their own way. Alex Grey's Tibetan teacher, Namkhai Norbu, taught him the simple sound "ah" many years ago. Grey repeats this sound every day before he starts to work: "It clicks me back into the remembrance of a condition that's beyond pollution, beyond the weak stupidity that I exemplify at other times. It takes me back to something that is perfect from the beginning, that cannot be harmed or taken away from its boundless beauty."

From there, he paints.

Grey feels that when any artist creates from this place of connection, it allows an "energetic download," which affects the object of art itself: "When this downloading has been happening through the artist, and through their chosen medium onto a surface, perhaps taking hundreds or thousands of hours, there is a devotional field of subtle energy that surrounds the object." Grey tells me that he has even asked friends to lead him through museums with his eyes closed. He can feel the energetic field and emanation from certain paintings and sculptures, from the intense focus of so many hours of devotional energy downloaded into the work by the artist.

Eckhart Tolle describes a similar experience of stepping aside when writing. At first he felt "some kind of tension building up" while visiting

California. He had written fragments over many years of teaching, but this was different. This was "an empowered energy stream." He bought himself a notebook and started to write. When he returned to his home in England, he got out his notebook again. Nothing happened, no more writing flowed. He could edit what he had written in California and British Columbia, but he could not write. The next time he visited the West Coast, the writing again started. This happened several times: the result was *The Power of Now*. Because the empowered flow occurred in one location, and not in another, Tolle realized he was obeying a force greater than himself, a choiceless activity: "I came to obey this, to the realization that 'This is what I have to do.' If I had questioned it, or said out of fear, 'No, I am not going to do it,' it would probably have led to illness."

> There is a point where I disappear. People who are not used to making music suddenly realize they are making it themselves. You feel it and you see it. Everybody is singing together and they're hearing each other. And when it stops the silence is simply holy. It's the most magical and nourishing thing.
>
> — Miten

When an artist in any medium opens to these channels, it often causes a break with tradition. The source of inspiration is now coming from beyond and through the artist. Although it may use their skills, it will do so in its own way. Grey described it this way: "Suddenly I didn't care where the art world was going. I was tapped into something real and wonderful. Something that obviously manifests through all the world's wisdom paths. This for me was a trail worth blazing in contemporary art: the path back to the sacred."

Dana Lynne Andersen teaches artists how to create in a more translucent way. To her, it is most important to abandon all of one's ideas of what art should look like or how it reflects what you see on the outside:

I'm trying to help people connect to an experience of the source of being within themselves, and to realize that that's the part that you experience, realize, or know. As soon as you find that and feel it and experience it, you know that it's an eternal source of being. Eternally present, present now, outside of time and space, outside of the constraints of time and history. That happens only when you can break the habit of trying to create for what it looks like.

OUTSIDE THE BOX: LIFE AS ART

Andersen has observed that when artists leave the well-worn path, they discover that the creative force flowing through them is not limited to one medium but can shift freely between the different senses and means of expression. She calls this "synthesia," the capacity to "smell" a texture, "taste" sound, or "see" the color of a word or a musical note. Like Deva Premal, the translucent artist lets go of the notion "I am a writer" or "I am a singer" and allows the creative current to flow. In working with all kinds of artists, Andersen and many others like her have come to radically expand their definition of creativity:

> There is an infinite number of possibilities for your expression. When you come to your center, there will be paths and avenues that are right for who you are. For one person it'll be gardening, and for another person, piano. That is a different issue than skill level. Channels, vehicles, avenues of expression come from your passion, your interest, your background. The creative urge will press out of whatever is your avenue. The water will flow through your custom riverbed.

Humor as Translucent Art

Translucent people may share the same wakefulness, knowing their original nature to be limitless, but it is hard to find traits that unify them in daily life. On the contrary, translucents display wildly ranging diets, standards of living, occupations, and lifestyles. But one translucent quality that seems to be universal, to cross all boundaries is a lively sense of humor. The fundamentalist mind has trouble laughing at itself; rigid belief systems create stagnancy. Humor is a kindly disrupter of normalcy, a way to keep from stagnating.

> If the awakening is taken out of the rarefied atmosphere of simply "a realization that I have," and taken *into* the level of "my human life, and humanity," it actually becomes an absolutely, totally unique expression of that truth. Nobody else throughout all of time is going to carry that uniqueness into life.
>
> — Adyashanti

Comedian Steve Bhaerman has found his "riverbed" through his sense of humor. He is best known to the world by his stage name: Swami Beyondananda. His book, an offering to the world of translucent art, is called *Driving Your Own Karma*. Bhaerman sees comedy as a great way of waking up and living translucently. To "get" a joke usually requires us to be an observer, to cultivate a detached enjoyment of the absurdity and at the same time the tenderness of life:

> *The power of humor is in stories. I call them Zen Cohens, because a lot of these are Jewish, like me. And I use them to ignite a moment of awakening with a spark of laughter. You are bumped out of your distress. There is an insight, like an exclamation point. You are liberated physically and emotionally through the laughter; the insight liberates you mentally and spiritually. You may think differently, you may see differently. All of a sudden you are looking at it from God's perspective. The greater perspective is very important, because we usually think we have to do something to get out of the situation. Often what people present with a problem is a sense of victimization. Part of the reframe is to ask, "What is this a consequence of? What is my role in that?"*

> If one's realization stabilizes, even just a little bit, the experience of the world is of appearance, coming from and made of this shining consciousness. Then a kind of humor toward one's participation in that world occurs, because it's seen for what it is rather than what we're conditioned to respond to it as.
>
> — David Deida

The Body as an Instrument

Michael Murphy, the co-founder of the Esalen Institute in Big Sur, California, is also the author of *Golf in the Kingdom*. Murphy has played competitive sports his whole life. "I wrote golf reference books," he told me. "I probably know more about peak experiences on golf courses than any person who has ever lived." For Murphy, any physical activity, from golf to wrestling to dance, is ultimately a means to express our latent divinity. He sees all sports as being "overdetermined." You might start running because the doctor tells you to or to help you quit smoking:

> *Pretty soon, you can't eat so many steaks. You want to be lighter, and steaks are just too heavy. So you pick up more motives. You start to feel better. Vanity kicks in. You look better, people are complimenting you, and you want to*

look even better. You work out every day. It becomes a positive addiction. You get addicted to feeling good. Whatever your motives are at the beginning, you deepen and broaden your motives. Behind it all is the drive for Divine Expression: the ultimate good, the ultimate ecstasy, the ultimate power, the ultimate beauty, the ultimate love.

George Leonard, an old friend of Murphy's, is best known for bringing aikido to the West. Aikido is his translucent work of art:

When I do one of those techniques, and really get it just right, the hardest possible strike feels just like a feather. If he hits this hard, or this hard, it's no difference; I do exactly the same thing and I feel no pain at all. It's just wonderful. And with randori — *that means multiple attacks when three or more people are coming at you as hard as they can and as fast as they can —*

that's where it really gets to be joyful. It's a state of not thinking. It has to do with what people call awakening, except it's in motion, rather than in stillness. In those moments, I can say I'm one with the universe. I'm not thinking — if I think, it won't work; if I look in the other person's eyes, it won't work.

> You are driven by many things; part of it is to wrest out of your soul what you were put on earth to do. That kind of passion helps in maintaining the ecstatic free imagination chute.
>
> — Alex Grey

In fact, if I look at anything in particular, it won't work, because if you stop to think in randori, *in about twenty seconds you'll be flat on your back.*

Sofia Diaz teaches yoga and sacred Indian dance in Boulder, Colorado. All of her work is based on a deeply translucent approach to the body. She describes her entire life's motivation as:

the obviousness of what people need to do with their bodies in order to be harmonious or commensurate with what they feel in their heart. This means approaching all bodily experience as kindling for the fire of your deepest realization or deepest yearning for realization. The actual practice is aligning the body into the lines of light that already live it, and feeling what the difference is between absolutely perfect light and what we tend to do with that light. The feeling of light is love.

Diaz believes that at all times we affect everything around us with the energy and movement of the body, whether we like it or not. She sees both Hatha yoga and dance as skillful means to bring more awareness to what we are actually expressing through the body, moment to moment, and to what degree that expression reflects our deepest heart in an honest way. For Diaz, this is not a question of mastering the perfect yoga asana, or the perfect dance form, but simply of restoring innocence and freedom of movement to the body so that it can become a vehicle of gifting:

> *It comes down to how much one is just present to what one is feeling in any given moment. Trust isn't perfection of movement, trust has to do with someone acknowledging that their movement is imperfect, but it happens to be the most they can give. That's what I call dance, it's offering the most that you possibly can through feeling the limitations of this moment completely. It's how aware you are, how you're perfecting reality through your bodily disposition and feeling. That engenders trust, and it is also what the greatest bodily art has come out of. It doesn't have emotions erased from it; it's actually the revelation of deep emotion, so deep that love is bled through every emotion and every healing experience of the moment. Dance does not have to do with perfecting your places of closure, but with giving your revelation, your realization in this moment.*

NUDGING ART INTO TRANSLUCENCE

Several of the artists I have interviewed also teach other people how to bring deeper translucence into art. Here are some of their suggestions:

NUDGE
Go Deep and Wait

Peter Makena advises us to relax all effort to make something happen, and to become quiet and wait for the impulse of creativity to come. In deep silence, in prayerful surrender, the songs sing themselves. It takes a quiet mind to hear them.

NUDGE

Break Boundaries

Dana Lynne Andersen suggests that her students paint on newspaper to get away from the idea of a blank canvas. Sometimes she gives people just eight colors, and two minutes to cover the paper. Not much time to think: "As an art teacher, I'm a midwife, a facilitator. You can gauge the process and tell, this person is ready to abandon the rules altogether, go for it. Just paint. You need a road from the inner to the outer, and once that's there, once you can get a feel for it, it's more about learning how to nuance it so you stay in it, and, when you start to get out of it, how to get back in it."

Whatever your medium of expression, find ways to catch yourself off guard, to allow your expression to be spontaneous.

NUDGE

Stay Fresh and in the Moment

Andersen also suggests being aware of "production mode." She gives the example of drawing a mountain. You can draw the mountain shape and then color it in, which immediately becomes an invitation to lose presence, to become repetitive. Instead she suggests that every movement can be filled with presence, even if it seems repetitive.

Be vigilant in your consciousness. You're taking the brush and you're following the curve of the mountains and you're flowing in; even if you're covering the same character, you're flowing it in. And if you have a line of a tree, you look at the tree, observe it, or feel the tree inside and you're letting each line be felt. And as soon as you start to fill in the leaves, you've come up with something that flattens.

PART THREE

COLLECTIVE TRANSLUCENCE

CHAPTER ELEVEN

THE WISDOM OF NOT KNOWING

Translucent Education

Jenny was halfway through her second year of college when she reached her limit. A business major, she would go to the library to read, and the words would just dance on the page; she'd lost the ability to make the symbols mean anything anymore. She lost weight, became nervous and jumpy, and even stopped sleeping. Finally, Jenny went to a counselor, who recommended she drop out for a year, which she did. At first, Jenny was disoriented. She had no idea what to do with herself. Then a friend encouraged her to attend a gathering of one of the teachers featured in this book. Jenny was introduced to self-inquiry and awakened to a dimension of herself that was limitless.

For a while, though, she continued to drift, not knowing what to do with her life. Then she discovered a number of different translucent practices. She explored the layers of unconscious beliefs she'd held about herself, about her world, and about why she was getting an education.

Two years later, Jenny went back to the university to finish her degree. This time her experience was completely different. She had a sense of direction, a sense of why she was alive. She was interested in finding practical means for expressing what she felt inside and became only peripherally interested in all the models and business approaches. As she describes it, she *returned to her university interested in how to harness and express her inner creativity rather than in how to adhere to external models.*

Jenny graduated with straight As, moved to California, and flourished as an entrepreneur. She launched several different businesses successfully by applying the tools and principles she'd acquired with her degree, but always in service of her own deepest truths.

The previous chapters primarily focused on how translucence affects an individual's actions, thoughts, and feelings. As these individuals move through their lives, influencing those around them, we also begin to discover translucent qualities in organizations. In this chapter we will explore the translucent approach to education, and how just a few translucent people can transform a much larger environment.

> People have two philosophies about education. One is that you come into the world as empty, or even negative, with a tendency toward evil and therefore children have to be shaped, developed, contained, and made into a good person. The other is that you are born naturally life affirming, learning oriented, and cooperative. We simply need to create safe learning environments, and students will naturally develop.
>
> — Jack Canfield

Linda Lantieri is the editor of *Schools with Spirit*, an excellent primer on translucent education. She has worked in mainstream education for more than thirty years in the New York area, advocating a translucent view of education. "To nurture the spirit," she says, "is to cultivate a realm of human life that is nonjudgmental and integrated. It is about belonging and connectedness, meaning and purpose."[1]

Lantieri differentiates between two possible approaches to education. The view we call Iago-based she calls "filling the pail." In this perspective, the child is seen as inherently empty, albeit a potential cog in the machine of established commerce. Education's first goal is to program children's as yet empty hard drives with those facts and time-tested formulas that will help them learn to earn and consume. The teacher has two connected roles: as the provider of knowledge, and as disciplinarian who will deal with the wayward tendencies in every child to rebel against this process of force-feeding.

In contrast, Lantieri calls the translucent view "lighting a fire." In this perspective, the child is seen as inherently full — of creativity, energy, play, and imagination. Translucent education provides the optimum soil in which these seeds can grow to maturity and blossom. The translucent teacher is a custodian, a midwife to this process of unfolding. Rather than stuffing facts and opinions into a child's empty brain, the teacher draws out potential creativity from within the child's full spirit. This, in fact, is the original meaning of the word *education*, derived from the Latin *educare*, "to draw out."

Jack Canfield, who worked for many years as a schoolteacher before becoming a chicken soup chef, describes these different systems:

> *Depending on which philosophy you adopt, you end up with two very different systems of education. One says, "We've got to control the little bastards, pump a lot of knowledge into them, which they probably don't want to learn but they need it. We've got to cultivate them." The other says, "Here are all these wonderful little beings, and our job is to create an environment where they can evolve and learn." The first one is the old system way, but it's shifting, little by little. As individuals change, the institutions slowly have to transform to contain them.*

SURVIVAL TRAINING

When we're caught in Iago's grip, life is about survival. We see the world as competitive and hostile and feel an obligation to prepare our children to make money, acquire the right skills, and to succeed. Hence the entire educational process is one of preparation. From kindergarten onward, every grade, with its accompanying tests and requirements, becomes the foundation for moving up to the next level. The danger of failure, of being held back, hovers over children from an early age.

In France, in the preparation of pâté de foie gras, geese are traditionally force-fed six to seven pounds of grain, three times a day, through a funnel wedged into their beaks. They suffer unimaginable pain. Finally, after weeks of agony, when the bird is no longer able to move, it is killed, and the gigantic liver, considered a delicacy, is removed. The practice

> Education is making kids into objects, little learning machines. It seems that the main purpose is to make them all give the same answer to the question, so as to make everybody the same. That's what you call a machine.
>
> — George Leonard

has recently been outlawed for its cruelty in many countries. Some feel it is hardly more cruel, however, than taking a small child, full of wonder and play and delight, and force-feeding facts and skills from a young age. Once that child becomes a teenager, the pressure shifts: make it into the right high school and the right college, get the right job, and succeed in life. Many of us, even having done well at every stage of the game, later end up asking ourselves if we ever consciously chose the direction our lives took.

Education is fueled by the drive for success. But who decides what that success should look like? Is it the young child? Or is it parents and society, full of ambitions, and an educational system, all dominated by the Iago trance? Even to begin to free ourselves from the confines of an Iago-based approach to education, we need to take the notion of success down from its pedestal. What does success really mean? Who provides the definition? Unless we restore this inquiry, for both children and their teachers, to the very core of education, we are left with an information machine, one that creates unimaginable pressure for everyone involved. The educational system has become increasingly polarized in recent years. At one end of the spectrum is an abundance of resources, support, information, teachers, coaching, and encouragement to do well. At the other, a child is "left behind."

Two seemingly well-meaning efforts have been made in recent years to bridge this gap between the over- and underprivileged in the United States.

> The primary emotion these days is fear: I'm gonna get caught, I didn't do homework, I've failed a test, It's not okay to be me. God forbid you're gay or creative or on the feminine end of the continuum, or you want to grow long hair, have an earring, and be in the arts instead of play football.
>
> — Jack Canfield

The Head Start program, initiated in the mid-sixties, endeavors to "increase the school readiness of young children in low-income families." While this sounds like a great idea, when we seek to define and implement such an idea, as often as not it translates into "read and write at an ever-younger age."

The No Child Left Behind program of 2002 sets uniform standards and testing across the nation, for children from all incomes and cultural and linguistic backgrounds. The program seems logical, if you view education as purely and simply a way to train children to perform specific standard tasks. Then success is measurable: they must read by five, write essays by seven, and perform specific math tests by nine. But according to the educators I talked to, the program has created more problems in schools than it has solved. School is reduced to a means of testing performance, for administrators, teachers, and children. And the values that determine the specific content of those tests are all drawn from the Iago-based society as we know it, rather than from a vision of how we could be living.

The Problem of Relevance

Jill Moss has been a schoolteacher for more than thirty years. She has taught in both the mainstream educational system and in a more translucent alternative. Moss described to me the specific problems created by an approach based on standardized testing.

> The basic idea of today's education is to make everyone the same; it's hope breaking. It's not expanding the ability of children to explore and find out new things, to discover the essence of existence; it's just so they can get the same answers that everybody else in that class is going to get to the standardized question. And that is a tragedy.
>
> — George Leonard

The paramount problem is one of relevance. When teachers are obliged to enforce a curriculum aimed at reaching specific test scores, the entire process becomes irrelevant, removed from anything interesting to that child. When information loses obvious relevance, children rebel, not because they are bad or because they intrinsically want to sabotage their own welfare, but because they have no natural motivation to participate. As long as the test result is more sacred than the child, the only solution is discipline: to enforce the curriculum through punishment and reward.

As a child I was required to learn Latin, Greek, and French at school. At first I had no energy for any of these languages, for a simple reason. My immediate needs were to communicate with my friends, my family, and my teachers. I could do that in English. My life was in no obvious way changed or improved by learning to say the same things in a language spoken in another place by other people, much less by people who had been dead for more than two thousand years. Then I went to France for two weeks. I was able to put the little French I had learned at school to a useful purpose, like ordering ice cream. I learned as much French in those two weeks as I had learned in years of academic rote learning and testing. As a teenager, I visited Italy. Then I got the point of Latin; it was close enough to Italian to become relevant. I could talk to beautiful girls. That was useful. I never made the jump with Greek, simply because it remained a topic whose only logical purpose was to help me pass tests and avoid punishment.

The problems of irrelevance are almost all solved as soon as learning is laid at the feet of a child's creative expression. Anything they learn that allows them to actualize the latent creativity locked within them, which they have an inward motivation to express, will be relevant and will therefore not require discipline or forcing on the teacher's part.

When children do not feel engaged in the educational process, when they fail to see the relevance of information or testing, all kinds of other problems face school administrators and teachers. Truancy rates go up when students feel they have no chance to succeed at performance tests. They are less likely to pass the tests if they do not study, and less likely to study if they have no natural yearning for the information because it appears irrelevant. Irrelevant information creates boredom, and teachers have to rely more on disciplinary measures to compel students to pay attention. Children are forced to choose to either conform to the standards and the information offered, or retreat into feelings of isolation and failure. Very often this dynamic creates an atmosphere of continuous conflict between peers: those who conform and those who rebel.

> I've never met a stupid child. I've met incredibly stupid and reductionist systems of education.
>
> — Jean Houston

Once children reach their teenage years, they are faced with two seemingly contradictory pressures. The first, which generally comes from teachers, family, and the educational system, is to succeed. This requires them to work hard and be highly motivated so that they will be able to pass test after test, to graduate to a university, and to pass more tests, all to get the right job, to make money, and to consume.

The other force generally comes from within students and from their peers. Students see the state of the world; they begin to discover that the notion of success they have been sold has a price attached. With greater access to a wide range of information, they discover a whole variety of new things about the world in which they are preparing to participate. Rapid extinction of animal species, corrupt corporations and governments, global warming, increasing economic disparity between the rich and the poor: all lead teenagers to question the validity of succeeding within a system that has gone mad. The overall effect of waking up to the realities of the society they are preparing to join is a sense of meaninglessness. Jean Houston reflected with me:

> *Consider the problems that young people today are going to face — terrorism, global warming, worldwide unemployment, more than a billion people living in deprivation, disappearing soils and forests, oppressive governments and corporations, stratified economic systems that reward the most greedy among us. . . . What kind of education do we need to develop the skills to cope with a world in which so much can go wrong? Is going wrong? The world shadow is horrendous. It would be the greatest of tragedies, in the midst of the fact that we know so much now about the brain, about the mind, about spirituality, if we agree to a very limited vision of our possibilities.*

> The biggest dilemma in education today is the differing visions of what an educated person means. To do well on tests is often more important than helping young people really be prepared to deal with the tests of life.
>
> — Linda Lantieri

Today all high school students find themselves somewhere within this dichotomy. There are ways to blunt this sense of meaninglessness: drugs, alcohol, sex, even violence. But still both these pulls remain — to find the motivation and enthusiasm to participate or to deeply feel the Iago trance state of the world and to lose any sense of purpose. To the degree that a school is driven by Iago-based values, this polarity is more evident, and the student body more factionalized.

This split, both within and between students, came into a sharp and horrifying focus on April 20, 1999, in Columbine, Colorado, when friends Dylan Klebold and Eric Harris killed themselves, twelve of their fellow students, and a teacher and seriously injured twenty-two others. A year before, they had both completed a juvenile court diversion program, receiving high praise from their supervising officer. Dylan was described in the report as a "bright young man, who has a great deal of potential" and "intelligent enough to make any dream a reality." Eric's prognosis was "a very bright young man, who is likely to succeed in life. He is intelligent enough to achieve lofty goals."[2] Both boys came from affluent families: Dylan drove a BMW only a few years old. Both had access to the best facilities imaginable as well as extra classes out of school.

The question on everyone's mind in the aftermath of the shooting was, Why? When they had everything that less privileged children might dream of, what would lead two boys to commit mass murder and suicide? The answers are not as deeply hidden as one might imagine. Psychologists Patricia Greenfield and Jaana Juvonen investigated the events leading up to the tragedy. They reported that "bullying and victimization were not just individual phenomena, they were part of the school culture at Columbine High."[3] Former students at the school reported "a lot of tension between groups, almost continuous conflict, anything from verbal abuse to attacks and violence."[4] As in almost every school, this tension was between the highly motivated high achievers in sports or schoolwork and those who did not fit in and were ostracized as "weirdos" or "creeps."

> Columbine was symptomatic. It was the tip of the iceberg of a much bigger phenomenon that may not lead to violence or suicide, but may lead nevertheless to a pervading sense of depression and meaninglessness, which is just as insidious.
>
> — Linda Lantieri

Harris was described only a few years earlier as "a motivated young man, interested in many things."[5] He never missed a creative writing class. He acted in school plays and made his own video films. But his alienation from others, his experiences of not fitting in, led him to channel his creativity into hatred. His diaries are full of tremendous resentment toward the establishment, toward our present economic structure, toward the government, toward corporations, and particularly, in his immediate environment, toward other students who appeared to conform and succeed, whether in class or in sports.[6] "I hate you people," he wrote, "for leaving me out of so many fun things."[7] Klebold also excelled at school and had even picked out a room at a college dorm. But he too filled his diaries with accounts of not fitting in, being frequently depressed, and hating his life and existence. Both boys wrote repeatedly of Columbine as a "worthless place" and of their lives and the world around them as meaningless.

It is easy to dismiss these two teenagers as evil or mad, to blame their families, lack of gun control, the media, or even gothic music bands. But many see Columbine as symptomatic of a much more pervasive malaise. Similar incidents have erupted in other parts of the country, as well as in Europe. Violence in schools is an extreme result of the dominant paradigm in education, one that creates a profound feeling of failure and irrelevance in students and that makes conforming and getting ahead more important than self-expression. "The school culture — not just individual behavior — must be changed," Greenfield and Juvonen conclude. "Schools must moderate their obsession with academic standards and achievement and be given resources to adopt preventative programs."[8] As we will see, to be effective, such a shift in priorities must begin long before children's resentment has hardened into adolescent rage, as it did with Harris and Klebold.

Children are not the only victims of an Iago-based educational system. Faced with the daunting prospect of forcing children to perform in tests they resent, many teachers suffer above-average levels of stress and a high rate of job turnover, and many opt for early retirement. Even though schools contain some of the most creative and generous people in our culture, curriculum requirements can make teaching a thankless task.

> We've got more than anyone in the world, we've actually got what belongs to other people in the world, and with all that, people are suicidal, so what's wrong here? That's the question to pose to our whole culture. We've lost our sense of connectedness, of belonging to ourselves and to one another.
>
> — Linda Lantieri

SPIRITUAL MYTH #15: After a spiritual awakening, there is no need to learn anything; you already are everything.

TRANSLUCENT EDUCATION

Translucent educators have a profound intuition, based on direct experience, of their own deeper nature. They have discovered their luminous core to be an infinite source of creativity and light. When you know yourself to be full, it is natural to see that same fullness around you, to see young children as whole, intuitively knowing what is right and good. The educator who is more awake simply provides the context to evoke this innate brilliance.

Translucent education begins from this premise. Rather than viewing a child as unprepared and unresourceful, needing to be filled with knowledge to be able to survive, translucents recognize that children are born with a natural curiosity, interest, and creativity. Neither force nor discipline is needed to wake up this innate brilliance; it simply has to be seen, respected, and harnessed.

A translucent educational model encourages children to question, to create, to become learners rather than knowers. Rather than preparing children to participate in the existing economic and social system, translucent educational environments help children to question the status quo, and so prepare them to change it. It creates awakened co-creators instead of somnambulant consumers. Jean Houston observed:

> Education that is hands-on, experience-rich, that calls forth the whole mind and body of each child, and develops human, mental, spiritual, psychological capacities. These are the tools I believe can allow us to cope with the transition we're in. Schools can lead the way, providing a model for education continuous throughout life. Schools at all levels can teach us, and allow us to find our hidden potential that will enable us to explore the morass of our present time.

At the core of a translucent educational environment lies a reverential respect for each child as sacred and unique, and for each child's gifts as distinctly her own, not to be reduced to the conformity of standardized testing. This approach respects the essential divinity of each child as the source of wisdom as much as the recipient of knowledge. It respects the mystery each child embodies, as a living representation of something far deeper and more alive than any syllabus could ever solidify.

> What nurtures is age-appropriate learning that doesn't push, not a kind of abstract intellectual learning too early, but one that allows them to explore their senses and develop their imagination in a time when that's what's natural and appropriate.
>
> — Eric Utne

For Lantieri, translucence means bringing spirit into education. She makes the vital distinction between religion and spirit: "Religion can be an expression of one's spiritual nature, but many people nurture the spiritual dimension of their lives without adhering to a specific religion. Spiritual experience cannot be taught. But it can be uncovered, evoked, found and recovered."9

The blurring of this distinction between religion and spirit has been the greatest impediment to bringing more translucence to education. Of all those I interviewed for this book, more had a background in education than in any other field. Educators are, on the whole, a more translucent community than, say, people in the military or in business. The challenges of bringing translucence into education are not due to a lack of translucent parents or teachers but to an entrenched bureaucracy with fixed notions of what education can and cannot include.

We can find vibrant examples of translucent schools springing up, like shoots of grass through the concrete, all over the United States and in Europe. Many, like the ones in which Lantieri's work has had such an impact, are to be found right in the heart of the mainstream system, and often in less privileged areas. Two other movements, both of which have gained ground in recent decades, have provided a particularly fertile soil for translucent schools to flourish: one is the Waldorf system of education created by Rudolf Steiner, and the other is the charter school movement. Both have attracted translucent parents and teachers like bees to honey, and we have even begun to see these two models overlap.

> I started teaching high school in 1968. What's going on now compared to then is like night and day. Back then you couldn't do yoga; now it's being done all over the place. You couldn't talk about quiet time/meditation; now there are a whole lot of places where you can do that. It's very spotty, and it's not like you can call it a national phenomenon, but I've trained thousands of teachers over the years who are doing this stuff.
>
> — Jack Canfield

Waldorf Education

Rudolf Steiner, an Austrian philosopher and teacher, began his exploration of a new model of education by accident. He was hired as a tutor to the four sons of a wealthy Viennese family. One of those boys, Otto, had a severe learning disability. He had already been labeled unfit for schooling. Steiner saw something deeper in Otto; he saw the boy's essence and knew that he had great potential. Steiner believed his task was to bring Otto back in touch with his body and knew he could only do so by gaining the child's respect and love. Steiner was successful, and Otto went on to become a doctor. This experience created the basis for Steiner's educational philosophy: that the human soul and spirit are deeply connected with the body. The nurturing of this connection became primary to Steiner, far more important than rote learning. After World War I, the Waldorf Astoria Cigarette Factory, in Stuttgart,

Germany, invited Steiner to start a school for their workers based on these principles, and the first Waldorf school was created. Today there are more than 150 Waldorf schools in the United States, and over nine hundred in the world, more than double the number ten years ago.[10]

Waldorf education is grounded in respect and love. The first question Steiner asked the students in his schools was "Do you love your teacher?" and the first question he would ask the teacher was "Do you love the children?" Waldorf teaching methods respect the natural developmental steps that a child passes through, waiting for a child's thirst for learning at each stage to kick in before meeting it with skills or information. Up until the age of nine, children are encouraged to enjoy the fantasy world of childhood and teaching happens through stories and mythology. Children are taught a wide variety of skills using their hands: knitting, crocheting, painting, drawing, and woodworking, as well as exercises to encourage coordination of the mind and body. Children learn to play the recorder and the violin. Great emphasis is placed on color and texture. A Waldorf classroom is permeated with soft colors and lighting; it is comfortable and inviting. It is not until after the "nine-year change" that emphasis is placed in earnest on reading and writing.

From the mainstream perspective of preparing children to compete in today's technological world, school inspectors might throw up their hands in disbelief to see the kids learning about Norse gods and medieval tales, and acquiring skills like cooking, knitting, gardening, and music, when they can barely read at eight years old. Children in first through fourth grades perform well below the average in standardized tests. But patience pays off. By waiting until a natural curiosity about the world kicks in, Waldorf teaching methods create much less resistance than other models. Truancy is almost nonexistent; in fact, students beg to go to school, even when they are sick. By the time Waldorf children reach seventh or eighth grade, they perform in the ninetieth percentile on state tests and their enthusiasm and self-confidence are through the roof.[11]

> The protection of childhood is so critical to the future of humanity and the world. If we don't lay the foundation for these beings to unfold their gifts and be free human beings, then our hope for the future is really jeopardized.
>
> — Terry-Anne Paquette

Teachers in the Waldorf system stay with the same group of children from first through eighth grade, so they grow together as a community of friends. The relationship grows deeper than that of educator and pupil, and in many of the schools I investigated, the teachers take extended field trips with their class, sometimes even becoming part of the child's extended family. They become friends and mentors to a group of children they will know deeply for eight years.

Innovative educational alternatives such as this were, until a few years ago, the prerogative of those who could afford private education. That changed with the implementation of charter schools in the United States. In the late 1980s, a research project compared academic standards throughout the world. One might assume that the United States, as the wealthiest and often most smug global presence, would rank close to first, but in fact it ranked twenty-sixth, after most European nations. As a result, some local school boards created "charters," giving small groups of teachers the freedom to explore innovative, alternative models of education, which could then be tested. In 1991 Minnesota passed the first charter school law, enabling the development of schools that fostered "opportunity, choice, and responsibility for results." California followed in 1992, and there are now charter school laws in forty states.

> Schools that are turned on and awake do exist in pockets here or there. There are more and more, but often are only available to a small number of people. With the separation of church and state, when we threw out religion we threw out spirituality. I think that's a huge distinction that American culture hasn't learned to make yet.
>
> — Jack Canfield

A Translucent School

In 1993 Terry-Anne Paquette was running a preschool out of her home in the Sierra Nevada foothills in California. She looked at the alternatives facing the kids as they entered the school years. The wealthier families could afford the local Waldorf school, one of the best and oldest in the country, while the one-size-fits-all information-feeding machine awaited the rest. She and a group of other translucent educators gathered together to see if they could create a public school that would respect the sacredness of each child. They applied to the superintendent of the Grass Valley School District, and their first meeting filled the town gymnasium with families eager to participate. Initially their proposal was accepted by the school district. Until things took a turn:

That very night, there was a closed-session meeting of the school district board. They fired the superintendent of schools who had accepted us, and called us the next day to say our school had been canceled. They didn't really talk about the needs of children; they only talked about business. That was new for us; we were used to having our focus on the child. Just looking at the whole child is critical. My experience of working with the government, with the school districts, is that they were not in that place at all, and it made it even more critical in my mind. My goodness! Not only are they not looking at the whole child, they're not even talking about children at all!

Thirty families were prepared to enroll their children in kindergarten. "We will have a school," Paquette told them. They were finally accepted by a neighboring school district with declining numbers, and so the Yuba River Charter School was formed in 1994, the first public charter school in the United States to combine Waldorf and mainstream teaching methods.

In 1998, when I first visited the school, I cried. It embodied everything I had longed for in my own schooling and that had been sorely missing. As I visited each classroom, I found children obviously happy to be there. The walls were painted in soft colors, often with several shades blending onto one another. I saw first graders playing their flutes under the tall pine trees, I saw second graders cooking together, with dedication as well as laughter. In the eighth grade, the teacher sat on his desk, pondering a student's question. This balding, rosy-cheeked man had no apparent need to impose an authoritarian discipline on his students; the teenagers in his class were relaxed, fully engaged in the topic they were chewing on together. I enrolled my own children for the following year. To research the chapters on business and health care I've traveled far and wide, but to discover a vision of translucent education, I only had to visit the principal after giving my sons a ride to school.

American schools often recognize "honor students," children who have

> We want children to experience, with their heads, hearts, and hands, the whole sweep of human consciousness. From the very beginning of the dreamtime, to the Industrial Revolution, they have a picture of humanity that they have discovered through practical work, through stories and the experience of going out in the world with their class and doing things.
>
> — Terry-Anne Paquette

excelled academically in some way. Some schools even provide parents with a bumper sticker or license plate frame: "My child is an honor student at Hometown High." In contrast, the license plate frames for sale to parents in this school office read, "Every child is an honor student at Yuba River Charter School." At Yuba River, they have gone to extraordinary lengths to help every child feel unique, included, and valued for who he is more than how he scores. Paquette talked of a recent incident in which a boy, Johnny, was sent to her office after a "big tiff" in the schoolyard:

A boy got hurt. Johnny apologized to him, but he was in tears and totally in despair, so Johnny came up here so we could have a talk about it. Of course I told him it shouldn't happen again. I asked him if he understood, and all that . . . but what is most important for a child to remember is that we are all good people here. We are part of a whole, we can look at how we can do it better next time, and talk about that. Maybe there's a letter of apology that needs to be written. Yes, the parents will have to be called, because someone was hurt, and we will have a meeting, but it's not that anyone is bad. It doesn't help if the child doesn't feel good about himself or herself; then they can't move forward, and they stick themselves in a box, which gets harder and harder to get out of.

> When you have art in the curriculum, you are also going to have a sense of the whole person being deeply involved in the creation of their own mind.
>
> — Jean Houston

Freeing children from boxes seems to be the name of the game here: "We do the same with schoolwork. If a child is struggling, rather than labeling them or treating them as different, we have a tutoring program set up so they can be helped right away and get back into the classroom."

Preserving the Divine Essence

Steiner's primary question to his early teachers, "Do you love the children?" has been preserved to this day. Eric Utne, best known for his progressive magazine, the *Utne Reader*, trained as a Waldorf teacher himself after seeing miraculous results in his sons at a Waldorf school:

As teachers, we are encouraged to consider each child just before we go to sleep at night, to hold them in our consciousness, in our dream life, and to ask for help. We are searching to see the essence in that child, who they really are. I wouldn't claim to be able to see that on demand, but I see a little glimpse in my students of who they are going to be. I have become convinced, after a couple of years of teaching now, that this is the job of a teacher. That is what we are here for, to learn to see this archetype in each other, and in ourselves. I think that is what is missing in conventional education.

During my interview with Paquette, she reached into the corner of her office and grabbed a long walking stick, made from the branch of a tree. Gnarled here and there, not perfectly straight, it had been sanded down to a perfectly smooth finish. "Let me tell you the story of this stick," she said:

I first met Josh when I was teaching kindergarten, here at the school. He was on Ritalin; he was a wreck. From the beginning, I suggested to his parents that he come off the medication. I also asked that they eliminate all television and electronic games. I said he needed to get out and dig in the ground and play. I had to carry him to the school assemblies, as he wouldn't go on his own, it was just too intense. But he'd get there, and then he'd love it.

> Children have a mind, emotions, imagination, and intuition. They have a creative impulse, a will that they need to learn to harness, and they have a self. We need to teach them how to be aware of, appreciate, accept, express, and learn to control, those aspects of themselves. We also need to align them with their "high self" or "soul."
>
> — Jack Canfield

Josh is in the sixth grade now and doing great. He still has his problems; just the buttons on his shirt could bother him! He's just one of those people who is very sensitive. But he is brilliant and interesting, and he's fabulous. Now his mother runs our preschool program, and his father is on the school council. They are very dedicated to the school because of what has happened.

At one point I said to his dad, "Josh needs to do something with his hands. He needs to be in nature, doing some activity regularly with you, every day." So when he graduated from two years of kindergarten, they presented me with this walking stick. Josh and his dad had gone and cut it, and he had sanded and sanded and polished and polished. So now I keep it in here to remind myself of what can happen. The miracle.

Translucent schools like Yuba River are full of miracles. They create an atmosphere that allows every child, from the most gifted to the most challenged, to be valued as essentially good and whole, as making a unique and essential contribution. A father was carpooling a group of children to the school. Prompted by his own competitive school days, he asked them, "So, who is the smartest in the class?" The kids looked at each other, a little confused. Finally one of them said, "Well, Jeremy is the best at math, Ruth Anne is the best recorder player, oh, and Hannah is the best storyteller, and, yes, John is the best artist." Soon everyone in the class had been mentioned. Together they created a whole. Translucent parents and teachers tend to recognize that all children, indeed all human beings, are distinct expressions of the same creative source. Each contributes unique strengths and weaknesses. In this way, standardized testing seems a superficial and limited, if not irresponsible, way to address the sacredness of the blossoming child.

> The children being born today are different. We need to interfere as little as possible. Our education system is designed to contaminate them. It's designed to reduce their potential, to take away their creativity.
>
> — Paul Lowe

HOLISTIC EDUCATION

Translucent schools emphasize the development of the whole person more than the acquisition of specific skills. The curriculum often includes activities that activate the connection between the deeper spirit of the child, the brain, and the body. Knitting, crocheting, and specific physical exercises all integrate the left and right sides of the body, which research has demonstrated activates the whole brain. In the Novato Charter School, north of San Francisco, one year the children in second grade grew their own wheat, threshed it, ground it, and then baked bread with it. In third grade they built a small house together, from the foundation to the shingles on the roof. On the last day of third grade, Molly ran to greet her mother: "Mom, I can do everything now. I know how to make my clothes, I know how to build my house, I know how to make my food." There is an infectious satisfaction in this feeling of "I can do it," very different from the familiar "Oh, I'm so bad at math, I'm never going to get my times tables, I'm failing in my tests, What's this all about anyway, It's so boring and what does it mean to me?" Says Eric Utne: "Many of the students in this kind of school come away feeling like they can do anything. When they get to college, they are shocked by their contemporaries who don't have that attitude. They have the expectation that life is something they can really participate in; it is not going to overwhelm them."

A school infused with translucent vision sets the stage for a sense of empowerment and lifelong learning. It used to take decades, or even centuries, for new discoveries and inventions to change the way we live. Today, much technology becomes outdated in eighteen months, and our lives are run by innovations that were unimaginable even a few years before. A holistic education trains the child to be a flexible and open learner, in an ongoing relationship to a changing world, while an Iago-based system only emphasizes knowledge. "In times of rapid change," said Eric Hoffer, "it is the learners who inherit the future. The learned usually find themselves equipped to live in a world that no longer exists."[12] Training to be a learner means learning to meet each new moment in a way that is open, intelligent, responsive, with a wisdom that runs deeper than beliefs and information. You learn how to remain endlessly able to learn and adapt. There is no point in passing on to children the ways we have done things before. Most of them have proven not to work very well. Better to equip children to change the world with a fresh and flexible intelligence than to prepare them to produce and consume in a system that is in any case dying.

> I'm passionate about the use of theater in the classroom. If children play something out in theater and drama as part of the curriculum, practice social behaviors from comically disastrous to courtly, they internalize appropriate behavior.
>
> — Jean Houston

Many translucent schools incorporate music, theater, and art into the curriculum as a way to allow children to fully realize their potential. Studying the theory of music as well as playing specific instruments even enhances abilities crucial for both engineering and computation. Says Houston:

Why do children in southern India show such ability in both math and music? It has to do with the ragas, which fill the air, the complex rhythmical and tonal patterns that call forth the geometries of the mind, the algebras of consciousness.

If you give children singing lessons and keyboard instructions, their mathematic abilities soar. If you have them using their whole mind-body psyche, their spirit rises, their self-esteem, their sense of the moral flow of the universe. The highest scores in science for children through ninth grade are in Hungary, of all places, because until recently they had the most intensive school music program in the world.

Dance energizes the whole system, stimulates the mind and body. Houston told me of a recent study in Southern California, conducted in 250 elementary schools, which showed that students improved significantly with language arts when movement and dance activities were expanded. Theater allows children to act out stories and poems to internalize specific behaviors. When they enact history, rather than just read about it, they internalize huge lessons from our collective maturation of thousands of years. They learn greatness through imitation. When a child plays Caesar or Juliet, the brain is transformed. What begins as a metaphor engages the mind in spectacular ways. Houston feels we can learn a great deal about holistic education, not only from playing Shakespeare's characters but also by feeling into what kind of man this must have been:

> The heart is where you have to make the child. It sets the stage for empowerment, for lifelong learning. They feel "I can do it, I can do anything." They are there. They have had the village around them, with the festivals and the parents helping.
>
> — Terry-Anne Paquette

Why is Shakespeare Shakespeare? Why is there so much there? Why are there so many levels of understanding? He looms out of Elizabethan England with an astonishing abruptness. This is a man from someplace else, who has been touched by the shining light of consciousness. How on earth, and under heaven, can such a mind of incomparably greater powers than anything that had gone before him have so mysteriously appeared? From someplace else, from some great unbounded cavern of the soul.

Shakespeare's education was multidimensional. He performed in plays all the time; his education was not academic, but visceral. He grew up in a small pocket in time. The early seventeenth century was one of the most intellectually and artistically stimulating times the world has ever known, as society woke up from the superstitions of medieval theocracy. The lid was off every belief system. Kings and queens were intimately involved with scientific and literary fashion. It is, perhaps, the best parallel we can find to our present time of emerging translucence. Young Will was right in the middle of this human-istic transformation of education, performing multiple roles in both Latin and English, memorizing poetry, and developing and moving freely between an enormous inner library of characters, feeling, and settings. Houston goes on:

> To get a whole being that's healthy and alive and integrated has to do with letting the child follow their own intuition, learning how to trust their own bodies, to express but not be run by their emotions, to think clearly but not be run by the mind. Give them the skills that would make the world work better, teach them to trust themselves.
>
> — Jack Canfield

The best schools of all, the ones that I try to develop, are the schools where children run in delight and expectation. They are schools where learning is like Shakespeare's, learning is creation, performing, thinking across subjects, exploring ideas through images, sounds, songs, dances, artistic expression. Then children become like Shakespeare: myriad-minded, soulful, spirited, conscious participants in their own unfolding. Yes, they need to learn to read and write, but they are also encouraged to imagine, to dream, and to expand the limits of the possible.

Cultivating Compassion

The holistic vision expressed in translucent schools is not limited to more expansive ways of learning and creating; it also embraces the unfolding of the heart. Linda Lantieri co-founded the Resolving Conflict Creatively Program, an initiative of Educators for Social Responsibility, which teaches children, teachers, and administrators about the possibilities of living beyond separa-tion. Her program is now taught in four hundred schools nationwide. Right after Columbine, she was interviewed extensively.

For one interview, Lantieri asked to bring in a fifth grader from a school where she had been sharing RCCP, in an economically disadvantaged part of New York City. His name was Mark. The interviewer asked Mark about Columbine: "Two kids killed a lot of other kids. They never told anyone what was going on for them. What would have happened if that were your school?" Mark paused for a while, silent. Then he said, "Well, you know, I'm having a hard time figuring out how that could happen at our school. Because those guys were angry and upset. If that happened at our school, we would go over to those kids and say, 'Brother, something's happening for you. You've got some really strong feelings that you need to talk about, to get out. Do you think you should go to mediation?' But I probably wouldn't stop there, because if he'd never been to mediation, he probably wouldn't go. So I would tell one of the adults in the school what was going on for this boy." The interviewer asked him whom he would tell. "I would tell one of the adults who cared." The interviewer pressed on: "Who is the adult you were thinking of?" And Mark said, "Well, sir, I don't have to think of one adult, all the adults care in my school."

During a training session in another elementary school, Lantieri was on her way to the bathroom during a break, when she overheard two fourth-grade boys talking. One was comforting the other, who was crying, saying that another kid had said he was going to beat him up the next day. The boy who was listening exclaimed, "Wait a minute, wait a minute. I know what's happening here, this kid must be new to our school!" Their school had implemented Lantieri's program, creating such a different sense of community that this small boy couldn't even imagine one schoolmate threatening another. "He must be new." That was the only explanation.

When kids leave schools such as these they will have a whole set of innate assumptions about what kind of world they can live in, and what kind of world they can create. They know what is possible. Lantieri has endless success stories like this. They demonstrate how one motivated translucent person can have a huge impact on a community. As later chapters will demonstrate, whether in business, health care, politics, or education, one person with a proactive translucent vision can cause a community to shift dramatically in a more translucent direction. We are all, underneath the layers of our Iago conditioning, natural translucents. We simply need a nudge.

> Cultivating a child's social and emotional skills is much more important than pushing their abstract reasoning and rational skills. Those tend to come along naturally with the children's ability to manage their own emotions, to be aware of what they're feeling, and to be aware of what others are feeling.
>
> — Eric Utne

Lantieri, who works primarily with underprivileged children in New York City, has seen how her program can have a ripple effect on the community at large. She told me this story:

Seneca lives on the seventeenth floor of a housing project in the South Bronx. Every day, when he took his younger brothers and sisters to school, they had to pass drug dealers sitting near the elevators. Seneca hated it that his little siblings had to see this every day. We taught him the RCCP skills to create win-win solutions. The next morning, he approached the dealers and said, "I can't tell you what's right or wrong here, but I'm going to ask you if you would be willing to do your thing on another floor. I take my brothers and sisters to school every day, and I hate for them to see this as an example." They didn't say much to him, but the next day they weren't there, or the next day. Two weeks later, they still had not come back to his floor. "I still don't sleep that great at night," Seneca told me. "Now I'm thinking about the kids on the sixteenth and the eighteenth floors, because that's where they probably went."

He was not only learning skills to help him stand up for himself, he was doing something that even to me, as the facilitator, seemed impossible. He began to realize that this wasn't only about skills for himself, but about a change for everybody. He awoke within himself a commitment to social action.

> Today we approach the classroom a little differently. Kids start trusting themselves more. Now they do yoga, they get in touch with their bodies more. As individuals transform, the institutions slowly have to transform to contain them.
>
> — Jack Canfield

The School as Community

It is not only the children who benefit from a more translucent educational model. When we shift the emphasis of education to one that respects the whole person and that draws out each child's brilliance, a teacher will meet almost no resistance to learning. Being a teacher changes from a highly stressful job to a deeply rewarding one. Carol Nimick sees teaching as her vocation. She takes her group of twenty-six children on several trips a year, sometimes involving two or three nights, organizing transportation, food, and a full itinerary. She produces several plays each year with the class, with costumes, scenery, and several packed performances. While her time in the classroom lasts from eight till three every day, she is often still at the school in the early evening. During vacations, she is preparing handicraft projects and other materials to make her classes more engaging. When the state of California went through budget cuts in 2002, she voluntarily took a reduction in pay to help the school survive, funding many extracurricular activities out of her own pocket. But she feels like a winner: "I get rewarded in so many ways by these children," she says.

Running a school is a challenging affair. Yuba River has been faced twice with lawsuits from right-wing religious groups, as well as with severe financial pressure. I asked Terry-Anne Paquette what most helps her to keep going, what are the moments when she knows it has all been worthwhile. She mentioned the festivals, which happen four times a year. The whole community comes together on these days: children, teachers, administrators, parents, and visitors:

I remember the harvest festival. Alistair was playing his fiddle, Karen had her big drum. All the children of the whole school made a big parade, bringing things they had brought for the food bank, to help less fortunate people in our community. They brought it up to a gorgeous table the parents had prepared; so many parents were there to receive the food on behalf of the community. Some adults started dancing, and the children joined in. Even the teenagers were dancing, which is quite unusual; they are usually so self-conscious. There was a play performed by the second grade, and the fourth graders came as an enormous dragon, with forty legs. We ate food together; there were so many games everyone played together. It felt like the place where we had found our true nature, in those few hours. As I looked over that scene, I saw that we have a place, all of us, to discover our true potential together.

> Art-based education facilitates the capacity to travel in inner space through drama, music, and the potent richness of the language for the development of the whole child. Making that kind of education available requires a shift from the idea of cramming with facts and quick skills to help them survive in a me-against-them universe, to a view of education's purpose being not just the survival of the fittest, but a divine expression of sharing.
>
> — Jean Houston

All kinds of schools are emerging, all over the country, that offer this same context to discover human potential. We have focused here on Waldorf and charter schools, since they provide an obvious magnet for translucent

Steiner said the wound is the gift. When struggles are faced and met, they are going to be the greatest gifts. In my oldest son's class, he had several classmates who in any other system would have been labeled and categorized as having special needs. But they were always referred to among his class as just one of the kids; they weren't singled out as being different or disabled or handicapped in some way, and therefore they became healthy kids.

— Eric Utne

parents and teachers. But they only act as flag-bearers for the possibilities of a broader translucent influence in our schools. Linda Lantieri, Eric Utne, and thousands of other teachers and administrators give us a glimpse of an alternative to the dominant paradigm. Here is Jean Houston again:

If children can learn to self-orchestrate along a continuum of states of consciousness, traveling interior highways through realms of fantasy and imagination, and spelunking through caves of creativity, then they will discover how to focus, how to concentrate, how to have access to levels of high creativity, also to the space in which the personal self seems to disappear and one enters mind at large. It's a unitive condition in which you discover yourself to be the knower and the knowledge and the known.

I have met hundreds of families who have chosen such an alternative approach, and it is virtually impossible to find any who regret their decision. The majority of problems that plague conventional education simply evaporate. Truancy doesn't exist. Even excused absences are less than half of the state average, as kids in translucent schools want to be there every day. Disciplinary problems become less frequent and much less serious. Teachers stay for decades and feel replenished by the quality of contact they have with their children. And, most important, such schools are successful at the job they set out to do: to kindle the flame of confident inquiry, curiosity, and creativity in children, so they may grow up to be innovators of a new world rather than obedient participants in the existing one.

TRANSLUCENT HIGHER EDUCATION

The same differences we have described in schools can be found in colleges, where alternatives with a strong translucent influence are also emerging.

Stephen Dinan received his undergraduate degree from highly competitive Stanford University: "The average person going to Stanford had to have been at the top in his class; they are hardwired for high achievement. The dominant culture there is definitely oriented toward the next success or challenge, whether it's becoming a doctor or getting the top scores on the MCATS. It can be a playful culture, yet I felt a spiritual emptiness about the place."

Dinan describes himself as the typical type A personality when he got to Stanford: "Show me a mountain, and I'd run up it faster than anyone else. I had to be number one at everything. The first year, though, I got crushed. The place was full of geniuses from all over the country. I was no longer number one. My ego took a bashing."

In his second year, Dinan's best friend from high school was killed in a car accident. "It pulled the rug out from under my whole goal-oriented 'climb the ladder faster than the next guy' world. I had to ask myself, 'What am I doing all this for?'" After a period of disillusionment, Dinan discovered Tibetan Buddhist meditation, as well as many other methods, and experienced a radical awakening. At first he was disoriented. "When I stepped out of the rushing river of achievement there was a tremendous feeling of aloneness."

> Young people grow up with too little meaning, still committing suicide in large numbers, still having mental health disorders, mainly because they're also not able to fulfill the deeper aspects of what it means to be human.
>
> — Linda Lantieri

Dinan discovered that other students were also waking up from the achievement trance and questioning the ultimate purpose of academic pressure. There are, however, many factors built into higher education in the United States and other countries that promote a success-driven approach. Over the last thirty years, the cost of a college education has risen between 50 and 110 percent faster than inflation. More and more working families have difficulty paying for this education, even with assistance. Most students will graduate with a debt for which they are personally responsible. This increases the need to decide, early in the process, on a specific career path, such as becoming an attorney or a doctor, so as to be able to repay the loan. It discourages self-exploration or the development of the whole person.

Dinan was one of the few who chose to go on to a holistic school, one inspired by a translucent vision. He did his graduate work at the California Institute for Integral Studies: "CIIS has a whole different orientation. It is largely populated by people who have seen through the highly ambitious, achievement-oriented mainstream culture. Students there are seeking and exploring in a more introverted direction. CIIS does not have the rocket-thrust, the 'achieve the next, biggest, brightest' thing. It is more of an unwrapping, an unraveling."

> The best athletes cross train, and the same process applies in life. You can be rigorous about using tools for an extended period of time, without believing that any particular tool is going to take you to where you need to go. Instead of being loyal to a certain path, you start to become savvy about the process.
>
> — Stephen Dinan

After graduating from CIIS, Dinan wrote the book *Radical Spirit*, about translucent innovations made by people under thirty. He was involved in Dennis Kucinich's bid for the 2004 Democratic presidential nomination and works as a consultant with many environmentally, politically, and socially transforming projects. Like other translucent colleges, such as Naropa Institute in Boulder or JFK University in Pleasant Hill, CIIS creates graduates like Dinan, more of a renaissance man than a twenty-first-century specialist.

Joseph Subbiondo is the president of CIIS. He has a prestigious academic background, including positions as dean at Santa Clara University, academic vice president at the University of the Pacific, and dean at St. Mary's College of California. When he interviewed at CIIS in 1999 and first met the faculty, he was skeptical of their extraordinary enthusiasm. Many of them had been professors at some of the best institutions in the world and could earn much higher salaries elsewhere:

I was very curious as to why they would be here. I had some suspicion that what they were telling me was not so. They would tell me, it's the mission. Now that I've been here for five years, I can also say that it is the mission. I've never been with a group of faculty who are more committed to the mission of the institution than they are to their own discipline. Mostly, in higher education, if you're a philosopher, you couldn't care less where you taught philosophy just as long as you got to teach what you wanted to teach and you had decent students. Here, they want to teach philosophy within the context of this mission. It is the same with the students. I've never been in a community where vision is so much a part of the daily existence of the institution. We're very mindful of it. I don't believe I have been at an institution where I have felt more liberated than I feel here.

In our conversation, Subbiondo articulated the founding vision that makes CIIS so unusual and such a magnet for both distinguished faculty and students. He calls it an "integral vision," which he expressed to me in a number of ways:

1. It incorporates wisdom from both Eastern and Western roots: "As the founder of CIIS, Haridas Chadhuri, realized, the world will not know peace and unity until East and West understand and respect each other. That vision continues to address issues underlying the tensions and divisions that cause global instability at the present time. CIIS provides an integral education for changing the world; we're committed to the pursuit of meaning by integrating the wisdom and traditions of East and West."

    > We all have a drive to make an original contribution: a form of service and sharing, a way for a human incarnation to fulfill its destiny. As an educator I have a feeling of completeness, I have pulled together something from a certain aspect of my life, I've made that available, not just for myself but for anyone who's interested in it.
    >
    > — Stanley Krippner

2. It is a holistic education, exploring the integration of mind, body, and spirit: "So often in higher education it's not about the inner life. Here, we put a great value on inner life and reflection while maintaining academic rigor. For example, we begin many of our classes and meetings with a meditation."

3. It is a vision that seeks to integrate opposites: "There is a middle path — it's not either/or. We are interested in moving away from dualism, in looking at extremes and beginning to see what they have in common. We can envision a world that is enriched by an inclusive panorama of many cultures; CIIS honors diverse paths to knowledge."

4. Learning is seen in an evolutionary context: "Our core vision is that

consciousness is always in an evolving state; part of the role of higher education is to be able to track the stages of consciousness and to recognize that in its evolution we will, hopefully, arrive at a better place."

With this highly translucent vision, both as its founding mission statement and as its ongoing expression, CIIS attracts both translucent students and faculty. Subbiondo continues: "We are creating a collaborative community; we have committed, active, forward-thinking scholars and practitioners who hold to integral and transformative values and experience and are drawn from many parts of the planet. People are drawn to us because they really want to deepen themselves, to connect to others, and to transform the world."

CIIS boasts an extraordinary graduate body. John Paul Lenney, for example, is now the president of McGraw-Hill, one of the foremost publishers of textbooks in the country. At a recent alumni gathering, Lenney told Subbiondo that he feels that it was the kind of translucent education he gained at CIIS that empowered him to become who he is. He feels that it was the inner work, learning to listen well, to understand people in terms of their values, and, most important, that he was able to come to know himself. Other graduates include Jorge Ferrer, an authority on transpersonal psychology, Dan Hamburg, elected to the House of Representatives and now a political activist with the Green Party, and Mike Riera, an authority on teenage issues.

> What is learning? To learn is to change. Education is a process that changes the world. Or else it's not education.
>
> — George Leonard

The focus of a translucent school has shifted from acquiring specific worldly skills to the unfolding of the whole person. CIIS has helped hundreds of its students become licensed therapists and psychologists. Says Subbiondo:

If one is studying psychology at another college or university, even though there is a distinctive founding mission, I doubt very much that one is studying psychology differently than one would at any other place. But if you're studying psychology here, you are studying it in a different way because you not only can take courses in psychology, you are also able to choose from a full range of courses in social and cultural anthropology, philosophy, and cosmology. You have such a rich draw of electives from so many other programs and courses, you're going to have a richer education. Most important, you will be studying psychology informed by an East/West perspective.

Many of the students at CIIS take postgraduate degrees with concentrations in subjects like cosmology, philosophy, or East/West psychology: "They're not coming here to be a cosmologist, they are coming here to understand themselves better, and in doing that they will perform better at anything else that they attempt to do."

Typically, translucent schools like CIIS do not receive the same kind of funding as state schools do, and they are not cheap. A student who chooses this kind of educational model must have tremendous clarity, integrity, and commitment. In an Iago-based world that encourages separation above all, they are willing to place a high value on their own wholeness.

Linda Lantieri offers these ten important questions for educators in assessing how translucent a school is:

1. Is there a sense of community in your classroom?

2. Do you and your students feel comfortable sharing thoughts and questions about values, meaning, and purpose?

3. Do you encourage respect for diversity of opinions, beliefs, and cultural backgrounds among your students?

4. Are there opportunities in the school day or week to appreciate the beauty of a work of art or to allow students to make art — poems, pictures, sculptures, music, and drama — themselves?

5. Do you provide regular activities to explore and spend time in nature? Are elements from nature present in the classroom?

6. Do you and your students have ample opportunity through studying history or through storytelling to honor the power of ancestors and the past?

7. Is there some free time in the school day, including time for silence and reflection?

8. Do you have the flexibility to allow for moments of spontaneity in which intuition redirects a discussion or an activity?

9. Are there opportunities for students to become involved in volunteering or community or social action projects?

10. Do you and your students feel that most of what is being taught and learned is authentic, meaningful, and useful?

NUDGING EDUCATION INTO TRANSLUCENCE

More than anything else, any educational model that values the whole person as highly as specific skills encourages greater translucence.

NUDGE

For Parents

Consider these questions about your child's school:

Are the children valued for who they are as well as for what they achieve?

How much parent involvement is encouraged in the direction and vision of the school?

How much corporate influence is allowed?

Are teachers encouraged to take care of themselves, for example, with times for rest and stillness, yoga, or other means of regeneration? Does your child's teacher seem stressed or balanced?

Is the classroom, and the school generally, aesthetically pleasing? Do you feel soothed and calm there?

Are body-centered activities like dance, stretching, or even martial arts, part of the curriculum?

Are art, drama, and music respected as a powerful part of your child's life?

Are the children taught to resolve conflicts in a creative way?

NUDGE

For Teenagers or Young Adults Still in the Education Process

What kind of world do you want to live in?

What sort of world do you want to see in twenty or thirty years?

If the world continues on the course it is on now, can you relax and know this is as good as it gets?

What kind of contribution do you want to make?

What gift do you want to give?

Is your education helping you to deeply consider these questions and to find creative answers, or do you find yourself on a conveyor belt in an information machine?

Does the process of learning serve the unfolding of your gifts, or are your gifts subjugated to the process of learning?

NUDGE

For Teachers and Educators

Feel into the deepest unique gift of each child or student you are guiding. Do you love them for their hidden potential? Do you hold them in your heart?

Can you let the unique flame of each child, as it bursts forth in its own way, be just as important as any curriculum or test result or notion of where they should be by now?

Many of the translucent writers and teachers I have talked to view the schoolteacher as the most important caretaker of our mutual future. A teacher may have more influence on how we grow as a race than a politician or a priest. Just now, please receive my thanks, and the thanks of so many who care about our future, for what you have chosen to do with your life. Take very good care of yourself. It is a stressful job, and when your students remember you in years to come, it will be for the translucent brilliance that shines through you as much as for the facts and testable skills you are able to impart.

CHAPTER TWELVE

THE WAR IS OVER

Translucent Business

"If you lose a little money, or your credit cards are maxed out, you still can be in denial about it. But if you are in charge of a company that loses six or seven times its net worth in one deal, you can't deny that you are an idiot." David Neenan started his own architecture and construction company. Their first big contract was constructing an athletic club in Casper, Wyoming, for $1.5 million. They created a magnificent building, but it cost them $2.2 million. "I lost $670,000 on my first big job. We started out with $90,000 and ended up $580,000 in the hole. I didn't know what to do, so I tried to work out a plan with the bank and with my suppliers.

"The president of the bank asked me out to lunch, before he knew just how bad my situation was. Between the time he invited me and the time he took me, he found that out, so we went to lunch at a Burger King. He didn't even know how to order — he'd never eaten there before. He just didn't want to be seen with me.

"Everybody said, 'You should claim bankruptcy,' or, 'Hang up another shingle,' or, 'Leave town.' That's what most people do. Instead, I called a meeting of the employees. There were thirty of us then. I told them, 'I have no idea what to do.' I drew a picture of a tombstone on the flip chart, and I wrote 'knower rest in peace.' One of the employees said, 'So, why don't we work together?' And I said, 'You mean satisfy customers and make money with dignity in this industry?' And everybody started laughing. They said, 'Yeah, why not?' So I said, 'Hey, we've got nothing to lose. Let's try it.' All the ideas came from somebody else. I don't think I had an original thought at that time."

Within three months, the Neenan Company turned itself around and was making money. The company has gone on to become one of the most successful commercial construction companies in Colorado as well as a role model of translucent business.

Roger Bayliss is up before 7:00 every day. He grabs some breakfast and the paper before driving to the local station and taking the commuter train into Seattle. He gets to his job, at the corporate offices of an international retail chain, by 9:00. Lunch is often spent with sales reps. If he can get out of the building by 6:00, which is not every day, he's home by 7:30, just in time to kiss his two kids good night. He eats the plate set aside from the family dinner and often falls asleep in front of the TV, his way of unwinding, or at least trying to.

Roger will probably repeat this routine 250 days a year for close to forty-five years. Maybe more. Like most of those who have gone before him, by the time he retires he will probably be too exhausted to find anything else to do with his spare time. Roger will spend more than 135,000 hours in work-related activities in his lifetime, almost one-third of all his waking hours. Work is so central to Roger that the quality of his work determines the quality of his life. If his work is stressful, he will lead a stressful life. If his work is meaningless, even family and recreation will not compensate enough to allow him to live a full life. If his work is a compromise, simply a way to make ends meet, Roger will lose his sense of integrity. And, if Roger is lucky enough to work with integrity, with vision, in a way that calls forth and expresses his deepest translucent core, it is likely that these qualities will overflow into every other area of his life.

> Very few people in business will confess to their disappointment with where they are. In fact, they're always focused on the future, the next leap, because there's always something you can do next. Always.
>
> — Fred Kofman

Fred Kofman has worked with tens of thousands of people like Roger.

As the founder of Axialent, an international consulting firm, he works with companies like Shell, Microsoft, and General Motors. A founding member of the Business Domain of Ken Wilber's Integral Institute, Kofman sees "work" as the primary arena where translucence can manifest itself:

> It's fundamental. At the heart of translucence is the question: Are you going to put yourself in the hands of love or fear?
>
> — Anders Ferguson

Everybody works, except for a very few independently wealthy people. Work targets basic needs and puts us in touch with very primal feelings. Survival, your public identity, power, money, politics, it is all there. Work is a very ripe domain for people to play out their worst neuroses. Marriage is not that different, but you don't have to be in relationship. People can get sick and tired, and say "I'm out of here" for a couple of years. Very, very few people can say, I'm sick of this; I'm not going to work ever again.

Kofman is one of a growing number of visionaries working with corporations to bring more translucence into the workplace. I asked him what he could offer a CEO to be a more translucent business agent:

First, I would help them get in touch with their desire and commitment to become a more translucent agent of life. Then, I would invite them to see business as a realm where they can manifest that commitment, where they can offer their deepest gift, as opposed to a place where they go to get something. The main shift from opacity to translucence is going from acting out of fear and lack to acting out of love and fullness.

IAGO-DRIVEN BUSINESS

The great majority of business environments are dominated by fear. We use the same language in contemporary business as we do in warfare. We launch campaigns, we target a market, we develop strategies to attack the competition, strategies we guard like military secrets. If our offensives are successful, we "make a killing." This highly competitive environment, driven mostly by the male psyche high on testosterone, creates stress, stifles creativity, and encourages an atmosphere of crisis, distrust, and separation.

Although Kofman sees this atmosphere of Iago-driven fear and lack as pervasive in every business environment in which he works, he also sees the workplace as ripe with possibilities. He describes the Iago trance in business as a vacuum into which every participant is sooner or later unwillingly swallowed. A few lucky people, like artists, writers, and inventors, do what they are most passionate about, but the majority end up working for someone else and resenting it:

> Mullah Nasrudin, the wise fool of many Sufi stories, was eating a poor man's diet of chickpeas and bread. One of his neighbors approached him and said, "Mullah, why are you eating like this? If you only go and bow to the emperor, he will give you so much money that you'll never need to eat chickpeas and bread again." Nasrudin replied, "That's true, but if you only learn to eat chickpeas and bread, you won't have to bow to the emperor again."
>
> — Fred Kofman

The deepest separation I see in business is that people feel like they are missing something essential, and they believe they are going to get it from the outside. They need money to buy happiness, and they are going to earn it through meaningless work. They crave power to validate who they are, and they are going to get it surrendering to those in authority positions. They want respect, and they are going to get it by fulfilling other people's expectations. Of course, none of this works. They are trying to fill up an infinite black hole that swallows everything.

Kofman sees this black hole as an addiction. Driven by fear, Iago offers us the idea that the fear will stop when the hole in the soul has been filled. People sacrifice more and more, choosing jobs that are not really their calling. They act in ways that violate their deeper integrity for material reward or career advancement:

Every time we get what we think we want, there is a temporary blip of happiness, a temporary illusion that our strategy is working. The fear abates for a while, just long enough to validate the hope. Then, of course, the illusion collapses, and we start feeling as much fear as before. Over time we throw more and more life into this hole.

It's like renovating a house. You do more and more projects, and then at some point you get a nagging feeling that you built the house in a swamp or in an earthquake area. This is really a house of cards that will collapse. But you've invested so much money and energy, you can't even consider the possibility that your house will break down.

This pervasive atmosphere of fear and greed makes business a fiercely competitive environment, both within and between companies. *Their* failure is the collateral damage for my success. There are only so many senior positions to go around, only so many corner offices. Increasing our market share must inevitably leave less for others. The pie can only be cut so many ways. The results of working day in, day out in this kind of environment are no different from the results of being in a protracted war for a long time. Almost everyone Kofman works with in large corporations suffers from high levels of stress, the primary motivation for bringing in a consultant. Productivity goals and deadlines leave little room for relaxed playful creativity.

In a hierarchical chain of command, with superiors to please and limited seating in the boardroom, we are less likely to be honest or to behave spontaneously. An emergency environment creates distrust, separation, and competition within the company. Most companies encourage competitiveness. They set one employee against another, they give bonuses based on performance, and they may pay employees on commission. All these tactics encourage people to compete rather than support and co-create with each other.

> When you're acting out of fear and lack, you're trying to fill up a hole, a black hole eating anything around you. It feels like you're fighting for your life. Survival is a primary driver because you believe that if you don't sacrifice everything to the black hole, it will suck you in.
>
> — Fred Kofman

Statistics for both job absenteeism and rate of job change show a deep malaise at the heart of the corporate world. People at all levels of business complain to Kofman about feelings of meaninglessness at work, disconnection from co-workers, lack of empowerment in the direction the company is taking, and job insecurity in a workplace, where almost everything can be distilled down to the bottom line: profit. "Profits to a company are like oxygen to a human being," said Singer Russell Ackoff. "If you don't have enough of it, you are in serious trouble, but if you think that life is only about breathing, you're missing something."

Kofman reports that people at all levels of business suffer from two parallel fears. One is the fear of not having enough money to support their lifestyle. The other is the fear of being caught at the same rung of the corporate ladder and not progressing fast enough to a higher level in the hierarchy. Very rarely, he says, does that fear ever stop, no matter where you are in the organization: "Most people don't realize, until it's too late, that they're climbing a ladder leaning against the wrong wall. If you ever get to the top, then you realize that there's no happiness there. It's as old as humanity, this illusion that you're going to get something from the outside that is going to finally fill that black hole."

A plethora of business solutions are available. Most of them attempt to bring about a change in the external environment: to make it more relaxed and informal, friendlier. Better coffee, better doughnuts. Few make more than a superficial dent in the prevailing paradigm. If the core issues of meaninglessness and irrelevance are overlooked, if the business is still a juggernaut designed to reward shareholders, the central malaise in business goes unaddressed. You can rearrange the furniture in the cell as much as you like, but you are still in prison. Most business solutions, in Kofman's experience, are an attempt to make an activity that is essentially meaningless to the employees more palatable. But the meaninglessness itself is not being addressed. They are addressing symptoms rather than the cause.

> Humankind struggles and frets, but despite itself it gets pulled in a positive direction. Integrity is now becoming one of the mainstays of business. Those companies that lack integrity are falling by the wayside. Throughout the centuries, winning and gaining was the dominant yardstick for success. We have a new standard by which we evaluate things now.
>
> — David Hawkins

In this chapter we will explore several business interventions that move beyond cell decoration to significantly shifting the business environment from jail to temple.

SPIRITUAL MYTH #16: Business and spirituality are two separate arenas of life; it's inappropriate and embarrassing to mix the two.

SPIRITUAL MYTH #17: After any kind of spiritual awakening, money will flow easily and effortlessly into your life, with little or no effort on your part. In the words of Swami Beyondananda, "Everything I eat turns to money, and my drawers are full of cash."

SPIRITUAL MYTH #18: Money corrupts. Anyone with real spiritual integrity should not be concerned with money, success, or the world.

FERTILE GROUND

Anders Ferguson, founder in Spirit in Business and Uplift Equity Partners, has consulted with hundreds of corporations, large and small. He sees our world as dominated by four social systems: established religions, government, NGOs, and business. Of these four, he sees business as the most potent agent of change, first, because it is less tied to entrenched belief systems and written dogma than the other three, and second, because of the radical feminization of business, which we will address later in the chapter.

In fact, thousands of new businesses are springing up all over the world, and established ones are being transformed into instruments of translucent change. Judy Wicks, owner of the White Dog Café in Philadelphia, is hailed as a trailblazer for a new and conscious business. Despite phenomenal success with the restaurant, Wicks decided to limit the size of her operation to fewer than 150 employees. She feels that if the organization expands, it will no longer be family. Like many translucent business leaders, Wicks blends a high quality of product (food, in this case) with community service, consciousness-raising, and environmental awareness. In the summer, she brings her organic growers into the café, so customers and farmers can meet each other. She does her best to keep the same growers from year to year, buying organically from local farms. When you eat at the White Dog Café, you can read about where everything was grown, where the chickens (and their eggs) came from, how they lived, and what they were fed.

> When I look at translucent business I see companies that are concerned for the whole. They are trying to take care of and develop people inside their large generative operation, to change their operations so that they're healthy and whole and working in their communities in a good way. They see that we're all living in an interconnected web.
>
> — Anders Ferguson

There are, in fact, thousands of such conscious businesses all over the United States and Europe. Contrary to popular myth, they compete quite well with the global giants, because they offer something that economies of scale can never purchase on the cheap: heartfelt integrity. Until quite recently these stories were rarely reported in the business press.

WHAT IS A TRANSLUCENT BUSINESS?

Companies become translucent when they are influenced by translucent people. The influence may come from the CEO or top management, but it may just as easily come from an outside consultant, the shareholders, or the collective wisdom of the employees. It requires only a very few instrumental translucent people to begin to transform an entire organization.

People become translucent when they wake up from their contracted self-preoccupation and feel themselves to be bigger than their personal story. They discover they are both no one in particular and at the same time part of everything around them. From this recognition of connectedness, translucent people become more humorous, more honest, and less fearful. Their lives get reorganized around service and contribution. It is possible for the same awakening process to happen to an organization. When a business starts to awaken from its self-preoccupation with profit as the only justification for its existence, it starts to display translucent qualities.

Translucent businesses wake up from the myth of lack, of our gain at the expense of others' loss, and explode with possibilities: Of course! This is where all these creative people gather every day, where they spend most of their time. It could be a place of inspiration, of creativity, a place of community. It could even be a place to feel love, to feel spirit! Translucent businesses demonstrate a recognition of connectedness. They too are more humorous, more honest, and less fearful. They too become reorganized around service and contribution, to their own employees, to society and the environment, and to their shareholders. And, as it does when an individual becomes more

> I think what we've seen in a more widespread way is that the idea of personal balance and well-being has become legitimized. That is no small step.
>
> — Bruce Cryer

translucent, the awakening of a business brings as many challenges as it does triumphs.

HeartMath

One group having a dramatic translucent influence on a wide range of businesses is a small firm in Santa Cruz, California, called HeartMath. Founded by researcher, author, and consultant Doc Childre, HeartMath offers an array of simple techniques and technologies to reduce stress and improve health and performance, with its unique hallmark an emphasis on research. Since 1991 HeartMath has accumulated rigorous scientific validation for the benefits of one simple intervention: shifting our attention from the mind to the heart. They have proven what we already know but do not always dare to trust, that the heart is more than just an organ to pump blood; it is a vital instrument of healing that brings us back to ourselves, back to our senses, back to the present moment. As soon as we shift back to the heart, it sends messages to the brain that change our perceptions and behavior. HeartMath proves in a host of studies that this process launches a cascade of beneficial nervous system, hormonal, and immune system activity "in a heartbeat." Their PC-based software system, *Freeze-Framer,* uses a unique heart-monitoring technology to create a form of biofeedback that helps the user rest in a more relaxed and open state.

Bruce Cryer, CEO of HeartMath, has taken their tools to hospitals, federal agencies, and hundreds of other companies like BP, Hewlett-Packard, Cisco Systems, and Boeing. "At the end of the day," says Cryer, "people feel more in touch with who they really are. While the approach is based on scientific principles, it's really a way to help people relax." HeartMath takes what Cryer describes as a "Trojan horse" strategy toward transforming large organizations. They found out early on that most organizations are not very interested in being transformed until they can see the benefits in practical ways: "The idea of transforming their

> Love overcomes fear. This is not a biblical tenet or a "feel good" thing, or something you do just at home between your family members. Increasingly, science demonstrates that coming from a place of love, appreciation, and kindness in business significantly improves performance rather than coming from a place of fear and lack and scarcity. That's very powerful.
>
> — Anders Ferguson

culture is maybe appealing to a small group of human resources people, but it doesn't play well to most CEOs, especially if it has a spiritual slant to it. Most people who run organizations today are concerned about business, about bottom lines, and about themselves, their own health and viability."

In 1997 the chief medical officer at what was then British Petroleum — later renamed simply BP — asked Cryer and the team at HeartMath in the U.K. to consult with their company. The issue was stress. Because of high stress levels the performance of the company was dropping. "They were intrigued that we had a technology that could help their senior people effectively deal with the pressures of running a rapidly expanding global business," says Cryer. "They recognized that HeartMath tools were a powerful way to rebuild the health and vitality and resilience of their leaders." The entire board of BP went through the HeartMath program, and from there the program rolled down through the ranks. Cryer feels it was easily accepted throughout the company because of its strong scientific basis: "This technology is very intriguing and interesting to people who would otherwise never touch a spiritual or self-help topic, or would not necessarily say they're interested in personal awareness. The instant feedback and hard data make it extremely compelling to otherwise skeptical executives and engineers."

> I think for all of us who are experiencing this transformation, it is rooted and driven in the reintegration of spirit and science.
>
> — Anders Ferguson

In the case of BP, our work has been to help them see the connection between individual well-being and corporate effectiveness. Many corporate leaders are still in the model of believing that if an employee can't hack it, the company needs to get somebody new. They don't necessarily see that the decisions, the image, the social responsibility of an organization is necessarily linked to how individuals feel about themselves, about their organization, about their life. At BP, we've seen a strong recognition that the health and well-being of the individual does impact organizational performance and does lead to the kind of decisions that are in the long term more sustainable.

Bruce Cryer has been inspired by the transformation HeartMath has catalyzed, not only at BP but in dozens of other corporations as well:

We've found that this emotionally based approach, with the foundation of physiology behind it, can help leaders to validate some subtle promptings they're already getting inside themselves but don't know how to talk about. The average CEO can't relate to the concept of spirit in business, but they can relate to their own health and longevity. They can relate to the disconnect they feel between the kind of legacy they want to leave behind and what they have to do on a daily basis, the stress and the pressure they're under. We come into an organization to help them where they're hurting, which are the areas of stress and performance.

When HeartMath steps into an organization, they see a pattern to reward the "stress athletes," those who work their tails off at great personal cost: "At BP, we have been playing a key role in helping a conversation begin to happen. We have seen the birth of the recognition that it is legitimate not only to talk about stress but also to do something proactive about it, and that makes good business sense."

Many people refuse to believe that a company like BP can embrace translucent ideas. Our image of oil companies is of entities only interested in raping and plundering the land for the almighty dollar. Cryer himself is amazed at how much benevolence and goodwill are stored away in the recesses of a large company like BP, just waiting to be recognized:

In fact, there are good people everywhere, dealing with the same pressures and anxieties and personal-growth challenges in oil companies as anywhere else. They aren't necessarily only interested in digging black stuff out of the earth. That's been an important part of our approach, to recognize the humanity, the goodness in people everywhere, to recognize that people are the sum total of what they've learned. Obviously, as a planet we've got to learn some new stuff, some new intelligence and new ways of thinking and being and feeling.

> Every result you get in your life is the combination of the challenge you receive from the reality around you and your capacity to respond to that challenge.
>
> — Fred Kofman

This willingness to recognize the goodness in people has borne ample fruit at BP. Change a few trees, and sooner or later you have a whole new forest. In 2000, after working with HeartMath for three years and acquiring several other companies, the company changed its name from British Petroleum simply to BP, adding the slogan "Beyond Petroleum." They instituted a campaign, largely completed by now, to power all their gas stations in Europe, as well as their office buildings and refineries, with solar-power panels installed on the roof, making them the single largest user of solar energy in the world. BP has initiated numerous wind-power projects in Europe and is actively exploring the role of hydrogen in its pursuit of a sustainable energy future. Although the project is highly experimental at this point, with DaimlerChrysler they created a ten-city European Bus Project, to fuel public transportation in London, Barcelona, and other big cities with fuel cell, zero-emission vehicles. Their "Sustainability Report" for 2003 is startlingly realistic, honest, and responsible. BP does not avoid the fact that it is still a major contributor to world pollution: the report diligently lists all the damage they are still creating. But it also offers a road map out of that position, along with a vision of energy sustainability.

MULTIPLE BOTTOM LINES

Joe Kresse, with the Foundation for Global Community, is another translucent activist who perceives business as a ripe arena for transformation. He reports that translucent values emerge in businesses when they are willing to question the traditional idea of the bottom line. The more Iago-driven an organization, the more profit determines every decision. "True enough," says Kresse. "Business does have to make a profit, but more and more businesses are developing multiple bottom lines. In many cases these are People, Environment, and Shareholders." He observes that all are served best when prioritized in that order.

> All of the best business data that we have right now indicate that companies that focus on the environment, social issues, workplace issues, women's issues . . . on improving life, are outperforming their competitors financially.
>
> — Anders Ferguson

Kresse cites the Danish company Novo Nordisk, the world's leading manufacturer of diabetic drugs, as a prime example. Their 2001 annual report is aptly titled *Reporting on Three Bottom Lines: People/Planet/Profits*. Out of sixty-eight pages, a full twenty-eight are devoted to social responsibility: investigating the company's contribution to global issues, including universal health care, human rights, and bioethics. Another eighteen pages are devoted to the environmental impact of the company.

Like the BP sustainability report, this is a far cry from what one expects in a corporate annual report, prepared primarily for the shareholders. The document is frequently critical of the company's ability to meet its own ethical standards. It presents seven dilemmas and then publishes critical responses from people outside the company. For example, they invited the editor of *Newsweek* to respond to the question "How can we do ethical business in an unjust, unequal world and also respect its diversity?" The question "How can we improve access to health care and make our products affordable, and yet continue to operate a profitable business?" was answered by a doctor in a small medical center in Tanzania.

While Kresse sees many more examples of this kind of translucent approach to business in Europe than in the United States, he notes that even companies like Dow Chemical and Philip Morris, at one time the quintessential villains of environmental and health-related irresponsibility, are starting to change, albeit at a snail's pace.

Kresse maintains that for a company to perform well in the emerging translucent paradigm, it must put profitability as its *last* priority, almost as a by-product of other, more important contributions. Profit is something like happiness. If we make life about trying to be as happy as possible, we become very self-absorbed and often miserable. But we all know people who have made their lives about service, community, and making the greatest contribution they can: they end up happy almost by accident. Some companies, like BP, may pass through bumpy periods of transition in shifting from a single to multiple bottom lines, but once they do, says Kresse, they will become more profitable.

> You can't create a coherent organization that has a sense of balance, without individuals in your organization — your leaders, your workers, and your administrative staff — themselves trying to become more balanced and more coherent. There just is no way you can do it.
>
> — Bruce Cryer

THE FIRST BOTTOM LINE: PEOPLE

Most people in America know George Zimmer, founder of the Men's Wearhouse, as the bearded affable character on television who promises the right suit at the right price. Zimmer has a huge commitment to bringing translucence to the corporation he founded in 1971. His care for people, both within the organization and in the local community, eclipses any fixation on profit. At a conference on Business and Consciousness in Santa Fe, Zimmer emphasized *servant leadership*, a term I have repeatedly heard used by translucent business leaders.

The CEO's role is to steward the company in the realization of its vision, in this way allowing the people within the organization to live at their highest potential. To this end, Zimmer fosters a spirit of "reciprocal altruism," which he says requires trust and fairness, for people to act as a team. Although his sales force works on commission, he has created an environment where people feel, "If I can help you get a sale, I'll do it, because I know the next time I'm going to be on the receiving end." Zimmer believes in promoting from within the company, whenever possible, rather than bringing in outsiders to manage workers who have been there much longer. He has created a college fund for the children of his employees, and gives away more in scholarships each year than he earns.

> You have to treat everybody with respect. My social experiment says that if anyone comes and cares and works hard, then I have a spot for them. A lot of people say you can't afford to do that anymore. But I don't know, I think I'm way ahead of my time. I think I've paid a handsome price for that, but so be it. I'm glad I did.
>
> — David Neenan

Zimmer's primary motivation in taking care of people is not making a profit, although that has been the by-product. Reciprocal altruism is a core value, a natural quality of his self-discovery. Says Joe Kresse: "Zimmer puts the stockholders last. He sees five groups of stakeholders: the employees are the most important, the customers are next, suppliers are third, other stakeholders are fourth, and financial investors are last. He believes that if you do the first four right, the stockholders will be just fine."

Like many translucent business leaders, and in stark contrast to the habits of Iago-driven business, Zimmer limits his salary to ten times that of the average worker at Men's Wearhouse. Kresse reports that many companies in Europe also put limits on this ratio, while the average for larger corporations in the United States exceeds 1:700.

Delnor Community Hospital

As it is in most hospitals in the United States, staff retention at Delnor Community Hospital, outside Chicago, was a huge problem. The hospital was losing 35 percent of its staff each year, including nearly half the nurses. This loss of staff, of course, seriously affected the quality of health care. Only 73 percent of the patients described their stay at the hospital as a positive one. In an environment designed to promote healing, this is not an encouraging statistic. Delnor embarked on a journey to reinvent itself, retaining HeartMath to help them create an environment that places care for the staff and for the patients above any other objectives.

To date, nearly 70 percent of the Delnor staff has been trained in the HeartMath approach. Overall staff turnover has dropped steadily over three years to 14 percent, while among those who have done the training, it is now at an astounding 4 percent. Patient satisfaction has risen from 73 to 98 percent. In two out of the last four years, Delnor has been rated the number one hospital in the country in employee satisfaction. And this happened with tools that, in Cryer's words, "help people feel more in touch with who they really are, to help them become more balanced, less stressed, and more caring."

Today Delnor is a friendly place, a happy place. People enjoy working there, and they are proud of what they have achieved together. Their chief nursing officer, Linda Deering, says the HeartMath tools "help me to recognize when I am allowing my energies to work against me. I really shift my attitude, perception, thoughts, and then, of course, my ability to stop reacting and start responding effectively."

> You realize how smart the other people are around you. My gosh, if we could get some real synergy going here, we could add a lot of value — there's so much waste in the way things happen in business. People are at war. If you can stop the war, you can add a lot of value and that's what we've been doing.
>
> — David Neenan

By making staff well-being a higher priority than profit, they have actually made more money. The hospital saved more than $2.2 million in the first year alone, and the savings have continued. In four years, the hospital has grown, adding 50 percent more staff, building new buildings, and modernizing their equipment. Delnor's efforts were recognized nationally when, along with Pitney Bowes and Lockheed Martin, they won the 2002 Corporate Health and Productivity Management Award. In 2004 Delnor became only the third hospital in Illinois to achieve Magnet status for nurse excellence.

Green Mountain Coffee Roasters

Bob Stiller, the CEO of Green Mountain Coffee Roasters (GMCR), is personally committed to the practical application of higher consciousness in his leadership abilities. He has introduced a practice developed at the Weatherhead School of Management of Case Western Reserve University called Appreciative Inquiry, which asks us to pay special attention to "the best of the past and present" in order to "ignite the collective imagination of what might be." It promotes "heightening our collective awareness of the value, strength, and potential of ourselves and others — and overcoming the limits that we impose, often unconsciously, on our own capacities."[1]

By drawing on the collective vision of his employees in this way, Stiller has stewarded a remarkable transformation of his own company. In 1981 GMCR was a small café in Waitsfield, Vermont. It now trades on NASDAQ, and 2003 sales exceeded $113 million. Despite this phenomenal financial success, profit is not what drives the company. Stiller has stimulated the translucent wisdom inherent within his company, involving his employees in crafting its vision and direction. Their Fair Trade Coffees, grown organically, establish price guarantees to ensure that small-scale farmers in developing nations receive a fair price for their efforts. The company sponsors seminars for the local community, where they invite speakers to explore consciousness-raising issues. Their environmental committee, comprised of the company's employees, regularly travels to coffee farms in Costa Rica, Mexico, Guatemala, and Sumatra to ensure that the quality of the farmers' and their families' lives, as well as of the coffee itself,

> We are co-create colleagues in this, because nobody's got the whole story. Not even close. Everybody matters, everybody is bringing forth their own unique flavor to truly meet and honor one another. It's really a work out. We'll all do a lot better when we can get more toward regarding one another as fellow scientists in the lab of being.
>
> — Saniel Bonder

meets the company's ethical standards. In 1997 GMCR funded a hydro-plant in Peru to serve sixteen farms. Their Coffee Kids micro-lending project has grown to include 270 participants in Mexico.

Co-Creation

Carolyn Anderson and John Zwerver, the founders of a UN-affiliated organization called Global Family, call this model of people working together "co-creation." Anderson is the co-author of *The Co-Creators Handbook*. She defines co-creation as "co-participating consciously with the laws or patterns of life itself, conscious alignment with the essence of others and with nature."[2] Anderson and Zwerver offer several other examples of co-creative businesses, where the CEO or president has come to a position of stewardship, drawing out and giving voice to the innate wisdom of the collective.

> I knew in my heart that it wasn't just me adding value. Everybody was adding value. I promised myself that if I was ever in a position to share with my employees the value that they had helped me create, that that would be the honorable thing to do.
>
> — David Neenan

For as long as we can remember, Iago-based business has used a dominator model. Decisions are made by the CEO and senior management, who are retained by investors to represent their interests: to make as much money as possible. The dominator model of doing business may make money, but the hidden cost is high. First, everyone in the company, from middle management down to the shop floor, is placed in a position of subordination. Divorced from their own vision, their integrity and inspiration become entirely irrelevant in this ask-no-questions environment. If you want to keep your job, you don't question company policy. People feel used. Absenteeism and job turnover rise, since those doing the hands-on work feel little or no loyalty to the company, to its reputation, or to what it produces. Second, with dominator models the source of innovation is restricted to senior management, which may be quite out of touch with the realities of what it really takes to care for patients in a hospital or to produce widgets on a factory floor.

In a co-creative model, the source of new ideas can come from anywhere in the system. Rather than simply handing down orders, senior executives are responsible for creating an open listening environment, in which the voice of every participant can be heard. Anderson and Zwerver emphasize the necessity to create what they call a "resonant field," an invisible space that can resound, echo back, and affirm the highest good in one another. This frequency aligns individuals heart to heart, calling forth the gifts and creativity of each person. Hence the need for HeartMath tools, for Appreciative Inquiry, and for other companies to explore a whole host of spiritual practices. Co-creation happens when enough members of the organization are able to resonate at a translucent frequency together.

> We can't take the "dominator attitude" any further. What we need now is partnership. We forget, and we end up making stupid decisions that hurt other people and the earth. We've got to remember our Spirit in every moment. We *are* Spirit, it is our nature. We are beings of Spirit, but we often don't act like it. And Spirits don't harm each other or the earth. We are partnerships.
>
> — Marc Allen

Co-creation doesn't mean that everyone performs the same function. There is still a place for some to lead, for some to keep track of accounts and statistics, for some to keep the environment clean and beautiful, and for some to serve the customers and their needs. Just like the organs and limbs of a body, every component of the system is recognized as equally valuable and necessary for its survival. Salary ratios reflect that recognition. The walls separating the different parts of the organism begin to come down.

David Neenan literally brought down these walls of separation in his construction firm:

> We were all in departments at the time. The department heads and I sat in the conference room and agreed on what we were going to do, then each department went its own way and everybody closed their door. This is the old way of doing business. It aggravated me so much that I got to thinking about it. I realized the reason we were not working together was that we could all close our doors, and that was really not okay. So I went to the janitor and asked him to take all the doors off over the weekend. By Monday morning there were no doors left, except on the bathrooms. Nobody said a word about it. A few days later, we were having a meeting in my doorless office. I had to pee. I had a little executive bathroom, and when I went in, I saw they had snuck in and taken the door off the bathroom, too. While I was peeing, my secretary came in the office and gasped. They had got me.

That's co-creation. Innovation can come from anywhere in the system.

New World Library

And now, a word about our sponsors. Marc Allen started New World Library (under the name Whatever Publishing) in the 1970s. Everyone told him, "You can't make money in publishing, or if you do, it's very stressful." Allen has proved them wrong on both counts. He built New World with as much partnership as possible. Everything, from the books they choose to publish (including this one), to the titles and covers, is decided in meetings, often involving the whole company. "I've never had to make a top-down decision they didn't all feel good about," says Allen. On his desk he has his personal mission statement as the CEO: "We are creating wonderful success in an easy and relaxed manner, in a healthy positive way, in its own perfect time, for the highest good of all."

And Allen keeps to his mission religiously. "I'm one of the few people I know who gets enough sleep," he says. He spends roughly a third of his time with his family, a third alone, and a third at the office. "And when I feel lazy, I sleep and relax." But this is not a case of the boss sitting by the pool while his minions run themselves into the ground. Marc encourages everyone at New World to take great care of themselves, to take vacations and "wellness days." "What arises naturally is this great energy, a wonderful activity that arises out of our inaction. As soon as we have any ongoing stress, then it's time to relax again.

> The trick is to pay attention and review each day. Like in martial arts, see where fear comes up. See where it's not flowing, where effort gets strained. It's an opportunity to feel how to create a way to work better.
>
> — Jack Canfield

"Every business should have a generous profit-sharing program, as well as the best possible pension plan and benefits." With titles like *The Power of Now* and *The Way of the Peaceful Warrior*, New World also demonstrates that a business can be financially viable and maintain integrity.

Corporate Mystics

What is the logical extension of putting people first? Once an organization has taken care of the basic well-being of its employees, it begins to glimpse the highest potential of a work environment, ultimately an arena where people can experience their spiritual potential. Anders Ferguson feels that a

surprising number of larger companies are moving steadily in this direction.
He and his partner, Sander Tideman, have done extensive work with Unilever,
the largest consumer products company in the world and perhaps the last
place you would expect to find corporate
mystics. But Ferguson describes their top
management in Holland as "dedicated
people exploring every kind of meditative
and spiritual practice, looking at how to
really constructively bring translucence into
the business world." He reports that their
decision to purchase Ben & Jerry's but to leave its political, environmental,
and ethical stands intact, was made in order to learn more about doing business in a translucent way. "They have worked mightily to create compassionate, heart-opened, and practical business leaders," Ferguson says. In 2004
Unilever launched a campaign to rebrand themselves, with a new logo and
new environmentally friendly products built around the concept of Vitality.
Their annual report is now organized around issues such as "environmental
management," "environmental reporting," and "social responsibility."

> My business became my spiritual path,
> the fast track to spiritual growth.
> Because everything I was not clear
> with surfaced.
>
> — Jack Canfield

As the structure of a business reorganizes itself to reflect a co-creative
organism rather than a hierarchy dominated from above, the innate translucent qualities within that organization emerge naturally. When David
Neenan wrote "knower rest in peace" on the flip chart, it was not the result
of a mystical awakening, but rather an act of surrender, of giving up the need
to control his environment: "It used to be, I would call everybody in, ask
them how they did that week, and give them orders for the next week. I was
convinced that even if I died, I could still control them. I could make a videotape and say, 'In the event of my death get out the videotape and it'll tell you
what to do this week.' They say you can't run it from the tomb, but I was
ready to try." Now the Neenan Company is a pioneer for co-creative business
practices.

When any company shifts into greater translucence, it mirrors the experience of an individual. It recognizes itself to be part of a bigger whole.
Operating as a conscious organism, it starts to tear down not only its internal walls, but also the walls that separate it from its community and the
world.

THE SECOND BOTTOM LINE: ENVIRONMENT

When an individual is caught in the Iago trance, everything contracts down to "my" needs. There is never enough, I am always on the verge of some calamity or other, I have to watch out for me. In this way, we have very little energy for anything outside our own survival. After an awakening, the impulse to serve others follows naturally. This is equally true for a company. When the obsession with profit, lack, and survival in the marketplace has relaxed, the company begins to display natural altruism. When Bob Stiller opened up

> It's important to have a lot of time to yourself. Our culture has a lot of neurosis about "not enough time and money." I've found there are plenty of both. Our beliefs about these things become self-fulfilling.
>
> — Marc Allen

to his employees' collective wisdom at GMCR, the environmental initiatives the company explored were not strategic but natural. Feeling beyond the preoccupation with profit allows any organization to respond to the needs of its local community and the world of which it is a part.

Interface Carpet

Ray Anderson started Interface Carpet in Atlanta, Georgia, in 1973. His goal was to make his carpet business the biggest in the world. He succeeded. By the late 1980s, Interface was the largest commercial carpet manufacturer worldwide, with sales in 110 countries and production on four continents. But this success had a price. Every year, Interface's factories produced hundreds of millions of gallons of wastewater and nearly nine hundred pollutants. Carpet accounts for 30 percent of all landfill waste.[3]

While he was building his company, Anderson was not concerned about the environmental impact of his economic growth. "For the first twenty-one years of Interface's existence," says Anderson, "I never gave one thought to what we took from or did to the earth, except to be sure we obeyed all laws and regulations."[4]

In 1994 Interface's customers began to question what the company was doing for the environment. In response, Anderson appointed a task force to examine their worldwide environmental position. He was invited to be a keynote speaker at the task force's first meeting and to offer an "environmental vision." "I then realized," says Anderson, "that I had no environmental vision beyond the typical 'obey the law, comply, comply, comply.' I had heard statesmen advocate 'sustainable development,' but I had no idea what it meant. I sweated for three weeks over what to say to that group."[5]

Anderson's moment of awakening came when he read Paul Hawken's book *The Ecology of Commerce*. Hawken's book suggests that industry is systematically destroying the planet, and that the only people in a position to stop this destruction are the industrialists themselves. The book's argument spun Anderson's perspective 180 degrees. "It was like a spear to the chest," he says. "'The death of birth,' meaning that species are disappearing, never ever to be born again, it was those kinds of revelations that created the epiphanal experience for me."[6] For Anderson, this was not just a shift in business strategy, or a revision of company policy to zip out before golf. It was transformational. It changed his whole perspective on life.

> When you act in integrity, you are always willing to subordinate success to the alignment with the truth. You have an unwavering commitment that manifests itself in your day-to-day actions. Love, freedom, and truth are more important than anything else, and you will not subordinate those to the achievement of some secondary goal. I call that integrity "success beyond success."
>
> — Fred Kofman

As is often the case when someone becomes more conscious of the consequences of their actions, the first phase of Anderson's rebirth was to face the damage that he and others like him had caused in the name of more at any cost: "People who steal are put in jail today. We haven't yet figured out that what we're doing in industrialism is stealing from future generations. We created America to get away from remote tyranny, but we haven't figured out that with industrialism we're imposing the worst form of remote tyranny on our progeny. When our values change and our yardstick changes, I think that we will see our present-day actions as criminal in the light of a future sense of justice."[7]

Anderson began to look at his company with fresh eyes and to introduce his employees to the awakened responsibility he was feeling. He first addressed the task force. "That little group of people went away sensitized," he says, "but only them."[8] It took quite some time for this new consciousness to permeate the entire company. First, Interface looked at recycling. Its LaGrange, Georgia, plant alone sent six tons of carpet trimmings to the landfill every day. By June of 1997, less than three years after that first task force meeting, they were sending *none*.9 At a Maine division of Interface, computerized controls installed on boilers not only reduced carbon monoxide emissions by 99.7 percent, but also improved the boilers' efficiency. As a result, waste decreased and profits increased.

"It took a while to move beyond the heart, the 'This is the right thing to do' sense of responsibility, to 'Hey, this is good business. This is smart — as well as right,'" says Anderson. "It took a while, but once we understood that reducing waste was the same as boosting profits — two sides of the same coin — that realization probably crystallized the transition from heart to head."10

> Ask yourself, What is my gift? What do I want to offer to other people in the world? What's my love? What am I overflowing with, that I need to find a means of expressing? Let go of asking, How am I going to get something external that will finally make my life meaningful?
>
> — Fred Kofman

This second bottom line, environmental integrity, not only takes care of the third, shareholders, but also the first, the people in the company: "When our employees began pulling together to make the firm operate more sustainably, they also had a renewed sense of purpose. Operating responsibly was a galvanizing force for us. Abraham Maslow said that people want to work for something more than subsistence, even something beyond personal development. They want to work for a higher purpose. And our drive to be sustainable has provided that higher purpose."11

Interface is rapidly learning to harness solar and wind energy in place of fossil fuels and to plant trees to offset the pollution caused by trucks transporting its carpet. The company creates raw materials by harvesting and recycling carpet and other petrochemical products, while eliminating waste and harmful emissions from its operations. Their vision is to shift from being a petro-intensive company, as they are now, to never needing to take another drop of oil from the earth by 2030. The company has even found a way to make carpet out of corn, and plant-derived products now make up 10 percent of their business. Furthermore, Interface uses carpet tiles for commercial installations, making it possible to replace only carpet in high-wear areas. They have also developed recyclable carpet; the fibers can be salvaged, washed, and reused.

Anderson has faced various challenges from different groups. With his suppliers, his approach is blunt: "This is how we are going," he says. "If you want our business, come along." He follows up with the softer incentive, that it is also the right thing to do. With customers, he elicits support: "Help us increase our leverage up the supply chain. You can have a role in this mountain-climbing expedition." To his community, he says, "Hey, we're involved. Our people are your people. Our rivers are your rivers, and your rivers are ours. This is our community. Let's work together to make it a better place." And finally, to the financial community, he can say with conviction, "The companies that are going to survive in the long run are the resource-efficient ones. We intend to be among those. Think of us as a good long-term investment."[12]

Anderson is a herald for sustainable business. He has been showered with awards and praise for his work. His book *Mid-Course Correction: Toward a Sustainable Enterprise* has inspired many other companies to follow suit. He founded the Alliance to Save Energy, helping children design energy-saving campaigns for their schools. "The new course we're on at Interface," he says, "is to pioneer the next Industrial Revolution: one that is kinder and gentler to the earth."[13]

> A true leader who operates translucently is somebody who can maintain their awareness even in a situation of high stakes.
>
> — Fred Kofman

Interface acknowledges there is still much to be done; they estimate they are less than a quarter of the way to their ultimate goal of environmental sustainability. But like many other visionary business leaders, Anderson believes the tide has turned. "It's a wave that's forming. I have no way of knowing how fast or how big the wave will be, but businesses that don't move in this direction won't survive."[14]

Odwalla Juice

In 1980 Greg Steltenpohl and two friends started Odwalla Juice as a way to pay their way through college. They squeezed their first box of oranges in a backyard shed in Santa Cruz, using a $200 used juicer. "We were a loose-knit group of friends, looking for a legal way to make a living together," Steltenpohl recalls with a laugh.[15] They delivered fresh juice to local restaurants in their Volkswagen van. From the beginning, environmental and social integrity have been central to their vision. They have always used fresh, local, organic ingredients and kept the turnaround time from picking, to juicing, to delivery, at a minimum. As a result, they've developed what Steltenpohl calls a "FedEx" kind of operation, ensuring a quality of freshness unequaled in the juice business. Odwalla quickly became a poster-company for the environmental community, regularly honored for its pioneer recycling, organic cultivation, and community investment programs.

Like GMCR, Odwalla encouraged an active conceptual participation of its entire community of workers, including delivery drivers and warehouse packers. The reigning metaphor, of "conversation" rather than policy, has been borne out for more than two decades. Steltenpohl has recently moved on from Odwalla to co-found "The Interra Card," a forthcoming environmentally conscious credit card. Coca-Cola purchased Odwalla in 2000, and it will be interesting to see if they have the intelligence to maintain the company's translucent direction.

> My last doubts about the shift into awakening were whether I would be able to hold it in the face of intense business. My business life gets more intense as my understanding gets deeper. I take on more and more, there's much more action because of less doership. Things are happening at a level I could never have imagined or tried to bring about.
>
> — Satyam Nadeen

Fetzer Vineyards

Paul Dolan, CEO of Fetzer Vineyards in Mendocino, California, is a third-generation winemaker. After participating in the Landmark seminar, he experienced an awakening shift and woke up to the potential of the business he was stewarding. He has since steered Fetzer Vineyards in a sustainable direction. They have moved toward growing their grapes organically, using drip-feeding methods to preserve the area's water table. They have introduced electric vehicles and run the winery on solar power. Dolan has introduced a program to offer his employees — many of them immigrants — free English lessons. He views his workers as human beings, worthy of respect, rather than cogs in an industrial machine. Dolan also believes in ad hoc decision-making, where employees who know most about the problem, rather than an elite management at the top of the pyramid, institute innovation. Dolan would eventually like to see all vineyards grow organically and practice sustainable agriculture, and Fetzer has instituted educational sessions for other winemakers to promote these practices.

Corporate Karma

Yvon Chouinard, who founded Patagonia in 1974, understood from the very beginning that the earth's resources are limited. Patagonia has one of the highest levels of environmental integrity of any company today. Their top-selling fleece material is made from recycled plastic soda bottles. They use organic cotton and launch countless environmental initiatives. They donate 1 percent of their gross sales, or 10 percent of profits, whichever is greater, to environmental causes.

Even Nike, at one time criticized for being one of the worst culprits in using sweatshops in Asia, has launched a campaign to end sweatshop use. As with BP's concentration on the damage caused by burning fossil fuels, and Interface's focus on landfill waste, often the companies who have most lagged behind in specific areas later pioneer their cleanups, giving rise to the term *corporate karma*.

> The best research tells us that what we see emerging — and the break is becoming bigger — is companies that are doing the right thing, putting into practice translucent values, are breaking away from the pack and doing better across the board . . . including financially.
>
> — Anders Ferguson

Today hundreds, and perhaps thousands, of companies like Patagonia, Fetzer, and Interface are reversing conventional corporate thinking. The old wisdom, embodied in current governmental policies, puts economic growth as the sole aim of business, ignoring its effect on people and the environment. This is the Iago ethic, driven by fear. In contrast, translucent companies place values before shareholder greed. And the result, ironically, is better news for the investors.

THE THIRD BOTTOM LINE: SHAREHOLDERS

However translucent a business, it still needs to make money. Shareholders expect a positive return. How, then, has the translucent revolution affected investors?

"In the past, 'conscious' investing was fairly simplistic and primarily used 'negative filters' — the simplest ones and the dumbest ones: weapons, alcohol, and tobacco. The portfolio manager simply says, 'We're not going to support any of that stuff,' " says Joe Kresse. Of course, negative filters can still allow all kinds of questionable integrity. In the past decade, the growing number of translucent investors has created a demand for increasingly sophisticated investments, using "positive" filters that favor environmental sustainability, social and economic equality, and cultural diversity.

Instead of filtering things out, more conscious filters look for positive trends: service to the community, limited salary ratios between the highest- and lowest-paid workers, employee health and well-being, respect-based communication, and environmental responsibility. According to Ferguson, there are now more than two trillion investment dollars using positive screens. Kresse estimates that one-eighth of the money invested in Wall Street now has a positive social or environmental screen on it. He points out that in the past, such investments meant giving up a measure of performance. "In the last five years," Kresse says, "these positively filtered investments have done at least as well as everyone else and have often outperformed the market."

> We will not win this case because it's simply the right thing to do. Not in business. Not in the cost-conscious world we live in. We've got to combine profit and integrity, and we shouldn't be fearful of combining the two.
>
> — Anders Ferguson

The Domini Index

Amy Domini has been a stockbroker since the 1970s. Many of her clients shared her unease about investing in companies with questionable policies. Her clients had a wide variety of concerns: one, an avid bird-watcher, discovered that the paper company she was investing in was using chemicals that harmed wildlife; another, a pacifist, was unknowingly investing in a defense contractor. Domini discovered a smattering of mutual funds that applied screens to their portfolios, but their efforts were not coordinated. Was it possible, she wondered, to pursue investment goals without violating one's conscience?

Domini recognized the need for a benchmark for conscious investors, an index, like the S&P 500, that could be used to track the performance of investing with awareness. With two other partners, she created the Domini 400

> It is now at the tipping point, from what we won't invest in, to what we will. It's shifting to the positive, investors pointing their dollars to the positive instead of the negative. How could you create a future that's generative or translucent from investing in the negative?
>
> — Anders Ferguson

Social Index, using 400 large-capitalization U.S. corporations, selected for a wide range of positive environmental and social criteria. Launched in 1991, the Domini Index was the first of its kind.

Over the past decade, the Domini Index has reported an impressive average annual return of 12.03 percent, compared to 11.10 percent for the S&P 500. Domini and her associates are proving that socially and environmentally conscious investing is soothing not only to the soul but also to the bank balance. Today, other investment funds, like the Calvert Group and Trillium Asset Management, apply the same principles to investing.

Shareholder Initiatives

As well as putting dollars into the right companies, funds with translucent values can influence a company's behavior through shareholder initiatives. Says Joe Kresse: "Until quite recently, shareholders had very little influence on companies. There were relatively few initiatives proposed by investors at annual meetings, and they only represented about 5 to 10 percent of the vote. Shareholder meetings would see carte blanche voting for whatever the management proposed."

That has changed dramatically in the last ten years. Firms like Domini and the Calvert Group are highly active, both in proposing and in passing progressive shareholder resolutions. This shift in investment values is a compelling indicator of a real change in the direction taken by business. When shareholders, either as individuals or represented by funds like Domini, can demand that companies respect multiple bottom lines, they remove the very foundation for unethical business. A CEO puts profit before people or planet to please the shareholders. If those same shareholders demand higher social and environmental standards, the tide has effectively turned.

Domini has filed more than ninety such shareholder resolutions in ten years, with more than forty corporations. In addition, she has engaged in dozens of long-term dialogues with various companies. The impact of these initiatives may be more powerful than any other single factor we have examined here. For example, Domini was able to persuade Gap, Inc. to review its policies on cheap overseas labor. The resulting Social Responsibility Report transformed Gap's business practices and set a new high bar for the rest of the clothing industry. Domini persuaded three large companies to amend their corporate policies to prohibit sexual discrimination. Time Warner and Tribune agreed to disclose information to the public about donations to political parties and their possible effect on news reporting. Domini was able to put limits on executive pay at AT&T through proactive dialogue, without the need for a formal initiative.

In addition, Domini has implemented policy changes affecting global warming, global labor standards, indigenous people's rights, fair trade, and responsible water use. Today, half of Domini's proposals are agreed to by management before they even come up for vote at shareholders' annual meetings. With baby boomers coming into wealth, 60 percent of them women, the percentage of money managed by funds like Domini is rapidly increasing. Conscious investment now stands at about 15 percent of all money market funds. These types of shareholder initiatives become the most powerful way to influence business practices, and hence our planet, in a translucent direction. They are often far faster and more effective than through government regulation.

Money talks.

> If you want to honestly look at where the goddess has most appeared, in the United States anyway, she's appearing in business. There are far more women in business, getting ready to make the shift, than in any of the other major social arenas.
>
> — Anders Ferguson

THE GODDESS ON WALL STREET

Amy Domini is not the only woman bringing feminine sanity to corporate America. In living memory, wealth was traditionally passed down through families to the firstborn son. Money stayed in the hands of men. At least in the Western world, this practice has become more or less completely obsolete. Because women live longer than men, perhaps because they invest more intelligently, Anders Ferguson estimates that at least 60 percent of investment assets will be in the hands of women within ten to twenty years. He points to the power of Oprah Winfrey, for example, to galvanize and give voice to feminine wisdom. "The feminine is gaining power," he says. "Power is not a bad thing. Force is a tough thing, the traditional male thing, but empowerment is a very different part of the puzzle." James Berry, the founder of the Business in Consciousness Conference, has seen it become much easier over the years to find women in senior executive positions willing to speak from a place of the empowered feminine.

> I see over and over again, in microsettings or even in countries, when women are given voice, it doesn't just change their lives, it changes everybody's lives. The outcome is miraculous.
>
> — Lynne Twist

When a woman controls the checkbook, her spending habits are different from a man's. How many women buy guns, large machines, or poisonous chemicals? At least in my house, when Chameli goes shopping she is likely to come home with things that smell good, taste good, look beautiful, and make us healthy. Give me the credit card, and we end up with better power tools. As more translucent people, particularly women, have more control over investment, we are seeing the emergence of increasingly sophisticated filters that favor environmental sustainability, social and economic equality, and respect for cultural diversity.

The goddess is not only transforming business as shareholders, of course. In the last decades we have seen women take stewardship for businesses, and the different environments such a change can create. "The infusion of women into positions of leadership," says Ferguson, "is central to the translucent transformation of business." He feels that the traditional trajectory of moving up the ladder is very masculine. The feminine style of leadership nurtures the people in an organization, nurtures the environment, and places profit as a by-product of integrity instead of a substitute for it. The masculine obsession with "more, more, more" is replaced, in the translucent balance of masculine and feminine, with nurturing what is already here.

LIMITING GROWTH

Ironically, the Iago obsession with lack manifests itself in business as a fixation on the need for growth. Iago economics, dominated by the masculine, is not about sustaining or downsizing; it is always about expanding. Politicians are elected to and removed from office over the "growth of the economy." More is better. Everyone needs to work, of course, to have a certain level of security before they can feel more deeply into why they are alive, but our obsession with endless growth triggers more consumption, more depletion of resources, more pollution, and, possibly, a more distracted and stressed populous.

Basing national economic success on economic growth is like rating your children's well-being solely on their grades. Terms like *consumer confidence* and *national productivity* simply reinforce Iago-based values. Duane Elgin is a proponent of voluntary simplicity. He feels that an individual, a business, and finally our global community are all more sustainable with less growth and more integrity. For example, cars today have built-in obsolescence. We expect to trade in our cars after less than a hundred thousand miles. Building longer-lasting cars would contribute toward a shrinking economy (people would make that particular purchase less often, and so car sales would drop) but a healthier environment. The shift to fuel cells, slowed by pressure from both the oil industry and auto manufacturers, is a move toward elimination of the oil industry, less commerce, and zero pollution. Lowering production and consumption, and focusing on the quality and longevity of a product, are still coun-

> The first thing you need to do is make peace with yourself. Sink into that black hole of luminous space to find who you really are. Find your true identity, not an identity that's borrowed or filled from the outside, but an identity that is luminous and radiant in itself.
>
> — Fred Kofman

terintuitive to the mainstream Iago culture but will be inevitable as more of the population, and business, shifts to translucent values.

Measured by traditional economic standards, many of the business entities we have examined appear to be shooting themselves in the foot. Patagonia refuses to endlessly expand its product lines to "new" and "different." BP has publicly committed to finding alternatives to oil production. Judy Wicks has decided not to duplicate the White Dog Café, even if it would make more money. Green Mountain Coffee Roasters would make a lot more money if it turned a blind eye to the living conditions of farming families in Sumatra. Although not all these businesses are run by women, they all demonstrate a balance of masculine and feminine energy. Just like giving a quarter to someone living on the street, or visiting an AIDS hospice, these choices make sense because they feel right to the awakened heart, not because they necessarily lead to "growth."

Wicks is a member of Responsible Wealth, a group of affluent individuals, including Bill Gates, Sr., who favor retaining the inheritance tax. Responsible Wealth exemplifies putting integrity before greed. As well as opposing tax cuts for the highest income bracket, they have created multiple programs for a more equitable distribution of financial resources.

> I do feel that the addiction to money is part of what causes business to go awry and wreak havoc rather than make a contribution, as it can and often does.
>
> — Lynne Twist

WHAT DOES IT TAKE?

Businesses can be transformed in a more translucent direction in a number of ways. Like Interface Carpet or Fetzer Vineyards, the change may start with a shift in consciousness from the CEO and trickle its way down. As with the Neenan Company or GMCR, translucence may grow through co-creation, eliciting the collective wisdom of its employees. Crippling executive stress may prompt a call for outside help, as BP and Delnor did from HeartMath, leading to more translucent practices. For other companies, like Gap, Inc., change resulted from investor initiatives. No matter what the instrument for change, when an organization begins to wake up from its Iago trance, as with an individual, it can initiate an uncomfortable process of facing reality.

The Transformation of Shell

Shell, the British-Dutch oil giant, received a slew of bad press in the mid-1990s. In Nigeria they were implicated in the murder of an environmental activist.[16] Off the Shetland Islands, Greenpeace caught them trying to sink an oil rig.[17] By the late 1990s, Shell had a terrible reputation with environmentalists worldwide. Activists organized successful boycotts of Shell products in both the United States and Europe. Their environmental policies were threatening the company's profits.

The sharp contrast between Shell's annual reports from before and after

the crisis offer an extraordinary window into a company's waking up from
Iago domination. The predictably upbeat tone of the 1997 report is set by the
president: "Our goal is to achieve strong growth in production and sales volumes, and in revenues — with a 15 percent return on capital employed by
early next century." There is no evidence of any environmental or social
responsibility. The level of denial, and delight in profiteering, is reminiscent
of an addict on a binge.

The 1998 report reflects the addict's crash. "Nineteen ninety-eight was a
bad year," the president laments, no longer lost in his feeding frenzy.
"Business conditions were difficult. They
may continue so for some time." His report
is full of discouraging phrases: "difficult
conditions," "profits down," "exploration
and production badly hit," "chemical earn-
ings badly affected." His outlook for the
future is just as gloomy: "Difficult condi-

> Most businesses today only talk about creating shareholder value. All the rest is secondary — they don't realize that they've put the cart before the horse.
>
> — Joe Kresse

tions may persist." "Economic growth is likely to be slow." One imagines him
stumbling around in the kitchen, clutching his head and desperately searching for the aspirin.

In the late 1990s, initially perhaps as a Band-Aid measure, Shell entered
a period of self-reflection. They hired HeartMath's European-based team to
work with them, as well as Fred Kofman and a number of other consultants
with a translucent approach. They adopted a policy of open-ended self-
disclosure about company practices and their effect on the environment.

Shell's annual report for the year 2000 is titled, "How Do We Stand?
People, Planet, Profits." "Their recent reports," comments Kresse, "are show-
case documents of what is possible when a company transforms itself from
clandestine profit-based operations to openness." Reading their 2000 report is
like meeting your alcoholic uncle, whom you have not once seen sober in thirty-
seven years, after a year in rehab. He seems clean and sober, he smells good, he's
smiling, optimistic, and above all, honest. You may feel a little suspicious and
wonder what he's hiding, but things certainly seem to have changed. "My colleagues and I," reports Mark Moody-Stuart, then Shell's chairman, "are totally
committed to a business strategy that generates profits while contributing to
the well-being of the planet and its people. We see no alternative."[18] The report

is openly critical of Shell's effect on the world. It questions its own values and track record, without necessarily supplying answers.

The report even includes negative e-mail from disgruntled critics: "Your products have made a significant contribution to the destruction of the environment on a global scale," wrote a German activist. "You shrug it off with excuses like 'it's not our responsibility what our customers do with our product.'"[19] "Shell does NOT encourage open communication internally," writes one of their employees.[20] "I'm sorry, but if you expect any self-respecting activist to believe a word you say about your commitment to human rights, then you are as arrogant as the PR firm that came up with this strategy,"[21] writes an anonymous critic.

Shell's 2000 report uses the words *sustain* or *sustainability* 169 times in sixty-eight pages. Their newly discovered environmental integrity has not always sat well with shareholders: "It has sometimes been suggested that our commitment to contribute to sustainable development is an unnecessary distraction from our central task of delivering shareholder value," said Jeroen van der Veer, Shell's chairman, in 2003. "In fact, I believe that the reverse is true. Our efforts to contribute to sustainable development will play an important part in rebuilding trust, managing risk, and delivering the strong business performance our shareholders demand, in both the short and long term."[22]

> People can say, well, Shell is just greenwashing. But corporate leaders don't like to make statements like this if they're not going to be able to at least look like they're close to living up to them. They don't like people coming back and embarrassing them.
>
> — Joe Kresse

The company's transformation is extensive. Here are a few random highlights of the innovations they have introduced in just a few years:

- Participation in the Sustainable Mobility Project run by the World Business Council

- Clean air initiatives in Asia and Africa

- Opening the world's first hydrogen refueling stations accessible to the public in Iceland and Holland

- Tripling wind-power capacity to 650MW, enough for two hundred thousand homes

- Producing the most efficient thin film solar panels available commercially

- Providing solar power to fifty thousand homes off the grid

I know, I know, enough Shell already. You want more Eckhart Tolle, more Ram Dass and tantric sex. The transformation of Shell is useful to focus on because it highlights the many stages a company may go through in becoming more translucent and serves as an icon for bringing translucence to business.

> What's most important right now is encouraging people to practice and to break their hard shells. We live in a really tough world, and there are hard decisions to be made. The more hard decisions we make out of love, the faster the unfolding will happen. The human experience right now is *really* precarious. We don't have a lot of years to turn around the enormous Titanic we are all co-sailing.
>
> — Anders Ferguson

NUDGING BUSINESS INTO TRANSLUCENCE

We met Fred Kofman way back at the beginning of this chapter and left him wandering around talking to stressed executives. Kofman has worked with numerous Fortune 500 companies at all levels, from the shop floor to the executive suite. Kofman believes any business is a co-creation, and that its transformation requires the participation of everyone in the organization. His advice on how to nudge your work life in a more translucent direction depends on your position in the company:

NUDGE
At the Base of the Pyramid

For any service position — workers on the shop floor, nurses in a hospital, or those working directly with the public — Kofman has the following advice:

1. Get out of debt. As long as you are in debt, you are enslaved to your organization, you often sacrifice your own integrity, and you will probably feel resentful.

2. Whatever your relationship to the company, ask yourself, "Do I really want to live like this?" Not, "Do I want to go where I think I am going?" but "Do I want to live as I am living now?"

3. Ask yourself, "What is my greatest gift? What do I have to offer this world?" If your work now does not reflect your deepest gift, stop. Ask if your ladder is leaning against the right wall.

> You need to learn to love the job that you have, because today it's the best expression that you have found of what's meaningful to you. And if you hate your job, your job is going to hate you back.
>
> — Fred Kofman

4. You are better off downscaling your life to preserve your own vision than upscaling it to fit someone else's.

5. As you clarify your core values, learn to love the work you have now. Even if you plan to change it, do not resent your job.

NUDGE

For Middle Management

Supervisors and managers are caught in the middle, between the boardroom and the factory floor. Here are some of the nudging tools Kofman suggests for middle management:

1. Listen. Become a hollow channel between the needs of those above and those below you in the organization. Make it your practice to stay out of the way in listening and passing on their needs.

2. Honor your core values. If you are asked to do something, or more important, to instruct other people to do something, value your core translucent beliefs more than keeping your job at any cost. Today, whistle-blowers are becoming our national heroes; they make it onto the cover of *Time* magazine.

3. Be a role model. You have a leadership role with respect to the people under your supervision. Instead of giving them orders, listen to them and do your best to understand their problems and concerns.

4. Tell the truth. When you look up, you are going to be responding to people who are fairly separated from day-to-day operations. They don't understand what's happening on the front lines and yet they have a responsibility to give direction and overall strategy alignment. Your job is to honestly convey to your superiors what's going on in the company.

> The magic of all this is when we get ourselves into a place that's focused and quiet — and we can take action, definitively and powerfully, out of that place — then we can be in relationship with other people. So it's a twofold process: improving our own health, our wellness, our leadership, our creativity, and then being able to combine that across a whole company to produce superior results.
>
> — Anders Ferguson

NUDGE

For the Executive

According to Kofman, translucent leadership means consistently maintaining one's awareness and core values, even in situations of stress.

1. Encourage co-creation. Transform your company from a hierarchical system into a listening and learning organization. Find ways to allow every employee's voice to be heard.

2. Honor your core values, whether you are dealing with employees, clients, the environment, or yourself. Arrange your life and your business to mirror these values.

NUDGE

For the Investor

1. Be informed. Ask about the screens placed on money invested on your behalf. Look for portfolio managers with positive screens, like the Domini Fund or Calvert.

2. If you have large investments in a company that does not fully align with your values, find out how you can implement shareholder initiatives.

NUDGE

For the Rest of Us

Put your dollars where your heart is. Sometimes you may need to pass up the cheapest deal, produced by slave labor in China or with unrefined petrol products oozing into local rivers, for the best deal for everyone. Use your money to support companies that have chosen to do the right thing, even if it costs them immediate profit. Fill your car up at Shell or BP before Exxon, and know that you are supporting fuel-cell research for the future. Take a stand for voluntary simplicity. Participate in a more sustainable economy so that our children can lead richer lives.

CHAPTER THIRTEEN

MORE THAN LIFE AND DEATH

Translucent Health Care

In 1990 *Robert Dickinson was thriving. His Seattle acupuncture practice was booming, and he was in high demand as a tai chi teacher and as a lecturer in Oriental medicine. When he started to get headaches, his doctor attributed them to muscle tension. But they got worse and more frequent. Finally, an MRI revealed a large noncancerous tumor on the left side of his brain.*

"From that moment on, it seemed like the possibility of death was just around the corner," Robert says. "I got my affairs in order, addressing potential situations and conflicts that needed to be resolved before my operation. It was a letting go: of material possessions, relationships, future expectations — a process of cleaning up unresolved issues from the past and anticipation for the future, and residing more and more in this moment."

He recalls that when he came around from his first operation, he had no thoughts. There was only deep silence and what he calls "a peace that passes all understanding." For Robert, this was his moment of awakening. He calls the tumor, of unknown type and origin, his real teacher. "It was the guru within. It showed me the truth of who I really am." Back at work, at first he was afraid that he would not be able to teach. How could he remember anything without thought? But his students reported his classes, in fact, were the best ever. When Robert gave acupuncture sessions, he knew the right point for the needle purely from intuition.

The tumor returned, and Robert had two further operations. During the last, in 1994, he passed through a near-death experience. His heart and breathing stopped for almost a minute before he was revived. When he awoke in the recovery room, he no longer had control of his body, nor could he speak. Still in his thirties, he had now lost everything, not only his mobility but also the possibility of continuing his successful career. Then his fiancée broke off their engagement. "At that point, it really didn't matter too much," he recalls. "I'd had lost so much, I felt, 'Well, one more loss? Okay!' I just kept practicing letting go, letting go, letting go."

Today Robert lives in the countryside near Seattle. Although his speech returned slowly, he is confined to a wheelchair. The awakening that followed his first operation has only deepened. "I have experienced the expansion of consciousness on many different levels, the most profound being one of compassion for seeing the suffering in this world. Many people suffer and do not want to let go of the real cause of suffering. In the last ten years, I have spent a lot of time observing different aspects of humanity and learning to experience compassion and love, an unconditional love for even the more abhorrent aspects of humanity." Robert still consults with patients and students and has come to recognize that the essence of healing is in the transformation of consciousness. "Many times," he says, "it is specific beliefs and patterns that are related to the cause of the illness." While the world labels Robert as handicapped, he feels he has been truly healed. He knows himself to be that which is beyond birth and death. He is whole.

> Most physicians know they are not, fundamentally, mechanics. However, our culture compels them to behave and act as if they are. There are enormous disincentives for physicians to peer out of the box of the limited problem that is in front of them. Ultimately, their choices and attitudes will be profoundly affected by the degree to which they recognize the interconnectedness of all beings.
>
> — Jeremy Geffen

A visit to the doctor, the dentist, or the hospital is on most people's list of their least favorite activities. For most of us, going to the doctor is at best uncomfortable and at worst traumatic. You didn't feel too good to start with; that is why you showed up. And there you are, interacting with a bunch of strangers asking intrusive questions. You may spend what seems like hours sitting in the waiting room with a clipboard, trying to remember your mother's medical history, signing waivers that say, in legalese no one could possibly decipher, that whatever happens, you will not hold them responsible. Before you even get through the doctor's door, you'll need to answer more questions about how you are going to pay. Over forty-five million people in the United States do not have a very good answer to that question. Then, the big moment. You get your fifteen minutes with the expert. If you are part of a cost-conscious HMO, this will probably be someone you have never seen before and whom you will probably never see again. Someone whom it seems very unlikely will lose any sleep over what happens to your condition.

IAGO-BASED MEDICINE

The many health care professionals I spoke to in researching this chapter tell me that the Iago trance affects medicine from three points of entry: the patient (especially one who's aging), the doctor, and the medical system itself.

Why Me?

The spell cast by Iago causes the sick patient to want to avoid responsibility. In the Iago-driven world, everything is "out there." We are more or less always the victims of something that has happened *to* us, for we are cut off from our creative source. Our relationship to medicine is further overshadowed by the fear of death, in fact, by our fear of any change at all. When we have lost connection with our real nature, only the story remains the soap opera of me: my life, my needs, and my things. That is all that we know, and we will pay any price to keep its fleeting appearance in place for as long as possible. Since his stroke in 1997, Ram Dass has been active in visiting other stroke survivors in hospitals. One of the greatest impediments to healing, he told me, is that people want their life back exactly

> Our health care system is largely designed to pay attention to what can be directly seen and measured. The deeper, more intuitive levels of feeling and being are generally discounted or ignored. As a result, on a subtle energy level, interactions between patients and the system as a whole can be, and often are, quite violent.
>
> — Jeremy Geffen

as it was before. But that will never happen; we have to be willing to die and be reborn with every new phase of our lives.

Iago and Aging

As we grow old, still in the clutches of the Iago trance, the process can be one of great fear, regret, and isolation. Watching the mind slowly losing its faculties and the body its vitality is terrifying when that is all one has with which to identify. The most obvious way to deal with aging is to numb oneself, gradually dissociating from life, from the body, and from feeling. In this way Iago kills the spirit long before the body dies. We age as we have lived. Whatever Iago-based habits we have not attended to in our life will become more accentuated as we grow old. Aging is the sad ending to an unhappy story, or, as we will see, it can also be the blissful completion of a life lived translucently.

> I see people having a very painful yearning to live more out of their true Self, and to find their life's purpose. I see most people too caught up in their materialistic life to let go of what we need to let go of in order to do it. I see that all the time.
>
> — Jacquelyn Small

Connie Kishbaugh has worked with cancer patients for thirty-two years as a clinical specialist, a clinical educator, and as senior research nurse at U.C. Davis Medical Center. She also founded a community cancer program and developed a cancer program for home health and hospice. She told me many heart-wrenching stories of watching people growing sick and old, fully in the grip of exclusive identification with the body.

Kishbaugh reflected on the most common qualities she saw in her patients as they grew old:

- *Isolation and loneliness.* Strongly identified with a personal view, our values and beliefs become more rigid. As humanity continues to evolve and mature, those beliefs become increasingly irrelevant to younger people. The musical tastes, political views, morality, religious beliefs, and even aesthetics of an old person still caught in Iago's whisper can become outdated and even ridiculous to younger generations.

- *Numbing and withdrawal.* Kishbaugh told me of a man she had cared for in a hospice, who took it on himself to annotate old texts in his bed. He stopped communicating with the staff, even with his family during visits. She noticed that his task gave him no apparent pleasure; it became a strategy to be too preoccupied to feel real connection.

- *Dependency.* Kishbaugh feels that we treat old people like children; we don't give them credit for their life experience or for the knowledge they have gained. Another of her patients had been a celebrated artist, displayed at galleries in New York and Philadelphia. Finally her adult children were not able to care for her, and they put her into a nursing home:

The staff did not acknowledge any of the things she had done in her life. They spoke down to her, called her "honey" and "dearie," and dressed her in the most garish, outlandish colors. She was so frustrated. But they would not listen to her; they would say, "No, this is what I have already put out for you, so you are going to wear this today." I talked to her about art, about literature. She told me how she wanted to be remembered — for her art, not as an old woman withering away in a nursing home without any say left in her life.

> In modern medicine, patients are often made to feel like children. They must go as supplicants to the doctor, who will dispense information and prescriptions. Patients are relegated to being passive recipients of health care as opposed to being recognized as co-equal partners.
>
> — Jeremy Geffen

- *Fear.* People are afraid to lose the people they were connected to, the things they were attached to, because that would be the end. There would be no chance of ever having that again, or anything similar. Aging does not only presage the death of the body, it points to something much bigger than that — the annihilation of everything we have ever used to define our identity.

When we did our interview, Kishbaugh had just decided to retire early from mainstream medicine. She now works as a complementary healer, focusing on the patient's emotional and spiritual journey through the cancer process. She works not only with the patient but with the whole family, helping them to clarify misinformation they may have about the disease process, to know when it is time for more treatment or when it is time to stop, and to focus on symptom management so the patient can live out the rest of her life in a more fulfilling way.

The Healer Needs Healing

The Iago virus also infects doctors by defining for them a role that severely limits their potential. The fifteen-minute visit, without any established ongoing relationship between physician and patient, reduces medicine to the level of Jiffy Lube: in and out in a few minutes, thousands of franchises all over the country, open long hours. All very well, we might respond, but where is the *love*? Our contemporary medical environment reduces the doctor to being a mechanic. Furthermore, the cost of receiving an education in medicine in the United States also turns every doctor, willing or not, into a businessperson.

> Many healers are unaware of their own codependent emotional drives: their need for significance, their need to feel powerful, their need to feel needed. This is often part of the shadow side of healers and doctors.
>
> — Jeremy Geffen

With years of student loans to be repaid, escalating malpractice premiums, and fewer reimbursement dollars from insurance companies, many doctors forget their original high ideals to heal and help people. Each new patient who walks in the door becomes another figure in the balance sheet, another payment to the car loan or the house loan or the student loan. Many doctors, particularly those in mainstream medicine, have had to cut themselves off from their hearts and spirit to survive in the marketplace of modern medicine.

The Spoils of Sickness

Finally, the Iago trance permeates the system in which both patients and doctors find themselves caught unawares. Drug companies, insurance companies, hospitals, pharmacies, and medical practices are all eagerly waiting for the next time you get sick, looking for a cut of the pie. The cost of health care insurance has risen astronomically in the last decades, so much so that many families cannot even afford to be prepared at all. Kishbaugh comments:

The emphasis is on treating the body, not on treating the person. Research is always going for the new thing, pushing for further treatment. I found that we just were not able to support the patients emotionally and spiritually, because of time constraints and simply because of the way the medical system is structured. The primary reason is because of the way reimbursement occurs. The facility is reimbursed per patient, so the more patients we could see in the least amount of time, the better the reimbursement. The whole economics of the situation is slanted away from treating the whole person and towards quickly addressing symptoms.

SPIRITUAL MYTH #19: Awakened people are always in perfect health; they never get sick.

SPIRITUAL MYTH #20: Those awake to their real nature have spontaneous healing powers. Like Jesus, they can cause the sick to rise up and walk.

SPIRITUAL MYTH #21: After an awakening, no one needs psychotherapy; there is no ego and no personal life remaining.

SPIRITUAL MYTH #22: Awakened people are beyond attachment to the body. They have no care if it lives or dies.

INTEGRATIVE MEDICINE

Dr. Jeremy Geffen is a widely respected oncologist and the author of the celebrated book *The Journey through Cancer*. He makes the important distinction between the relative and the ultimate purposes of medicine:

When we encounter a health problem, whether it is a minor one like a cold or flu, or something very serious like malignant cancer, there is a natural desire to move from feelings of fear and discomfort back to comfort and certainty. The relative purpose of medicine is to address the physical problem

> The illusory sense of being separate from our true nature, our true essence — the source of existence itself — is the ultimate cause of sickness, pain, and suffering. Recognizing and understanding this, and responding with insight and mastery, is the great promise and opportunity of the spiritual journey.
>
> — Jeremy Geffen

with as much skill and integrity as we can. This is a worthy objective, but it is only part of the picture. It does not recognize that medicine has another purpose as well, an ultimate purpose, which is to address the deeper needs and concerns of human beings with as much skill and integrity as we bring to the care of the body.

Geffen points out that until the last few decades little attention has been paid to the mental or emotional realms of being, let alone the spiritual ones, and we have suffered as a result. He acknowledges, however, that medicine has begun to shift in recent years to encompass more than just the physical dimensions of health and disease. He sees that more attention is finally being brought to a patient's mental and emotional experience. He offered me the example of a woman in her mid-forties who discovers a lump in her breast. She has two children, a career she has only recently revived as the kids got older, a beautiful home, and a husband she loves. Understandably, she wants to remove the problem as quickly and efficiently as possible:

There is so much more we can do to help this woman heal as well as become cured. Along with removing her tumor and administering chemotherapy, we can also try to help with emotional issues, including fear, anger, depression, sadness, and any others that might arise. We can help her to explore what it means to her to have a lumpectomy or mastectomy, and how this might affect her self-image or her sexuality. We've only recently begun to enter a new era of medicine where it's acceptable to acknowledge these issues, explore them openly, and begin to find effective and empowering ways of dealing with them.

> Conventional medicine works with the iron filings, whereas a deeper form of healing would attempt to influence the magnetic field. Most doctors don't see the field, so they're trying to figure out the relationship between the filings without even trying to incorporate the energy field in which they exist.
>
> — Bruce Lipton

Dr. Geffen applauds this new willingness to address emotional issues of healing. But like other translucent healers at the cutting edge of medicine, he goes further, believing that even many alternative modalities never get to the deepest truth:

Most doctors and healers still aren't plunging into the ultimate purpose of medicine, which has to do with a deep awakening to the truth of who we all really are. As long as there is a separation between who we are holding ourselves to be and who we really are, there remains an opening, into which more reaction and misidentification can occur, which creates the opening and context for more illness and suffering.

Without consciously taking the final step, we are always abiding in the realm in which sickness and health, pleasure and pain, hope and fear, and life and death come and go in an endless cycle. These phenomena all occur in the domain of doing *as opposed to the domain of* being. *They don't touch the timeless, transcendent dimension of existence, the silent and most radiant aspect of ourselves.*

Now these may sound to you like the flowery words of a new age miracle healer in Berkeley or Los Angeles, the kind who gets their medical diagnosis by channeling Lady Diana, or who would have you live only on green algae gathered at new moon from a specific lake in Mongolia or perhaps raw, organic quail eggs. But they are not. Dr. Geffen is a physician with impeccable medical training and credentials. He is a board-certified medical oncologist, a Fellow of the American College of Physicians, and a gifted writer. He is also the founder of a renowned cancer center and research institute, which he ran for ten years, and has testified before Congress as an expert witness on integrative medicine and oncology.

> If we don't understand and consciously acknowledge our oneness with spirit — and our ultimate identity with spirit — we're never going to get to the deepest levels of what's really going on in our lives and our health. We're going to stop at a more superficial level. This is one of the reasons why so many of the conditions in our bodies, our relationships, and our world are currently the way they are.
>
> — Jeremy Geffen

Dr. Geffen has probably spoken at more medical conferences than most of us have gone to the movies. I asked him how his colleagues respond to his views. "For most physicians," he told me, "this perspective is simply not part of their reality. They have been conditioned, particularly in their professional lives, not to venture too deeply into the realm of thoughts and feelings, let alone spirituality." Others, he says, have had awakenings and have begun to cultivate a translucent life. Their number is growing. But it is when he speaks at conferences where the public is also present that the response is usually overwhelmingly positive:

> *Many people love to hear that there is a physician who is standing up and saying that we are more than our bodies and ultimately, even more than our thoughts and our feelings and emotions, as important and compelling as they are. As much as we want to feel good all the time, and as worthy as it is to strive to learn how to do that, there's a vital dimension of life, of who we really are, that's beyond all striving. As human beings, we deserve and are well advised to spend some of our time and energy focusing on that dimension as well.*

An Integrative Approach in Action

When Geffen was still a medical student in the mid-1980s, his father died of cancer. The pain, frustration, and turmoil fueled in both of them by this experience inspired him to search for a more complete and more compassionate approach to cancer care than the one his father received. He eventually became one of the leading experts on integrative cancer care in the country. In 1994 he founded the Geffen Cancer Center and Research Institute in Vero Beach, Florida. Over the next decade, thousands of patients were treated at the center, which became renowned for

> Everyone with cancer gets the invitation to look within. A growing number of people are RSVPing to that invitation with a "yes." Still, many people don't say yes. They don't accept the invitation to go deep inside their own mind and heart, to experience whatever pain is there, and also discover the deeper truth of their essential self.
>
> — Jeremy Geffen

its high-quality medical care as well as its pioneering integrative medicine program.

Dr. Geffen feels that cancer is one of the spiritual wake-up calls of our time. The second leading cause of death in the United States, it is expected to become number one within a decade, surpassing even heart disease. Cancer evokes deep and compelling challenges in patients and their families:

> *People with cancer are often staring into the abyss of the unknown. They don't know if the cancer is going to come back or if the treatment is going to work.*

They often have to navigate through great turmoil and uncertainty. Along the way, they need medicine and technology, but they also need kindness, compassion, wisdom, and unconditional love. Cancer, fundamentally, is not an external event that happens 'to you.' It is a profound dysfunction of your own cells that can ultimately destroy your body from within. That's one of the things that make cancer such a spiritually intense illness.

Dr. Geffen closed his center in 2003. He now devotes himself full-time to writing, speaking, conducting seminars and retreats, and consulting with hospitals, medical centers, and other organizations, to educate others about the need for, and benefits of, a truly integrated approach.

THE SEVEN LEVELS OF HEALING

Geffen feels that every dimension of one's being must be skillfully and effectively addressed for healing to occur at the deepest levels. This is the goal and purpose of his work — to fulfill both the relative *and* the ultimate purposes of medicine. After years of searching for the most comprehensive, meaningful, and effective ways to respond to cancer, Dr. Geffen saw that the needs and concerns of cancer

> Suffering is one of the major catalysts for awakening. And the awakening many times resolves the suffering.
>
> — Robert Dickinson

patients and their families fell naturally into seven areas. He developed a program, the Seven Levels of Healing, which he offered to his patients and their families as an adjunct to their mainstream medical care. These levels are not necessarily sequential but represent multiple dimensions of healing that can, and often do, occur simultaneously.

Level One: Education and Information

A diagnosis of cancer, or any other serious illness, prompts a multitude of urgent questions requiring as many clear and coherent answers as possible. Dr. Geffen points out that unless patients have a fundamentally adequate understanding of the nature of their disease and their treatment options, they will not be able to derive maximum benefit from those treatments. And until the mind has been sufficiently quieted and comforted, patients cannot relax enough to enter into the deeper dimensions of healing. This information has to be given, of course, with great sensitivity and compassion.

Level Two: Connection with Others

Just holding the hand of someone in crisis can have powerful physiological effects. It slows the heart rate, lowers blood pressure, and calms the mind. Dr. Geffen points to volumes of clinical and scientific data that document the adverse health consequences of social isolation. He encourages patients not only to foster their connection with family and friends but also to find support from a wide variety of other sources.

Level Three: The Body as Garden

Dr. Geffen tells me that there comes a point when patients have all their treatments in place, they have their drug regimen, and they are aware of the options within allopathic medicine. Then they ask him, "What more can I do to help myself? What should I eat? Should I exercise, and if so, how much? What vitamins should I take?" When patients begin to ask these questions, Dr. Geffen knows that the next level has been activated. This is where the healing process can go even deeper, where the patient begins to have a feeling for cleansing, toning, and detoxifying the body as a whole organism rather than

> There came the intense realization that I was not my body. But the body is important to care for as long as you're going to have one. It's like having a car. Many people take better care of their cars than their bodies.
>
> — Robert Dickinson

simply trying to make diseases and symptoms disappear. Patients begin to shift their notion from the body as a machine to be "fixed" by drugs and surgery to that of a sacred garden that can be nurtured and cultivated through a variety of complementary approaches to healing. Along with conventional medical therapies, Geffen's center offered a full range of complementary therapies, including yoga, acupuncture, massage, and nutritional counseling.

Level Four: Emotional Healing

Dr. Geffen regards emotional healing, an element grossly overlooked in Western medicine, as pivotal. It was at this level that he was able to achieve some of the most dramatic breakthroughs, in part because here the strong feelings and emotional needs of cancer patients, often ignored in mainstream arenas, were consciously addressed:

> Many patients complain bitterly about the health care system — and understandably so — for a wide variety of reasons. However, many are unwilling to acknowledge the role that their own mind, heart, and spirit play in their lives and health.
>
> — Jeremy Geffen

For many people, this is the hardest area, because it often involves getting in touch with feelings and emotions that are painful and scary. As a result, people often strongly resist going to support groups or even working privately with a counselor or therapist. Consciously or unconsciously they are afraid of what might come out, what they might feel, or what they might have to confront in themselves. This is very human and understandable. But sadly, this resistance can create an even deeper sense of separation, which can cause even more pain and suffering and, ultimately, more illness.

Laura came to the center when she was fifty-one. Four years earlier she had been diagnosed with breast cancer. After she received a wide variety of conventional treatments, including a mastectomy and chemotherapy, her cancer went into remission for a year. Then it returned and spread to her lungs, liver, and chest. She tried even more aggressive treatments, but it returned again. Dealing with her illness had become almost a full-time job for Laura and Steve, her husband. They came together to Dr. Geffen for yet another opinion about treatment. In their initial visit, they asked question after question about the relative merits of different treatment protocols, drugs, growth factors, and other technical matters. During the discussion, Dr. Geffen noticed that Laura's legs and arms were crossed, she and Steve were both very tense, and there was virtually no contact between them. They never touched, and rarely even looked at each other.

Finally, he said to them both, "You know, your questions are valid and important, and we will address them all. But right now I'd like to ask you a different question: *How are you feeling about all this?* How are you feeling about what you've been through, and what you are going through right now?"

At that moment, they stopped talking and became very still. The energy in the room changed radically, as did the entire tone of the discussion. A short time later, they both burst into tears. "We have been all over the country," they said. "We've been to major cancer centers. We've seen expert after expert. We have had surgery, radiation therapy, round after round of chemotherapy, and various hormone therapies, too. But through all of this, and in all these places, *no one ever asked us how we were feeling.*"

> At the core of cancer, and many other diseases, is a longing for love, the longing to be reconnected with one's true nature, which is love. Cancer cells are fundamentally crying out for love — an expression of the derangement of feeling separate from our source.
>
> — Jeremy Geffen

Geffen invited the couple to explore what was really going on inside; they both began to share their deep, inner emotional experience. For the first time, Laura was able to truly articulate her fear and pain and not focus only on her blood counts and treatment side effects. Steve was able to talk about how the ordeal was affecting his life as well as hers — and how much of his time and energy had been focusing on her medical condition.

These dynamics are so poignant, so human — and so common — and yet they had never been addressed. Over the following weeks and months, Laura and Steve developed a level of trust, emotional honesty, and caring between them that they had never imagined, let alone experienced, before. This became a centerpiece of their experience at the center. Geffen saw shifts like this in hundreds of his patients. He emphasized how, for so many individuals, it was only when the emotional dimension was opened up and explored that the real healing could begin.

Level Five: The Nature of Mind

Patients are shown how they can begin to examine their thoughts, beliefs, and the meanings they give to their condition, their treatments, and the healing process. Jim believed he had gotten metastatic melanoma because he was a "sinner." He believed that God was punishing him for his sins, and that he deserved to suffer. It was clear to Geffen that this belief was impeding Jim's ability to heal, that it actually had become, to some degree, a self-fulfilling prophecy. Geffen offered to work with Jim on his beliefs. That's not a service I remember being offered by any doctor: "I gently helped him to look at the beliefs he was having about his illness and to see whether or not they were really true, and whether there might be some deeper truths that could be more supportive and nurturing for him. This one process alone

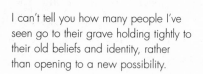

I can't tell you how many people I've seen go to their grave holding tightly to their old beliefs and identity, rather than opening to a new possibility.

— Jeremy Geffen

shifted his experience dramatically. It did not change the outcome of his illness, but it significantly changed how he felt and how he lived and experienced the remaining months of his life."

Level Six: Life Assessment

Patients in Dr. Geffen's care were invited to consider deep questions about their lives: *What is the meaning and purpose of my life? What are my top goals and priorities for the next year? How would I like to be remembered when I am gone from this life?*

John, a sixty-four-year-old hard-driving lawyer, came to the center with metastatic lung cancer. His diagnosis was completely unexpected, and it shook him to the core. He had all the money he ever dreamed of, and all the legal skills necessary to make him admired by his colleagues and feared by his adversaries — but he couldn't buy or litigate his way out of lung cancer. Assessing his life was a powerful turning point. When he read his life mission statement to his wife and kids, he started to cry — for the first time in many years — and so did they. In contemplating how he ultimately wanted to be remembered, he discovered that he wanted to be recalled as a great father and a loving husband. He realized that if he wanted to be remembered this way, he would have to start spending more time with his kids and to stop criticizing his wife.

No one at the center told John what he should do, what his goals or purpose should be, or how he should change. On the contrary, simply by asking himself these questions and taking the time to find the answers within his own heart, John recognized what he needed and wanted to do differently, how he wanted to *be* a different kind of person.

Level Seven: The Nature of Spirit

For Dr. Geffen, the final level, the level of spirit, is the doorway into the deepest core of healing: the return to one's innermost self. It allows patients to return to their essence, where they are untouched by their outer circumstances. For many patients at his cancer center, Dr. Geffen was able to bring them out of their story of illness and suffering to a place of radiant translucence. In this last level of healing, the ultimate level for Geffen, it is the translucence of the doctor, and the unwavering certainty of who the patient really is, deeper than her story, that affects the transformation, through a process of spiritual osmosis.

> Our society is based on having more, no matter how much we get. People are realizing that this is not going to get them what they truly want, which is health and peace of mind. People are becoming willing to do the inner work necessary, realizing that the healing is not going to come from outside of themselves.
>
> — Marc Halpern

Sally came to the center with metastatic colon cancer. She was afraid and looking for a quick cure and to get back to her life of high-powered real estate. The treatments initially worked well, and she went into remission. For six months. When the cancer returned, it had spread to her liver, lungs, and bones. In the ensuing months, while undergoing more treatment, she carefully explored all of the seven levels of healing offered at the center and experienced a deep awakening. As she slowly came to accept that her condition was not, in fact, curable, she spent more time going within. Dr. Geffen recalls the day when they decided to stop her treatment:

She was absolutely fearless. Her eyes filled with tears and light poured from her face. She went around the clinic and offered love and reassurance to everyone else whose hearts were broken because no one wanted to say good-bye to her. We invited her to our weekly staff meeting. She spoke for a few minutes, thanking everyone, and then a wave of silence came over us all. This deep silence was coming through Sally — everyone was moved to tears, and to stillness, with no words being spoken. By then the cancer had spread throughout her body. She was very weak and barely able to walk on her own. And yet she was absolutely radiant. Here was a woman dying of incurable, chemotherapy-resistant, metastatic colon cancer, and yet she was abiding in a place of radiant, silent joy and harmony.

CURING AND HEALING

Not everyone who came through the Geffen Cancer Center was cured or went into remission. And while their quality of life and overall survival were, Geffen believes, consistently higher than they would have been at many other centers, this was not the most important point for him. Sally died. So did many others who came with serious, advanced cancers of all kinds, often far past any reasonable hopes of reversal. But Geffen feels that many were indeed healed. Like other physicians on the cutting edge of consciousness and medicine, he sees a vital distinction between mere symptom alleviation and genuine healing.

When clients are cured, their diseases appear to have been removed from their bodies, and they hope to return to the lives they were leading before. They may have postponed the grim reaper's knock for a few more years, but there is no way to assure that they have been relieved of the deeper malady. Genuine healing, for Geffen, is a liberation from the Iago-based entrapment in the cycles of thought and emotion. Life-threatening illness, especially cancer, can be an opportunity for a radical awakening, to discover one's true nature, to touch what is most real and unchanging, and to find the ultimate source of healing that lies within.

> If you recognize all states as a part of yourself, as manifestations of consciousness and light, if you don't pull back from them but are willing to just be with them, they transform into love, into light, and you enter into them more and more deeply. It becomes a religious experience.
>
> — David Deida

Geffen sees that a true healer is much more than a body mechanic. It is someone who can see past the inevitable fluctuations of good and poor health and the inevitable progression toward death. True healers have discovered a deeper, more abiding dimension of themselves and are able to see that in their patients, and to help that to awaken. They can see that the body is sick, but that the patient is more than the body, and in his essence he is whole and missing nothing. Jon Kabat-Zinn and his wife, Myla, bring this quality of translucence to the way they train medical students at the University of Massachusetts Medical School:

We teach medical students that being really present is absolutely critical. The sacred bond between doctor and patient is always spoken about, the Hippocratic oath and all of that, but is usually reserved for the admissions brochure and brought out again at graduation. We are trying to train young doctors to practice being present, to step outside of time with their patients. That is actually very useful when you've only got six minutes with somebody. It should be six timeless minutes. Then you have an infinite number of moments in a relatively short period of time. When you are driven by your agenda, you may get your agenda accomplished, but you are going to alienate the patient. These principles apply to virtually every arena of life, whether it's parenting, or medicine, or law, or work, or love relationships, which are also such a mystery and so difficult.

A true healer is multidimensional. Dr. Geffen did not come to discover the possibilities of integrated healing only through his Western training. He also spent years studying yoga and meditation, as well as exploring the traditions of Ayurvedic and Tibetan medicine. This combination of perspectives and experience informed and transformed Geffen's understanding of healing.

> Many illnesses are about some inner lessons that need to be learned, some aspect of oneself that needs to be embraced and looked at, and ultimately illuminated by the light of consciousness. Many times I have had a patient in very dire situations, and in one situation they chose to die rather than look at the deeper level of the issue.
>
> — Robert Dickinson

Along the way, Geffen learned that by using alternative forms of medicine, we are not necessarily being more holistic, as people sometimes assume. It is quite possible, for example, to go to the acupuncturist or the homeopath to get "fixed," just as one would go to a Western doctor. Shifting modalities does not necessarily mean that the patient is taking more responsibility, let alone feeling into the emotional, mental, or deeper dimensions of their condition.

Ayurveda

Some of the modalities gaining prominence in the last decades do, however, have a holistic and translucent quality built into them. The most obvious of these is the ancient science of Ayurveda, which practitioners claim dates back over seven thousand years in India. Dr. Marc Halpern is the founder and director of the California College of Ayurveda, which offers training for practitioners. He described Ayurveda to me:

> *The focus of Ayurveda is the alleviation of suffering, and symptoms are part of that suffering. That is the physical component of it, but remember, we also suffer emotionally, mentally, and spiritually. Ayurveda makes no distinction between these levels. In Ayurveda, we recognize that you can't separate the body, the mind, and the spirit; they're integrated together, and so all treatments have to work on all levels. There's a much bigger picture. We are trying to eliminate the roots of disease, which cause suffering, and those roots are found in our lifestyles, they're found in our choices, and they're found in our inability to find stillness.*

An imbalance in the body, the mind, or the feelings, or just a disturbance in meditation, would affect all these levels at the same time. That imbalance is addressed by working with every dimension simultaneously. In Ayurveda, every patient is seen as made up of three basic *dosha*, or elements: *vata*, *pitta*, and *kapha*. For most people, one of these energies is more dominant, which determines their basic constitutional type. And everyone has a tendency, or a weakness, toward imbalance. Dr. Halpern's clinic determined that I was 60 percent *pitta*, (i.e., fiery, forceful, driven), 30 percent *vata* (speedy, etheric, mental), and 10 percent *kapha* (docile, earthy, slower). My weakness, however, is toward a *vata* imbalance. The symptoms of this imbalance, which sounded all too familiar when first described to me, include irregular digestion and an inability to gain weight (physical symptoms), rapid thoughts that change subject very easily (mental), and feelings of anxiety or panic (emotional). And, no doubt, a tendency to take on overambitious book-writing projects.

> Ayurveda looks at things a little differently; it raises the stakes a little bit. It says that the path to perfect health parallels the path to awakening. There is a word in Ayurveda, "Svastha," which means "perfect health." It also means, "to be established in the self." Perfect health comes when we're established in both our true nature as spirit and in our nature as physical beings.
>
> — Marc Halpern

The path back to balance in Ayurveda is totally client-centered. Clients take full responsibility for every aspect of their healing. They need first to fully understand the nature of the imbalance and its ramifications in every aspect of their life. A regimen for a *vata*-imbalanced person incorporates changes in diet, including how much one eats, how often, and at what times in the day; awareness of breathing patterns; awareness of thoughts and beliefs; the frequency and kinds of sexual activity; and kinds of mental stimulation. My Ayurveda practitioner has even brought to my attention the effect of watching certain movies after a particular time of day. I added a good editor to the prescription. All these choices are seen as vital parts of the return to balance. When the imbalance has been restored, the patient will still have a basic constitutional predisposition. You know that the treatment has been successful not only because the physical symptoms clear up but also because the patient experiences emotional balance, mental clarity, and most important of all in Ayurveda, easy access to their translucent core as silent, vast, and luminous.

> In the Tibetan tradition a physician's ability to be a deep healer is directly proportional to the degree of their spiritual awakening. The mark of the master healer and teacher is reflected in the degree of loving kindness and compassion they've cultivated in their own heart and consciousness, and the depths of sincere and spontaneous desire they have for the well-being of others.
>
> — Jeremy Geffen

Ayurveda is both a system of physical healing and a basis for a sophisticated spiritual discipline, which takes into account the unique constitution and needs of each person. With its essentially integrated vision, many see Ayurveda, like Tibetan medicine, as the flavor of the translucent medicine of the future.

Quantum Healing

Dr. Bruce Lipton's research on the mechanics controlling cell behavior points to a radically new way of understanding how our bodies, as well as how the healing process, works. Lipton has been researching and lecturing on cell biology since 1971, including as a research fellow at Stanford. For centuries, Lipton explains, science has attempted to understand the body based on the principles of Newtonian physics. This approach views the body as a mechanism consisting of parts. Pressing button A creates an effect on B, which will affect C, which affects D. If the body is malfunctioning, it follows that, as with any machine, one of the parts is broken and needs to be replaced or repaired. This theory has led to the attempt to disassemble and analyze all the parts, an approach called "reductionism":

> *Knowledge of the body's mechanism would enable scientists to determine how an organism works and how to "control" the organism by altering its "parts." Biologists have analyzed the individual cells down to their component parts: proteins, sugars, nucleic acids, and lipids. They also discovered that the body establishes its internal communication (and hence its capacity to display life) through the interaction of proteins. They found that protein action was not random; it was controlled by an overriding element.*

In 1953, this discovery led to the unveiling of the genetic code, the discovery of DNA. Science assumed that the workings of the body, including its predisposition to illness, psychological characteristics, and longevity, were all controlled by DNA. This dogma, known as the "primacy of DNA," concluded that DNA determines the character of an organism. The Human Genome Project, a multibillion-dollar program, next attempted to map all the genes. It was assumed that with a complete genetic map in place, we could repair or replace "defective" genes, in the process gaining full control over every aspect of an organism's expression.

> When someone has a sudden shift of belief, it can radically change the epigenetics, which means that the same cells in the genetic code will now be interpreted completely differently — this could be the difference between cancer and remission.
>
> — Bruce Lipton

Dr. Lipton is at the forefront of a discovery that is starting to totally transform our understanding of the body. He has shown that genes do not, in fact, control an organism's behavior. It would take hundreds of thousands of genes to control the activities of the more than one hundred thousand proteins, whereas we now know that there are fewer than twenty-five thousand. We had assumed that a human being's behavior was determined by his or her genetic code. In fact, says Lipton, the *interpretation* of the genes (known as epigenetics) is determined by belief. When those beliefs, or the external environment, change, the interpretation of the genes changes, and ultimately, as he has shown, the genetic code can change as well.

Dr. Lipton is creating a completely new paradigm for understanding biology. By looking at the body from a quantum perspective rather than a mechanical one, he is the first scientist to provide evidence that consciousness is primary over matter in the functioning of the body. Medicine is riddled with blind spots, he says, events with no obvious explanation within the current flawed model. Patients have spontaneous remissions, or abruptly get sick for no apparent reason. Conditions can worsen suddenly or disappear overnight. We have all heard of miracle healers and cures, which completely defy modern science and are usually therefore discredited as quackery. In a quantum model of the body, what we now call miraculous becomes commonplace. All physical events, including the functioning of the genes, are overdetermined by consciousness. A change in belief — including one that says whether a condition is curable or not, how long it would take to heal, how long a life would last — all may determine how the cells behave. Dr. Lipton has shown that simply by dissolving belief, we can radically change conditions in the body instantaneously.

> Every cell, every living organism on this planet, has a biological imperative, a built-in innate desire to survive. When we put a belief in the way, that distorts the natural harmony, the balance, and that is where it all falls apart. If you put a cell free in an environment, it will seek the most happy, stable harmonious environment — which is love.
>
> — Bruce Lipton

Medical Magic

I first met Clarissa in 1982 in Europe. (Clarissa is not, in fact, her name, but she has been forced to keep her identity and physical whereabouts to herself, if she wants to avoid harassment from the Newtonian universe police. You'll soon see why.) She visited a residential therapists' training I was attending. Clarissa had a reputation as a "healer." Since I had been experiencing some pain and constriction in my colon for some months, I signed up. Clarissa was in her early forties, crisp, professional, and polite. She asked me to lie down on the table while she washed her hands with her back to me. She turned around, and without asking me a single question about my condition, she began to rub my belly. There was a small gurgling sound, like something you'd hear if you squeezed toothpaste very quickly from the tube, and then her hands were *inside* my body. There was no pain, but I could feel her pulling a rope of old mucous out of my belly. And, as quick as this short interruption of matter-as-we-know-it had begun, it was over. She again rubbed my belly in a comforting way, and that was that.

My belly was red for the rest of the day, but there was no scar. All the symptoms that had been disturbing me cleared up completely. You might think I imagined it, or that it was a trick. But later that day, many of my friends in the course and I watched her work on several other people. With my very own eyes, I saw her remove one man's eyeball and get rid of some dead cells from the back of it, before replacing it. We saw her open up hands, bellies, and a breast. Before she left that day, I asked her how she could possibly do this.

"I spent a good deal of time training with a teacher in the Philippines," she told me. "It took a few years, little by little, to deprogram my belief that matter is solid. Once I got free from that assumption, the rest was easy." Clarissa is by no means the only healer working in a way that completely defies mainstream scientific thought. Joao de Deus,[1] working in Brazil, has attracted tens of thousands of visitors in the last years, including Ram Dass and Dr. Haines Ely, a California dermatologist. Like Clarissa, he performs "surgeries" that seem impossible and "dangerous" from conventional understanding. Hundreds of visitors, every day, experience symptoms completely disappearing, including having tumors, previously evident in CAT scans, shrink to nothing in a matter of seconds.

> When something happens that doesn't fit the conventional point of view, it is ignored. But the exceptions are pointing to the fallacies of the law. The exceptions are eliminated because every one reveals some innate healing ability of the body that medicine says does not exist.
>
> — Bruce Lipton

Events like this are happening all over the planet, even though they defy everything we understand from the Newtonian perspective. As the translucent revolution ushers us into the recognition that we live in a quantum universe, the possibilities for physical healing will exponentially expand the possibilities of what the human body can do, and for how long.

TRANSLUCENT AGING

We see the fruits of a translucent life nowhere more vividly than when people grow old. Here, the contrast between a life lived in servitude to the Iago trance, and one that has been transformed through awakening, becomes stark. Just as Iago habits catch up with us and amplify as we grow old, so translucents experience old age as a time of harvest, when their translucent practice becomes a brightly shining inspiration and example.

George Leonard was seventy-nine when I first talked to him. As a trailblazer of the renaissance of awakening in the West, he has been passionate about spiritual practice for decades. He sees aging as a mind-set as much as a process in the body:

> People are looking around and getting discontented with how everybody is so focused on materialism and greed and how much money they can make and how powerful they can be. People are walking out of corporate jobs. We've got more people from corporate America coming to our workshops now than we've ever had before.
>
> — Jacquelyn Small

Aging is inevitable, but many people start acting old fairly early. There's a real advantage to it, and I can see the temptation. You get a little bored, and so you say, "Well, it's time for us old folks to go home and get to bed." Or people say, "Pretty good for an old guy." It's pretty good or it's not pretty good! Don't accept age as having anything to do with it. There's a lot of value in acting old, you get a lot out of it, and you get an excuse for all sorts of things. Don't do it. Eventually we're all going to get old, and we're going to die. But most people start acting old prematurely; even in their fifties they start using age as an excuse.

When I met with Leonard, he had just been in the hospital for a major surgery. He had lost twenty-two pounds. When he came around from the anesthetic, the doctors asked him some standard questions to see if he was disoriented. First they asked him where he was:

But then they had another question, which when I heard it was so bizarre I could not understand it. They said, "What did you used to do?" I said, "What? What did I used to do? Exactly what I do now!" They didn't get it. I said, "I used to play jazz piano with a group sometimes. I play jazz piano now; I play better now than I played a year ago, or five years ago, or ever. I sing. When I was fifty I had a baritone; now I have a big deep baritone. I do better now than I used to. I do aikido. I used to do aikido; I still do aikido.

I'm president of an institute. I used to be president, and I'm still president. Now tell me, what the hell do you mean by this question?" They just looked shocked. Isn't that terrible? "What did you used to do?" Think about that. As if it's all over, you tell them what job you used to have, and where you used to go. Good God!

Like every translucent over seventy whom I interviewed, Leonard feels that he is in his prime. Throughout our conversation, he was brimming with new projects, new plans, new creativity. I asked him how he felt about the fact that he would one day die, and his response was, "I'm too busy to think about it." His friend Michael Murphy was the co-founder of the Esalen Institute in the 1960s. Murphy is seventy-three and still walks four miles every day. Not long ago, his doctor said to him, "You've never been sick, and you have no heart disease, no diabetes, no cancer. What are you going to do for the rest of your life?" Murphy replied, "That's the least of my worries. I'm just getting started."

We might suspect that these men have simply been lucky to have avoided some of the ailments that often afflict the aging. But translucent aging is not a function of perfect health, but of how one lives within, and gives through, the body, whatever its condition. Ram Dass, for example, had a stroke in 1997, which left him partially paralyzed in a wheelchair, with his speech greatly impaired:

> When we cross a threshold of awareness, we become aware of our connectedness to something greater than physical reality. We perceive so much larger a picture that the stressors become infinitesimally small. They no longer have a harmful effect upon the body and mind.
>
> — Marc Halpern

Before I began to have awakening, even at the young age of thirty or forty, I was anxious because my body was aging. Then I realized that I was not my body, not the ego. I was much more a spiritual entity or spirit itself. There is no doubt that I am going through aging, and a stroke, and approaching death. But I am not identified with the person who is doing all that. I am enjoying my aging and my stroke. That is an enjoyment that would never have come if I had not awakened.

In 2004 Ram Dass led seven different retreats in a year. From a wheel-chair. When I got back in touch with him recently, he was away on a seven-city tour, giving a talk in a different place every night and flying to a new location the next day. He has been actively involved in the Zen hospice in San Francisco, training midwives to the dying, helping people to see the dying person as not the body-mind that is dying, but as the luminous conscious-ness, which cannot die. If anything, Ram Dass's stroke has increased his pas-sion to serve and inspire.

Barbara Marx Hubbard is seventy-five. Recently she had three serious illnesses within six months: walking pneumonia, a ruptured appendix, and a rare blood disease called CLL. She told me about her health problems with the enthusiasm and excite-ment one might hear from someone de-scribing a new hobby or a favorite movie:

> A woman's body is set for reproduction. After menopause, if she can identify with the deep Self and the pattern — the plan of action, the vocation — that is innate to her and says "yes" to it as she does to a pregnancy, she starts to give birth to the self at a level that the feminine never had the opportunity to do before.
>
> — Barbara Marx Hubbard

I took it as a signal that I had to pay attention to my body. I began to notice the effect of every thought on my body, to notice the toxic thoughts and to consciously transform them to evolutionary thoughts. One thought might be, "I'm a failure, I'll never finish my assignment." I was rushing all my life to finish something that was too big for me, and I think the white blood cells responded. I created a new thought, "The process is unfolding naturally, that my work with the local self is over, I am experiencing the divine process of creation within me." Gradually I changed the internal pressure on myself, and I became the experience of that ful-fillment. I felt lighter, I felt a gentle joy internally all the time. I began to discuss this with other women in their fifties, sixties, and seventies; they also felt they were heading into a whole new life. It really had nothing to do with ordinary aging.

Hubbard calls the new phase of her life, which has evolved out of her sickness, "regenopause." She sees menopause as the transition to the most active and creative expression in a woman's life:

Regenopause affects her body, her mind, her creativity, her spirit. It is the basis of the new feminine archetype, the feminine co-creator. Given the dangers and terror of current life on the planet, controlled by the dominator structure in large organizations and institutions and male patriarchal power, the rise of the feminine co-creator at the time of regenopause is necessary for the survival of our civilization. Women are being called forth into a new phase of life, because without that feminine expression, we don't have the way to evolve.

The sociologist Paul Ray also sees that our collective transformation rests in a transformation of the way we view aging and the way we treat older people in our culture. He talked to me about the need to create a "wisdom culture," in which elders have the same position of respect as they had in many older cultures:

The wise elder has learned to disengage, to disidentify from various occupational roles, perhaps even from the primary egoic structures. And those who have been sufficiently prepared have a very good chance of making a transition where they begin to see "I am part of a whole field of consciousness, and that field of consciousness is being terribly distorted by these corporate monstrosities and other bureaucratic monstrosities." They start saying, "What about the children and grandchildren of the future? What kind of world are they going to come in to?" The deep sense of connection to the future of life on the planet, the future of children, is a crucial signature of the wise elder function.

> It is important to meet people where they are. At the same time there's always an open invitation to go more deeply. This is done very informally and casually. I like to just sit quietly with people, gaze, and then see what comes up.
>
> — John Prendergast

TRANSLUCENT PSYCHOTHERAPY

No profession has been as affected by the translucent revolution as deeply as the practice of psychology. While Iago may still hold a tenuous grip on the mainstream — how insurance companies pay for psychological services, or the way that conditions are still pathologized in the *DSM IV*, the diagnostic manual used by psychologists — hundreds of psychologists have passed through a radical awakening and are introducing translucent psychology as an emerging force within the profession. John Prendergast, for example, is the senior editor of *The Sacred Mirror: Nondual Wisdom and Psychotherapy*, which includes contributions from ten prominent therapists whose work today is more influenced by their awakening than by old notions of pathology. Dozens of books published in the last decade redefine psychology as a celebration of awakening as the ultimate sanity, rather than the alleviation of defined dysfunctional states. Dr. Prendergast has been in practice for more than twenty-five years. Since his own awakening, he has experienced that the most powerful tool in meeting with clients is his own openness and presence, his capacity to connect with people and to experience people as that awareness. He says he now experiences a profound intimacy in his work with people "by really living in the unknown and engaging in a dialogue from that. There is a deep ease and enjoyment to dialogue from not knowing."

> We are redefining spirituality and therapy at the same time; that's where our work is. We are not interested in bypassing the human experience but fulfilling it; there's a groundswell now where more and more people are looking for greater meaning and a more profound contact with themselves as well as with the other.
>
> — Jett Psaris

Donna Hamilton, a licensed therapist in Reno, Nevada, agrees. When Hamilton began her training at the University of Nebraska in the late 1960s, she remembers one professor, influenced by Carl Rogers, suggesting that a therapist's role might be just to sit and reflect back love to the client. "When I was twenty-three years old," she says, "it didn't seem like enough to just sit there and simply reflect back and simply hold the space of unconditional love." In the intervening thirty-six years, Hamilton has continuously deepened and refined her training. While working with clients, she has explored every kind of body-centered, emotion-centered, and cognitive-centered approach I'd ever heard of.

Today she has come full circle. After Hamilton experienced a radical awakening several years ago, she reports that the way she worked with clients completely changed. Now, as she enters her sixties, she places presence above strategy. She speaks for the many translucent therapists I talked with in doing research for this book: "I now realize that this truly is the only gift a therapist need give a client — to simply sit in the presence, in that truth of unconditional love, and allow that person to simply witness themselves as they're held in that container. So that's what I have learned in all those thirty-six years.... That's all I've learned, that that's all that is necessary."

Hamilton reports having much more energy as she has shifted from doing to being: "I used to find, after seeing six or seven clients a day, my energy was very low. When I made the transformation into staying in this resource state of unconditional love myself, at the end of a workday, I have more energy."

Many therapists also recount that they experience less tension and less personal responsibility for the outcome of their work. Like an artist, for a translucent therapist the process happens through them, not from them. Stephan Bodian is a psychotherapist in San Rafael, California, whose work has been deeply affected by his awakening many years ago. He says that the most important shift for him has been to relax into trusting in presence: "You learn to trust that you don't have to keep reconstituting a sense of a separate self, doing something specific for everything to work out. Things work out; they unfold quite naturally if you just abide in presence."

> I don't think of myself as a psychotherapist anymore, because I don't take myself to be one. Even though I perform that function, I can no longer think of myself that way.
>
> — John Prendergast

Bodian says that early in what he calls his "awakening process" there seemed to be a choice: "Do I go into my usual psychotherapeutic mode here? Do I look at my notes, prepare a treatment plan for this session, and put on my psychotherapeutic hat? Or do I just trust? Just be?" He reports that this choice was actually a phase; after a while it evaporated, as trusting in presence became the flavor of every aspect of his life:

Of course, I'm going to be with my clients the way I am with every moment. What else is there to offer? Over time I've come to trust in presence to do the work, without having a plan, a preconceived idea of where we're going. I enter the session and just be, trusting that presence is the most transformative thing. It's not about the words; it's about the quality of the presence. And it's not my presence, it's the presence. Being in the presence together, words come out of that. Nothing has to be said, and nothing has to be done. Presence provides the words, the responses.

Many therapists concur that by "just being," they enter into a deep resonance and intimacy with their clients. Prendergast reports, "It is very easy now for me to enter into what feels like the inner world of the client." Sometimes, he says, once a client gets used to this way of being together, she will sit quietly with her eyes open and wait to see what comes up. He says he would never impose any of his own translucent views onto his clients. "I take people where they are," agrees Bodian. "I'm not trying to get them to some place, to any realization. Wherever they happen to be is where I meet them."

> Most people are very stuck in their stories and don't have much of a sense of the space within which these stories occur. As much as possible, I help people discover that sense of space as an entry point to revisit the story with open inquiry and a greater sense of freedom.
>
> — John Prendergast

Hamilton explains that most clients come to her office with a "story." They may have just gone through a divorce, or they are still dealing with the memories of a painful childhood. In conventional therapy, the story is the issue they are dealing with and becomes the force guiding the therapy. "I do not focus on the story," Hamilton says. "I'm very focused on the present time." Translucent therapists will often see the story as an impediment to the deeper potential of the client to awaken, and will support dialogue that moves more into the present moment. Says Prendergast: "The story begins to be seen as a story. That brings a tremendous relief in and of itself. There's less identification with it. The story can be seen as arbitrary and untrue. This brings a felt shift in the body — a sense of ease, of being more grounded, more present, and of feeling a core life energy."

He says that as soon as the grip on the chronology of events in the past, or at least the client's perception of them, has been loosened, all kinds of possibilities open up. The first is to come more into the fabric of now: "I invite a client to be very intimate with their immediate experience, with their body sensations, and to be as close to that as possible." Prendergast calls this "truth," with a small "t": "As a therapist wakes up deeply, therapy is much less about fixing a problem, and more about exploring what is actually true." He encourages his clients to become aware of what their experience actually is, in the present moment: to notice their body sensations, thoughts, feelings, and to be able to be honest about them and distinguish them from the "story."

Prendergast calls the second possibility that opens up "Capital 'T' Truth." This means guiding the client to become aware of who is experiencing this moment. More and more therapists are redefining their role in this way. They are as much a spiritual guide as they are a traditional therapist. Says Hamilton: "As people become more present, they begin witnessing their thoughts, witnessing feelings. As they move along you can start to ask them, "Who is witnessing this?" That's how people reside in the Self. Our responsibility is to return people to the real Self. That is the only relevant truth. Everything should be redirecting us, not to giving answers, but finding that deep return to the Self that knows."

The third role of a translucent therapist is to question and dissolve beliefs that keep reality locked into a certain gestalt. When Prendergast hears his clients voice a belief, he will ask them to innocently inquire, "Is it true?" He calls this a deconstructive movement.

But the most important work for a translucent therapist often comes *after* a client has experienced a radical awakening. Jacquelyn Small went through her shift in 1981, which turned her life upside down. She has gone on to become one of the greatest authorities on the translucent practice of psychotherapy. Through her Eupsychia Institute, in Austin, Texas, she trains therapists to be midwives to the embodiment of awakening: "There are stages to the awakening process. Usually it starts out with a real high; you feel like you're enlightened. Then the second stage can be very painful, because you start to go through a purification process. You discover that the emotional body is full of untruths; your thoughts are untrue, because they are based on societal hypnotism."

> I started out focusing on helping people to see what was wrong with them, a pathological approach to psychotherapy. Now a lot of what I do with my clients has to do with focusing on what's right. There's a very authentic powerful transformation that occurs when people focus on their successes, when they focus on their positive relationships.
>
> — Donna Hamilton

Small says that many of her students and clients pass through an initial period of feeling that because they have touched an impersonal and essentially free dimension of themselves, the personal has gone away forever: "The next thing you know is that you're bawling someone out, or you're mad because you didn't make enough money, or you're jealous. Then the danger is in discounting the awakening you've had. People need guidance because

Spirituality often frowns on psychology, or thinks that there's a transcendent approach that is actually more effective. I see them as highly complementary — they need to work together. We have habitual, early strategies of survival which manifest in our relationships. You can't meditate around them; you can meditate to the center, but still those issues get provoked.

— Richard Moss

otherwise they start discounting their awakening; they can get depressed, feel like a failure." Small feels that real "shadow work" begins after awakening. She calls it the process of becoming whole:

Everybody is looking for a quick, easy answer, so that they don't have to go through the purification process. "What are the ten laws of the self, what are the seven principles of enlightenment?" They want to buy a book and memorize something. You always have to buy another book, and then another book. You're not going to get it through books. They're definitely helpful, they can be road maps, but they're not the territory.

Like Small, psychotherapist Frances Vaughan also works as a midwife to deepen and embody awakening. The difference, for her, between meditation and psychotherapy is that therapy is interpersonal: "You are going deeper, but with someone else. If we can acknowledge all the 'negative' emotions, all the pain, all the fear, all the anger, that is what removes the obstacles to the awareness of the underlying capacity for love."

Hamilton adds that many people will experience awakening but then use it to avoid areas that have been painful or difficult:

Many people who come to wake up to their real Self, surprisingly remain quite disassociated. They may be very identified with spiritual states, even with out-of-body states. They may feel very special because they have a certain kind of attainment. But they also often feel very alienated. They flip-flop back and forth between alienation and spiritual superiority. These kinds of people really benefit from body-awareness work.

This kind of "unhealthy transpersonal state" that Hamilton describes is more common than one might imagine. Small feels it is, in fact, inevitable, even among well-established spiritual teachers. The more we hold onto an idea of "enlightenment" as a stable state, the less we are willing to allow this purification to unfold, and the more it may become repressed and distorted. We are discovering that the more "unenlightenment" a person is willing to embrace, the more actual "enlightenment" their lives will actually express. Richard Moss, for many years both a medical doctor and a spiritual teacher, puts it another way:

> *The greater degree of realization you have, the more you have to embrace despair. The heart of spirituality is the redemptive part: not transcendence, but embracing despair, claiming it in our lives. People don't want to hear that, if they're still in survival mode. "How can I have recognized the oneness of things, and then experience the feeling of being provoked by the really difficult process of relationships with people?"*

> One can hide out in the absolute and get stuck in emptiness. Awakening has no effect on day-to-day life unless conditioning drops away. After a real awakening, the deeper conditioning, even the core story that a person carries, can continue. Until it's directly paid attention to and worked through, one may continue to act out the conditioning in destructive ways.
>
> — John Prendergast

Perhaps for this reason, translucent therapists often find the recovery community is ripe with awakening. Says Small:

> *It's the sacred purpose of hitting bottom. Hitting bottom calls you back to yourself; it drops all the defenses that are in the way. You're just flat on the bottom of your psyche again, and there's nothing in between you and truth. That's why I like working in the addictions field, because people who come through recovery know about that better than anyone. Once you've hit bottom, I don't think you can ever be the same again.*

Hamilton, and many other therapists like her, uses a process of "titration" to dissolve traumatic contractions in a client after an awakening. First, she will guide the client back into their most wakeful resource state to be fully present in the body, in the environment, and to rest in the limitlessness of their original state. Then, she gradually starts to address a traumatic issue where there has been contraction. She does this very, very slowly. As soon as she begins to notice any kind of "emotional flooding," she will return the client to the resource state, to feeling the body in the present moment. In this way, she says, deep shock and contraction are released from the autonomic nervous system. She has released shock from accidents, hospitalization, birth trauma, and all kinds of psychological traumas in this way: "By dealing with them through resourcing, and going very slowly, they get discharged from the body, and this creates lasting and permanent change. In this way psychotherapy is transformed from a fixation on what is wrong with someone to a process of embodying what is already whole, and has always been so."

NUDGING HEALTH CARE INTO TRANSLUCENCE

Dr. Jeremy Geffen believes that we can nudge the healing professions into translucence from all three directions: patients, doctors, and the system in which they meet.

NUDGE

For Patients

Dr. Geffen suggests, for anyone receiving health care, whether physical or psychological, to make sure that the process is multidimensional. Ask yourself if all seven levels of healing are being activated:

1. Are you fully informed of your options, do you feel good about your treatment choices, and do you have confidence in your medical team?

2. Are you honoring your need for connection with others? Are you isolating yourself from family and friends?

3. Are you being kind and good to yourself? Are you nurturing and nourishing your body, and treating it as a precious garden, or are you treating it like a machine?

4. Are you noticing and expressing your feelings? Or do you feel emotionally stuck, depressed, frustrated, or bottled up?

5. Have you examined the underlying beliefs you hold about your condition? Have you explored the workings of your

own mind, and can you see how your thoughts and beliefs affect your experience of life? Are you sure that everything you believe is true?

6. Do you feel connected to the meaning and purpose of your life? What do you really want to live for? How do you wish to be remembered by those you love and care about?

7. Are you taking time each day to connect to your deepest spiritual core and essence? Are you awake to the real Self?

NUDGE

For Practitioners

Dr. Geffen reminds us of the instructions given to parents in an airplane: Secure your own oxygen mask first, before helping small children with theirs. He feels that we can only heal other people when we are willing to heal ourselves. Ask yourself, he advises, which areas of your life are out of balance. Which are less than full? If we are to be effective and empowered healers, he says, we have to commit to healing ourselves first.

He especially advises doctors and their staff to spend some time in silence every day. Sometimes, he says, do this with patients as well. In his Cancer Center the entire staff meditated together regularly, and he saw it as the most important time of the whole week: "This was where we connected with our deeper, inner nature as humans, where we could look at each other and be present with each other with kindness and compassion, and allow our roles and identities to melt away. If we didn't do this — individually and as an organization — we could not skillfully guide others into the magnificent silent ocean of love and tranquillity which everyone is ultimately seeking underneath their desire to get well."

> The awakening gave me something bigger than my personal life to focus on. It gave me a stronger sense of purpose and a reason to be here. My personal life as I'd known it was just over at that point. My life now is more dedicated to service, and my personal life is full of loving support.
>
> — Jacquelyn Small

NUDGE

For Society

Geffen points out that it is very difficult for either patients or doctors to come fully into translucence in a health care system that regards human beings fundamentally as physical objects and that has made health into a for-profit business: "I believe we need a nonprofit national health system that provides fundamental care to everyone," he says. Just as an individual with a diseased liver cannot expect to have healthy skin, since we are all connected in the web of life, on some level we all suffer when some of us are in pain. Geffen encourages translucent doctors, as well as their patients, to recognize that it is impossible to be in real health unless every part of us, all of our six billion human incarnations, are healthy, too.

CHAPTER FOURTEEN

STRAIGHT TO THE GOAL

Translucent Religion

*C*laudia was flipping through TV channels one Sunday morning. Sports and preachers, she wanted neither. Her son, Sam, was out with his friends. Even though she hadn't been to Mass in years, Claudia felt huge waves of guilt when she thought about the Church. Her mother still reminded her, from time to time, what awaited her after death. Would her sin be passed on to her boy? Perhaps it already had been; he had dyed his hair blue and wore an earring now. They were probably both damned, and it was all her fault.

Claudia got pregnant in high school. The wedding was hastily arranged, with everyone in the family under strict orders not to gossip. "Just look at all the expense and trouble and embarrassment you put your family through with your sins," her mother told her. How could she do this to them? They had brought her up a good Catholic girl.

Claudia soon got used to the fact that she was a sinner. Her husband left her and the baby when Sam was only two: more proof of her sins. There was never enough money, Sam had asthma, the job at the factory was long hours for little reward. Now, at thirty-three, she had little hope that anything would change. Surely, God was punishing her.

"The same light dwells in each and every one of us." The words broke through Claudia's thoughts. She looked at the television. The preacher was a woman in her fifties. There was a band. People looked happy, they were laughing. Definitely not Catholic, or anything like it. The preacher went on, "It does not matter who you are, or what you have done, you cannot separate yourself from the love of God." Claudia started to cry. She had spent her whole adult life listing the ways she had pissed off God.

Claudia watched again the next Sunday, and the Sunday after that. Finally, she found her way down to the church, the Living Enrichment Center, where three thousand people came together every week. Happy people, people who hugged each other and told her there is no sin except in the mind of man. At first, Claudia hid in the back of the church during the service. She was worried that if the TV cameras picked her up, her mother or someone else she knew might see her and make things worse.

But Claudia went back every week. She got to know the minister and started attending a Course in Miracles class. Now Claudia teaches Sunday school. She also goes to Mass with her family now and then. She listens to her mother's fears about hell, and her sister's concerns that she has joined a cult. "For the first time, I actually love Mass with my family," she says. "I love the singing and the smells of the incense. I think I've learned to take the essence, and smile about the rest. It's not bad, it's just missing a few pieces."

> Religion and spirituality have to be a force for harmony in this world, not a force for strife. We need to really go deeper and connect as authentically and truly as we can, and dedicate ourselves to really finding meaning and purpose through spiritual practice. Not just being a member of something, part of a new fad, or a team. Not just being a Buddhist, but becoming a Buddha.
>
> — Lama Surya Das

In our Iago trance, many of us turn to religion out of feelings of shame and unworthiness. There remains within us a cellular memory, an intuition, of being limitless, connected with everything, essentially at peace, essentially good. But we feel separate, disconnected from ourselves and from everything else, and the contrast between vague memory and present actuality validates the notion of our fall from grace. Iago-based religion becomes a way to reinforce that sense of incompleteness. It places our real nature far away, either in the future, in something that will come after death, or in another person, separated from us by time, culture, and disposition.

Iago-based religion rests on the solid platform that in some fundamental way something is wrong with you. The distance between where you are now and your natural state requires a long journey, one you may never complete. All Iago-based religions are future oriented. We need to involve ourselves in practices, we need to punish or discipline ourselves in the hopes of a later reward. Whether we call the carrot heaven, salvation, rebirth, or enlightenment, the most important fact is that we are not ready now.

LOST IN TRANSLATION

The problem at the core of organized religion is not one of malice, but of misunderstanding. A mind habituated to problems, to lack, to striving for something that is missing will hear a statement about now, about perfection, about connection, and translate it into a future state.

The essence of every liberating teaching is to turn to your own true nature. When the teacher says, "I and the father are one," and then says, "Come follow me," the Iago trance does not allow us to consider that what is true for the teacher could also be true for us. So we follow the teacher's words, but not his example. He walks in connection, in oneness; we follow in separation. The teacher says, "Seek ye first the kingdom of heaven, and everything else will be added unto you." The teacher is even kind enough to tell us where to seek: "The kingdom of heaven is within." But for the Iago mind, there is no within, there are only endless thoughts and desires and fears, all pointing outward. That's the problem; everything is without. So the mind holds onto the kingdom of heaven part, ignores the "within" part, and then creates an entire fictitious universe: one place called heaven, where you play golf and enjoy moderate year-round temperatures, ornate floral arrangements, and room service, and another where it's hotter than Texas, the

> Christianity needs to hear its own message. Every tradition needs that. The monks who trained me used to say, "The trouble with God is that God has absolutely no taste. He loves everybody." This is radical inclusiveness, this is unconditional love.
>
> — Father Alan Jones

air-conditioning is always on the blink, and the neighbors have violent arguments in the middle of the night.

It is reported that Buddha's last words were, "Be a light unto yourself." In other words, find guidance from within, not by following someone else. But still, hundreds of millions of people cling to the Buddha's words and follow precepts. It is as though the teacher speaks in color, and the Iago mind hears in black and white. We distort the original teachers and teachings to fit them into our own collective assumptions.

Let me tell you a story. There was a monastery in the Middle Ages where scribes were making copies of the Bible. This was before the printing press was invented, so they would write it all out by hand. Every now and then the abbot would do a random quality-control check, calling in a scribe and flipping through his pages. "No!" he cried on one such inspection, hitting his hand to his forehead. "The teaching is 'celebrate,' not 'celibate.'" The mistake is unintentional; the Iago mind can only hear things that conform to its view of the world.

> Sometimes it's more juicy and more fragrant and more clear and more loving to give puja to the dung bug than it would be to go to church every Sunday, and just sit around, and "here we are, and we just bring our families for appearances."
>
> — ShantiMayi

I saw this happen with my own eyes many years ago. I was in England, attending a weeklong retreat with J. Krishnamurti. One morning he spoke about the perfection of the present moment: no need to do anything, no need for practice or meditation, it's all already here, just relax and be what you already are. He talked for more than two hours: he became so passionate that his whole body was shaking. "Don't do anything!" he cried into the tranquil English morning. Finally, he opened the talk to questions. There was a little old lady in the very front row, a longtime follower. "Krishnaji," she began, with utmost devotion, "thank you so very much for your most edifying talk today. It has made everything so very clear, and my only teeny little question for you today is, ahem, how should we practice meditation, in order to get to where you are describing?" Krishnamurti hit his forehead with his hand. The Iago-bound mind must distort. The trance of emergency makes it impossible to experience now; everything becomes about a path to somewhere else.

THE ONE AND ONLY PATH HOME

"Behold the lilies of the field, neither do they toil nor do they spin." Jesus' teachings are about love; we don't find much of a catalog of do's and don'ts in them. The teachings of every awakened prophet point to the sacredness inherent in this present moment. Since the Iago mind knows nothing about this, it transforms the original teaching into beliefs, dogma, and moral codes about what you should and shouldn't be doing.

> I no longer "do" religion as a divine imperative. I come out of passion and not out of duty. It's been a lovely gift to get this kind of discovery in my sixties, that this prison door is open.
>
> — Bishop Richard Holloway

Dogma translates a living mystery into something concrete, something that will survive the passage of time. Of course, what we really need, to keep the teaching alive, is more and more awake people, living their own direct connection to now, to the source of things. Once the mystery gets written down, formulated, then what was fluid and alive becomes solid and dead; it becomes dogmatic, hierarchical, and organized. Out of living spirituality is born the institution of religion; the living Buddha becomes Buddhism; the living Christ, Christianity.

Once such a creed is developed, it almost always claims to be the one way to heaven, to end suffering. Fundamentalist Christians believe that Jesus is the only way to God, Muslims believe the same about Muhammad, devotees of Krishna claim they've got an exclusive too. Any fundamentalist group assumes that the rest of the world's populations are heathens and infidels, with no possibility of salvation. Obviously, from a rational perspective, they can't all be right. The number of groups who could possibly be right about having an exclusive license on liberation is either one or zero. As Neale Donald Walsch pointed out in our interview:

> *Each claims to be the single and sole source of divine revelation and divine wisdom, of divine insight, and divine understanding, of divine clarity and divine power. And nothing could be further from the truth. Many of the world's religions insist that this is so, ignoring completely the contradiction in terms, that it cannot possibly be true of all of them. Somebody must not be clear about this, or perhaps none of them is clear, and the truth is that God is*

communicating with, sharing his power with, bringing his insight to, and sharing his wisdom with everyone. And that only a few people have had the clarity to see that, to accept that, to receive that. And to embrace that.

The more fundamentalist and exclusive a religious teaching, the more hostile it becomes to any other viewpoint. It's us against them; we're right, they are wrong. What could be more explicit than "When your enemy strikes you on the cheek, turn and give the other cheek"? It's a powerful and unambiguous dictate: when someone attacks you, don't attack back, don't retaliate, but show your vulnerability, and that will transform the situation into love. Muhammad was a teacher of peace. "Allah loves not transgressors," says the Koran. Yet even before the Crusades, and right up to the present day, horrific wars have been fought in the name of defending these religions of love and forgiveness. "If Jesus came back today," said Cynthia Kemper, "I think the thing he would have most trouble with is the institution of the Church."

> The Roman Church loves mystics, but only when they're dead, because you can't control them alive. It's an issue of power and control. Now we're realizing that you cannot have hierarchical systems. Knowledge is diffuse, and how things organize themselves is much more complicated. Even if you wanted to be authoritarian, it's not going to work.
>
> — Father Alan Jones

Following an exclusive path to salvation, based in dogma, inevitably creates tremendous fear and disempowerment. Generally, the only way to connect with divinity is through a complicated structure of intermediaries, who in most religions are men. The more you believe in the dogma, the less trust you have in your own innate intelligence as a reference. In our dialogue, Stephen Post put it like this:

Every reasonable person has to be ambivalent about belief systems and about religion as organized worship. Religious beliefs can bring out the very best in people. And human history is littered with the bodies of universal altruists who have been dispatched by local altruists who felt threatened by the idea of universality. Religion can bring out the most positive aspects of human spiritual and moral behavior, and on the other hand they can bring out the worst. They can play on hatred, on deeply ingrained in-group/out-group tendencies and the demonization of the outsider as a reality. We have to hold belief systems up to the critical light of a common humanity.

Transforming original expressions of liberation and insight into moral codes is counterproductive. As soon as you try to repress anything, you create an equal and opposite resistance. The Catholic Church's denial of sexuality, for example, has created a plethora of sexual scandals within the priesthood. More than eleven thousand allegations of sexual abuse were filed between 1950 and 2002 against forty-five hundred priests in the United States alone.[1] If we can bring ourselves to imagine how many other cases of abuse never resulted in official allegations, or what these figures would be like in a predominantly Catholic country, we can see that making any activity off-limits as part of a moral code only raises the temptation factor a thousandfold. Moral codes create perversion; they morph a natural activity, otherwise a portal to know the divine, into a pocket of shame and denial.

> I happen to like dogma a lot, but dogma has had a bad rap. It should be the first word about something, not the last word. It should be a platform from which you leap into mystery. Rather than closing conversation, it should open it up. It should give you the grounds for discussion.
>
> — Father Alan Jones

Many of the translucents I interviewed and surveyed over the last years were raised on fundamentalist dogma, the staple diet of the 1950s. Dogma presents us with the choice either to obediently follow moral dictates, which feel restrictive, or to have no values at all, which leaves us feeling lost, without any reference points. Then you have no rituals left, no feeling of direction, no wise authorities to turn to for advice. Faced with this dilemma, many of us became adherents to moral codes from other cultures. Because they were not the stuff of our own family and environment, because they smelled and sounded exotic and unfamiliar, they seemed to provide more meaning. But sooner or later, we end up in the same place, following a moral creed, still longing for real connection. Only now we're up at the crack of dawn handing out books at the airport. In the last years, many have fallen into a real awakening, an opening of the living core. Then we begin to discover the possibilities of living as a Buddha, not as a Buddhist, of walking as the living Christ, not as a Christian.

SPIRITUAL MYTH #23: After a spiritual awakening, there is no more need for religion. All churches are just for sheep to blindly follow rules.

SPIRITUAL MYTH #24: Only very few people in all history have ever known real spiritual experience. The rest of us must be content with a contact high.

SPIRITUAL MYTH #25: There is a specific state, in the future, that you can aspire to, where evolution is complete. Then you will flatline, and nothing will ever happen again. Till then, you know nothing.

TRANSLUCENT RELIGION

In a moment of radical awakening, you have a head-on collision with the present moment. Even though it may still drive, the vehicle of past and future is irreparably damaged. Translucent religion is now-based; it begins in and takes its expression from what is discovered in this present moment, outside thinking. Although translucent spirituality may bear some superficial resemblances to Iago institutions, it is actually an antidote to fundamentalism. It replaces "ism" with "is-ness," with devotion to what is real. Rather than looking to the future for salvation, we look to now for what we might have overlooked. Rather than looking to dogma or dusty books for the truth, we learn to trust our own intuitive response to this moment and know that it is more infused with wisdom than any text.

> Belief systems and, in particular, traditions are useful and good only insofar as they shape and form their adherents toward an absolute love of all humanity without exception, which is a world completely free of conflict and divisiveness. Insofar as they move their adherents away from that goal and toward hatred and in-group/out-group conflicts and polarity, they fail.
>
> — Stephen Post

The Living Enrichment Center

Mary Manin Morrissey was the senior minister of the Living Enrichment Center, outside Portland, Oregon, for twenty-two years. She talked to me about the kinds of people who attended her services:

My church has services filled with people who have left traditional forms of theology without leaving God, without leaving a sense of deep connection to that which is eternal and imminent and present. They have a deep connection, a personal relationship with that. The people who come to the Living Enrichment Center have a deep respect and honoring for the many traditions that have given rise to that sense of the sacred, throughout all people, throughout all time and history.

Morrissey's teaching is Christian at its core. Those who have been guided by her seek to be "Christ-like," taking very seriously his teaching that light dwells in everyone, that we are to do the things that he did: "There's a scripture that says, 'Jesus thought it not robbery to stand equal with God.' And he says, 'Now follow me.' And so the work that we do seek is not so much to make Jesus the great exception as the great example and that we are then to not only follow but embody the same capacities."

She tells me that many people come to churches like hers because they carry wounds. They are hurting; they have recently divorced, lost a job, lost a loved one. Many are what she calls "recovering Catholics":

> There is a curriculum raining down on the planet. Anyone who is half awake is picking up on it. More people are aware and awakening to these energies. More and more people have a sense that life has a higher purpose, a sense of connecting to something more deeply spiritual, something beyond the theological concepts they've been taught in church.
>
> — Jack Canfield

All we do is give them what Jesus said, versus all the dogma. We give them what Buddha said, we give them the core of Hinduism. It's all about the power of God's love, and the transformation that it brings. We all yearn for it; we seek for it in so many ways. We seek for it in materiality, we seek for it in prestige or praise, we seek for it in all sorts of misguided ways and all we really want is to learn how to live in and live from the love of God. And interestingly, we find that when we tap into and touch the passion to create within us, which is our particular godliness, then we allow ourselves to be one with the creative principle that is life itself.

Churches such as the Living Enrichment Center are collectively called "New Thought" churches. The term includes Unity churches, and churches of religious science. Many are independent and simply emphasize direct spiritual experience, embracing all religious traditions, without fixating exclusively on any one approach. Such churches are, on the whole, remarkably successful in replacing dogma with awakening. Says Morrissey: "When people have had enough awakening to their real nature, they stop looking outside themselves for a reflection of who they are or a direction for what they are to be or do. There's an identification with the divine that is ever present and revealing itself everywhere. The access to its wisdom and guidance is found in the deep self."

> They say, "Will you come?" and I say, yes. I know that everyone knows what I know. So my work is simple. I can't ever tell what I know. I ask people questions and they realize for themselves what they know, which is what I know.
>
> — Byron Katie

I have taught at many New Thought churches. In the last years, I have been speaking about the kinds of awakening I have been researching for this book. I always ask if anyone there knows what I am referring to from direct experience. A few years ago, half the hands would go up. Recently, at the Unity Church in Fort Worth, Texas, all but one hand, out of more than a hundred, went up. The sole exception, it turns out, spoke only Spanish. When the question was translated, she enthusiastically waved both her hands in the air. It is happening everywhere.

I spoke with Reverend Morrissey a second time, shortly before the manuscript for this book needed to be turned in. The Living Enrichment Center, which she founded, had passed through some rocky times, in part due to financial mismanagement of which she had been unaware, and they had been forced to sell their building and eventually close the church. I was deeply touched by the way she took absolute responsibility for what had occurred, even for events quite outside her control. She was committed to making sure that everyone involved in her church would be properly taken care of. The apparent collapse of the outer forms she had created did not put even a small dent in her trust in, and commitment to, what her heart knows to be true.

All in the Now

This transformation of religion from dogma to direct mystical awakening is not limited to a small bunch of Unity churches on the West Coast of America. Richard Holloway was the Bishop of Edinburgh till he retired in 2000. His attitude toward religious life has been totally transformed since his awakening a few years ago, which he described to me with radiant innocence.

> *I describe it as living in a state of expectant uncertainty. It's a kind of potentiality toward the future and an unprogrammed excitement about it. It's not being externally guided by some prepackaged program. It's like a new discovery of the world, a fresh sense of wonder, as in childhood. If you like, Adam and Eve leaving Eden's gated community, but without the sense of the "fall." A fresh, anticipatory feeling — a new world to explore.*

He told me that he used to conceptualize God as a superbeing outside the human continuum to whom one sends letters and tries to make contact: "I no longer have that idea of a divine object projected onto the blank screen of space with whom I can be in touch by sending letters 'to him who lives, alas, away,' as Hopkins put it. For me, prayer is no longer a specific activity; it's a mode of attention, sensitivity towards the other, whether it's a human being or a rowan tree on my beloved Pentland Hills." Bishop Holloway feels he can find God everywhere, behind his own eyes, and in everything he sees. The boundaries of what is spiritual and what is not have melted.

> I'm still uncomfortable with the idea of religious experience — the notion of me having a private experience of the divine. I know that for many people that is a valid description of what the divine is, but it's no longer valid for me. For me, religion has carried a number of important values, like a rocket propelling a satellite into orbit. Though the rocket has fallen away, the values remain. They cannot be commanded, but they can be experienced.
>
> — Bishop Richard Holloway

Father Alan Jones is the dean of Grace Cathedral in San Francisco. The giant stone structure reminded me of Canterbury Cathedral, where I went to school. It brought back memories of listening to the catechism in the damp, dark crypt. So I was amazed at this energetic upbeat man in a God collar, sitting in his study overlooking the gothic arches, sipping his tea as he told me:

God is being democratized. You can't do things based just on authoritarian religion anymore; if it isn't freely given, it is not spirituality at all. We are moving from the tribal to the transformational. We want communion with each other, but it's not going to be based on someone else's say-so. I love the tradition, but I think you have to be a revolutionary, you've got to be subversive, you've got to be in conversation with it all the time.

> The tendrils of a new, deeper form of spirituality are growing. It's the greening under the surface crust of consciousness and social paradigm.
>
> — Jean Houston

For Christians like Holloway, Jones, and Morrissey, everything has been distilled down to the discovery of divinity within the ordinary and the human. It is not "out there" anymore. Buddhists call this the jewel in the lotus. Says Morrissey:

We live in God. God is living and moving and having being as each one of us, and we are living and moving and having being as God. It is ever present, there's not more of it here and less of it there. There is a beautiful experience called human life, filled with drama and comedy and pathos. The universe is evolving itself also. We are full of God. Every one of us. As we are awakening, so is the universe awakening itself, through us.

This willingness to pay close attention to what is real now, to the actuality of the human experience, takes the "futuring" out of religion. Whatever is worthy of our worship is here in the moment, and the rest is a figment of imagination, a creation of the mind. Eckhart Tolle talked of it like this:

Don't seek where you cannot find, in the future. Bring the intensity that is behind the seeking into now, and seek in now. Because the portal is here. There seems to be a future, but ultimately there is no future because it never happens; it never arrives; nobody's ever met it. The future is a mind form. Then seeking gets trapped in mind forms. If you seek in the now, at first it might be disconcerting. The now seems so insignificant, or it seems to be an obstacle to my wanting to get somewhere or to be something. Seeking is transformed into alertness. That intensity becomes alertness in which arises whatever form this now takes.

Translucent religion is based on a deep respect for, and attention paid to, our moment-to-moment experience.

Jeffrey Miller left his life in Boston in the early 1970s when he was twenty-one and traveled to India. He met many spiritual masters, including the Hindu sage Neem Karoli Baba, who gave him the name Surya Das. He lived and studied with many Tibetan masters, going on to establish Tibetan monasteries in the United States in the late seventies. In 1980 Surya completed two traditional *dzogchen* (literally, "great perfection") retreats, each one lasting three years, three months, three days, and three hours: almost seven years of monastic reclusion. He was the first person born in the West to become a lama in a lineage of Tibetan Buddhism. Lama Surya Das is steeped in Tibetan Buddhism. He is one of a great number of people who turned their back on the religion of their

> The idea that there is a divine realm outside the human realm no longer has any meaning for me. It's not operational in my life, though I recognize that it still works for many people, and I want to respect that.
>
> — Bishop Richard Holloway

upbringing and wholeheartedly embraced the religion of another culture. But today, like Bishop Holloway, Surya Das has also come to value the essence more than the form:

I am a Buddhist deep down, but it's not like it is the core of my being. I would like to be not too attached to that idea and to recognize that it is just one more affiliation or -ism. With -isms come schisms. That is why I think spirituality is so important today: based in personal experience, verging on mysticism, going inward and deeper, not just going outward from spirituality to religion and institutions. We have had too much of that, we are top-heavy. We are out of touch with the inner life thread, the mysticism that is the heart thread. Religions are like the body, the church, the temple, but the God that animates it is the heart.

While translucents unanimously value spiritual experience over dogma, they also recognize that any experience can become plastic within nanoseconds. There is always the temptation to hold onto an insight or glimpse of connection, and to make it into a treasured memory. Then Iago uses moments out of time to distract us from the present moment, returning us to living in the past.

It was through meeting ministers within the established church that I realized how widespread the translucent revolution has become. It is no longer a subculture, an alternative to the mainstream; it has infiltrated the mainstream itself. When Bishop Holloway began to speak more openly about his own awakening, he found that many people in the Anglican Church were very critical, but he also experienced, in many others, an enormous sigh of relief:

> *I'm not trying to persuade anyone into anything or dissuade anybody out of anything; I'm just trying to be true to my own experience. But I do find that people who read what I've written tell me that it has given them permission to say "yes" to what they are experiencing in their lives, to own what is happening to them as well. It's one of those lightbulb experiences, unique only in that we are all having it in our own way. There does seem to be the sense that this is happening to a lot of people. I think that they're discovering that the prison door was never actually locked. I don't quite know what it is that made them get up and push it, and see it swinging open and discover that all the prison guards had disappeared. There is a sense of having been a prisoner to one's delusions and of finally realizing that the snake is just a rope.*

> Spiritual experience can actually lead to inflation. There's no one more insufferable than someone who thinks they're more enlightened than anybody else, without a certain sense of humor. I know people who on one level are deeply at peace and enlightened, and yet go crazy if they miss a bus. We may still be five years old, and on another level be a saint. That's what keeps us humble. That's why religion is very funny.
>
> — Father Alan Jones

I spoke to Jean Houston, Eckhart Tolle, and the ministers from churches of several denominations, encompassing congregations of tens of thousands of people. I spoke to longtime meditation teachers like Christopher Titmus. I found unanimous agreement that they have been witnessing a massive shift from dogma to direct spiritual awakening in the last ten to fifteen years. Since the phenomenal success of his *Conversations with God* books, Walsch has met with tens of thousands of people:

> *Not only do all people have the potential for having this precise experience of connectedness with the divine, people in fact have the experience of it, but they*

simply do not know it. And because they do not know it, they do not experience their own experience. More and more people are giving themselves permission to truly open their eyes and see what is really there. And to believe what they are seeing. As more and more people believe that it is possible, more and more people see what was always there.

THE CONVERGENCE OF RELIGION

The huge wave of radical awakening, both outside and within organized religion, has tended to polarize people either into an increasingly rigid fundamentalism or into the vast open waters of translucent mysticism, where we no longer know with our thoughts and beliefs but we truly *know*, with our whole being. Paul John Roach is the senior minister of the Unity Church in Fort Worth, Texas. Since September 11 he has seen people respond to more uncertain times in one of two ways:

> There are two Christs for me. There's one in me waiting to be born and there's one in you waiting to be recognized. As the early Church said, God became man so that we might become divine. Instead of the language of salvation, it was the language of divinization. We become transparent to God. We greet the God in each other. It's about loving what you are, loving that you were born to love.
>
> — Father Alan Jones

Some adopt a rigid system that answers all possible questions and so you don't have to think beyond its systems. The other response is much more seemingly fragile but much more expansive, because it doesn't lay down a rigid framework. It allows you to move within the mystery of it. And that seems to be flowering right now. I think people are more and more interested in embracing that because they've been through everything else. It is a willingness to embrace mystery, a willingness to embrace not knowing, allowing that intuitive awareness to speak.

This willingness to sit in mystery has become hugely accelerated since September 11. Pamela Wilson is a spiritual teacher who travels extensively in the United States, Europe, and Asia; just looking at the teaching schedule on her Web site can give you jet lag. She describes a dissolving of boundaries between what she calls "messengers of the truth":

So many people have dropped their identification with their role in recent times. All the messengers and traditions are relaxing and melting their identification and separation. I see a dissolving into oneness of tradition, the teacher-student polarity melting back into one medicine. This is, for me, a very blessed time to be a messenger. There isn't a hierarchy and there isn't a rigidity of "my way is the only way." Different paths are all melting into each other, and that is really living the truth. Nature seems to be the ultimate satsang giver.

Alan Jones refers to dogma as "conceptual lust," the "agonizing desire to have a conceptual control of reality, one way or another." Religion becomes tremendously more intelligent when it is freed from such control and can connect again to the core vision we all share.

> We're at the early stages of creating the hybrid spiritual culture that is fusing disciplines and practices and perspectives from all over the world. There is more of a vigor and strength and more transformative power than any of those traditions have on their own. You have to develop your own real navigational compass and your own common sense to do these things.
>
> — Stephen Dinan

Sitting next to one of the largest Christian cathedrals in America, Jones stated with a twinkle that he is much less interested in what people believe and much more interested in how those beliefs function: "My first test with anyone to orthodoxy is, 'If you were in charge, would I be safe? If you were in charge, would there be room for me?' If the answer's yes, then we can argue about anything. I love an intellectual argument."

He tells me he has as many Buddhist, Jewish, Hindu, and Muslim friends as he does Christian and finds common ground with all of them:

I know so many wonderful people in other traditions who for me seem so authentic, and I would say that they bear Christ for me. I don't mean to baptize them and be imperialistic. One of the best little talks I've heard on "I am the way, the truth, and the life" was from a Hindu. "Yes," he said, "Jesus is saying, 'I am the way,' but what is the I? Who is this Jesus? The life of self surrender, the life of compassion is the way, the truth, and the light."

Like Bishop Holloway, Jones says he loves the teaching stories of Jesus, and in that sense he remains a Christian. For example, the virgin birth, he says, is not only about Mary's sexual status: "It is saying, look at this woman with a baby. Look at any woman with a baby, at her breast or her cheek, and ask yourself, 'In the light of that image, how should I be in the world? How should I behave? How should I treat people?' "

Awakening from rigid dogma allows us to embrace a theology that is evolutionary, that is always discovering more about the possibilities of living as love. "God is infinite. Go from glory to glory, in endless revelation," says Jones. Fundamentalist anything pins the truth down to words in a black book (never mind that they are the translation from the Latin, which was translated from the Greek, which was translated from the Aramaic, from the spoken word of someone who never met the original prophet), and makes that book a higher authority than what we see and feel and trust in this very moment. Buddhists compare the present moment to the Dhammapadda, making that the higher authority. Muslims do the same with the Koran. Evolutionary spirituality sees every teacher who has lived as a significant landmark on an endless journey of consciousness, experimenting with its own possibilities at incarnation, discovering how manifest consciousness can reflect the splendor of its unmanifest face.

> We are reconnecting to the Universe, not as a dead scientific system but a living Universe. To the extent that we reclaim the aliveness of the universe we are reclaiming our capacity to engage naturally in spontaneous religious experiences.
>
> — Duane Elgin

When we shake free of dogma, we find all kinds of evidence of the natural goodness of humankind, of the Goddess energy of creation. Translucents who have given up the rigid beliefs of religion, while staying true to their own experience, have a far more positive view of humanity than those who cling to ideas of original sin.

The most translucent expressions of every religious teaching converge on the same essential message. Jesus, Buddha, Lao-tzu, and Krishna all said essentially the same thing, which is to come back to who you really are and rest there. Translucents find common ground in all these teachings, so they find it easy to talk to one another. An explosion of conferences, magazines, and Web sites in the last decades has brought together religious leaders from all different parts of the world and traditions in dialogue. At events like the Prophets Conference and the Parliament of World Religions, the Dalai Lama,

Deepak Chopra, Thomas Merton, and the Indian teacher Ammachi all found common ground. Father Alan Jones shares his thoughts:

> I'm not going to throw the pictures out; I'm going to keep the picture book. And then when I'm with Hindus or Buddhists or others, we just exchange family albums. It's like getting the old wedding pictures out. Instead of clobbering each other with dogma, we say, "Have you heard the one about the prodigal son?"
>
> — Father Alan Jones

The divisions in religion are not between traditions now but within them. I'm not interested in "Is this Christian?" I'm interested in "Is it true?" I have more in common with Rabbi Pierce than I would with a TV evangelist, who I feel is living on a different planet. Even to say "following Christ" doesn't have much coherence, because there are so many Christianities, there are so many Judaisms. That's where the splintering is; part of it is good and some of it is frustrating. It's a very exciting time.

Every religious tradition today is experiencing the internal distillation into translucence and fundamentalism. The more translucent elements resonate with the original spirit of Jesus or Buddha or Moses and with personal awakening. They find it easy to be in conversation with other traditions, and become different flavors of the same universal religiousness. The more fundamentalist interpretations, of the same religious traditions, cling to literal readings of written scripture, dogma, and moral codes. Walsch put it this way:

> *Religions are now talking to each other. We have heard it, and we have seen it. With great sincerity they are finding areas of commonality. The Catholic Church reached out after September 11 to all the different faiths to congregate at the Vatican to determine in what ways we might unite under the common flag of humanity, for the common belief in a single loving God. Those are profound sociological experiences and events that would have never have occurred even five years ago.*

The Potential of Religion

If the translucent revolution prevails, can we expect to see churches and synagogues closing? Will Grace Cathedral be remodeled as the world's largest

Ikea (come to think of it, the Ikea outside Stockholm could contain several cathedrals), with millions of translucent people set free and wandering aimlessly on Sunday mornings, filled with an ecumenical devotion? Absolutely not. Many translucents love their roots, their traditions, and their rituals but see them as flavors of a universal religiousness. Any religious ceremony reminds you that you are whole, not broken, and there is a divine and beautiful world waiting to dance with you in the very moment. All that is asked of you is to shake off the shackles of dusty belief and lose yourself in celebration.

Any kind of gathering in spirit, be it a church, a synagogue, a Twelve-Step meeting, or a silent meditation, is an antidote to the dense smog of Iago-based thinking that overshadows our world. Television, advertising, the speed of life, even our families and our work can seem to pull us away from ourselves. In the Iago-driven model of religion, we need an intermediary between divinity and us. The priest represents the dictates of the church, the moral code that we must follow, and reminds us of the consequences of our actions in the life to come. The translucent minister or rabbi reminds us of the power of now. Translucent religion brings us back to ourselves, to our innate divinity, and indeed back to its original meaning: *religare*, "to tie back." The translucent religious leader has a specific role: to facilitate an environment that can be a fertile soil to bring people back to themselves. Mary Manin Morrissey described her role:

> I really don't feel that human beings are foreign to love. I think they've become foreign to love, but I think inside them is true, open, deep love. I never will give that away. Even when I am totally frustrated with the world, I will never give that away.
>
> — ShantiMayi

I have a gift for speaking, and a gift of inspiration. I also have a gift of being able to see through the crust of our misconceptions about ourselves, so I don't attach myself to people's stories or their past experiences, but I help midwife their own understanding to a much truer sense of themselves that isn't attached to or bound by or restricted by the experiences they've had or the stories they've been told about themselves. My role is to expand in the high remembrance of the whole being, which is in every person, to tell stories about that, to create services, music, and experience.

But ministry is not restricted to one person in a church that is alive with its original awakened core. Everyone becomes a minister for the mystery outside time to become embodied as love. That is not to say that everyone goes off to a seminary or rabbinical school, but that we each find our unique way to be a vehicle for the Big Love. Morrissey pointed out that in her church, one woman's ministry was her motherhood and her passion to create a home, another's was her business, and one man was a minister for the living truth through his photography. "He's a wizard with light," she told me. "That is when he is most alive and it's his ministry."

> We come together, discover and uncover who we really are, and then ground ourselves in service. The deeper levels of spiritual growth only occur through service. People come for reminders. We gather together on Sundays for reminders and encouragement and examples, to have an anchoring someplace on the planet where we can practice the principles that give rise to this kind of awakening on an ongoing basis.
>
> — Mary Manin Morrissey

When the leader of a religious gathering is willing to sit back in the saddle, to be a facilitator, almost a bystander, to the collective awakening, a spirit of democracy arises in religion that has often been dreamed of, but rarely realized. At the Unity Church in Cincinnati, groups meet every night bringing people back into themselves from their complicated lives. On Saturdays alone, you can attend the Men's circle, the Women of Wisdom circle, the Diamond Heart Work group, the Sacred Heart Circle. Each of these groups allows people to invoke the awakened teacher as a meeting rather than as a particular person. Eckhart Tolle's book has reached more than two million people, and groups based on *The Power of Now* have popped up all over the world. The people who come together have read the same book, and they rely on their shared direct experience to be their teacher.

The great benefit to gathering with other translucent people in this way is that the teacher emerges as the meeting itself. Anyone with a question, or needing support, can offer that to the circle and let the circle become the teacher. There is no guru in the room, spread evenly like hot butter. Rather, the body of the teacher is made up of everyone present and can only speak or move when all come together. The musician Peter Makena sings:

> *Whenever two or more of you are gathered*
> *In the name of that which loves*
> *That which is compassionate,*
> *That which liberates*

Great blessings shower on you,
Great blessings radiate from you.

Before the historical Buddha died, he reportedly predicted that a teacher named Maitreya would be the next to turn the wheel of dharma twenty-five hundred years after the Buddha's death, which is right about now. Maitreya is often pictured sitting in a chair, rather than cross-legged like the previous Buddha. Some have interpreted this to mean that a man named Maitreya would be born in our time, offering teachings and enlightening humanity while seated in a La-Z-Boy. But the word *Maitreya* means "the friend." Today people like Vietnamese monk and author Thich Nhat Hanh feel that the Maitreya has come and is actively teaching all over the world, as I write and you read these words. Today it is the spirit of friendship that turns the wheel of dharma, the spirit of honest and open investigation into and testimony to the truth. It is the gathering itself that is the guru, friends meeting friends.

Millions of people have come to discover translucence through recovery from addiction. One of the core tenets of the Twelve-Step programs is the recognition that since you are powerless over your addiction and your life is unmanageable, you need to invoke a power greater than your separate identity to deal with it. Recovery communities emphasize the power of coming together in a spirit of friendship, where everyone can simultaneously be both student and teacher, both helper and helped. In this sense they are also "churches," just as much as Christian gathering places or synagogues.

> I find when I travel around lecturing, I see the audience as part of myself. I feel that I am really talking to myself. I say to the audience: "My name is Ram, which is a name for God, but Ram is an acronym for 'Rent a Mouth.' You and I have rented my mouth to say things we all already know." And I know that because no matter how far out I get, there are people who are nodding in the audience.
>
> — Ram Dass

Phil's teacher is his men's circle. A group of eight men have been meeting for several years every week. They get together in each other's homes. The meeting begins with ways to center themselves. They may sit quietly, or go round the circle for a check-in, to see how each man is doing. Most of the meeting is "open time," when anyone who needs support or guidance can turn to the whole circle as his teacher. Over the years, they have learned to become sensitive to the dangers of offering advice or doing a sales rap for any particular viewpoint.

"I don't trust my own mind too much," says Phil. "It changes its position with the wind. And I don't trust the mind of any one of the men in the group too well either. But there is something about collective wisdom that I will surrender to every time. If I'm caught up in something and they tell me to take action of some kind, I'll always follow it. Especially when they all agree, when it's unanimous." Phil has had several more traditional teachers in his life. Now, he says, the circle of men performs the same role for him. The circle is the guru. Phil's circle performs the same role for him as a church or synagogue might. It is, in the deepest sense of the word, his religious experience. It binds him back to himself, dispels his doubts, and helps him to move forward with confidence.

Catherine, his wife, is part of a women's group:

> Our lives are the marvelous possibility. Our lives, our children, our gurus, our work, our creativity, even our doubts are the ground for really expanding ourselves as far as we possible can, to see how deep we can go in ourselves. Every instance gives us that opportunity, no matter where we are. I just can't imagine that there's an end to the ripple. It's wonderful
>
> — ShantiMayi

Women have been meeting in circles forever. The dynamic of the circle brings everyone into a depth. It's not any one of the women who does that, it is the circle itself. We all meet with the intention of showing up and being honest with whatever is true. The intention is sacred. It is like a free playground for the feminine to show its face in whatever form. It's exciting to see what will happen next. In the women's circle there is huge acceptance and empathy — you can see yourself in all the different feelings that everyone is going through. We have a commitment to support each other to be with feelings, and to remind each other if we get lost in the story. I become so present, so present, life is taking over, I'm being taken over, and at the same time I support the other women to just be with what arises.

These groups, free from dogma and tradition but infused with sacred respect for what is real in the present moment, are also part of the new translucent church. Without the sacred tribe, we may easily feel lost at times. When the Iago trance swoops in on us, as it can for everyone, we become a little person with no mast and no sail, tossed aimlessly on the waves. The only anchor we can find is "my truth," which, as Phil testified, can seem unreliable and fleeting. In a wisdom circle — of men, women, people in recovery, or simply budding translucents — every small moment of awakening in each person contributes to the translucence of the circle. As a participant, you may find yourself speaking in spite of yourself. When you are done, you may wonder where the clarity came from. It was not the "you" you are familiar with, it was Maitreya using your lips and tongue to turn the wheel of dharma again.

And finally as you expand beyond the confines of religious tradition, the whole of your life becomes the teacher, everywhere you go is the temple, and every moment is a sacred event. ShantiMayi asks: "Who can say anything about anything? Terence McKenna was a shaman, plants were his

> It is always accessible and direct. Access is one of the things that is most important in spiritual teaching. It doesn't depend on a church, a priest, a mediator, or any particular form. The sixth patriarch in Zen got awakened when he was sweeping. A piece of tile went flying, hit a bamboo, and went "clunk." Who is the guru, the teacher, there? The bamboo.
>
> — Lama Surya Das

teacher. Ramana Maharshi's guru was a mountain. Some people are taught by the core of their own heart. Some people's gurus are their children. And some people are dedicated to a living master, or one who has passed away, for a lifetime."

THE PARADOX OF TRANSLUCENT PRACTICE

Whatever the catalyst, after any radical awakening the translucent finds herself sitting in the middle of a paradox. A moment of awakening is a moment outside the mind, a moment outside time. Surya Das says of such a glimpse: "Things are already perfectly at rest and in place, they are not expanding, evolving, improving, or anything. That is the ultimate absolute reality, the unconditioned, the true nature of things. We all come home to it, and it feels like home. Houses come and go, but home is a state of mind." Whenever we rest in our original state, there is clearly no need to do anything, to improve anything, or to go anywhere.

The other side of the paradox is the actuality of our human day-to-day life. We see where we are being unconscious, insensitive to other people's needs, or just getting lost in stories and trivial details. We intuitively know our human potential is greater than this. Surya Das continues:

We need to integrate awakening into our jobs and our families and our health and our community action, and social action and connect with the environment. That is why I find teachers like the Dalai Lama very inspiring today. They are willing to entertain new applications of the timeless truth. It is true that our own innate divinity is always and already perfect. But it is not true that our human nature is perfect, and therefore there is nothing we can do about improving ourselves, or this world. There definitely is plenty that we can do.

It is easy to become dogmatic on either side of this razor's edge. On one side, we can become fundamentalist about there being nothing to do. Everything is already perfect as it is, not only because we have intuited it in a glimpse but because we have also heard so from various teachers and books. So it becomes "unenlightened" to initiate any action at all. No need to practice; who you really are is divine already, and the rest is illusion. No need for prayer; there is nobody to pray to, it is all you anyway. Although this position is based on authentic realization, our own or someone else's, its interpretation through the mind cripples us from acting with common sense, and in fact buffers us from the divinity of this present moment.

The other side of the paradox is to become fanatical about fixing ourselves. Looking at our day-to-day life, we tend to compare ourselves to spiritual heavyweights like the Dalai Lama or St. Francis and feel that we are far from living wakefully. Then there is no time to waste; we need to work hard if we are ever going to make it. When we can embrace both ends of this spectrum, we enter translucent spiritual practice in devotion to the present moment, not to get somewhere later.

> I believe in tailor-made spiritual clothes, so depending on who comes and what they come for I try to facilitate their next step. That's all. I try not to have an idea for where everybody should go and have each do the same thing, the way that I did it. I try to be open, helpful to facilitate their next step on their true spiritual path.
>
> — Lama Surya Das

Says Michael Barnett: "One doesn't sit to get somewhere; one sits because sitting is *it.*" Rather than using practice as a means to get there, it is a means to come home to here, again and again and again. However deep our glimpse may have been into our real nature and the real nature of things, we are still living in a Iago-dominated culture. Through television, advertising, the whole nature of our economy, our culture is continuously attempting to generate more desire, more of a feeling of lack. That is how the commerce machine keeps going.

We need practice not because there's anything wrong with our realization, but as an antidote to our contact with the collective Iago mind. It's like cleaning the kitchen. You can deep-clean the kitchen, scrub under every cabinet door, but it doesn't mean you never have to clean the kitchen again. You clean it, and then it gets dirty. So you clean it again. We are used to the fact that we have to clean the kitchen regularly to bring it back to its pristine condition. In the same way, we enjoy practice regularly, not to get to a place where we no longer need to practice anymore, but because we recognize the outgoing pull of the world around us. Here's how Richard Moss speaks of his practice:

> These are the two extremes: "there's nothing you can do" and "it's all up to you." There is an intensity behind seeking, but that intensity is distorted through the filter of thought and becomes translated into seeking for something to be added to me through the future. The intensity may well be the evolutionary impulse of the Universe, and then the old mind forms make that into a future.
>
> — Eckhart Tolle

After the radical awakening I had a reference in my reflection, which was emptiness, infinite. Now, there is a basic practice of self-reflective awareness. So my practice has been to look at myself when I'm in a contraction or reactivity and find out where that started in myself. I have a natural love of meditation, but I don't like sitting per se. I like to sit up when I wake up in the middle of the night. I always keep some big pillows at the side of the bed, and I just put them up against the back of the bed and sit myself up into a semireclining position. I open my eyes and rest into the night and listen, watch, and let movement happen. You can call that my practice. It is a calling. I create an environment for being. Every moment of my life is a practice.

Translucents love to practice. Lama Surya Das loves to sit, to meditate every day. He loves to chant and to do the many things he has learned in his years as a Tibetan Buddhist: to pray, to study texts, to do inflections, to do self-inquiry, to practice yoga. He conducts many retreats a year, and in this way he spends long periods with his students enjoying practices. He is awake. He knows his true nature to be limitless, always at peace, outside of time.

"So why do you practice?" I asked him. "Is it to deepen the realization, is it to reach some further state?"

"I don't know," he answered. "I have no other choice. That is who I am, that is my karma. I love it. I am moved to do that, for no good reason. And for every reason I can think of. I don't find anything else I would rather do. I have looked...I have traveled around the globe six or seven times."

Jack Canfield is another veteran of spiritual exploration. He has collaborated with some of the more mature teachers and writers of our time for his *Chicken Soup* series of books:

What I'm seeing is a lot of my friends don't go to church or belong to spiritual movements. They don't go to satsangs. A lot of us have reached places where we have spiritual practices, maybe not just one but a smorgasbord of practices to draw upon. We have dipped into many traditions. I've done Sufi retreats, Christian retreats, Vipassana sessions, and sat in Hindu temples. But now it's just me and the practices that bring me back into a state of fullness — sometimes in community and sometimes alone.

> We're in the Divine Deli, in the global cafeteria of religion where you can find spiritual technologies and modalities that help you access your depths. We have access to the genius of the world's modes of finding your place in this larger universe. That's why so many of the really interesting spiritual books are transreligious.
>
> — Jean Houston

Translucent practice is generally tailor-made in this way. The Iago mind loves to find the "right way." It loves dogma, uniformity. Thirty years ago, we were offered a variety of universal panaceas. Feeling depressed? Repeat this mantra twenty minutes twice a day and everything will be okay. Low sex drive? Repeat the mantra. Want world peace? Same mantra. Want to lose weight, make more money? Got gangrene in your leg, ants in the basement? Repeat the mantra. Some were peddling mantras, some advising we chant in the streets, some had a two-weekend deal to "get it" and leave all your troubles behind forever. That was the time of one-size-fits-all, off-the-rack, Kmart spirituality. What's good for the goose...

Translucent practice is subtler. You order made-to-measure clothes according to your size and need, instead of one teaching, one-practice-suits-all. Lama Surya Das loves to sew fine clothes for his translucent students:

> *Everybody has to find the way themselves. It doesn't mean that they have to invent the wheel from scratch, but one has to find what works for oneself. People often ask me, "If I were going to have one spiritual practice, what would it be?" And I say, "How about taking a walk in nature every day? Or connecting with animals or pets, something simple. Or lighting candles, putting flowers on an altar." You know, simple. Of course, if you want to do yoga, if you want to do meditation, if you want to do tai chi, of course those are great. But then you have to talk about learning them and further practicing them. Anybody can walk outside and connect with nature. That is one of the most available, always accessible spiritual experiences. On the other hand, it might not be for everybody. So you have to be open to that, for others it might be reading scriptures, or any number of other things, which may or may not be my bag.*

> I just can't see how people can grow unless they start inside. A teacher creates the possibilities and sets up the situation, but the teacher can't do it for them. New esoteric Christianity is to do practices; they say don't worship Christ, they become him.
>
> — Gay Luce

Prayer

Translucents pass through many relationships to prayer, a special flavor of practice. In the Iago trance, everything is external. God is far away; he's got a naughty twinkle in his eye and a joystick on his knee controlling what happens next in our adventure. So we beg: *Please, give it to me, give me a new truck, make me richer and smarter and safer, please God, give me more pleasure and less pain.* After a radical awakening, the whole exercise seems futile. You discover yourself to be limitless, the source of everything; you extend everywhere, you are one with God. There is no one out there to beg, and besides, you are totally full, missing nothing at all. Translucents pass through a period, usually soon after an initial awakening, when prayer is dismissed as the infantile projections of a mind calling out to Daddy for help. As the awakening matures, however, prayer returns in a new way.

Translucents can embrace the full spectrum of who they are from the vast, eternal spaciousness to the personal, immediate, and temporary. When we look back all the way into ourselves, behind our own eyes, we find an endless ocean of consciousness. When we look out through these same eyes, we see the world, and we are willing to be a human wave in that ocean. We are both. The dialogue between the wave and the ocean is called prayer. Being consciously connected with the ocean of which they are made, translucents tend to speak and take action more in alignment with that oceanic source. They want things that the ocean wants them to want. They think things that the ocean is thinking. As a result, they experience a much higher degree of synchronicity than they do before an awakening. Things happen easily, with less effort. The right thing happens at the right time. There's a feeling of benevolence, as though something or someone very loving is taking care of you.

> Pray as you can and not as you can't. I don't think the form matters. Some people can empty themselves into a wordless silence, and some people do it by looking into an object with depth. I have a friend who's a musician, and that transports him. I'm a word person, and poetry does it for me very easily.
>
> — Bishop Richard Holloway

The old way of praying: *Please, Lord, Father, Daddy, Pop, give me what I want* is replaced by *Thank you, whoever you are, for giving me more than I need.* Prayer becomes a song of thanks, a song of surrender, a song of devotion to a source that is both the depths of who you are and at the same time just separate enough for there to be a flow of gratitude, worship, and surrender. The Iago prayer sees half a glass of water and thinks about the future: *I have only half a glass, I may die of thirst. Please Lord, give me the rest of the glass, please, do not let me die.* The translucent prayer sees the same glass and, in a voice that calls within to the infinite cavern of the heart, says: *Thank you, God, Goddess, my own true heart, thank you for the half glass I have, and thank you in advance for the rest of the glass, too.*

Service: Prayer in Action

The teachings of Jesus and others remain relevant today because of the emphasis on service, a form of prayer in action. Twelve-Step programs see service as essential to ongoing recovery, and most spiritual teachings include the vision of generosity of spirit. When our spiritual life is about getting something or arriving at some destination, it reinforces a trance of lack, of not being "there" yet.

Wanting anything, including enlightenment, solidifies a universe in which you are missing that which you want. The cures for endless aspiration are service and gratitude. When you are giving away, helping someone, inspiring someone, you are giving from what you have, and you enter a universe where you are overflowing. Service is the antidote to the beggar mentality.

Morrissey shared with me stories of many people who came into her church looking for something. As they felt more connected with themselves, they connected with "the place where the love of God moves from." And so, she says, after some time you naturally put yourself in the service of that which is within you. Which is the same as putting yourself in the service of that gift in every single person. Which is the same as putting yourself in the service of God.

Compassionate service is the inevitable and natural perfume of a translucent life. It does not take morality or effort. When you put you finger into the flame of a candle, it takes no effort or willpower to pull it out. You feel the pain, and the action is spontaneous. When you feel out a little more, expand your circle of life, you feel those close to you as yourself. When a mother sees her child in danger, standing in the path of an oncoming car, she does not need religious dogma to know what to do. The intimacy she feels with her child makes her action spontaneous. As our translucence deepens, so the sense of a separate identity becomes thinner, and the recognition of one spirit everywhere becomes stronger. Every sentient being becomes part of us, and we know ourselves to be part of one humanity. Then we live in Jesus' teaching, and Buddha's and Krishna's too, and the teaching lives in us.

> When people fall into that awakened love disposition, and are no longer struggling to get out, then there's a discovery, a landing in what I refer to as "an inherent bodhisattva impulse that needs no vow." This to me is a natural human being. We were built to participate in the furtherance of life, for everyone, and unless everyone is included, it ain't complete.
>
> — Saniel Bonder

THE RETURN OF THE GODDESS

The translucent transformation of religion is not only the product of more people experiencing radical awakening. After all, religion has always and everywhere been born of awakening. It is also the result of a balance of the masculine and feminine expression of that awakening. When anyone, man or woman, experiences the truth of their original nature, that realization is always the same; it is the recognition of limitlessness, silence, peace, infinite possibility. That which is realized is neither masculine nor feminine. The expression of that realization, however, in human life, will always be expressed through a human form. Hindus express their awakening in a Hindu way, sitting cross-legged perhaps, chanting *Om*. An American, like Byron Katie, will do so in an American way. A well-educated scholar will express awakening with great erudition, while a simple, uneducated person will express the same awakening with great simplicity. In the same way, masculine and feminine people will express the same awakening through the particular filters of their human incarnation.

> I knew I had to do something in this world to help other people. I realized there was nothing else to do here on this earth. That was all that really matters. We've all come here to do that. We're all here to live the purpose of humanity by becoming human and waking up through the human process. We *be* it; that's how we change it, by being it.
>
> — Jacquelyn Small

Religion, like almost everything else in our culture, has been dominated for millennia by the masculine psyche. Every organized spiritual path has been created by a man, and the stewarding of it into the world has been in the hands of men. Not only Jesus but all twelve apostles were men. In the Catholic Church, every priest, including every pope, has been male. Until a few decades ago, this was true in other schools of Christianity as well. Buddhism was founded by a man, and all the original *bikkhus* were men. When the Buddha was finally persuaded to create an order of nuns by his stepmother, Prajapati, he reportedly said his teachings would have lasted for thousands of years, but with women involved they would last for less than a thousand. Islam was founded by a man and has no place for women as imams. Leonard Shlain, the author of *The Alphabet Versus the Goddess*, put it like this: "Look at the founders. Almost without exception, they were misogynists. It's hard to find a friendly word for women among the teachers: Buddha, or Paul, or Moses, or the prophets. Even if the founder did say something nice about women, the scribes that came and wrote down what they thought he said, many centuries later, completely obscured the original message, and we'll never know what it was."

The masculine psyche turns religion into a quest for liberation. Life's purpose is to break through all boundaries to freedom, to get out of here and transcend the material realm. Traditional concepts of enlightenment imply a complete detachment from the world; the literal meaning of the word *nirvana* is to "snuff out." Masculine religion emphasizes discipline, renunciation, celibacy, solitude, asceticism, and the fixed authority of dogma and the written word. In many traditions, love and compassion are seen as the fruits of a spiritual life, but not as the life itself.

> The feminine invitation is about being kind inside and including the arising emotions and contractions. Rather than inquiring them away, there is a gorgeous balance of the fiercer Shiva aspect and the warm feminine: this too, this too, this too.
>
> — Pamela Wilson

Leonard Shlain has demonstrated the extraordinary concurrence of literacy rates with the dominance of the masculine psyche in society. According to Shlain, the more we worship the written word as the ultimate authority, the more we move into the left hemisphere of the brain. This hemisphere is associated with logical reasoning, rules, and dogma, which controls the right side of the body, thought of in many cultures to be more masculine. He postulates that at the time when the Old Testament was first put into written form, the feminine face of God was lost. Later, the invention of the printing press in 1454 allowed written books, including Bibles, to be circulated in massive quantities. This caused a huge rise in literacy among working people. Within thirty years, says Shlain, we witnessed the widespread persecution of women, with more than three million burned at the stake as witches during the Inquisition. Today, fundamentalist religions, dominated by the masculine, all rely heavily on the written word and emphasize the importance of literacy.

The feminine religious spirit in all of us is quite different. It is much more attuned to the present moment. It has the view that "we are all connected to nature, we're not outside of nature, we are part of it," says Shlain. It connects us with our bodies; it brings us back to our senses. Rather than trying to transcend human life, the feminine discovers the divine by entering fully into life with love and devotion. While the masculine is set on achieving a goal in the future, the feminine is relaxed in a continuous flow, one that has no defined end to it.

Shlain points out that just as the invention of the alphabet and the printing

press allowed for the domination of religion by the masculine, so there have
been equally germinal changes in the way we get information just in the last
few decades, which herald the return of the Goddess. In little more than a
single generation, we have seen the global advent of the cinema, of television, and now the Internet. We are receiving as much information through still and moving images and sounds as we are through words. This activates the right side of the brain, associated with the left side of the body and the feminine. Along with this increase in image-based information has come a decline, especially in Western countries, in literacy rates. The dogmatists, horrified, are doing whatever they can to encourage reading at ever-younger ages. "Heck, if you can't get them reading by five years old, we'll cut off your funding." To those who value a whole brain, a decline in literacy is not a bad thing. It allows for the balance of the left and right hemispheres, the masculine and feminine, and the return of the Goddess in our lives. Says Shlain:

> The feminine brings intuition, trusting your own inner guidance rather than having to go outside yourself, and a responsiveness to that guidance. As we bring more feminine energy, we see a rise of compassion and acceptance, a full expression of the love of God, which can express itself as a love of humanity. It is the mother energy, love expressed on planet Earth, so there is no lack of what is needed for the family of humanity. It is the manifestation of compassion.
>
> — Mary Manin Morrissey

> I'm well aware that there is a major movement all over the world today, the Goddess movement, where women and men are wanting to reconnect with nature and the feminine principles by having rituals and trying to define a new religion. It no longer says to you, "Some guy ate a meal a long time ago, here's the menu, I'll let you read the menu but we don't want you to eat the meal, we don't want you to have an ecstatic experience, because we wouldn't be able to control that. We want you just to have a very dull, boring religion, where you stand up, sit down, stand up, sit down in a big, dark, gloomy building every Saturday or Sunday. That's the religion." Well, that doesn't have much soul in it and that's one of the reasons why so many people are wanting religion that is experiential.

Sherry Anderson is a pioneer in rediscovering the feminine face of God.
True to the feminine spirit, instead of filling my tape machine with theories,

she told me a wonderful story. "The feminine face of God is a koan," she says. "What is interesting is what women experience. I cannot talk about the feminine in abstraction."

Anderson was the senior teacher at a Zen center in Canada from 1977 to 1982. She had been practicing Zen meditation for many years. She told me she had many deep experiences of "the ground of being, the boundless eternal reality." She said, "I guess I was living in a very silent spacious depth, but there wasn't any joy." She wrote to her Zen teacher, a Korean master, to tell him how she was feeling. "More hard training is necessary," came the reply. She was already getting up at 4:30 every morning, doing many hours of hard practice. "Something else was needed," she told me, "although I didn't know what it was. I had developed a capacity to be very present with attention, but a true openness, a true curiosity, and a true longing to really be in contact with what was true and real for me hadn't happened until that time. I felt that I was a great failure."

Anderson left the Zen center and moved with her husband to Lone Pine, California. She spent a great deal of time in the desert. She danced, she prayed, she worked with heart. She would spend many hours among the red rocks, singing, yelling, doing the Sufi turn: "I was still very lost. You could say that being lost is really being found, and that thinking you are found is really being lost. I was open in a way like when you bang your finger, there's nothing else that you can think about except that finger all day. The finger is hurting and so all day your awareness is with that finger. I felt a really deep and continuous open longing for something real. And I had no idea what it was."

> How tenuous life is, how delicate it is in its preciousness — it's sacred. It's not something you put on an altar, but more like a bird. It's alive and worth caring for.
>
> — Aneeta Makena

Then she had a dream. She was flying around on a gold and white dragon, quite contentedly, when she had the thought: *Is this all there is?* At that moment the dragon descended to a beautiful lake with a small temple next to it. An old man came out of the temple and indicated that she must enter, and he would follow her in. She walked down a long corridor into a very large room, which was empty, except for a dais at the end with a cabinet. Anderson opened the doors and was shocked by what she saw. It was a Torah, the sacred book of the Jewish people. It did not have the traditional cloth covering it.

She was born Jewish, and was a prize student at Hebrew school. Women never touch or hold the Torah, but in the dream Anderson lifted it in her arms, like a baby.

> With the former dominance of, the stamping out, and the burning at the stake of the feminine expression, my hope is that we don't have to go to another pole to heal it. As much as we've had centuries of dominance by the masculine energy, we don't have to go to the other extreme. There's enough awakening that we can come from a healed masculine and feminine. There's a move to balance, a full masculine and full feminine.
>
> — Mary Manin Morrissey

The old man indicated that she should break the seal and open it. She rolled it out, and again she was astonished. It was empty. The old man told her that there was nothing written in this Torah because it was a teaching for our time, a teaching that had not yet been written. He told her to take it into her body. As she picked it up, it entered into her body. Suddenly, she heard great joyous sounds; she looked up and saw the room was filled with patriarchs. They wore ceremonial dress, and they were dancing. Behind them now were tables laden with fruit and wine and all kinds of beautiful food. They reached out and invited her to dance. Joining them and dancing around and around, laughing, she finally paused and asked them what all this was for.

"We are celebrating your initiation, as someone who will help to lead the way for our time," they said.

"But how can I be initiated?" she protested. "I'm a woman. How can you initiate me?"

"This is the time for women. You are not the only one. Many, many, many women are coming forward now to show the way."

"Will you help us?" she asked them. At that point the room was filled with the most delicate kindness.

"We are your brothers, and we will help you in any way we can, but we no longer know the way. You women need to find a new way."

This dream proved to be prophetic, not only for Anderson but for many other women also. About a month later, Anderson began to hear an unusual word in her head: *Shechinah, Shechinah.* She had never before heard the word. She asked her friends, but no one knew what it meant, until her friend Joan McIntyre found the word in a library book, *Tarot and Kabbalah.* Shechinah, in Judaism, is the feminine face of God. The feminine started to reveal itself to Anderson and her friend Joan:

From that point on we did it together. We understood that what needed to come forward was something that we couldn't do alone, because the time of the lone wolf is over. Something connected needed to happen. We sat together, we asked, What is this feminine face of God about? I entered a meditation where I felt like an infinite black vastness. For a very long time the vastness remained and then began to take the form of the feminine. A black, loving mystery was holding us, like we were suckling her breasts, but her breasts were made of flowers. It seemed very clear that the infinite reality is simply itself, but when it comes into the infinite variety of its forms there is an infinite variety of feminine; that quality of "yes," from the infinitude into the ten thousand things, and from the ten thousand things into that Absolute Oneness, is all utterly seamless and continuous.

Anderson and her friends felt they received guidance from this newly born feminine spirit. It spoke to them: "What the feminine is in this time is emerging. It's to be discovered. You have to come with your not knowing. You have to come with your longing to know and loving to know. When women come together, it will emerge through you, you will be teachers for each other. You'll all be teachers."

Sherry and Joan began to travel, to New York, to Boston, to San Francisco, meeting with women in sacred circles. They met in living rooms, with no curriculum, just in the shared longing and openness to find out what God is like when she is allowed to regain her feminine form:

> We now live in a world that is saturated with images. As a result, we're seeing an extraordinary surge of the feminine coming back into our society with women becoming priestesses again, being elected as judges and law makers. This pattern will continue because we've shifted from a text-based society to an image-based one.
>
> — Leonard Shlain

People were speaking, and as they spoke we took the masks off, took our veils off, and just dropped them. I think it was because we were feeling the urgency to find our voices, to hear from each other about what it means to be living in this life now as women, wanting to be our sacredness, wanting to be our wholeness, our fullness, wanting to be with what's real. One woman said, "I don't give a damn about spirituality, I want to know about reality."

Anderson now teaches the Diamond Approach, developed by A. H. Almaas, in the United States and Europe. Her book *The Feminine Face of God*, written with her friend Patricia Hopkins, has influenced thousands of women to trust their deeper intuition of feminine spirituality. Looking back on the shift she has been instrumental in provoking, she said:

What women are bringing today that our world needs so profoundly is an embodied openness. And what I mean by embodied is a way of being that is emotional, physical, subtle, and connected to the earth. It's a longing to really be in intimate relationship with, engaged with, what's truly natural, our true nature. And when you are in touch like this, questions arise that come not just from thinking, but from the depth of your soul and that includes all of you — your vulnerability and strength, your heart and your belly. Our questions are about what's real, what really matters, and what's true in all our relationships. Not that time for solitude isn't very important, but there's not some single savior or avatar or anything that is going to be able to show the way for what we need now. We are discovering it together. It's that quality of openness in relationship to our human life that women are bringing forward now.

Women's wisdom circles have grown up all over the world. Anderson's book has been followed by a plethora of similar literature. But the power of the feminine gift will never be in the written word, it dwells in the realities of the body and connection. Although many women now lead large congregations throughout the world, Mary Manin Morrissey explains that we are not seeing the replacement of masculine domination with feminine. We are seeing a balance: "While dominance and control is at the far end of the unhealed masculine, so seduction and manipulation is at the far end of the unhealed feminine. What is being called for, and what is rising up in the new theology, is balance, a retraction of any form of fundamentalism."

> I think the whole gamut of spirituality is simply to have a very soft and open heart and to have a very vast and open mind, which are just natural states for human beings.
>
> — ShantiMayi

The expression of this whole, balanced spirituality is a spirit of celebration. The traditional organ and worn hymnal have been replaced with a rock band and new songs every week. People dance. People share with the community. They want to make a difference. Translucent spirituality embraces the compassionate love of the divine feminine with the clarity and focus of the divine masculine, in a way that has, perhaps for the first time, the power to heal the world. Bishop Holloway told me:

> I've always felt in myself that we're not here for personal enlightenment; we're here to awaken the world. People say, "Shouldn't we start first with ourselves?" You are the world. The world is you. This is something that envelops everyone, beginning with you. If you don't think so much on your thoughts and desires, there is nothing you do not have.
>
> — ShantiMayi

God has finally become human. The incarnation has finally happened. The reference is now to what happens in the human continuum; now it's life before death, not life after death. This is It, this life we're in; it's filled with beauty and terror, just as we ourselves are capable of grace and terror. There is a desire to amplify the human experience prior to death, to have abundance. It propels you in the direction of wanting to mend the world. But you're not just doing that out of a sense of duty, you're enjoying it too. It's right to enjoy the world, the beauty of it, and the pleasure it provides.

My old spirituality had a lot of prayer by rote to it, trying to force myself to meditate. My prayer now is more of attention to the world and the people within it, and a new interest in animals and the beauty and horror of the natural creation. The wow factor has come back!

NUDGING RELIGION INTO TRANSLUCENCE

NUDGE
Solitude

The first place to discover translucence is in your own awakening, again and again. It begins with connecting to yourself. This might be for fifteen minutes in the morning, or it might mean spending a few days alone in retreat. Some great translucents have spent forty days and forty nights in the desert. Whenever we take time to go within, the Iago mind will arise and try to tempt us with desires. It will offer us visions of power, money, sex, and fame. The practice is to keep listening more attentively to the music of your own heart than to the fleeting whisper of Iago. Like Jesus, you can nudge in the direction of saying, "No thank you," and diving deeper into the heart, where you are one with God.

NUDGE
Connection

From this connection with yourself comes connection with another. If periods of solitude go deep enough, we can still feel that we are alone when we are with another. We look into the eyes of the other, and recognize the same silence we found within ourselves.

> I am five feet off from perfect, but I try to put whatever talents or abilities or possibilities I have in service. I don't think we can wait until we are perfect before we try to act, or teach, or serve. So, the question then becomes, who is my master and who am I serving? Am I serving just myself or my ego or my own individual selfish agenda, or a greater good?
>
> — Lama Surya Das

After you return from the heart cave of meditation, take the time to look deeply into the eyes of someone close to you: your spouse or child, a friend, or even a colleague. There's no need to stare, but really look, really pay attention. As yourself, ask, "Who is this other? Who is looking back at me? Who, or what, is behind the eyes?" Sink into this koan and it will unlock the fathomless wellspring of natural compassion.

NUDGE
Community

The connection with the beloved can grow from a meeting of two to a circle. We are still alone, with many hearts and eyes and hands. Seek out the people in whom you can recognize greatest translucence, and who can recognize the translucence in you. Meet, not in dogma or hierarchy, but as friends, in mutuality. We can find ways to help each other release the bonds of Iago around the heart, and to live with greater art and humor. Create a wisdom circle.

NUDGE

Found Your Own Religion

Find your own song, be the founder of Fred-anity or Amanda-ism. Let rituals arise out of your own heart; let understanding arise from your own wisdom. Let your spirituality be totally original, a fresh gift to the world, instead of a borrowed means to get something for yourself. Gay Luce calls this "autonomous spirituality" and feels this impulse will generate a whole new brand of ritual:

> Just accept, because in the end you have absolutely nothing to do with it at all. And the words *trust* and *allow* and *forgive* go out the window about as fast as a speeding bullet. Because trust is not a question. And who is there to allow anything? And who is there to say what is right or wrong? All of it, *all* of it, is only a step, a good step, but only a step, because it all dissipates. There's just nothing that can hold or condition that perfect sense.
>
> — ShantiMayi

I see that I want to create ritual out of something inside me, and I think I have wanted to do this all my life; as a child I used to want to create ritual to celebrate and say thank you. Sometimes it's to mourn, too. As a child it was mostly to say thank you; thank you for this excitement of life, thank you for this beauty, thank you for all these possibilities. And I think that that urge is still there and that as people become more autonomous, they find the rituals that work for them.

TICKLE

Be a Joke unto Yourself

When the Buddha was on his deathbed his last words were, "Be a light unto yourself." Two and a half thousand years have passed since then, and we need to update things now and then. We are in a time in which all kinds of rigidity of thinking are dissolving: a time, above all, to find humor in our spirituality. The contemporary mystic Osho offers us the advice to be a joke unto yourself.

A mother woke her son up on Sunday morning and told him he needed to get ready for church.

People have bought into Fundamentalism, with the accent not on the fun, so their universe can be explained and outlined to them. You know, here's your manual for being alive — follow these rules exactly. It's a way of pathological safety. Humor is disruptive to structure, disruptive to the structure of language, to the structure of meaning. It constantly puts ideas together that don't belong together. The nature of humor is to bump us out of dualities and bump us out of structure.

— Steve Bhaerman
(Swami Beyondananda)

"I don't want to go to church this morning," he told his mother.

"Nonsense," she replied. "You have to go."

"But Mom," he said, "everybody hates me, the sermons are boring, and none of my friends ever come."

"Now, son. First of all, everybody doesn't hate you, only a couple of bullies, and you just have to stand up to them. Second, the sermons mean a lot to people. If you listened to them, you'd be surprised at how good they are at helping people. Third, you have lots of friends at church. They are always having you over to their house. And finally, you *have* to go, you're the minister!"

CHAPTER FIFTEEN

PERFECT IMPERFECTION

A Vision of a Translucent World

Barbara Marx Hubbard was a mother and homemaker when she experienced a radical awakening in her forties. It changed her life completely. While she still maintained her responsibilities to her family, her heart was set aflame with the possibilities of a different world. She was nominated for the vice presidency at the 1984 Democratic National Convention. Since then, she has written many books and traveled and taught extensively. Yet a still deeper revelation came just two years ago.

"At a time of deep personal change and crisis, I came to see that all my efforts are, in a sense, in vain. Something beyond all of us is guiding the change we are passing through, and we have no choice or say in that. Our only responsibility is to surrender, and to allow that to do its work. Humanity is going through an evolutionary leap we have never dreamed of, but neither you nor I can stop it or help it. I have surrendered."

In 1990 Václav Havel, the playwright who became president of the Czech Republic in 1993, told a joint session of the U.S. Congress, "Without a global revolution in the sphere of human consciousness, nothing will change for the better...and the catastrophe towards which this world is headed — the

ecological, social, demographic, or general breakdown of civilization — will
be unavoidable."

We live at a pivotal time in human history. The dominant Iago trance state
has never been so pervasive: economically, environmentally, politically, in the
expression of religious fundamentalism —
you name it; we have never been poised so
perilously on the edge of the cliff. Read
back over the list of Iago qualities defined in
chapter 1; they define the state of today's
world. Certainly there has been greater cruelty, inequality, and imperialism in our history, but it has always been localized to a
despotic regime here or an invasion there.
Hitler, Genghis Khan, and Stalin may have
yearned for global domination, but their
insanity was isolated. Today the Iago cancer
has become systemic rather than localized. The dominant paradigm affects
everyone, seeming perpetrator and victim alike. We are all in this together.

> We don't really live in the world, we live in the conversation we have about the world. The conversation is totally malleable. The world may not be a changeable place, but we are completely omnipotent over the conversation. That is where transformation occurs, where health, well-being, and love occur, where compassion and forgiveness happen. That is where the future lives, where possibility is available.
>
> — Lynne Twist

At the same time, every writer, teacher, researcher, and translucent-
on-the-street I have spoken with is aware of a countervailing "emerging paradigm," with the potential to transform every sphere of life in every part of
the world. The birth pangs of *Homo lucidus* may sometimes cause us to yearn
for the familiar, but for most people it is too late. The head of the new
human being has pushed through, and its first cries are already in the air. We
are riding the crest of a worldwide wave whose consequences are unimaginable, and which holds perhaps the only real basis for optimism for our planet
and its inhabitants. We can sense the possibility of a quality of life that has
seldom been dreamed of. If we fail to take advantage of this opportunity, our
present habits may well destroy us.

As a boy, I loved James Bond movies. Don't groan, it's a guy thing. The
plot always followed the same basic template. A "bad guy," usually very rich,
greedy, and slightly mad, has malicious intentions to take over the world,
causing widespread destruction in the process. Every one was a man, as I
recall, with a name like Dr. No or Goldfinger. He usually heads up some
sort of global clandestine corporation, often with a benevolent facade. His

operatives are dark, inhuman, and robotic. And then there is Bond: suave, centered in his body, living totally in the moment, and free of fear. He is humorous, even in the face of death, and brings a lust for life to every situation. Again and again, against all odds, Bond will save the world. Its usually a race against time. Will Dr. Destruction detonate his mother of all bombs and turn us all into plasma, or will James single-handedly wrestle hundreds of meanies to the ground and save the day? Bond always comes through, with seconds to spare, and the movie ends with yet another liaison with the goddess of the day. Dozens of movies in the last decades have had the same theme: Indiana Jones, Superman, even Austin Powers.

In one way these far-fetched scenarios have prepared us for the situation we face at the start of this new millennium. The threat to our world's stability comes from a collective expression of greed, most pointedly embodied by global corporations, which put profit before integrity. Like Bond, translucents are heavily outnumbered. But also like Bond, they are sleek, sexy, cool-headed, humorous, and increasingly activated toward social change. So here we sit, on the edge of our seats, at the last and most gripping act of the movie. Will we see life as we know it irreparably mutilated by corporate greed and fundamentalists bent on proving themselves right and the enemy-of-the-month wrong? Or are we finally at the dawn of a collective shift into sanity? No point in twiddling our thumbs in anticipation, the final pages of the script are still being written, and you and I have been handed the job of finishing it off.

> It is a very dangerous time, but childbirth is dangerous. We are looking at the birth of a new consciousness on earth. These dangers are a part of the birthing process. I don't think the birth would take place without them.
>
> — Chris Bache

COLLECTIVE IAGO

Since we have bad and good news to discuss here, let's get the depressing stuff out of the way so we can move on to our creative solutions. I have heard every imaginable interpretation of the facts in the course of researching this book, but I cannot remember talking to anyone who entertained any doubt that we are coming close to a time of crisis in several independent and parallel dimensions. Duane Elgin has done an extraordinary job over many decades of compiling both the indicators of global crisis and the emerging paradigm that could balance it.[1] I am indebted to him for making me aware of a great deal of the research referenced here and his openhearted generosity in allowing me to piggyback on his efforts. Elgin comments:

Although human societies have confronted major problems throughout history, the challenges of our era are unique in one crucial respect — they now embrace the entire earth as a whole system. Never before has humanity been on the verge of devastating the earth's biosphere and crippling its ecological foundations for countless generations to come. Never before has the entire human family been required to work together to build a sustainable and meaningful future. Never before have so many people been called to make such sweeping changes in so little time.

> The acceleration is happening of the new arising, but the old still has its momentum and even that seems to accelerate. We are coming to the end of an evolutionary cycle for humanity, and the closer you get to the end of a cycle, the more dysfunctional that way of being becomes. There is nothing wrong with it, but all part of how it should be. When you close a cycle, it doesn't work anymore.
>
> — Eckhart Tolle

Let's look at a few of the tracks, laid down by the Iago trance over many decades, that are leading us over the cliff. Each one of these alone is a trajectory heading for disaster.

Commercialization

Today's world is no longer primarily controlled by monarchs, dictators, or even elected governments. We live in a world controlled by international corporations. Most of us work for them, we eat and drink what they provide, we are exposed to their persuasive and carefully crafted advertising, and we live on the earth that provides the raw materials for their endless "production" and the depository for their endless refuse. Corporations have become much more powerful than the governments that we hope might regulate them, and in fact they pay for the mechanisms by which a government can afford to get elected.

A few years ago I visited Urgen Tulku Rimpoche, a renowned Tibetan teacher who was living in the refugee section of Katmandu. The first morning, I walked around the stupa at Bodhnath, one of the largest monuments of its kind in the world, housing a relic of the Buddha. All around the stupa, which was 350 feet in circumference, an endless stream of maroon-clad monks, reciting *om mane padme hum*, keep thousands of prayer-wheels constantly turning. Sweet incense was in the air; cafés were selling tea made from yak's milk, flavored with salt. I was definitely not in Kansas anymore.

To the long, drawn-out sounds of Tibetan horns and the clash of symbols from a nearby monastery, I turned the corner heading toward the foothills of the Himalayas and bumped into...a Coke machine. Not so far from Kansas as I'd thought.

Throughout Europe, Asia, and Africa, McDonalds, Coca-Cola, and corporate marketing are invading local cultures. The danger of this increasing corporate presence lies in its basic motivation. Even totalitarian governments begin with some sort of intention to serve the deeper well-being of a population. Corporations are primarily responsible to their shareholders. Profitability is a higher value than environmental or social integrity. Creating and satisfying short-term desire eclipses long-term sustainability and sanity.

> The corporate "bigs," whether it be big media, big finance, big government, big corporations, or big armies, have an antihuman worldview. It's so pervasive that it hypnotizes most of the culture. When people start withdrawing from their occupational engagement, they realize that they've been caught up in something that they not only don't believe in but they think is abominable.
>
> — Paul Ray

The fruits of the earth, plants, animals, even water are all being patented and made into commercial products, including even drugs to create new feelings. This trend is increasing exponentially. But there is a finite limit to how much one can possess, and we are running out of anything new to patent and own.

The Trance of Lack

An oppressive political regime, like the British in India or that headed by Milosevic in Yugoslavia, takes advantage of a population and can eventually be rejected by revolution or the intervention of an outside force. The power of commercial interests is more insidious. Like the relationship between a drug pusher and an addict, this power runs on the immediate addictions of a population, without necessarily serving their deeper well-being. The collective trance of consumption, and the global economy it creates, only works because of you and me feeling lack. It thrives on our sense that there's a problem, that something's missing, that something's wrong with your life, and with you: *It's quite simple, buddy, you need to buy our product. Drink this soda, buy this barbeque, this house, this car; fly to this great place for a vacation and you will feel better. Look at these very happy smiling people in this photo here. They feel better. See?*

The global economy as we know it would not work with a contented population. You would have a hard time selling endless plastic gizmos to people who feel connected to themselves, who feel whole, who feel generous and grateful, and who know that they have enough. The trance of lack endlessly re-creates itself; it never reaches a plateau of contentment. More, more, more, more... it is an exponential curve that does not bode well for our future.

Economic Disparity

Thanksgiving dinner. Your whole family is there: parents, children, uncles, aunts, cousins, in-laws, your closest friends. Look at your plate. It is piled with turkey, potatoes, stuffing, ornately carved vegetables, rich gravy. You've got several glasses of different European wines in crystal glasses. Exotic seaweed salad, imported from Japan. On a nearby table are many different kinds of dessert. Yes, all for you. Now imagine that the people seated closest to you didn't do quite as well. They each have a microwave turkey dinner, $3.99, from Safeway. And Coke. The rest of the table really missed out. Some have bread or gruel and water — contaminated. Some have nothing.

Could you enjoy your meal under these conditions?

> We cannot live divided anymore; we need to bring wholeness within ourselves. If people are awake, if we can get by our habits, and defenses and certainties, there is an opportunity for all these things to converge and for there to be a tidal wave. I don't think we have an inkling of what is possible when we come from wholeness and move toward wholeness.
>
> — Wink Franklin

More than two billion people in the world live on less than a dollar a day, while the CEOs of many big corporations make millions of dollars a year.[2] Eighty-five percent of the world's wealth is held by 1 percent of the world's population.3 A 1998 United Nations report shows us that the cost of compassion and balance is far lower than we might think.4 Universal worldwide access to clean water and sanitation would cost $12 billion a year, less than the amount spent on perfumes in the United States.5 Basic health care and nutrition for everyone would cost $13 billion, less than the annual spending on pet food in the United States6 and 5 percent of the cost of the 2003 invasion of Iraq.

The imbalance between the haves and the have-nots also exists within the United States. In 2000 the wealthiest four hundred families in the States made an average of $29 million *each*, which would require the combined paychecks of 504,600 retail clerks to match.7 It is this kind of disparity that led to revolution in Russia in 1917. As the gap continues to grow worldwide, logic tells us it will end when the disenfranchised finally say "enough," ushering in the collapse of the economic system we now have — another indicator that life as we know it may be in for some bumpy times.

> We're living through the fall of Western civilization. It's going to be the heaviest fall of any civilization. What comes out on the other side, I have no idea, or how deep that fall is going to be. But in the meantime, I have great optimism for who we can become in that process.
>
> — Peter Russell

Debt

Today the average credit card debt in the United States is over $9,000, up from an average of less than $3,000 in 1990.8 American consumers owed a grand total of $2,053 billion by the end of 2003, not counting mortgage debt, an increase of more than 400 percent in twenty years, and an average of almost $20,000 per household.9 The number of people filing for bankruptcy hit 1.6 million in 2003, almost six times as many as those who filed in 1983, as more and more people are unable to keep their heads above water.10 Credit card companies lure customers with a sexy honeymoon zero interest rate, and then sock it to you with interest rates as high as 29 percent once you are hooked.11

National debts are also rising. The U.S. Senate set a new $8.18 trillion cap in 2004,12 when we had used every last cent of its previous limit of $7.38 trillion, more than eight times the debt in 1981.13 It added an additional deficit

> Debt is an accurate reflection of the belief in scarcity. We have no attention on our inner riches, but in accumulating outer riches, which puts us in debt. It is an accurate reflection of a society that's lost touch with its soul.
>
> — Lynne Twist

in the 2004 budget of $413 billion.[14] Many even less fortunate countries are in far bigger trouble. Tanzania, for example, has an external debt of more than $7 billion,[15] while their Gross Domestic Product is only $21 billion, or a mere $600 per capita.[16] According to guidelines set down by the International Monetary Fund, it is theoretically impossible for many countries like this ever to get out of debt.

Bribery and Corruption

By the end of 2004, there were 30,402 professional lobbyists in Washington DC, almost three times as many as there were in 1996.[17] In 2000, the last year for which we have such records available, they spent $1,557,545,531.[18] That is a ratio of fifty-six lobbyists to one elected Congressperson, and an expenditure of $2.85 million per elected politician. The total amount spent in the 2004 presidential election was $717 million, ten times the $66 million spent in 1976.[19] Each "special interest" group, like the National Rifle Association, the tobacco industry, and the oil companies, will demand a payback from the recipients of their generosity. They buy their way into power with the help of the same advertising agencies that persuade us to buy SUVs or to drink the latest carbonated beverages. In return, legislation makes it ever easier to make money. Hence, government is not so much elected as sponsored. In earlier and more innocent times this would have been named for what it is: bribery and corruption.

Who Owns the Press

One might hope that the media would alert us to these multiple dimensions of decay. But the same commercial organizations that bribe the government own the media. In 1945 80 percent of all American newspapers were independently owned and locally operated. By 1989 that ratio was inverted, and fully 80 percent of newspapers are run as media outlets by corporate chains.[20] The top ten newspaper owners control 51 percent of daily circulation.[21] A single company, Clear Channel, brazenly sympathetic to the policies of the neoconservative right, owns at least one station in each of the top markets, meaning they reach more than one third of the U.S. population.[22]

The average American spends a whopping 4.2 hours a day, or almost thirty hours a week, watching TV. For women over fifty-five, that figure goes up to forty-five hours a week. Almost a quarter of airtime is devoted to persuasive pitches to · buy more stuff.[23] At our house we only watch videos, so some other family is using up our share. That's 8.4 hours a day in their house. Imagine! The corporate buyout of the media further accentuates the complete control of commercial interests. Not only is the government bribed to ignore their misdemeanors, but the population's access to information is filtered to stoke the appetite for more consumption gloss over the price paid by our planet.

> To perpetuate a state of mind, you don't have to do anything other than prevent any other possibility from entering the public mind. In our consumer-oriented society, when large numbers of people are dissatisfied but can't express it publicly, then they don't really exist. In the public sphere the only thing acknowledged is consumerism.
>
> — Duane Elgin

Destruction of the Environment

While you and I may feel concerned over the trends created by the Iago trance, it is not you and I who are in the most trouble, but our children and grandchildren. In 1992, over sixteen hundred senior scientists, including most of the living Nobel Laureates in the sciences, signed and released a document entitled *Warning to Humanity*.[24] "Human beings and the natural world are on a collision course...that may so alter the living world that it will be unable to sustain life in the manner that we know....A great change in the stewardship of the earth and the life on it is required if vast human misery is to be avoided and our global home is not to be irretrievably mutilated."[25] The EPA estimates that 40 percent of U.S. lakes, rivers, and estuaries are too polluted for such basic uses as drinking, fishing, and swimming.[26] Three million people, the majority of whom live in India, die prematurely every year due to outdoor and indoor air pollution.[27] While air pollution has been curbed in more affluent nations, in Mexico City it is still at more than twice the maximum levels deemed safe by the World Health Organization.[28]

Global Warming

One particular effect of a consumerism-gone-bananas-economy that should cause us the most concern is the release of carbon dioxide (CO_2) into the atmosphere at a rate faster than the earth can reabsorb it, which causes global warming. When this phenomenon was first predicted in the 1970s, scientists warned us that long before we would be affected by the actual raising of temperatures, we would experience a major disruption of the earth's weather patterns. Severe drought, flooding, and storms over the last few years have signaled the start of that change. Mt. Kilimanjaro has lost 82 percent of its ice cap, and studies predict its glaciers will be gone completely by 2020.[29] The Arctic ice cap is melting at an unprecedented rate, with potentially dire consequences. According to a report conducted by 250 scientists, Arctic ice is only half as thick as it was thirty years ago and has shrunk by about 1 million kilometers, or an area about the size of Texas and Arizona combined. Scientists predict it will vanish completely in summer months by 2070, with temperatures rising 7 to 13 degrees Fahrenheit during this century, as a result of the CO2 already released.[30]

> We are being drawn into an historical crisis of unprecedented proportions, a global meltdown that is going to hurt terribly. If we repeat the choices from the past, we'll lose the race and extinguish life on the planet. We also have the potential to accelerate ourselves into an unbelievable positive future. We'll be as far beyond *Homo sapiens* as they are above *Homo erectus*.
>
> — Chris Bache

This is not even considering an increase in industrialization. Despite these warning signs, average gas consumption in the United States has increased. The fuel economy peaked in 1987, at an average of 26.2 miles per gallon, with light trucks and SUVs making up 28 percent of vehicles sold. Today they account for more than 50 percent of new vehicles, and the average fuel economy has deteriorated to 24.4 mpg.[31] Today's family vehicle resembles a tank. How many car commercials promote lower emissions instead of size and power?

We do have an increasing range of potential alternative technologies to reduce our CO2 emissions: hybrid cars, hydrogen-powered vehicles, solar heating, and wind and water as sources of energy. In 2001 the United States pulled out of the Kyoto Treaty, dedicated to limiting CO2 emissions, citing that it was "bad for the U.S. economy." This is like refusing to fix a gas leak in your children's bedroom because it would put too large a dent in the family entertainment budget.

The Rise of Fundamentalism

Were the great minds and hearts of the world to suddenly unite and pool their resources, we might feel more optimistic about fixing all these problems in our existing global society. But in fact the lemming race over the edge of the cliff has been marginalized in recent years in favor of creating wars of fundamentalisms. In every instance, all sides feel religiously justified in committing all kinds of degradation. From suicide terrorist attacks to indiscriminate military bombing of innocent civilians, everybody is willing to participate in mayhem, believing they have the God-given endorsement to kill their enemies. Meanwhile, the ice caps are slowly melting. The volatile combination of fundamentalism and weapons of mass destruction, *whoever* is holding them, is another of the many factors that make pessimism about our future seem like the most realistic point of view.

> Fundamentalism is a meaning system in a deep death moment; it cannot relate successfully to other meanings. It becomes more and more self-contained, more and more rigid, more and more absolute in its claims, because it is unable to stretch and breathe in the company of other meanings.
>
> — James O'Dea

Despair

We could fill a book, and many have, with endless statistics showing the rapid spread of the Iago cancer in mainstream global society. We have not even mentioned the extinction of animal species (fewer than five hundred thousand African elephants remain, less than 1 percent of the number a hundred years ago,[32] and only twenty thousand African lions)[33] or the depletion of the rain forest, or the abandonment of corporate and government integrity. Your bookshop is filled with far better informed researchers than me who can provide all the details: Duane Elgin, Michael Moore, and Arianna Huffington, to name just a few.

The obstacle is not a lack of available information but collective apathy and denial. If some mean, greedy men in dark suits were to show up one day and threaten my children, I would defend my kids with my life without hesitation. In fact, multiple gray meanies *are* threatening our children's future, but the effect is so slow and subtle that we are lulled into complacency. Some of us even vote for the gray meanies if they promise us lower taxes and more stuff *now*. Really opening our minds and hearts to what we are doing as a race requires such a fundamental change of lifestyle, such self-examination and remorse, that we generally feel too powerless and defeated to tune in at all. It is easier to bury our heads in the sand, to remain absorbed in an addictive trance of escapism, and to hope it is all a bad dream.

> Spiritual people have to wake up. They have too much fear about the world, too much not knowing what to do. When I see people being afraid to engage in politics, they're not willing to "walk the talk" of the spiritual life. If you get involved in politics, all your stuff may come up.
>
> — Corinne McLaughlin

Hitting Bottom

Anyone who has comes to terms with an addiction knows a great deal about awakening. In fact, many of the translucents I have interviewed have been, or still are, involved in Twelve-Step programs. Addiction is progressive. It is possible to cruise along for years managing a state of socially acceptable addiction. There may be outbursts of anger, occasional loss of control or collapse, but the addiction exists within the parameters of a "normal" life. People close to the addict may overlook or even endorse the creeping malaise. Most addicts have to bottom out before they begin to wake up. Many have to lose their health or their marriage, or face bankruptcy or a nervous breakdown before they are able to address what has been happening for years. Bottoming out is actually the beginning of a healing process. Those who understand addiction see this painful dead end as a very healthy sign, the essential prelude to being honest with oneself and moving toward real change.

Some of the most celebrated translucents today had to reach rock bottom before a radical shift: Byron Katie had her awakening in a halfway house; Eckhart Tolle hit the depths of despair before his awakening. First comes a free fall into darkness, a total immersion in Iago's universe. Then sudden freedom. When we reach the end of the road, we find deliverance.

Many translucent visionaries believe that this is now happening to humanity as a race. James O'Dea, the president of the Institute of Noetic Sciences,
calls the symptoms of extreme Iago expression the "death throes" of a paradigm we are now abandoning. As we exhaust every possibility of lack-based,
desire-based, separation-based living, we have no way out but to wake up and
take an evolutionary leap. O'Dea feels that those who can recognize the
process have a specific responsibility. Their job is to hospice the death of
the old ways, with dignity, with compassion, with patience, and to midwife
the emergence of the new human being.

Those skilled in facilitating transition
know how to interpret the signs. When
people buy fewer goods, the Iago mind
labels this "weakened consumer confidence," which creates panic. To the translucent midwife, this same trend indicates that
we are growing out of our addictions. The
breakdown of the World Trade talks in
Cancun in 2003 was seen as a setback to the

> It's no accident that people are awakening. The intensity of the problems we are facing is precisely what we need to awaken us. If the body responds very quickly to a symptom, it can heal and transform. If it doesn't respond, it'll get more and more symptoms. Every symptom is actually what the body needs in order to awaken.
>
> — Barbara Marx Hubbard

Iago merchants, and as a victory for the voice of civil society to the translucent midwife. Everything looks different when you welcome death and
rebirth rather than resist them in terror.

WHERE'S THE BAD GUY?

Once we recognize the collective Iago trance, we often want to pin it onto a
specific organization or person, and then to feel that once we eliminate them,
our troubles will be over. This has happened three times in Russia in less than
a hundred years. First the czar and his associates were seen as the source of
suffering; they were overthrown in 1917. After a few decades, Communism
proved to be not much of an improvement, and once again getting rid of the
bad guys became the imperative. Since 1991 the party is gone, but the Russian
people do not appear to be any better off with a capitalist system than they
were under either of the two previous ones.

In the thousands of interviews and surveys I conducted between the years
2000 and 2004, the activities of the Bush-Cheney administration provided a

convenient icon, for many people, of our collective insanity. Ram Dass talked about forgiveness as a translucent practice, and confessed that George Bush was his greatest challenge. The temptation to cast Bush and his friends as the core of the problem is enormous. Between them, they do indeed vividly represent every aspect of the Iago trance we have described. Their foreign policy has been driven by separation, by an us-versus-them mentality. Their decisions have generally been determined by hard-core fundamentalism rather than open-minded inquiry. They have succeeded in polarizing the country, defining unquestioning loyalty as patriotism, and instituting erosions of civil liberties as a means to deal with dissent. The gap between haves and have-nots has widened dramatically under their policies, which have been strong on "conservative" but dismal on "compassionate." And, of course, ideologically and economically motivated violence on a massive scale was sold to their populous through gross distortions of information, often verging on simple lying.

> To create a spiritual politics is to find some higher common ground, to listen to different perspectives and come up with something that really meets the true need. That means everything is out in the open, not backroom politics. We need to shine greater light on politics so that there is honesty, and people can see what is really going on. Then they will make the right choices.
>
> — Corinne McLaughlin

The many translucents I interviewed were by no means uniform in their political affiliations. Many take no position at all. Most were lukewarm at best about John Kerry. The only candidate in the 2004 election who seemed to stand out as representing a significant proportion was Representative Dennis Kucinich, who ran in the Democratic primaries. Yet the great majority were unified in the recognition that the Bush administration did an admirable job of embodying the values with which they could *not* affiliate.

Lynne Twist, an extraordinarily compassionate and translucent visionary, sees the Bush administration as symptomatic of our malaise of lack-driven, rather than causative, living. We all have the not-enough-for-me disease, and those with the worst cases seem to have taken up residence in 1600 Pennsylvania Avenue:

> *One way that I can sometimes find to have even a smidgen of compassion for our current president, and I disagree with almost everything he says and does, is to try to imagine where he is standing. What is driving them? You could*

chalk it up to selfishness, or control, or a lust for power. But if someone really believes that there is not enough to go around, in the myth of the lie of scarcity, then it seems noble and responsible to garner as much of the resources of the world as possible for you and yours, whomever you consider that to be. You've got to have way more than you need, to protect your people from ever being in the position of being left out.

You'll do anything to others, including bomb them and rape and plunder their country, to provide for the people that you're responsible for, for the moment. You'll borrow from future generations, from the animal kingdom, the plant kingdom; you'll stop at nothing, and blind yourself to the consequences. Our current administration is deliberately blinding themselves. It is really important to reveal what they are doing. I think that what they are doing is wrong; I'm not for it at all. But if I make them into adversaries, and become an adversary to them, then I'm doing the same as what they are doing.

And Mary Manin Morrissey, for many a spokesperson for a return to the true heart of religious teachings, had this to say: "If George Bush weren't here right now, we'd have to invent him. He is giving us a

> I never stopped being a radical. But I came to understand that the only revolution that's going to make a truly transformative difference, not just change the cosmetics of this whole mess, is one that transforms us from the core, that makes human beings more capable of intelligent responses to the actual situation we're confronting.
>
> — Saniel Bonder

very clear picture of the old dying order. That has done more to activate and cause a real coherence of the new forms than anything else recently."

We wake up from the collective Iago trance by seeing its roots in ourselves, in all of us. When we can see the seeds of separation and problem-based living within, and awake from them, not only do we live translucently but we also are able to elect translucent leaders.

SPIRITUAL MYTH #26: Spiritual people are beyond the mundane activities of the world; they are just one with what is. Politics and activism are dirty and ignorant.

SPIRITUAL MYTH #27: Everything is happening on its own. There is nothing you can do, and no doer anyway. Nostradamus said there would be a big war, followed by two thousand years of peace. The

Mayans support this, and so did the tea leaves in my cup this morning. Involvement in the ways of the world is just interfering with the divine plan.

SPIRITUAL MYTH #28: We are entering a golden age; all we have to do is to meditate and love each other and chant *Om*, and the world's problems will evaporate automatically.

SPIRITUAL MYTH #29: Capitalists and big corporations are evil. We need an armed insurrection; we can overthrow the oppressors, and the enlightened ones will rule supreme. The world can only be changed through militant political insurrection.

THE TRANSLUCENT VIEW OF THE WORLD

I asked almost everyone I talked to while doing research for this book how they saw the state of the world. I discovered an interesting paradox. Translucents are extraordinarily nonfundamentalist, all right with things as they are and at the same time willing to do everything possible to make a difference. They take our global predicament very seriously and yet maintain a sense of humor about it all. This does not mean that they suffer from violent mood swings — serious one day and laughing the next — but that the translucent view of the world is *simultaneously* deeply caring and accepting of whatever happens, at once funny and seriously kick-ass. Many of today's most poignant political commentators are also comedians: writers such as Michael Moore emanate a palpable compassion and social conscience, while earning reviews like "hysterically funny" from the *San Francisco Chronicle*.

> We're not going to wake up individually anymore; it's about a collective effort. It's about coming together, and of course it has to start within. A person always has good and bad, and right and wrong, and acceptance and nonacceptance. That is the basic separation that keeps humanity at a certain level. When enough people wake up to oneness in themselves, it will run through the whole of the planet.
>
> — Paul Lowe

I asked Byron Katie about this a few years ago. We were both speaking at the No Mind Festival in Sweden, and she had just returned from Israel, where she shared The Work, for which she is famous. She had asked her hosts there to drive her over the border into the Gaza Strip. She described to me the tensions, the disoriented people. But there was none of the usual disgust or complaint in her voice that one expects in a description of human suffering. She talked about it as if it were a great film or beautiful painting she had seen and appreciated. After a while I got curious about her tone. Didn't she care; didn't she feel the people's pain?

"How can I know it should be different than it is?" she replied. "Would it serve anyone for me to suffer about this?" Katie has obviously given up arguing with reality; she has no resistance to things as they are. Yet she travels the globe tirelessly. She makes a profound difference in people's lives, without having any investment in saving the world. The same was said about the Buddha, that he came to earth to dispel the suffering of all sentient beings, and he was only able to do such a sterling job at it because he could see that there were actually no separate beings and no real suffering. Like Katie, he could take care because he did not care; he could make the greatest difference because it made no difference to him.

> I don't know that I am entirely optimistic about the world, whether our species is going to last very long. The funny thing is, either way is fine with me, but I will work for this earth. The more you care, the more you don't care.
>
> — Ram Dass

I heard this view again and again as I talked to translucents from Iowa to India, from Sacramento to Stockholm. The certainty that things are perfect as they are, that the global situation is exactly as it needs to be, *and* the simultaneous recognition of great imbalance and the need for urgent change have become one view, presenting no contradiction. The ability to live within this paradox is of great importance to everyone who talked about it. To fall into one side, that things are perfect as they are, while negating the other, is to take a position of complacency and spiritual denial. To fall into the other side, and busy oneself only with urgent action, is to become trapped within and driven by Iago. Much political and environmental action has gone on a downward spiral. A war on evil becomes an enactment of evil. Yet in the middle of this paradox lies the possibility to deeply care without caring, to take action without attachment to the outcome. When you don't see any suffering anywhere, for the first time you can really alleviate suffering. When you see all things as perfect, you can begin to help them get better.

Horizontal and Vertical Tension

I was woken at 7 A.M. in California on September 11, 2001, by my friend Neil, calling from the airport. He knew I was scheduled to fly out that day to teach a seminar in Colorado. "Don't bother," he told me. "All the flights are canceled. America is under attack by terrorists." I peeked nervously out of the window, looking for men wearing sunglasses and bandannas behind every bush. I turned on the radio and heard with disbelief first about the planes, later about the collapse of the towers. Suddenly everyone was talking about some guy called O'Sama. Sounded Irish. Since we don't have the TV hooked up to the outside world, I went online to find out more about him.

There was little available at that point, but I did find an interesting article on PBS by ABC's John Miller, conducted in 1998. There was a photo of a bearded man with a twinkle in his eye, looking like a mischievous uncle. I read the interview. It presented a well-educated religious man, versed in current affairs, with high moral standards. He felt that his religion and culture were being threatened by U.S. foreign policy in several ways: first because of U.S. troops stationed near Mecca and Medina, holy land to Muslims, since the 1991 Gulf War; second because of a perceived bias of the United States toward Israel in the Middle East; and third because of a U.S. plan to build an oil pipeline from Tajikistan through Afghanistan to the sea, which he saw as further proof of Muslims losing their resources to economic imperialists. Several times in the interview, he emphasized that the Koran forbids overt acts of aggression, and he saw them as a last resort to stave off an attack on his culture and people. So this religious Muslim fundamentalist was essentially opposed to violence but saw it as the only remaining option in a war of principle to defend his religion: a jihad, or holy war.

Three days later, I went back to PBS's site. The picture of bin Laden had been replaced with a much more menacing shot of him with a gun, looking like the classic bad guy. Later that day, President Bush delivered a surprisingly restrained and eloquent speech to Congress. No Muslim bashing, only statements of deep feeling. But as his position solidified, I was fascinated to see how similar these two men were, both in their fundamentalism and their

> At some point global opinion will reach a matrix where it will say "no" in such a resounding and clear way that it will be heard, and it will be heard around the world.
>
> — James O'Dea

logic. Both see themselves as "good" (a servant of Allah on the one hand and of freedom and civilization on the other), and both see the other as "evil" or the "leader of infidels." Both feel justified in making strikes against the other's people (even though it may not be condoned by their particular holy book) in retaliation for previous acts of perceived terrorism. Both see these acts as divinely inspired: a "crusade against evil," and a "jihad." Both inspire less-educated and poor people to do their dirty work, and call them heroes. Both use language such as "resolve…determination…awaken the wrath of our people." Both speak of a fight that will stop at nothing until it is won. Both see their victory in the other's defeat. Both try to pull unwilling nations into the brawl. Both describe the other as weak and cowardly, and justify this with examples. Both feel that they are fighting for principles much larger than themselves (Islam and Arabs on the one hand, and freedom and democracy on the other). And both of them, and their friends, just *love* that oil.

On the surface of things we are witnessing the unfolding of global conflict between polarized forces. We can call this fundamentalist Christianity against fundamentalist Islam, which proclaims that my God of love and peace is better than yours, and if you don't agree I'll kill you. Or capitalism against feudalism, or the morally corrupt West against rigidly puritan Islam,

> September 11 got more people thinking about the eternal questions. "Who is up there?" "Why I am here?" I call it fierce grace. It wakes a lot of people up. They look at their own lives, their own preoccupations, in the light of a death.
>
> — Ram Dass

or democracy against totalitarian regimes, or, perhaps most accurately, large oil corporations looking for a good deal, and the governments they own, versus some very rich Arab gentlemen wearing gold Rolexes and fancy headgear. None of this is very new or interesting. You can imagine equally dogmatic Christian and Muslim zealots pulverizing each other during the Crusades in Damascus in 1190. Only now the weapons have been upgraded from javelins to "smart-bombs" from boiling oil to chemical weapons.

Another polarity is playing itself out, for which we do not find an obvious precedent. In the spring of 2003, while Bush and Saddam Hussein were lobbing insults at each other in another global squabble, millions of people took to the streets all over the world to protest war. Those who spoke up were not backing one side or another; they were saying, with a global intelligence,

Enough. Enough of your bickering; we need to grow up now beyond all this name-calling, beyond all this self-righteousness, beyond all this black-and-white thinking, beyond the small mind that sees revenge and domination as the best strategy. We need to feel deeper than that. Enough already!

This was the first time that global sanity has been evoked in this way. It found its feet in millions of peaceful marchers, it found its intelligence in countless connected Web sites, it found its voice in dozens of languages, it found its heart in the recognition of one new humanity, one sanity that knows no borders. We are the first generation of global citizens.

As we look at the surface conflicts — Osama and George, Republicans and Democrats, Israelis and Palestinians, and so on — we wonder who is going to win. But does it matter very much in the long run? At the end of the day we are not counting who was right, but who is left to talk about it. The vertical dimension is what matters, the depth of our consciousness. Will the old dinosaur minds draw us all into their conflicts, destroying life as we know it in the process, or will the emerging translucent view midwife us into a new way of living? In the translucent vision of the world there is no other, no enemy. It is a political view that encompasses the well-being of all sentient beings, not just of one group or another. Either we all win, or we all lose.

> There is nothing more powerful than civil society, no government, no multinational, no company. And civil society is growing in its power as never before.
>
> — Lynne Twist

Spiritual Activism

Without an inclusive approach, environmental, political, or social activism can easily add to the feeling of blame, of us against them, and evoke resistance and a hardening of opposing positions. Once a group of well-meaning young friends was concerned about proposed clear-cut logging in our mountain community. They saw the lumber company as evil, money-grubbing, and inflexible, and they took to camping on company lands and building platforms in the threatened trees, inspired by Julia Butterfly. The logging company appealed to the courts and to local law enforcement. Arrests followed, and so did more protests. Finally, the county called in a specialist in environmental mediation. Through his help, the concerns of the community were peacefully presented to the logging company and widely publicized in the local press.

Under public pressure, the demands of local residents were respected, and a land swap was organized that satisfied everyone.

Achieving this took an inclusive view. I listened to the mediator being interviewed on the radio. He spoke of the need to erase blame and anger within himself before entering any mediation. When he could see the highest intention of all parties, he said that again and again people would respond at a higher level. Wink Franklin, past president of the Institute of Noetic Sciences, described the proponents of this translucent worldview as "spiritual activists."34 He defined spiritual activism as: "more a vertical activity. The deeper you go in your spiritual understanding, the clearer you see harmony or the path ahead, not only for you but also for humanity. The clearer you can get in your inner work, the more effective your outer work will be."

The Dalai Lama is an inspiring example of this kind of spiritual activist and a role model for the translucent political leader. He devotes hours every day to his own meditation and practice. During one interview when he was asked about the possibility of a free Tibet, the Dalai Lama's answer was extraordinary. He said that he was no longer even working to drive the Chinese out of Tibet. He realized that such a long time had passed since the invasion that several generations of Chinese had now come to see that region as home. He now saw peaceful co-existence in the region, and the creation of a fully demilitarized zone, as the best scenario for all. This extraordinary position must be understood within the context of almost fifty years of rape, torture, and imprisonment of the Tibetan people, many of them monks and nuns. Ample excuse for revenge. To feel concern for the well-being of both your own people and your invaders is a true example of compassionate sanity, of what might be possible in this world.

> If we're acting from a state of division, which has an enemy, we may be feeding one child today, but our own internal opposition is being transmitted into the whole, which will only ensure that there'll be ten more starving children tomorrow.
>
> — Adyashanti

Imagine what the result might have been after the attacks in September 2001 if we had responded without revenge, but with the same translucent dignity that the Dalai Lama embodies. Imagine if we had felt our pain and loss and grief, and then sought to understand what had motivated these

> I think living your life from a stand rather than a position gives you infinite power. It's a different domain of life; you discover a portal that gives you access to the domain of true power, tapping into the real truth and destiny of the human family.
>
> — Lynne Twist

horrendous actions. The United States had at that time the goodwill and support of the whole world to draw on. Imagine if we had worked with that support in a peaceful way, used international agencies to track down terrorism but avoided resorting to further violence and loss of innocent civilian lives. It is beyond the scope of possibility for politics today, but the Dalai Lama holds up a torch to show us what is possible when we shift from us-against-them to one big inclusive *us*.

THE TIPPING POINT

In 1520 everyone believed that the earth was the center of the universe, and that the planets as well as the sun revolved around us. Nicolaus Copernicus, a Polish astronomer, was the first person to suggest that the earth was a planet among others, which were all revolving around the sun. His theories were virtually ignored in his lifetime, and his major work was not even published until the year of his death. It took Tycho, Kepler, Galileo, and later Newton to prove that his theory was correct. His was the opening shot in a revolution whose consequences were greater than those of any other intellectual event in our history. Suddenly everything made sense; the motions of the planets, previously seen as random wanderings relative to a still earth, now were seen to be in predictable orbits around the sun. Copernicus's theory provided a basis for the development of modern science as we know it, and a universe that follows predictable laws rather than the whims of an unseen patriarchal deity.

Galileo was excommunicated from the Catholic Church for siding with Copernicus. The discoveries he made with one of the world's first telescopes shook every popular paradigm to the core. Yet by 1600, less than sixty years after Copernicus's death, everyone in the Western world knew that he was right, and we were headlong into the Renaissance. Neither Copernicus nor Galileo had to go door-to-door to persuade *everyone* that they were right. Although they met with great resistance from the Church and the government, it only required a very few intelligent people to test their theories, and within a few years one paradigm was completely replaced by another. Despite great resistance from those in power, their view prevailed because it was true, and because it was verifiable by open-minded inquiry.

We are now at the beginning of another paradigm shift, one just as powerful. Copernicus's theory was about the physical universe and laid the foundation for modern science. The translucent revolution is about human consciousness and could lay the foundation for an evolutionary leap in human life unlike anything we have known. Like the Ptolemaic universe, the Iago trance does not stand up to investigation. In this moment right now, is there any reliable proof that you lack anything? Can you find a problem in this moment, right now, without thinking about how things should be different? The sense of separation, of I and you as distinct, which is at the very basis of the Iago worldview and way of living, does not survive self-inquiry, the simple and innocent search for a thing called "me." Randomly take any of the preoccupations, desires, and fears of the mind about past and future, and test them to see if they are real, or even realistic. Every one of Iago's tenets, outlined in chapter 1, collapses in the light of investigation. Yet all the features of a radical awakening, listed in

> What is possible for us as a race if a critical mass shift from ego-based living to surrender-based living? Not everybody need do this; one percent may be enough to tip the whole culture.
>
> — Barbara Marx Hubbard

chapter 2, reveal themselves on their own when we pay attention to what is real. Like the behavior of the planets, in the light of inquiry, everything falls into place.

In *The Romeo Error*, Lyle Watson was the first to suggest that it might take only 1 percent of a population to undergo a shift toward greater coherence for the whole population to shift. More recently, Malcolm Gladwell wrote *The Tipping Point*, in which he credibly demonstrates how shifts in the collective start with the local. He shows how one man taking a stand against gang violence in New York was pivotal in a dramatic drop in the crime rate of the whole city, and how a few people can start a new fashion for shoes that takes over the country. It only takes a few people, the right people, to transform isolated events into widespread change. Research in marketing trends — for example, in the shift from cassettes to CDs as the preferred media for music

— repeatedly shows small steps of gradual growth building to a "tipping point," followed by a sudden jump to universal acceptance.

How many people in the United States and the rest of the world have been touched by a radical awakening? In how many of these people has this awakening precipitated a shift toward sustained translucence? And how many will it take for translucence to become the dominant paradigm? Duane Elgin has been researching this question extensively for several decades. He cites a Princeton/Gallup Survey showing an increase from 22 to 33 percent of people reporting they have at some time had "a religious or mystical experience."[35] Elgin tells me that more recent research, including a poll conducted by the *New York Times*, puts this figure as high as 40 percent.[36]

To measure how many of those have been transformed by such an experience into a sustained trend is more difficult. Paul Ray and Sherry Anderson, in their extensively researched *Cultural Creatives*, suggest that a new paradigm of values is represented by about sixty million people in the United States. In my conversation with Ray, he estimated that about one third of them, or twenty million people, are "in the process of awakening." Fewer than two million people live in what he calls "significantly reduced-egoic access to the divine or no-self," which we are calling translucent. He also estimates that there are about the same number in Europe, or about four million combined. Other estimates have been much higher. The writer and teacher Satyam Nadeen, who teaches both in the United States and in Europe, feels that most estimates are unrealistically low because we have ideas about what kinds of people would qualify and tend to look to people with a similar background and belief as our own. Nadeen estimates the number of translucents worldwide to be more than fifty million, or almost 1 percent.

> The universe is continuously regenerating itself; as a living system, the life that flows through a living universe goes through us and around us. To the extent that we quiet our thinking mind there is an opening and we see that we are beings with cosmic dimensions; we are beings that connect into a living universe.
>
> — Duane Elgin

While estimates of the numbers vary, I found unanimous agreement among those I spoke with that it would only take a very small percentage of the world's population to wake up for there to be a global awakening. It is the underlying reality of the translucent view, like that of Copernicus's astronomy, that leads many to believe that it would take very few living in this way to tip the global scale. Translucents have reality on their side. Peter Russell sees the global awakening as more of an exponential curve:

> *The more people clear their consciousness and wake up, the more those people will be affected by the collective awakening. And the more they are open to that, the more it will facilitate their own awakening, and that of others. So it becomes a positive feedback loop. It is like a snowball going down a hill. The more snow it gathers, the bigger it becomes, and the bigger it becomes, the more snow it gathers. And so it keeps going and gets bigger and bigger.*

> The tide probably has already turned. Just as in the depth of the ocean, the tide turns long before you see it on the surface of the water.
>
> — Lynne Twist

Personal awakening is always happening within the context of the collective; it is spurred on by the collective at the same time that it contributes to it. Barbara Marx Hubbard has been experimenting with collective awakening in Santa Barbara, where she lives. She has brought people together into core groups for several years to explore what she calls the shift from ego to essence:

> *One of the main results we have discovered about the percentage that would be required to shift consciousness on earth and awaken us is that the first part is the number of individuals that are awake, and the second is how many of them are in resonance with one another, with two or more. We have discovered an enormous potency of resonance resounding, echoing back, and affirming the essential being in each of us.*

She encourages people to listen to their "inspiration, their higher voice, to bring our creativity into form through our vocations." People of similar gifts have formed into co-creative groups, where they "maintain the resonance while doing the work." Her Foundation for Conscious Evolution therefore puts resonant translucence first, and action and results second. As a result, members of her community have played strong roles in increasing the energy sufficiency and sustainability of Santa Barbara. Others have made political, social, and artistic contributions. Their work may be one of the first models for an urban translucent community, a foretaste for what is possible for us all.

The Global Brain

There is another unprecedented trend in global consciousness, which alone will have an impact we cannot yet imagine. Less than a hundred years ago it took months to communicate with someone on the other side of the world, and many more months for them to reply. Today you can call any one of about three billion people, half the earth's population, and speak to them in seconds, usually for a few cents. In 2004 the estimated number of people regularly using the Internet was 940 million, or 14 percent. This has grown from forty million in 1996, and ten million in 1994.[37] The world is becoming interconnected much faster than anyone anticipated. In 1994 almost all Internet users were using dial-up modems, which were then offering speeds of about 10 kbps per second. Ten years later, DSL and IDSN connections offer most people about sixty times that speed, 600 kbps or more. We are just now beginning to see installation of fiber-optic cables for home use. An advanced fiber-optic cable today is capable of transmitting 1.2 gigabytes of information in one second (the entire *Encyclopedia Britannica*, with all its illustrations), and *War and Peace* on DVD in three. At this rate we will be able to transmit the entire contents of the Library of Congress in less than ten seconds by 2014. And remember, all estimates so far have been very conservative.

What does all this nerd talk have to do with global awakening? Many years ago, Peter Russell postulated the emergence of what he called a "global brain." Every one of the ten billion cells in the brain has the capacity to connect to every other cell in almost no time. When we combine the rapid increase of Internet connectivity, the speed of connection, and the increase of computer speeds, we can see the real possibility in the next years of this global brain. Russell describes this planetary consciousness as "billions of messages moving backward and forward in an ever-growing

> The planetary crisis we're facing is an awakening signal. If we don't shift our consciousness to feeling oneness, connectedness, the field, we can destroy ourselves. We are all members of a living body — we are all cells in the planetary system, and whether we know it or not we are being connected rapidly by that system.
>
> — Barbara Marx Hubbard

web of communication, linking the billions of minds of humanity into one single system."

This is just like what goes on inside your skull all the time. In this way, human beings will go through a shift of identity from being separate autonomous entities to knowing themselves as cells in a bigger organism, parts of a whole humanity. The first pictures of earth broadcast to us from space, in the 1970s, initiated that awareness of a global identity.

Brain cells also differ from the way human society operates in that they work in synchronicity. Unless someone has brain cancer, cells are working together, not fighting one another. As it stands today, the Internet is primarily a tool for consumerism and escapism. Thirty percent of the money made from Web sites is from pornography. Says Russell: "The values have not changed enough yet. It's one thing to wire it all up, but another to change what it is used for. For the global brain to really be of service, we need a corresponding awakening of consciousness. The old consciousness coupled with the new technology is headed for disaster." Conversely, the new technology in the hands of more and more active translucents opens up the possibilities for a global transformation of which we can hardly dream. Let's examine why.

> Humanity is becoming our indentification group, and not the ego, or ego spelled large as nation, as state. Life will take us beyond the communication stage, and it will give us the next step, the consciousness stage. We are going through a process of evolution.
>
> — Ram Dass

The Power of Dialogue

It was our ability to communicate that allowed us to move from one paradigm to the next, as each outlived its usefulness. Communication allowed us to evolve together from the hunter-gatherer to the agricultural era (thirty-five thousand years ago), and then again to the industrial era. Today it is communication that will allow us to evolve from the industrial era, which has become as destructive as it was once useful, to the consciousness era, or translucent humanity. Our ability to communicate with every other human being more and more effectively is both the result of the wiring of the global brain and necessary for the cells of that brain to be able to work as one organism without conflict.

Before becoming president of the Institute of Noetic Sciences, James O'Dea was director of Amnesty International in Washington, DC, for ten years, and director of Seva, a nonprofit organization dedicated to international health and development, for five. So he knows about bringing disparate parts of the world together. For several years now he has led a series of dialogues called "Compassion and Social Healing." He has brought together Israelis and Palestinians, environmentalists and corporate CEOs, and blacks and whites in South Africa. Again and again, O'Dea has seen what happens when seeming enemies have the power to experience each other's points of view.

> Emergent consciousness is essentially dialogic. We all have different narratives about how we came to the present: "This is my story of how I came to be here." And our capacity to hear the truth of the other person's narrative is the basis for dialogue.
>
> — James O'Dea

Gottfried Lief, for example, was a teenager in the Hitler Youth movement in the late 1930s. Carried along by the strong forces gathering at that time, on Kristallnacht he ran through the streets of Berlin smashing windows of Jewish shops and homes. He was caught in what felt like an inescapable momentum, which became one of the most horrendous nightmares of cruelty we have witnessed. Now in his seventies, Lief was brought into one of O'Dea's dialogues with Mary Rothschild, the only surviving daughter of Holocaust survivors. She lost countless relatives. Lief and Rothschild were drawn together because they shared a desire to heal their relationship to the past. Introducing herself to him as the child of Holocaust victims, she asked him, "Who are you? What did you do?" He replied, "I am Gottfried Lief. I was in the Hitler Youth movement." And Mary asked, "I don't care about that; all I need to know in our dialogue is could you, if you had been old enough, *could* you have been the one to open the gas taps in those camps? Could you have been a mass murderer? Could you have been the one to kill most of my family?"

It was quite a question. Gottfried looked down for a while, then looked back into Mary's eyes. "I don't know," he said. O'Dea comments:

This was a revolutionary moment for Mary. If somebody says to you, "I don't know, I could have been a mass murderer with others, I could have gotten involved in that level of cruelty," it pulls your attention, and you realize you are in the presence of truth speaking. This was her experience. She thought, "Well, wait now, there is truth coming out of the mouth of the perpetrator. It's a human truth, it is an honesty that I can relate to, and even admire in some ways."

Gottfried commented on the dialogue: "You are in the abyss of history, as the representative of the perpetrator." Not only the perpetrators but their children and grandchildren bear this burden. Gottfried then acknowledged that Mary offered a bridge across the abyss, a place where perpetrator and victim meet. And that, I think, is the beginning of a new pattern that says: "We can transform our relationship to the past, we can create bridges over the abyss. We don't have to continue in those patterns, we can shed them with a greater meaning around our unity, we can heal the wounds of the past that are so deep."

O'Dea told me many stories of this kind. Laura Jason brought together two groups of women who felt passionately about one side or the other of the pro-life/pro-choice debate. They represented factions that had shown great public animosity toward each other. Jason took them into private dialogue together for about a year. After that year, they held a press conference. They said: "We have not necessarily changed what we believe, but the difference is now we are friends. We would take care of each other's children. In fact, we do. We have discovered a shared ground of being that is able to contain us, and so our differences become much less potent, less divisive. The expansion of the shared ground of being is what nurtures us and carries us forward."

South Africa was an important benchmark in our history, because after a period of significant oppression the country's response was to establish a Truth and Reconciliation Commission. Similarly, it took ordinary Israeli and Palestinian citizens to initiate the Geneva talks in 2003. Avoiding politics-as-usual, they said, "Enough. We are ready to move to a new level of humanity." All the thousands of examples like this, of dialogue replacing conflict, are creating fertile soil for Russell's global brain to wake up. Each dialogue that brings mutual understanding

> There is a middle road that unites the inner and the outer, that involves collective wisdom, checking in with other people and getting other people's feedback, and learning from other people's spiritual path and their action in the world. All of that is important. Spiritual activism has to be part of collective wisdom and collective judgment and collective action, and it also needs a solitary spark.
>
> — Wink Franklin

We are moving toward a form of justice that is not just punitive, but that restores balance to society. The most important thing is to discover the truth, to speak it openly, to find reconciliation and forgiveness, to heal as a collective and move forward.

— James O'Dea

creates new cells in the global brain that are able to function in synchronicity rather than conflict. At the same time, the rapid access to news and information from all over the world makes it more and more difficult to turn someone else into the "other." When you can hear their music, their anger, and their pain, when you can see their children and homes and their blood on television in your living room, you have no choice but to acknowledge their humanity.

SCENARIOS OF THE FUTURE

All these trends are coming together at an unprecedented speed. Several environmental reports on resource depletion, the disturbance of weather patterns due to global warming, and the melting of the ice caps have targeted the start of the second decade of this century as the time when it will be impossible to overlook the damage already incurred. Based on a continuation of current trends, by 2012 we will also have the kind of communications connectivity in place needed to create Russell's global brain. Duane Elgin, among many others, estimates that we will see enough translucent people to tip global consciousness into a new paradigm by the beginning of the second decade of this century. And, by coincidence, for the more esoteric in our midst, the Mayan calendar comes to an end in 2012, and Vedic astrology also predicts it as a time of sudden global transformation.

Recently I asked Peter Russell in what direction he felt we were pointing today, and he outlined three possible scenarios. The first he calls total annihilation. In this scenario, it's already too late. The damage to the environment, the continuing violence fueled by blind fundamentalism, the disparities of our economic system are all so great, and the number and effect of translucents is so small, that we are heading for extinction within our lifetime. He sees this outcome as very unlikely, simply because both the natural world and human beings have built-in mechanisms to keep restoring balance. Still, he asks, were that to be the inevitable conclusion of the trajectory we are on, what would be the best way to prepare ourselves? "The best thing we can do is to continue with our own personal journey of awakening, and maybe that will transform the world, and maybe it won't. But we won't say we went down without trying. We can say we went down in a better state of consciousness, instead of playing casinos in Las Vegas."

The second scenario is a global crisis, which we survive. In this picture, Western civilization is beyond reform and crashes heavily, bringing the rest of the world down with it: "What would that look like? There would inevitably be a lot of suffering, pain, and hardship. It is realistically impossible to imagine how we can go another twenty years without some kind of discomfort. It would take a miracle. What would we need in that situation? Compassion, a centeredness in yourself to ride the change, to not be attached to things; a certain equanimity."

Along with a very flexible sense of humor, these are the qualities of translucence, and the same qualities required in the first scenario.

The third scenario is the miracle. In this perspective, we have already made the shift. Like the tide deep down under the surface of the ocean, it has already turned, and the translucent paradigm is already well in place. As external problems worsen, they will only fuel the global awakening, and the combination of exponential advances in technology and quantum leaps in human consciousness will clean up our messes in no time at all. Although seemingly hopelessly optimistic,

> If you can help people freeze-frame certain moments, they will recognize the sanctity of life. They will recognize peacefulness not as the opposite of war, not anti-war, but a fundamental state of harmony.
>
> — Robert Rabbin

scenario three got a surprising number of votes from many of the well-respected thinkers I interviewed about future outcomes. The celebrated microbiologist Bruce Lipton, for example, points out that the shift we are going through, as a race, is also the shift from a mechanical view of life to a quantum view. The old paradigm, based on logic and cause and effect, is predictable. In a quantum universe, magic is not the exception but the rule. In quantum physics experiments, things behave in alignment with how the observer expects them to behave, so as we change our collective story about the state of the world, the state of the world also changes.

We're going to be in severe crisis with magic at our fingertips, and for the first time the wisdom and compassion to understand what to do. It's a complete ending of the trajectory that we've been on for thousands of years. Something is going to shift that's so radical, I don't think our minds today can comprehend what it's going to be like.

— Peter Russell

So how could we best prepare ourselves for a quantum leap in collective consciousness, in which we learn, just in the nick of time, to wake up and live as one humanity? By living translucently. Says Russell: "Whichever scenario we get, we'll need the same remedy. This has allowed me to let go of how the future will be. Whether we want to affect the situation, or deal with it falling apart, or celebrate a new beginning, the same work is needed."

TWELVE WAYS TO NUDGE YOUR WORLD INTO TRANSLUCENCE

NUDGE

Be Reborn Every Day

Find your unique creative ways to step again and again beyond the personal perspective. Be willing to die every day to the person you think you are, to hand the wave back to the ocean. Learn to distrust your own mind. Awakening is not a single event in time; it is a river endlessly flowing in this moment now. Whether with meditation, self-inquiry, dance, martial arts, or sacred sex, make sure you come home to yourself as the prelude to all else.

NUDGE

Practice Translucence

Once we open the channel of awakening every day, to the present moment and to our oceanic real nature, the next step is to be open and feel how the Big Source wants to gift the world through us. Surrender to how love wants to love through you, rather than from you, and become an instrument of collective translucence.

NUDGE
Find Your Tribe

Humanity does not go through paradigm shifts very often. It can be a bumpy ride. Like waking up in the middle of an earthquake, you may sometimes wonder what is going on. In your immediate environment, become aware of who else is part of the new paradigm, and take refuge in each other. As you deepen in translucence, you may find old relationships dropping away, and new people entering your life. Translucents easily recognize each other, often without even needing to speak. Find your tribe, those with whom you can die to the old and rise up as the new. Be undertakers and midwives to each other.

> A spiritual activist is someone who is no longer using subtle spiritual ego to keep the world away. The world has come in and has settled easily and naturally and this person lives in an easy and natural and open relationship to the world.
>
> — Robert Rabbin

NUDGE
Allow Guru to Move in You

The word *guru* simply means "that which dispels darkness." You can let your meetings with your friends be carried by that, without having to become special or superior. If you remember that we are all in this together, equally part of the new paradigm, all equally letting go of our old skins, then your friendships, your marriage, your meetings at work, and your random interactions with strangers are all opportunities for deepening translucence. Sometimes gently asking someone, "Can you feel your body just now?" or, "Is this coming from the deepest place in you?" can help them shift back into the translucent flow with respect and humor.

NUDGE
Clarify Your Vision

Take some time away from it all. Go on retreat, or camping, or hiking in nature. Free yourself of the commercial marketplace so that you can let go of what they want you to want and fall back into your innocent vision. Go deeper than "I want, I don't want." If you were the world's savior, if it all came down to you to make a difference, what kind of world would you want to pass on? If you have children, grandchildren, nephews, nieces, heck, even if you've ever seen a child, what kind of earth, what kind of social system do you wish for them? What is your prayer for humanity, what is your vision of heaven on earth? Write it down; get specific and committed.

> Try to find out what you think is the truth, what is for the highest good, and then find a way to promote that idea without lying, manipulating, or getting into power trips with somebody who disagrees. That is a real spiritual practice, the true spiritual expression of democracy.
>
> — Corinne McLaughlin

NUDGE
Align Your Actions with Your Vision

Ask yourself if the way you live, day to day, reflects your vision of the world. Your vision should be known to others by how you live, not by what you say. If you can see the dangers of burning fossil fuels, it may be time to look at how you contribute. If you have a bumper sticker proclaiming world peace, look at your relationships. Do they demonstrate a contribution to that peace? Start with small steps; bring how you live in alignment with the world you want to pass on. No need to practice what you preach, just practice, and let your example be the only preaching you do.

NUDGE
Get Informed

There are very few ill-intentioned people in the world. Ask around. Everyone says they want a better world, less violence, more tolerance. Okay, almost everyone. Our problem is not an excess of bad guys, it's apathy bred through inadequate information. Many of the larger news organizations provide a particular interpretation of selected news, to tell you what to think. Rather than choosing one biased news source over another, try to get information about your world from a variety of sources. You can easily do this is by using Google's news page. The stories are chosen by an algorithm, from about 4,500 news sources, and grouped by topic: http://news.google.com.

NUDGE
Simplify Your Life

There is a growing movement of voluntary simplicity throughout the Western world. You can free yourself from the collective trance of greed by asking, When is enough enough? Take some time alone and ask yourself what you really need to be satisfied. What kind of house is enough, what kind of car, what kinds of clothes? Learning to practice voluntary simplicity is the fastest way to get free of debt and to return to the life your heart demands that you live, the life you can look back on one day with a deep sigh of "yes." Once you can feel the atmosphere of "enough," practice gratitude, altruism, and generosity as ways to deepen translucence.

> We're coming to a shift where we need to bring heaven down to earth, to embody the divine fully within physical corporeality. The lovers of earth and the lovers of spirit need to come together. We need to ask, What is the function of time and space? Why are we here?
>
> — Chris Bache

NUDGE
Talk and Share What You Know

Individuals are transformed through inward practice; the world is transformed through dialogue. To the degree that you free yourself of any strong bias, share what you know with others. Create debate around you; encourage other people to find out more about the peoples and points of view that are foreign to them. Have the courage to be a whistle-blower, and know that your voice makes a difference in ending apathy and misinformation.

NUDGE
Be Involved

Would you rather see the world run by Iago-crazed greed or by translucents?

> Social action is exquisite Karma yoga. In a Ghandi-esque way, we approach social service with spirit. The renunciate path does not work in the West, so we have to renounce inside. We have to play the game, and not be concerned with the score.
>
> — Ram Dass

Whether it's in your community, your state, or your nation, find a way to get involved. Make your voice heard. Be the voice of sanity and sustainability on this planet. Participate in the electoral process. Look for the candidates who come closest to your vision of a more conscious world and stand behind them. If you can't find anyone who even comes close, look for the people you do admire and encourage them to run. Dennis Kucinich and Arianna Huffington represent a new breed of translucent politician, and it is up to you and me to stand behind them.

NUDGE
Vote with Your Checkbook

You make a powerful statement every time you choose integrity over the cheapest deal. Before you buy meat or eggs, find out something about the conditions those animals lived in, and make sure you really want to endorse those conditions with your money. Companies like Ikea or Patagonia make this process easy for you; they make their environmental and economic policies readily available.

NUDGE

Appreciate Translucent Activity

Acknowledge translucence wherever you see it. It takes courage and commitment to live in a way that demonstrates wakefulness. Go out of your way to thank writers, artists, musicians, businesspeople, or schoolteachers who have taken a stand to help row the boat in a different direction. Every time you thank someone for her or his contribution, it is as though you have poured water on the roots of their gift.

The shift from Iago to translucence is no more than the shift from madness to simple sanity. Life lived in natural fullness in direct relationship to what is in this moment, rather than fear or desire for what could be, is just a return to the natural state. This awakening from a long collective trance may be happening at this time simply because it has to. There may be no alternative but extinction. There is no precedent for what is occurring now. The problems have never been so urgent, the resources have never been so rapidly depleted, and the planet has never been so rapidly raped before. At the same time, the earth's people have never before been so interconnected and so equipped to inspire, share information, and cooperate with each other. There has never before been this kind of widespread awakening in a secular context. With this kind of critical mass, something extraordinary is inevitable in our lifetime.

> The consciousness that was in the great religious geniuses is popping now in ordinary people. We are born at a time of a planetary integration. It is very apparent, if you look at our current crises, that they can't be solved in the state of consciousness that created them.
>
> — Barbara Marx Hubbard

You are the world. Each of us is the pivot on which our future balances.

> In the past we had to ask for help and guidance. When the awakening human recognizes and becomes aware of the context itself, he recognizes that it really depends upon him. It depends on us now, all of us, to take this next step.
>
> — Andrew Cohen

What you do, and how you live, is not as trivial as we sometimes think. What you choose to do in the next five minutes, and the spirit in which you do it, contributes to the difference between nuclear annihilation and the opportunity for this world to return to Eden.

The future rests in your hands, and the stakes are getting higher. It is time for all of us to wake up to our natural sanity, and to live it passionately, dangerously, intensely.

Translucently.

Don't wait for someone else to come and save us. You are the one.

EPILOGUE

In the spring of 2002, I took a year off to research and write this book. Two years later, the process was still just getting started. Everyone I talked to offered me five more names of people who had fallen into the same view, whose lives were an exploration of the same inquiry. Whenever I went back to speak with those I had interviewed, as often happened, they told me their process had deepened so much more since we last talked that now they had a host of new discoveries as well as a whole new list of budding translucents to refer me to. For every one person willing to talk about translucence publicly, I began to sense the presence of a dozen more in the shadows, quietly living this awakening. The translucent revolution is not a static phenomenon that can be neatly investigated, measured, reported on, and shelved. This is a raging, out-of-control epidemic of sanity.

Finally, the situation was resolved by Marc Allen, my publisher.

"It's still not finished," I confessed, as yet another deadline had been missed.

"Books like this don't get finished," he advised me, "they get abandoned."

So here it is, never completed, but abandoned; not the final word, but a line in a conversation that is ongoing.

I write these last words as I complete a one-week retreat in Puerto Morelos, on the Caribbean shores of Mexico. My friends Bernie and Adrianna Heideman have brought a group of about forty, and they are joined by local Mexicans and expatriates for the Dances of Universal Peace, held twice a day on the beach. I have been invited along to "help people deepen." On the first day the talk was primarily conceptual. "How can I understand more with my mind?" Day by day, one after another, everyone has been falling into themselves, some as a refreshing return, some for the first time. Now, as the week has unfolded, the conversation has changed. Eyes are sparkling, knowing smiles point to a shared ground of being. The question has shifted to "How can I live this mystery, this that is known beyond the mind, more deeply, more generously?" The conversation has become translucent.

Gatherings like this are happening all over the world every day. The more people relax into the natural state, the more they explore how to live and love from this wakefulness, the easier it all becomes. The change we are passing through is a mystery. Awakening is only the beginning; it is in *living* that awakening that we face new horizons. This book has described some fledgling steps: in our relating, our sexuality, our business life, and our impact on the world. What is the potential once we spread our wings and fly? No one knows.

When I started writing this book, I had plenty of ideas. In the process, I have unlearned a great deal more than I have learned. One concept after another has bitten the dust. Now I look forward with delight to knowing even less next year.

The more we explore the blossoming of human potential, the more mysterious and paradoxical it becomes. The more we abandon our ambitions to be enlightened, the deeper the endless enlightenment goes. The more we sink into despair, the more we are liberated from its grip. The more we abandon hope, the more hope we engender. And the more we relax into a dimension where nothing is happening, and where nothing ever has happened, the more we become translucent revolutionaries.

ACKNOWLEDGMENTS

There is a saying in Africa that it takes a village to raise a child. This book seemed to require the population of a bustling town, spread over many continents.

I am immensely grateful to the many translucent writers and teachers who have given so generously of their time in our interviews. They are all listed in the "Who's Who" section. In some cases the interviews took more than ten hours of conversations, as well as multiple meetings and audiocassettes. It has only been possible to include a tiny part of the wisdom, humor, and loving-kindness I experienced in these dialogues.

Thanks to Marc Allen, publisher of New World Library, who believed in this book from the beginning. I often called him for inspiration and reflection, and he was invariably just waking up from a nap. I am convinced that Marc is a direct reincarnation of Winnie the Pooh. And thanks to his wonderful staff, who have been every writer's dream support system, allowing me to push back deadlines many times, and always be there on the other end of the phone to cheerlead the project on to the finish: Georgia Hughes, Kristen Cashman, Elizabeth Rose Raphael, Alexander Slagg, Munro Magruder, Majorie Conte, and Kim Corbin. Great thanks to Mimi Kusch for such sensitive and precise manuscript editing, to Karin Mullen, Steve Anderson, and Norman Filzman for proofreading, and to Charlee Trantino for creating the index. Thanks to Idana Bluem for her gorgeous close-up photography on the cover (it is a flower through a macro lens) and to Mary Ann Casler for her great cover design. Thanks to Tona Pearce Myers for the interior design and typesetting.

Thanks to my many friends and colleagues who saw the book through from initial inception to final proofreading. Thanks to Barbara Joy, Eileen Cope, and Susan Brown for help with crafting the initial proposal. Thanks also to Eileen Cope for her valiant attempts to interest New York publishers in this book. And thanks to those publishers for all the rejection letters: I definitely ended up in the right hands. Thanks to Connie Kishbaugh, Kelly Hale, and Jeremy Montz, who put countless hours into transcribing the interviews. Kelly Hale, my assistant, also supported the book in a multitude of ways and earns the official Girl Friday Award.

Above all, thanks go to Tinker Lindsay, my editor. She went far beyond the call of duty with this project and poured her heart and soul into it at every twist and turn, lingering with every word and comma in pursuit of the mot juste. Thanks to her basset hound, Lucy, for desperately needed comic relief, late at night when we were fried.

My thanks to the thousands of participants in seminars, conferences, and festivals in both the United States and Europe who allowed me to research the translucent shift with much greater breadth. Thanks to all our wonderful organizers in twelve countries who have hosted and supported us. Though you are too many to list, you know who you are.

Huge thanks go to my family. To my father, John, and stepmother, Katinka, for their support of this book, both literary and financial, and for the legacy of a writer's DNA. To my beloved wife, Chameli, for her unwavering belief in this book and her mad-scientist husband, and her patience with my long periods of withdrawal to the cabin in the woods with my laptop. Chameli has been an integral part of this book at every turn, and I have no words to express my thanks for the multi-dimensional blessings she showers.

Gratitude, love, and devotion to my sons, Abhi and Shuba, for inspiring me to trust in a tomorrow that is saner than our yesterdays.

NOTES

Chapter Ten: Through, Not From

1. Mireille Silcott, "A Happy Man," interview with Leonard Cohen for *Saturday Night*, September 15, 2001. Used with permission of Leonard Cohen.
2. Elena Comelli, "The Virtueless Monk," interview with Leonard Cohen in *La Nazione*, translated by Andrea Della Rossa, November 25, 1998. Used with permission of Leonard Cohen.
3. Brendan Bernhard, "Angst & Aquavit," interview with Leonard Cohen in *L.A. Weekly*, October 4, 2001. Used with permission of Leonard Cohen.
4. Martin Oestergaard, "Leonard Cohen Gave Me 200 Francs," *Wadsholt Euroman*, translated by Niels Wadsholt Euroman, September 2001. Used with permission of Leonard Cohen.
5. Brendan Bernhard, "Angst & Aquavit."
6. Brendan Bernhard, "Angst & Aquavit."
7. Mireille Silcott, "A Happy Man."
8. Quoted from "Transcript from Leonard Cohen's Premiere Online Web Chat," October 16, 2001. Available at www.leonardcohen.com/transcript2.html. Used with permission of Leonard Cohen.
9. Quoted from "Transcript from Leonard Cohen's Premiere Online Web Chat."
10. Lyrics from Leonard Cohen, "Boogie Street" from *Ten New Songs*, compact disc, Sony, 2001. Used with permission of Leonard Cohen.

11. Jordi Saládrigas, "Leonard Cohen: We Are Instruments of a Will That Is Not Our Own," interview with Leonard Cohen in *ABC Sunday Supplement*, July 22, 2001. Used with permission of Leonard Cohen.

12. Lyrics from Leonard Cohen, "You Have Loved Enough," *Ten New Songs*, compact disc, Sony, 2001. Used with permission of Leonard Cohen.

13. Jordi Saládrigas, "Leonard Cohen: We Are Instruments of a Will That Is Not Our Own."

14. Alan Ball, from the screenplay for *American Beauty*. Used with the permission of Alan Ball.

15. From an interview with Jeff Shannon of Amazon.com, republished on the Web at www.spiritualteachers.org/alan_ball.htm. Used with permission of Alan Ball.

16. Alan Ball, from the screenplay for *American Beauty*.

17. Alan Ball, from the screenplay for *American Beauty*.

Chapter Eleven: The Wisdom of Not Knowing

1. Linda Lantieri, *Schools with Spirit: Nurturing the Inner Lives of Children and Teachers* (Boston: Beacon Press, 2001), 7.

2. Reported by Matt Sebastian and Jason Hickman, "Suspects' Neighbors Stunned by Shootings," *Boulder Daily Camera*, April 24, 1999.

3. Patricia Marks Greenfield and Jaana Juvonen, "A Developmental Look at Columbine," *American Psychological Association Monitor* 30, no. 7 (July/August 1999).

4. Greenfield and Juvonen, "A Developmental Look at Columbine."

5. Quoted from a former classmate on a memorial site: http://columbine.free2host.net/eric.html.

6. Diaries, including written quotations and drawings, can be seen at http://columbine.free2host.net/diary.html.

7. Quoted on http://columbine.free2host.net/eric/writing.html.

8. Greenfield and Juvonen, "A Developmental Look at Columbine."

9. Lantieri, *Schools with Spirit*, 7.

10. For information about Steiner's beginnings and the development of Steiner schools, see Christopher Bamford and Eric Utne, "An Emerging Culture," *Utne Reprints*, available by calling 1-800-736-UTNE.

11. Figures on Waldorf students' performance in standardized testing provided by Terry-Anne Paquette at the Yuba River Charter School and by Eric Utne.

12. For more information about Eric Hoffer, see www.erichoffer.net.

Chapter Twelve: The War Is Over

1. Quoted from www.appreciative-inquiry.org.

2. Carolyn Anderson, *The Co-Creators Handbook* (Nevada City, Calif.: Global Family, 2001), xiv.

3. According to Joe Kresse, in my interview with him.
4. Quoted from Interface Carpet's website:
   www.interfaceinc.com/getting_there/Ray.html.
5. Quoted from Interface Carpet's website.
6. Quoted from an interview with the Natural Resources Defense Council:
   www.nrdc.org/reference/qa/intande.asp.
7. Quoted from an interview with the Natural Resources Defense Council.
8. Quoted from an interview with the Natural Resources Defense Council.
9. Charles Fishman, "Sustainable Growth — Interface, Inc.," *Fast Company*, no. 14, (April 1998): 136. Also available online at: www.fastcompany.com/online/14/sustaing.html.
10. Quoted from an interview with the Natural Resources Defense Council.
11. Quoted from an interview with the Natural Resources Defense Council.
12. Quoted from an interview with the Natural Resources Defense Council.
13. Fishman, "Sustainable Growth — Interface Inc.," 136.
14. Kate Jaimet, "The Greenest Chief Executive in America," *The Ottawa Citizen*, October 20, 2000.
15. Quoted in Christine Waters, "Pulp Non-Fiction," *Metro Magazine* (January 11, 1996). Online at: www.metroactive.com/papers/cruz/01.10.96/odwalla-9602.html.
16. Ken Saro-Wiwa, a poet and environmental activist, was murdered by the reigning dictator for fighting against the exploitation of the Ogoni people and the destruction of their land, primarily by Shell. The company was implicated in the murder. They had extracted an estimated $30 million worth of oil from Ogoniland, in one of the worst cases of rape and plunder by a corporation in living memory.
17. Greenpeace boarded and "squatted" the oil rig Brent Spar in the North Sea, off the beautiful coast of the Shetland Islands, successfully intervening to stop Shell's plans to sink the rig, which would have caused unprecedented pollution. See http://archive.greenpeace.org/comms/brent/brent.html.
18. "How Do We Stand? People, Planet, Profits," Shell annual report for 2000, 4. Available at www.shell.com/annualreports.
19. "How Do We Stand?" 17.
20. "How Do We Stand?" 33.
21. "How Do We Stand?" 27.
22. "How Do We Stand?" 4.

Chapter Thirteen: More Than Life and Death

1. For more information about this extraordinary man, visit www.johnofgod.com.

Chapter Fourteen: Straight to the Goal

1. According to a 2002 report by the John Jay College of Criminal Justice for the U.S. Conference of Catholic Bishops.

Chapter Fifteen: Perfect Imperfection

1. For more information about Duane Elgin's extensive body of work, go to www.simpleliving.net/awakeningearth.

2. Craig Conway, former CEO of PeopleSoft, for example, received compensation worth $112 million in 2002. See http://money.cnn.com/2003/05/09/news/ceo_comp/. The median salary of CEOs like him that year was $930,000, while hundreds of thousands of jobs were lost and almost all less-developed countries went further into debt.

3. Estimate provided by Sylvia Allegredo of the Economic Policy Institute in a telephone interview, December 2004.

4. From the *United Nations 1998 Human Development Report*. Available at hdr.undp.org/reports/global/1998/en.

5. Duane Elgin, "Indicators of the Great Turning." Available as a download from http://www.simpleliving.net/awakeningearth. Elgin is referring to statistics from the 1998 Human Development Report.

6. Elgin, "Indicators of the Great Turning."

7. Donald L. Bartlett and James B. Steele, "Has Your Life Become Too Much of a Chance?" *Time* (February 2004).

8. Statistics from cardweb.com, reprinted in Kim Khan, "How Does Your Debt Compare?" Available at www.moneycentral.msn.com/content/SavingandDebt/P70741.asp.

9. Federal Reserve Statistical Release. Available at www.federalreserve.gov/releases/G19/hist/cc_hist_sa.html.

10. American Bankruptcy Association, www.abiworld.org.

11. MBNA, for example, charges $35 in late fees and 25 percent interest after the promotional rate has expired. While the customer service representatives who call to harass people about late payments earn $8.50 an hour (according to the one I asked who was calling me about my late payments), Charles Cawley, CEO of MBNA, received a compensation package of $65.9 million in 2002. That is a ratio of 4050 minions to one lucky CEO. See money.cnn.com/2003/05/09/news/ceo_comp.

12. Alan Fram, "Senate Votes to Let U.S. Borrow Up to $8.18 trillion," Associated Press, November 18, 2004.

13. Find the latest amount of the U.S. national debt at www.brillig.com/debt_clock/, or take a look at how the debt has risen every year at www.publicdebt.treas.gov/opd/opdpenny.htm.

14. U.S. Treasury, "Monthly Treasury Statement," October 14, 2004. Available at http://www.fms.treas.gov/mts/index.html.

15. United Republic of Tanzania, Ministry of Finance, *Quarterly Public Debt Report*, April-June 2002.

16. Borgna Brunner, ed., "Countries of the World," *Time Almanac* (2005): 874.

17. *BNA Money & Politics Report*, December 8, 2004. Available to order online at www.bna.com/moneyandpolitics.

18. Figures monitored by the Center for Responsive Politics between 1997 and 2000. Available at www.opensecrets.org.

19. Center for Responsive Politics, www.opensecrets.org/presidential.

20. According to Ben Bagdikian, dean emeritus at the Graduate School of Journalism at the University of California, Berkeley. Cited to me by Janine Jackson, of www.fair.org, a media watchdog group. These figures are widely cited, and attributed to Bagdikian.

21. Quoted on www.stateofthenewsmedia.org.

22. Quoted on www.stateofthenewsmedia.org.

23. Nielsen Media research, *Television Audience Report*, 2000. Available at www.nielsenmedia.com.

24. "Warning to Humanity." The entire text can be seen at www.worldtrans.org/whole/warning.html.

25. "Warning to Humanity."

26. *National Water Quality Inventory*, reported to Congress in 1996, by the U.S. Environmental Protection Agency. Available at www.epa.gov/305b.

27. World Health Organization, Fact Sheet 187. Available at www.who.int/mediacentre/factsheets.

28. U.S. Energy Information Administration, July 2001.

29. Ohio State University geologist Lonnie Thompson, quoted in *National Geographic* (Sept. 23, 2003). Available at: http://news.nationalgeographic.com/news/2003/09/0923_030923_kilimanjaroglaciers.html.

30. Arctic Climate Impact Assessment, an international project of the Arctic Council and the International Arctic Science Committee (IASC). Available at www.acia.uaf.edu.

31. Office of Aerospace and Automotive Industries' Automotive Team: www.ita.doc.gov/td/auto/cafe.html.

32. See www.bagheera.com and www.solcomhouse.com.

33. Reported by Dr. Peter Raven, "Promoting Biodiversity Conservation and the Sustainable Use of Resources" (Darwin lecture, London, May 21, 2003).

34. Wink Franklin died since our dialogue for this book. He was well loved and well respected and is missed by all who knew him.

35. Duane Elgin, with Coleen LeDrew, "Global Consciousness Change." Available at www.simpleliving.net/awakeningearth/reports.asp.

36. Cited by Duane Elgin, in our interview.

37. See www.glreach.com/globstats/index.php3.

BIBLIOGRAPHY

Thousands of books published today express the emerging translucent view. This list is limited to those written by the people I interviewed.

Adyashanti. *The Impact of Awakening: Excerpts from the Teachings of Adyashanti.* Los Gatos, Calif.: Open Gate, 2000.

———. *My Secret Is Silence: Poetry and Sayings of Adyashanti.* Los Gatos, Calif.: Open Gate, 2003.

———. *Emptiness Dancing: Selected Dharma Talks of Adyashanti.* Los Gatos, Calif.: Open Gate, 2004.

Allen, Marc. *Visionary Business: An Entrepreneur's Guide to Success.* Novato, Calif.: New World Library, 1997.

———. *The Ten Percent Solution: Simple Steps to Improve Our Lives and Our World.* Novato, Calif.: New World Library, 2002.

———. *The Millionaire Course: A Visionary Plan for Creating the Life of Your Dreams.* Novato, Calif.: New World Library, 2003.

Anand, Margot. *The Art of Sexual Ecstasy.* New York: Tarcher, 1989.

———. *The Art of Sexual Magic.* New York: Tarcher, 1995.

———. *The Art of Everyday Ecstasy.* New York: Broadway, 1998.

Andersen, Dana Lynne. *Born with a Bang: The Universe Tells Our Cosmic Story.* Nevada City, Calif.: Dawn Publications, 2002.

————. *From Lava to Life: The Universe Tells Our Earth Story.* Nevada City, Calif.: Dawn Publications, 2003.

Anderson, Carolyn. *The Co-creator's Handbook.* Nevada City, Calif.: Global Family, 2001.

Anderson, Sherry Ruth, and Patricia Hopkins. *The Feminine Face of God: The Unfolding of the Sacred in Women.* New York: Random House, 1991.

Bache, Chris. *Lifecycles: Reincarnation and the Web of Life.* New York: Paragon House, 1993.

————. *Dark Night, Early Dawn: Steps Toward a Deep Ecology of Mind.* Albany, N.Y.: SUNY Press, 2000.

Barnett, Michael. *Diamond Yoga Handbook.* Zurich, Switzerland: Cosmic Energy Connections, 1993.

————. *With It.* Freiburg, Germany: Cosmic Energy Connections, 2003.

————. *Hints on the Art of Jumping.* Freiburg, Germany: Cosmic Energy Connections, 2004.

Beyondananda, Swami (Steve Bhaerman). *Driving Your Own Karma: Swami's Tourguide to Enlightenment.* Rochester, Vt.: Destiny, 1989.

————. *Duck Soup for the Soul: The Way of Living Louder and Laughing Longer.* Naperville, Ill.: Hysteria Publications, 1999.

————. *Swami for Precedent: A Seven-Step Plan to Heal the Body Politic and Cure Electile Dysfunction.* Santa Rosa, Calif.: Wake Up Laughing Productions, 2004.

Blanton, Brad. *The Truthtellers: Stories of Success by Radically Honest People.* Stanley, Va.: Sparrowhawk Press, 2004.

————. *Beyond Good and Evil: The Eternal Split-Second Sound-Light Being.* Stanley, Va.: Sparrowhawk Press, 2005.

————. *Radical Honesty: How to Transform Your Life by Telling the Truth*, rev. ed. Stanley, Va.: Sparrowhawk Press, 2005.

Bodian, Stephan. *Meditation for Dummies.* New York: Wiley, 1999.

Bodian, Stephan, and Jon Landaw. *Buddhism for Dummies.* New York: Wiley, 2003.

Bodian, Stephan, and Georg Feuerstein, eds. *Living Yoga.* Los Angeles: Tarcher/Putnam, 1992.

Bonder, Saniel. *Great Relief: Nine Sacred Secrets Your Body Wants You to Know about Freedom, Love, Trust, and the Core Wound of Your Life.* San Rafael, Calif.: Mt. Tam Empowerments, 2004.

————. *Healing the Spirit/Matter Split: An Invitation to Wake Down in Mutuality and Fulfill Your Divinely Human Destiny.* San Rafael, Calif.: Mt. Tam Empowerments, 2004.

————. *The Tantra of Trust: Skilled and Superlative Intimate Sexual Partnership for 21st Century Woman and Man.* San Rafael, Calif.: Mt. Tam Empowerments, 2004.

Canfield, Jack, and Mark Victor Hansen. *Chicken Soup for the Soul.* Deerfield Beach, Fla.: HCI, 1993.

Canfield, Jack, Mark Victor Hansen, and Les Hewitt. *The Power of Focus.* Deerfield Beach, Fla.: HCI, 2003.

Canfield, Jack, and Janet Switzer. *The Success Principles: How to Get from Where You Are to Where You Want to Be.* New York: HarperCollins, 2004.

Cohen, Andrew. *Enlightenment Is a Secret.* Larkspur, Calif.: What Is Enlightenment? Press, 1991.

———. *Embracing Heaven and Earth.* Lenox, Mass: What Is Enlightenment? Press, 2000.

———. *Living Enlightenment.* Lenox, Mass: What Is Enlightenment? Press, 2002.

Cryer, Bruce, and Doc Childre. *Freeze-Frame: One-Minute Stress Management.* Boulder Creek, Calif.: HeartMath, 1993.

———. *From Chaos to Coherence: The Power to Change Performance.* Boulder Creek, Calif.: HeartMath, 1999.

———. *Pull the Plug on Stress.* Cambridge, Mass.: Harvard Business Review, 2003.

Dass, Ram. *Be Here Now.* New York: Crown, 1971.

———. *One-Liners: A Mini-Manual for a Spiritual Life.* New York: Bell Tower, 2002.

———. *Paths to God: Living the Bhagavad Gita.* New York: Harmony, 2004.

Deida, David. *The Enlightened Sex Manual.* Boulder, Colo.: Sounds True, 2004.

———. *The Way of the Superior Man.* Boulder, Colo.: Sounds True, 2004.

———. *Wild Nights.* Boulder, Colo.: Sounds True, 2005.

Dinan, Stephen. *Radical Spirit: Spiritual Writings from the Voices of Tomorrow.* Novato, Calif.: New World Library, 2002.

Dwoskin, Hale, and Lester Levenson. *Happiness Is Free… and It's Easier than You Think.* Sedona, Ariz.: Sedona Press, 2002.

———. *The Sedona Method: Your Key to Lasting Happiness, Success, Peace and Emotional Well-Being.* Sedona, Ariz.: Sedona Press, 2003.

Elgin, Duane. *Awakening Earth: Exploring the Evolution of Human Culture and Consciousness.* New York: William Morrow, 1993.

———. *Voluntary Simplicity: Toward a Way of Life That Is Outwardly Simple, Inwardly Rich,* rev. ed. New York: Perennial Currents, 1993.

———. *Promise Ahead: A Vision of Hope and Action for Humanity's Future.* New York: Perennial Currents, 2000.

Falcone, Vickie. *Buddha Never Raised Kids and Jesus Didn't Drive Carpool: Seven Principles for Parenting with Soul.* San Diego, Calif.: Jodere Group, 2003.

Geffen, Jeremy R. *The Journey Through Cancer: An Oncologist's Seven-Level Program for Healing and Transforming the Whole Person.* New York: Crown, 2000.

———. *The Seven Levels of Healing: A Body, Mind, Heart and Spirit Program for Healing and Transforming the Whole Person.* Niles, Ill.: Nightingale-Conant, 2001. Audiocassette.

Goldstein, Joseph. *The Experience of Insight.* Boston: Shambhala Publications, 1976.

———. *Insight Meditation: The Practice of Freedom.* Boston: Shambhala Publications, 1993.

———. *One Dharma: The Emerging Western Buddhism.* San Francisco: HarperCollins, 2002.

Grey, Alex. *Sacred Mirrors: The Visionary Art of Alex Grey.* Rochester, Vt.: Inner Traditions, 1990.

———. *The Mission of Art.* Boston: Shambhala Publications, 1998.

———. *Transfigurations.* Rochester, Vt.: Inner Traditions, 2001.

Halpern, Marc. *Clinical Ayurvedic Medicine*, 4th ed. Grass Valley, Calif.: College of
     Ayurveda, 2004.
———. *Principles of Ayurvedic Medicine*, 6th ed. Grass Valley, Calif.: College of Ayurveda,
     2004.
Halpern, Steven. *Gifts of the Angels.* San Anselmo, Calif.: Inner Peace Music, 1994.
———. *Chakra Suite.* San Anselmo, Calif.: Inner Peace Music, 2001.
———. *Inner Peace.* San Anselmo, Calif.: Inner Peace Music, 2002.
Hawkins, David. *Power vs. Force: The Hidden Determinants of Human Behavior.* Sedona, Ariz.:
     Veritas, 1995.
———. *Eye of the I: From Which Nothing Is Hidden.* Sedona, Ariz.: Veritas, 2001.
———. *I: Reality and Subjectivity.* Sedona, Ariz.: Veritas, 2003.
Hendricks, Gay. *Conscious Living.* New York: HarperCollins, 2000.
Hendricks, Gay, and Kathlyn Hendricks. *Conscious Loving.* New York: Bantam, 1990.
———. *Lasting Love.* New York: Rodale, 2004.
Holden, Lee. *Tai Chi Chi Kung for Fitness.* Santa Cruz, Calif.: Pacific Center for Healing
     Arts, 2001. Videocassette.
———. *Qi Gong for Healing.* Santa Cruz, Calif.: Pacific Center for Healing Arts, 2004.
Holloway, Richard. *On Forgiveness.* Edinburgh, Scotland: Canongate, 2002.
———. *Godless Morality*, rev. ed. Edinburgh, Scotland: Canongate, 2004.
———. *Looking in the Distance.* Edinburgh, Scotland: Canongate, 2004.
Houston, Jean. *A Mythic Life.* San Francisco: HarperCollins, 1996.
———. *The Possible Human*, 2d. ed. New York: Tarcher, 1998.
———. *Jump Time: Shaping Your Future in a World of Radical Change.* New York: Tarcher,
     2000.
Hubbard, Barbara Marx. *Conscious Evolution: Awakening the Power of Our Social Potential.*
     Novato, Calif.: New World Library, 1989.
———. *The Revelation: A Message of Hope for the New Millennium.* Novato, Calif.: Nataraj,
     1998.
———. *Emergence: The Shift from Ego to Essence.* Charlottesville, Va.: Hampton Roads,
     2001.
Ingram, Catherine. *In the Footsteps of Gandhi.* Berkeley, Calif.: Parallax Press, 1990.
———. *Passionate Presence.* New York: Gotham, 2003.
Jones, Alan. *Living the Truth.* Boston: Cowley Publications, 2000.
———. *The Soul's Journey.* Boston: Cowley Publications, 2001.
Jones, Alan, and John O'Neill. *Seasons of Grace.* Hoboken, N.J.: Wiley, 2003.
Kabat-Zinn, Jon. *Full Catastrophe Living.* New York: Delta, 1991.
———. *Wherever You Go, There You Are.* New York: Hyperion, 1994.
———. *Coming to Our Senses.* New York: Hyperion, 2005.
Katie, Byron, with Michael Katz. *I Need Your Love — Is That True?: How to Stop Seeking Love,
     Approval, and Appreciation and Start Finding Them Instead.* New York: Harmony, 2005.

Katie, Byron, with Stephen Mitchell. *Loving What Is: Four Questions That Can Change Your Life.* New York: Three Rivers Press, 2002.

Kofman, Fred. *Conscious Business.* Boulder, Colo.: Sounds True, 2001. Audiocassette.

Kornfield, Jack. *A Path with a Heart.* New York: Bantam, 1993.

———. *After the Ecstasy, the Laundry.* New York: Bantam, 2001.

———. *The Art of Forgiveness, Loving-kindness, and Peace.* New York: Bantam, 2002.

Krippner, Stanley, and Teresa McIntyre. *The Psychological Effects of War Trauma on Civilians: An International Perspective.* Westport, Conn.: Praeger, 2003.

Krippner, Stanley, and Montague Ullman. *Dream Telepathy: Experiments in Nocturnal Extrasensory Perception,* 3d ed. Charlottesville, Va.: Hampton Roads, 2002.

Krippner, Stanley, Etzel Cardena, and Steven J. Lynn. *Varieties of Anomalous Experience: Examining the Scientific Evidence.* Washington, D.C.: American Psychological Association, 2000.

Lantieri, Linda. *Schools with Spirit: Nurturing the Inner Lives of Children and Teachers.* Boston: Beacon Press, 2001.

Lantieri, Linda, and Janet Patti. *Waging Peace in Our Schools.* Boston: Beacon Press, 1996.

Leonard, George. *The Silent Pulse: A Search for the Perfect Rhythm That Exists in Each of Us.* New York: Dutton, 1978.

———. *Mastery: The Keys to Success and Fulfillment.* New York: Plume, 1991.

Leonard, George, and Michael Murphy. *The Life We Are Given: A Long-Term Program for Realizing the Potential of Body, Mind, Heart and Soul.* Los Angeles: Tarcher, 1995.

Lipton, Bruce. *The Biology of Belief: Unleashing the Power of Consciousness, Matter, and Miracles.* Memphis, Tenn.: Mountain of Love Productions, 2005.

Lowe, Paul G. *The Experiment Is Over.* New York: Roximillion Publications, 1989.

———. *In Each Moment.* Vancouver, Canada: Looking Glass Press, 1998.

———. *Sounding Silence.* Byron Bay, Australia: Watergarden, 2000. Audiocassette.

Luce, Gay. *Body Time.* New York: Doubleday, 1979.

———. *Your Second Life.* New York: Pantheon, 1979.

———. *Longer Life, More Joy.* North Hollywood, Calif.: Newcastle, 1992.

Makena, Peter. *In Love.* Pebble Beach, Calif.: Open Sky Music, 1995.

———. *Open to Grace.* Pebble Beach, Calif.: Open Sky Music, 1999.

———. *Heart of Kindness.* Hidden Valley Lake, Calif.: Makena Music, 2002.

McLaughlin, Corinne, and Gordon Davidson. *Builders of the Dawn.* Summertown, Tenn.: The Book Publishing Company, 1984.

———. *Spiritual Politics: Changing the World from the Inside Out.* New York: Ballantine, 1994.

Morrissey, Mary Manin. *Building Your Field of Dreams.* New York: Bantam, 1995.

———. *No Less Than Greatness.* New York: Bantam, 2001.

Moss, Richard. *The I That Is We.* Berkeley, Calif.: Celestial Arts, 1981.

———. *The Black Butterfly.* Berkeley, Calif.: Celestial Arts, 1986.

———. *The Second Miracle.* Berkeley, Calif.: Celestial Arts, 1995.

Murphy, Michael. *The Future of the Body: Explorations into the Further Evolution of Human Nature.* Los Angeles: Tarcher, 1993.

———. *Golf in the Kingdom.* New York: Penguin, 1997.

———. *The Kingdom of Shivas Irons.* New York: Broadway, 1998.

Nadeen, Satyam. *From Onions to Pearls: A Journal of Awakening and Deliverance.* Carlsbad, Calif.: Hay House, 1996.

———. *From Seekers to Finders: The Myth and Reality about Enlightenment.* Carlsbad, Calif.: Hay House, 2000.

Neenan, David, and Dudley Lynch. *Evergreen: Playing a Continuous Comeback Business Game.* Lakewood, Colo.: New Echelon Press, 1995.

Post, Stephen G. *Unlimited Love: Altruism, Compassion, Service.* Philadelphia: Templeton Foundation Press, 2003.

Post, Stephen G., Lynn G. Underwood, Jeffrey P. Schloss, and William B. Hurlbut, eds. *Altruism and Altruistic Love: Science, Philosophy, and Religion in Dialogue.* New York: Oxford University Press, 2002.

Premal, Deva. *The Essence.* Round Top, Tex.: White Swan Records, 1998.

———. *Embrace.* Round Top, Tex.: White Swan Records, 2002.

Premal, Deva, and Miten. *Songs for the Inner Lover.* Round Top, Tex.: White Swan Records, 2003.

Premal, Deva, and Miten. *More Than Music: The Deva Premal and Miten Story.* Round Top, Tex.: White Swan Records, 2004

Prendergast, John. "The Chakras in Transpersonal Psychotherapy." *International Journal of Yoga Therapy* 10 (2000).

Prendergast, John, Peter Fenner, and Sheila Krystal. *The Sacred Mirror: Nondual Wisdom and Psychotherapy.* St. Paul, Minn.: Paragon House, 2003.

Psaris, Jett, and Marlena Lyons. *Undefended Love.* Oakland, Calif.: New Harbinger Publications, 2000.

Rabbin, Robert. *The Sacred Hub: Living in Your Real Self.* Freedom, Calif.: Inner Directions Foundation, 1996.

———. *Echoes of Silence: Awakening the Meditative Spirit.* Carlsbad, Calif.: Inner Directions Foundation, 2000.

———. *Igniting the Soul at Work: A Mandate for Mystics.* Charlottesville, Va.: Hampton Roads, 2002.

Ray, Paul, and Sherry Ruth Anderson. *The Cultural Creatives: How 50 Million People Are Changing the World.* New York: Harmony, 2000.

Roach, Paul John. *Pocket Unity.* Fort Worth, Tex.: Fort Worth Unity, 2000.

———. *Pocket Prayers.* Fort Worth, Tex.: Fort Worth Unity, 2001.

———. *Pocket Wisdom of the Wayshowers.* Fort Worth, Tex.: Fort Worth Unity, 2002.

Russell, Peter. *Waking Up in Time: Finding Inner Peace in Times of Accelerating Change.* San Rafael, Calif.: Origin Press, 1998.

————. *From Science to God: A Physicist's Journey into the Mystery of Consciousness*. Novato, Calif.: New World Library, 2003.

Russell, Peter, Stanislav Grof, and Ervin Laszlo. *The Consciousness Revolution*. Las Vegas: Peter Russell, 2004.

Shapiro, Isaac. *Outbreak of Peace*. Munich, Germany: Arun Publications, 1997.

————. *It Happens by Itself*. Maui, Hawaii: Luechow Press, 2001.

Shlain, Leonard. *Art & Physics*. San Francisco: HarperCollins, 1993.

————. *The Alphabet Versus the Goddess*. New York: Penguin, 1999.

————. *Sex, Time, and Power: How Women's Sexuality Shaped Human Evolution*. New York: Viking, 2003.

ShantiMayi. *Gayatri Mantra*. Righikuoh, India: Sache Publications, 2003.

Small, Jacquelyn. *Transformers: The Therapists of the Future*. Marina del Rey, Calif.: DeVorss, 1981.

————. *Becoming Naturally Therapeutic*. New York: Bantam, 1993.

————. *Awakening in Time*. New York: Bantam, 1994.

Subbiondo, Joseph. *John Wilkins and 17th Century British Linguistics*. Amsterdam: John Benjamins, 1992.

Subbiondo, Joseph, Gary Quehl, and William Bergquist. *Fifty Years of Innovations in Undergraduate Education: Change and Stasis in the Pursuit of Quality*. Indianapolis, Ind.: USA Group Foundation, 1999.

Surya Das, Lama. *Awakening the Buddha Within: Tibetan Wisdom for the Western World*. New York: Broadway, 1998.

————. *Awakening the Buddhist Heart*. New York: Broadway, 2001.

————. *Letting Go of the Person You Used to Be*. New York: Broadway, 2003.

Targ, Russell. *Miracles of Mind: Nonlocal Consciousness and Spiritual Healing*. Novato, Calif.: New World Library, 1998.

————. *Limitless Mind: A Guide to Remote Viewing and Transformation of Consciousness*. Novato, Calif.: New World Library, 2004.

Titmus, Christopher. *An Awakened Life*. Boston: Shambhala, 1999.

————. *Mindfulness in Daily Living*. London: Barrons Educational Series, 2002.

————. *Transforming Our Terror*. London and New York: Godsfield Press, 2002.

Tolle, Eckhart. *The Power of Now*. Novato, Calif.: New World Library, 1999.

————. *Practicing the Power of Now*. Novato, Calif.: New World Library, 2001.

————. *Stillness Speaks*. Novato, Calif.: New World Library, 2003.

Twist, Lynne. *Fundraising from the Heart*. www.fundraisingfromtheheart.com.

————. *The Soul of Money*. New York: Norton, 2003.

Utne, Eric. *Cosmo Doogood's Urban Almanac*. Minneapolis, Minn.: Eric Utne, 2004.

Vaughan, F. *Awakening Intuition*. New York: Anchor, 1979.

————. *Shadows of the Sacred: Seeing through Spiritual Illusions*. Wheaton, Ill.: Quest, 1995.

————. *The Inward Arc: Healing in Psychotherapy and Spirituality*. iUniverse.com, 2000.

Vissell, Barry, and Joyce Vissell. *The Shared Heart*. Aptos, Calif.: Ramira, 1984.

———. *The Heart's Wisdom.* Berkeley, Calif.: Conari, 1995.

———. *Meant to Be.* Berkeley, Calif.: Conari, 2000.

Walsch, Neale Donald. *Conversations with God,* Books 1–3. Charlottesville, Va.: Hampton Roads, 1996–1998.

———. *Tomorrow's God.* New York: Atria, 2004.

———. *What God Wants.* New York: Atria, 2005.

Wilson, Pamela. *The Ocean, the Fish, and the Buddha.* Tesuque, N.Mex.: Flypaper Press, 1999.

WHO'S WHO

About the Interviewees

ADYASHANTI dares all seekers of peace and freedom to take the possibility of liberation in this life seriously. After fifteen years of Zen practice and a series of ever-deepening realizations, Adyashanti began teaching in 1996. His spontaneous and direct nondual teachings have been compared to those of the early Zen masters and Advaita Vedanta sages.

Open Gate Sangha is a nonprofit organization founded in 1996 to support the teachings of Adyashanti. Hosting events throughout the United States and Canada, along with retreats and gatherings in the San Francisco Bay Area, it has brought Adyashanti's teachings to thousands of people from diverse traditions. The organization is supported by volunteers who form the heart of the community.

Open Gate Sangha

P.O. Box 782, Los Gatos, CA 95031

408-356-5554

www.adyashanti.org

MARC ALLEN is an author, composer, and publisher. He has written twelve books and recorded five music albums. He is co-founder (with Shakti Gawain) of New World Library, one of the most vibrant independent publishing companies in the world today, and also of Watercourse Media, his record company. Originally from Minnesota, he now lives in Northern California with his wife and two children.

New World Library publishes books, audio and video projects, and gifts that inspire and challenge us to improve the quality of our lives and our world. Authors published by New World Library include Eckhart Tolle, Deepak Chopra, Shakti Gawain, and Dan Millman.

New World Library
14 Pamaron Way, Novato, CA 94949
415-884-2100
escort@newworldlibrary.com
www.newworldlibrary.com

MARGOT ANAND is the author of numerous books on spirituality and sacred sexuality and the founder of the path of Skydancing tantra, with Skydancing Institutes teaching her work in many countries. The Love and Ecstasy training focuses on transforming sexual energy into blissful meditation. Margot is a sought-after speaker at conferences worldwide, and has recently turned her attention to art and filmmaking with a tantric slant.

SpiritWorks Church is the guardian of Margot Anand's teachings, entrusted with the responsibility to see that they are preserved for future generations and taught by others in an ethical fashion.

SpiritWorks Church
P.O. Box 2967, San Rafael, CA 94912-2967
415-454-6030
skyoffice@infoasis.com
www.spiritworkschurch.net

DANA LYNNE ANDERSEN is a multimedia artist, writer, playwright, and teacher with a master's in Consciousness Studies. Pioneering the use of art and creativity as vehicles for shifting consciousness, she has offered her acclaimed programs at schools, universities, conferences, civic centers, and through her Awakening Arts Studio.

Awakening Arts is a worldwide artists network that supports uplifting the human spirit and awakening higher consciousness through the arts. Awakening Arts Institute nurtures "awakening artists" through an online resource nexus, traveling workshops and exhibitions, retreats and residencies, symposiums, and a small fine art press. It unites artists throughout the world who are seeking a deeper source of inspiration and aspiring to a higher vision of what the arts are meant to be.

Awakening Arts Studio
14618 Tyler Foote Rd., Nevada City, CA 95959
877-463-7443
www.awakeningarts.com and www.awakeningarts.net

CAROLYN ANDERSON, MA, is a co-founder and the co-director of Global Family. As a speaker, author, and global networker, she has coordinated activities for numerous global peace events, assisted with the development of social cooperation trainings, and helped facilitate a number of international conferences.

Global Family, founded in 1986, is a nonprofit international network of individuals and groups dedicated to experiencing unconditional love and the birth of a new co-creative society. Their intentional community, Hummingbird Ranch in northern New Mexico, is a living laboratory for the evolution of consciousness, where they conduct programs, trainings, and retreats, and model the processes and practices they teach.

Global Family
P.O. Box 90710, Santa Barbara, CA 93190
530-277-1037
connect@globalfamily.net
www.globalfamily.net

SHERRY ANDERSON is the co-author of *The Feminine Face of God* and *The Cultural Creatives*. She presently teaches the Diamond Approach to spiritual development. She lives with her husband in Northern California and teaches in North America and Europe.

The Diamond Approach is a contemporary spiritual path dedicated to discovery, development, and preservation of the Human Essence. For information on Sherry's Diamond Approach seminars, see www.ridhwan.org.

sherry@culturalcreatives.org.
www.culturalcreatives.org

CHAMELI GAD ARDAGH facilitates seminars and retreats in the United States and Europe and is a respected speaker at national and international conferences on spirituality. She guides women back to honoring the wisdom of the heart. Chameli has been deeply involved in women's work for many years, extensively exploring the implications of a feminine-influenced spirituality. She trained in Norway as a psychotherapist and as an actress, which adds an expressive and playful flavor to her work. She lives in Northern California with her husband, Arjuna, and two stepsons.

530-478-5985
contactchameli@livingessence.com
www.livingessence.com
www.wildlove.org

CHRIS BACHE is a university professor at Youngstown State University and the California Institute of Integral Studies. He gives workshops and presentations in reincarnation studies, psychedelic studies, the philosophical and spiritual implications of nonordinary states of consciousness, consciousness and the impending eco-crisis, transformative learning, and the field dynamics of group minds in the classroom.

Youngstown State University offers undergraduate degrees, and the California Institute of Integral Studies offers graduate degrees in a variety of fields. Bache teaches as adjunct faculty in the Department of Philosophy, Cosmology, and Consciousness.

Youngstown State University, Department of Philosophy and Religious Studies
One University Plaza, Youngstown, OH 44555
330-941-1463
cmbache@ysu.edu

ALAN BALL is the creator and executive producer of *Six Feet Under*, the critically acclaimed drama series on HBO. Alan's screenplay *American Beauty* received the 1999 Academy Award for Best Original Screenplay and the Golden Globe Award for Best Screenplay. Before becoming a screenwriter for television and film, Alan was a comedic playwright in New York.

MICHAEL BARNETT graduated with a top degree in math and law from Cambridge. He went from being a successful businessman to co-founder of the Human Growth Movement in Britain to a top therapist of Bhagwan Rajneesh (Osho). Out of all this his unique Energy Work developed. Today he is a spiritual teacher of thousands of people.

OneLife is a training institute for personal and professional development based on Barnett's teaching work. From here his many worldwide seminars and trainings are organized. His most valuable teaching words are made available on audiocassettes as well as in books. The intensity of his presence activates a profound resonance, which creates the ideal conditions for transformation and invites each individual to fall deeply into the well of their own Being.

OneLife
Hauptstrasse 22, 79211 Denzlingen, Germany
(49)-7666-8-801-801
Onelife@wildgoose.net
www.wildgoose.net

STEVE BHAERMAN. Swami Beyondananda is the "altered ego" of writer and comedian Steve Bhaerman. As the Swami, Steve has entertained millions with his comedy disguised as wisdom — or is it wisdom disguised as comedy? Swami's latest mission is to use his cosmic perspective to heal the body politic and to cure "electile dysfunction."

The Right to Laugh Party promotes cosmic comedy and healing humor to enable America — and the world — to wake up laughing and wake up loving. It offers resources and recourses to help us set the new precedent, which will ensure a new president will follow.

Steve Bhaerman
400 W. Third St., Suite D-144, Santa Rosa, CA 95401
707-525-0711
swamib@saber.net or info@wakeuplaughing.com
www.wakeuplaughing.com

DR. BRAD BLANTON is a psychotherapist, writer, and workshop facilitator. For twenty-five years Brad practiced as a psychotherapist in Washington, DC, where he worked with couples, groups, and individuals, and consulted with academia, the government, and private enterprise. He teaches that the primary cause of stress, depression, and anger is "living in a story and lying to maintain it" and that the escape from the story and therefore the cure of the afflictions is Radical Honesty. He is the creator of "The Course in Honesty Workshop," which he conducts at his place, Sparrowhawk Farm in the Shenandoah Valley of Virginia. He is also a novelist, a candidate for Congress from Virginia, and president of Radical Honesty Enterprises, where he runs workshops, publishes books, gives talks, and trains trainers in Radical Honesty.
Blanton for Congress
646 Shuler Ln., Stanley, VA 22851
1-800-EL-TRUTH
brad@radicalhonesty.com
www.radicalhonesty.com, www.blantonforcongress.com, www.usob.org, or
www.changeofheart.biz

STEPHAN BODIAN is a spiritual teacher, a psychotherapist, and the author of several books, including the bestselling *Meditation for Dummies*. In his satsangs, one-on-one phone counseling sessions, intensives, and retreats, he offers a vital, direct, practical blend of the timeless wisdom of Buddhism, Zen, and Advaita Vedanta with the insights of Western psychology. He's the former editor in chief of *Yoga Journal*, and his articles on spiritual themes have appeared in numerous national magazines, including *Fitness, Alternative Medicine, Tricycle,* and *Yoga Journal*. Stephan leads retreats at the Omega Institute and offers phone counseling to seekers worldwide. He lives and teaches in Sedona, Arizona.
P.O. Box 45, Fairfax, CA 94978
415-451-7133
stephanbodian@hotmail.com
www.stephanbodian.org

SANIEL BONDER has helped hundreds of people, since 1992, awaken directly and then learn how to live and evolve together in awakened freedom. Author of *Great Relief* and *Healing the Spirit/Matter Split* and founder of the Waking Down in Mutuality Work, he's also an activist, entrepreneur, and devoted husband. The national Waking Down community is now (in early 2005) collectively embracing a "redesign" process to more fully embody its principles of democratic empowerment and mutual accountability. Its many realized transmitter-teachers offer workshops and retreats, lead small group meetings, and welcome individuals into personal, transformational relationships.

Mt. Tam Empowerments is Saniel and his wife Linda Groves-Bonder's private publishing and personal services company.

The Waking Down Work

5530 N.E. 122nd Ave., #B302, Portland, OR 97230

1-888-741-5000

wakingdown@earthlink.net

www.wakingdown.org

Mt. Tam Empowerments

369-B Third St., Suite 162, San Rafael, CA 94901

1-888-657-7020

saniel2@comcast.net

www.sanielandlinda.com

JACK CANFIELD is co-author of the bestselling book series *Chicken Soup for the Soul*® and co-creator of *The Success Principles: How to Get From Where You Are to Where You Want to Be*™. To find out more about Jack's workshops, trainings, and books, or to inquire about Jack's availability as a speaker, visit his website.

Jack Canfield

P.O. Box 30880, Santa Barbara, CA 93130

805-563-2935

www.jackcanfield.com or www.chickensoup.com

ANDREW COHEN is a twenty-first-century spiritual pioneer whose teaching of Evolutionary Enlightenment is igniting an extraordinary passion for transformation in people all over the world. His teaching cultivates integrity in the individual and establishes a revolutionary context for freedom and authenticity in relationship with others. This context, once awakened, creates a foundation for wholehearted engagement with the challenges of an increasingly complex world.

Cohen is the founder and editor in chief of the internationally acclaimed magazine *What Is Enlightenment?* (www.wie.org) and the author of several books, including *Living Enlightenment* and *Embracing Heaven and Earth*. He travels frequently giving public talks and leading intensive retreats, and along with a growing international network of progressive thought leaders and teachers, he is endeavoring to catalyze a major shift in consciousness for the sake of a new and enlightened future.

Impersonal Enlightenment Fellowship
P.O. Box 2360, Lenox, MA 01240
413-637-6000
ief@andrewcohen.org
www.andrewcohen.org

BRUCE CRYER is a former New York actor who has spent the past twenty-five years leading organizations, writing books, and teaching people how to live a stress-free, joyful life. Bruce is now CEO of HeartMath LLC, an innovative research and training organization offering an array of products, training programs, and coaching services designed to help individuals and organizations reduce stress, lead healthier lives, and be more productive. Tested on five continents and validated by more than a dozen years of rigorous scientific research, the HeartMath® system includes books, music CDs, videos, and the award-winning Freeze-Framer® interactive learning system with patented heart rhythm monitor. Their organizational programs help corporations and health care systems reduce stress and employee turnover, while enhancing customer and patient satisfaction and long-term well-being.

HeartMath
14700 West Park Ave., Boulder Creek, CA 95006
831-338-8700
bcryer@heartmath.com
www.heartmath.com

RAM DASS is an author, lecturer, and spiritual teacher whose landmark book, *Be Here Now*, guided a generation of spiritual seekers. He has published eleven other books and has taught throughout the world about the nature of consciousness and about Karma yoga, or service to others, as spiritual path.

The Ram Dass Tape Library Foundation serves as the vehicle for the dissemination and preservation of Ram Dass's teachings. It sponsors programs, retreats, and workshops around the country. With nearly fifteen hundred audio recordings in the archives, the Tape Library holds the history of Ram Dass's oral teachings, and copies of the recordings, along with copies of his books and videotapes, are available. The foundation's website provides information about Ram Dass's background, activities, and teaching schedule.

The Ram Dass Tape Library Foundation
524 San Anselmo Ave., 203, San Anselmo, CA 94960
415-499-8586
RDTapes@aol.com
www.RamDassTapes.org

DAVID DEIDA. Described as a maverick, a true original, and one of the most provocative spiritual teachers of our time, bestselling author David Deida is known internationally for his revolutionary approach to the way that men and women grow spiritually and sexually. He is the author of ten books published in more than fifteen languages, including *Wild Nights* and *The Way of the Superior Man*. His website provides information and resources for David Deida's writings, teachings, and trainings.

888-553-1939
Info@deida.info
www.deida.info

SOFIA DIAZ is a gifted teacher of Hatha yoga, sacred movement, and feminine spiritual practice, as well as Bharata Natyam in the Balasaraswati lineage of Temple Dance. Sofia holds a bachelor's in dance from Mills College in Oakland, California, and a master's in religious studies from the University of Colorado. She teaches in the Somatic Psychology Department at Naropa University in Boulder, has published writings on yoga and sacred movement in both academic and popular journals, and travels frequently, teaching women's yoga intensives throughout the world.

Sofia currently teaches Hatha yoga for women and men and maintains a private yoga therapy practice at Prasad Yoga Studio in Boulder, Colarado.

Prasad Yoga Studio
1630-30th St., 390, Boulder, CO 80301
866-234-0437
Lasya@compuserve.com
www.sofiayoga.com and www.womenstent.com

ROBERT DICKINSON has studied, practiced, and taught holistic healing since 1979, specializing in TCM, (Traditional Chinese Medicine) and its many branches, including Taji/Qi gong, Acupressure/Acupuncture, and Diet and Herbs. Robert learned from many masters of the art, both in China, where he interned, and the United States, where he graduated from and later taught at the Northwest Institute of Acupuncture and Oriental Medicine. He also taught for many years at the prestigious Bastyr University. He now makes his home in the Pacific Northwest and does private phone consultations by appointment.

standtall@bigfoot.com

STEPHEN DINAN is a marketing consultant, political organizer, and visionary firestarter. He is the author of *Radical Spirit* and the founder of TCN, Inc., which aims to create a network of transformational communities. He is available for workshops, speaking, consulting, and coaching. Radical Spirit is a spiritual community that offers a full-spectrum approach to the transformation of self, relationships, and society.

Stephen Dinan
415-491-4492
stephen@radicalspirit.org
www.radicalspirit.org and www.stephendinan.com

HALE DWOSKIN, *New York Times* bestselling author of *The Sedona Method* and co-author of *Happiness Is Free* (a five-book series), is the CEO and director of training at Sedona Training Associates. Hale has taught the Sedona Method to tens of thousands of individuals and corporations around the world for more than twenty-five years.

Sedona Training Associates is an educational training organization founded in 1996 to promote the revolutionary discoveries of physicist and engineer Lester Levenson. During the almost three-decade history of the Sedona Method® Course, hundreds of thousands of people worldwide have benefited from this work through training seminars and home-study audio courses produced by Sedona Training Associates.

Sedona Training Associates
60 Tortilla Dr., Suite 2, Sedona, AZ 86336
888-282-5656 or 928-282-3522
release@sedona.com
www.sedona.com and www.sedonamethod.com

DUANE ELGIN is an author, speaker, and activist for media accountability. His books include *Voluntary Simplicity, Promise Ahead,* and *Awakening Earth.* As a speaker and workshop leader, he explores themes ranging from the big picture of our world approaching a tipping point in history to practical changes we can make in our everyday lives to live more sustainably. He has worked as a senior staff member with a joint Presidential-Congressional Commission on the American Future, and as a senior social scientist at the think tank SRI International, where he co-authored numerous studies on the long-range future. As a citizen activist, Duane co-founded "Our Media Voice" to work for an empowered democracy through televised electronic town meetings. He has an MBA and a master's from the University of Pennsylvania.

info@awakeningearth.org
www.awakeningearth.org or www.ourmediavoice.org

VICKIE FALCONE is the emerging voice for today's conscious parents. She translates the sometimes lofty ideas of the world's greatest masters of consciousness (from Einstein to Buddha and more) into practical principles parents can use to create more peace at home.

While many wise spiritual leaders may never have had to worry about achieving peace and centeredness while driving a carload of screaming children, there is profound wisdom in their teachings. Vickie shows parents how to apply the teachings of these enlightened masters to the everyday challenges of modern parenting.

Parenting With Soul works with parents who want more peace at home. For more than ten years, they have offered parenting programs around the country that offer a balance of inspiration, humor, and practicality. Parents leave with the motivation and the practical skills needed to improve their lives.

Parenting With Soul
P.O. Box 4391, Basalt, CO 81623
970-927-6866
Vickie@ParentingWithSoul.com
www.ParentingWithSoul.com

ANDERS FERGUSON is a founding partner of Uplift Equity Partners, a global private equity fund investing in integrative health and well-being businesses managed with generative leadership. He also founded Spirit in Business, which connects leaders in a world community of inquiry, learning, and action accelerating interconnectedness as the primary driver of high performance and lasting personal, organizational, and global prosperity. SIB accomplishes this by producing conferences and research worldwide with leading corporations and thought leaders.

Anders was CEO of New England Country Dairy and chair of Northeast Cooperatives in the 1980s. He was the founder and CEO of the Cooperative Development Institute in the 1990s. Anders graduated from Oberlin College with a bachelor's in history and environmental studies. He speaks globally on Generative Systems, Healing, and Sustainability. Anders is a Vipassana meditator and Qi gong practitioner. In 2000 he spent four months meditating and studying qi gong and traditional Chinese medicine in Szechwan, China.

P.O. Box 228, Greenfield, MA
413-586-8950
info@spiritinbusiness.org
www.spiritinbusiness.org

WINSTON O. FRANKLIN was the president of the Institute of Noetic Sciences, as well as a longtime board member. He was also a trustee of the Fetzer Institute. Before assuming his position at IONS in 1984, he pursued twenty years of public service and management of foundations, and governmental and nonprofit research organizations. He spent ten years as an entrepreneur and venture capitalist. A few months after his interview for this book, Wink died of cancer. He is loved and missed by all who knew him.

For information about the Institute of Noetic Sciences, visit www.noetic.org.

JENNIFER GARCIA is committed to the practice of opening through fears and cultivating deeper trust of a more vulnerable heart. She has been a longtime student and practitioner of both David Deida and Sofia Diaz. Jennifer has been co-facilitating an ongoing committed women's group in Boulder, Colorado, for several years and has worked with women to open more into the divine feminine throughout the United States and Europe. She is available for private sessions by phone and in person.

info@deida.info

DR. JEREMY GEFFEN, MD, FACP, is a board-certified medical oncologist, a pioneer in the field of integrative medicine, and a well-known author, speaker, and consultant. In addition to his academic medical education and training, he has more than twenty-five years of experience exploring the great spiritual and healing traditions of the world.

Geffen Visions International, Inc. (GVI) works with individuals, organizations, and communities throughout the United States and abroad. They offer a variety of books, audio programs, consulting services, lectures, and retreats. Their programs and services are directed to those who wish to experience wholeness, integrity, and authenticity in every dimension of their being, and to express these fully in their personal and professional lives.

Jeffrey Geffen
4450 Arapahoe Ave., Suite 100, Boulder, CO 80303
303-444-6814
jgeffen@geffenvisions.com
www.geffenvisions.com

JOSEPH GOLDSTEIN is a co-founder of the Insight Meditation Society in Barre, Massachusetts, where he is one of the guiding teachers. He has studied and practiced meditation since 1967 under the guidance of eminent teachers from India, Burma, and Tibet. Joseph lectures and leads retreats around the world.

The Insight Meditation Society was founded in 1975 as a nonprofit organization to provide an environment conducive to the practice of Vipassana (insight) and metta (loving-kindness) meditation, and to help preserve the essential Buddhist teachings of liberation. IMS now operates two retreat facilities — the Retreat Center and the Forest Refuge, which are set on 160 secluded wooded acres in the quiet country of central Massachusetts. There is a schedule of intensive retreats of varying lengths throughout the year.

The Insight Meditation Society
1230 Pleasant St., Barre, MA 01005
978-355-4378
ims@dharma.org
www.dharma.org

ALEX GREY is best known for his paintings of the human body that "X-ray" the multiple layers of reality, revealing the complex integration of body, mind, soul, and spirit.

Grey is the author of several books on art and spirit, and his Chapel of Sacred Mirrors, CoSM, opened in New York City in 2004. Alex lives in Brooklyn with his wife, the painter Allyson Grey, and their daughter, actress Zena Grey.

Chapel of Sacred Mirrors

540 West 27th St., New York, NY 10002

212-564-4253

www.cosm.org

DR. MARC HALPERN is a world-respected teacher and leader in the field of Ayurvedic medicine and is the founder and director of the California College of Ayurveda. He is also a founding director of the National Ayurvedic Medical Association and the California Association of Ayurvedic Medicine. Marc currently resides in Grass Valley, California.

    The California College of Ayurveda (CCA) is a California State Approved educational center for the study of Ayurvedic medicine. They offer full- and part-time programs leading to certification as a Clinical Ayurvedic Specialist. Additional certification programs are offered in Pancha Karma, Ayurvedic Body Therapy, and Ayurvedic Yoga. The CCA also conducts a full-time community clinic where services are provided by their intern and graduate staff.

The California College of Ayurveda

1117A East Main St., Grass Valley, CA 95945

530-274-9100

info@ayurvedacollege.com

www.ayurvedacollege.com

STEVEN HALPERN is an internationally acclaimed composer, recording artist, author, and sound healer. For over thirty years, he has pioneered a new dimension in modern instrumental music that balances and harmonizes body, mind, and spirit. Steven has released more than sixty albums that have touched the lives of millions around the world. By creating an experience of inner peace within the listener, he contributes to creating more peace on our planet. Steven's work has been praised by Swami Satchidananda and Lama Surya Das.

    Inner Peace Music is the independent label that brings Steven Halpern's healing CDs to the world.

Inner Peace Music

P.O. Box 2644, San Anselmo, CA 94979

800-909-0707

info@innerpeacemusic.com

www.stevenhalpern.com

DONNA HAMILTON is a body-centered psychotherapist in private practice in Reno, Nevada. She can be reached at www.livingessence.com/pracpage.htm.

DAVID HAWKINS, MD, PhD, is described as an enlightened mystic and founder of the Pathway of Devotional Nonduality. A spiritual teacher, he is well known as the foremost researcher on Truth and Levels of Consciousness. Previously a psychiatrist and co-author with Nobel Prize winner Linus Pauling, winner of numerous awards, he now lectures worldwide on his works, which represent the core of pure spirituality.

The Institute of Advanced Spiritual Research is a nonprofit organization that provides for the requirements of research as well as arrangements for speaking engagements and publishing of books and materials. It produces audiocassettes, CDs, and video recordings of all lectures and posts speaking schedules in the United States and other countries.

The Institute of Advanced Spiritual Research
P.O. Box 3526, West Sedona, AZ 86340
928-282-8722
www.veritaspub.com

GAY AND KATHLYN HENDRICKS have been partners in life and work for twenty-five years. Gay, PhD, and Kathlyn, PhD, ADTR, have raised two children, written more than twenty-five books, including *Conscious Loving* and *Lasting Love*, accumulated a million frequent flyer miles, and appeared on more than five hundred radio and television programs.

The Hendricks Institute and the Foundation for Conscious Living is an international learning center that teaches core skills for conscious living. Their work over the past three decades has been to assist people in opening to more creativity, love, and vitality, through the power of conscious relationship and whole-person learning. They are passionately committed to creating a worldwide community of people with whom they can explore new heights of love, creativity, and well-being. Kathlyn and Gay are also co-founders of the Spiritual Cinema Circle, at www.spiritualcinemacircle.com.

The Spiritual Cinema Circle
402 West Ojai Ave., Suite 101-413, Ojai, CA 93023
800-688-0772
www.hendricks.com

LEE HOLDEN is a senior instructor for the International Healing Tao. Lee has taught meditation, qi gong, yoga, and tai chi for the last fifteen years. He has been the chief editor for Master Mantak Chia for numerous projects. Lee has been on staff with Mantak Chia and Deepak Chopra, teaching, writing, and facilitating seminars and workshops. Currently, Lee teaches at a number of colleges and is the founder of Pacific Healing Tao in Northern California. Lee's video *Tai Chi for Fitness* has been featured on two television shows and in numerous magazine articles. Holden is a graduate of University of California, Berkeley, with a BA in psychology and is a licensed acupuncturist.

Pacific Healing Arts organization focuses on health and healing through holistic and alternative medicine. They publish books and videos on Qi gong exercises for specific health ailments.

Pacific Healing Arts

508 Hampstead Way, Santa Cruz, CA 95062

831-465-1128

lee@pacifichealingarts.com

www.pacifichealingarts.com

RICHARD HOLLOWAY is a writer, with twenty-five titles to his name, and broadcaster. He was Bishop of Edinburgh and Gresham Professor of Divinity till 2000. He is a Fellow of the Royal Society of Edinburgh and recently presented a BBC television series on the turbulent history of Scottish Christianity called *The Sword and the Cross*. At the moment, like just about everyone else in Scotland, he is trying to write a novel.

6 Blantyre Terrace, Edinburgh, Scotland EH10 5AE

doc.holloway@virgin.net

DR. JEAN HOUSTON is a philosopher, researcher in human capacities, worldwide lecturer, the published author of eighteen books, chief advisor to the United Nations Development Programme, founder of the Mystery Schools, founder and director of the Foundation for Mind Research, and founder and director of the International Institute for Social Artistry in Leadership.

Over the past thirty-five years she has established programs and trainings dealing with the exploration and development of human capacities that till now have not been recognized or applied. These programs, both national and international, include the Mystery Schools; workshops and guest lecturing in business, educational institutes, and government; the Social Artistry Leadership Institute; and the partnering with the UNDP, which sponsors her work throughout the world.

Jean Houston Seminars

PMB 501, 2305-C Ashland St., Ashland, OR 97520

541-488-1200

bridgetthebrit@aol.com

www.jeanhouston.org and www.socialartistry.com

CATHERINE INGRAM is the author of *In the Footsteps of Gandhi* and *Passionate Presence*. She leads public events called Dharma Dialogues as well as residential retreats in the United States, Europe, and Australia, and currently resides in Los Angeles. Living Dharma is an educational nonprofit organization that sponsors Ingram's work as well as her retreats throughout the year.

Living Dharma
P.O. Box 10431, Portland, OR 97210
503-246-4235
LivingDharma@comcast.net
www.dharmadialogues.org

ALAN JONES. The Very Reverend Alan Jones has been the dean of Grace Cathedral in San Francisco since 1985. Before that he served as the Stephen F. Bayne Professor of Ascetical Theology at the General Theological Seminary in New York City from 1972 to 1982. Dr. Jones was the director and founder of the Center for Christian Spirituality, at the General Theological Seminary. Dr. Jones took a doctorate in 1971 at the University of Nottingham, England, and was awarded an Order of the British Empire in June 2002. He is a prolific author.

Unique among cathedrals, Grace Cathedral serves not only as a notable tourist destination and prominent gathering place in times of civic celebration or distress but also as home to a vibrant, active, and diverse resident congregation. It is a community based in fellowship, witness, spiritual development, and service. Encompassing the full spectrum of human experience, membership in the congregation at Grace Cathedral offers the opportunity to explore virtually any interest or affinity within the context of a nurturing Christian community.

Grace Cathedral
1100 California St., San Francisco, CA 94108
415-749-6321
alanj@gracecathedral.org
www.gracecathedral.org

JON KABAT-ZINN, PhD, is a scientist, writer, and meditation teacher. He is Professor of Medicine emeritus at the University of Massachusetts Medical School, founding executive director of the Center for Mindfulness in Medicine, Health Care, and Society and founder (in 1979) of its world-renowned Stress Reduction Clinic. Kabat-Zinn is the author of several bestselling books. His work has contributed to a growing movement of mindfulness into mainstream institutions in our society such as medicine, health care and hospitals, the law, schools, corporations, prisons, and professional sports. He is a board member of the Mind and Life Institute, a group that organizes dialogues between the Dalai Lama and Western scientists to promote a deeper understanding of different ways of knowing and probing the nature of mind, emotions, and reality.

University of Massachusetts Medical School
55 Lake Avenue North, Shaw Building, Worcester, MA 01655
508-856-2656
mindfulness@umassmed.edu
www.umassmed.edu

BYRON KATIE. In 1986 Byron Kathleen Reid suddenly woke up to reality, which she experienced as a state of unending love, gratitude, and joy. Out of this experience came a simple method of self-inquiry that she calls The Work. Katie's Work — four simple questions and a turnaround — gives form to her awareness and has helped hundreds of thousands of people in over thirty countries to bring radical understanding to their lives. As Katie says, "An unquestioned mind is the only world of suffering." Byron Katie International, Inc. offers free events throughout the world in which Katie does The Work with as many audience members as time allows. It also offers two-day intensives and the nine-day School for The Work with Byron Katie. The Work of Byron Katie Foundation is a nonprofit organization that provides educational materials free to all who request them and sponsors the training of educators, therapists, and prison-workers.

The Work of Byron Katie Foundation
P.O. Box 2110, Manhattan Beach, CA 90267
310-760-9000
info@thework.com
www.lovingwhatis.com

CONNIE KISHBAUGH, RN, BSN, OCN, has been a nurse working with people with cancer for more than thirty years. She feels she was awakened to the truth and beauty of the human spirit by her participation in their journeys. She is currently in private practice in Sacramento, California.

Her practice of healing the human spirit focuses on the person with cancer, as well as their family and loved ones. Connie provides a loving environment in which Living Essence sessions and bodywork with Reiki and massage are used to awaken and deepen her clients' experience of their truest self. Loss and grief sessions, as well as counseling in nutrition, fatigue management, and treatment-symptom control are intricate parts of the practice. Close communication with the client's oncologist is maintained throughout the course of care.

2607 Portola Way, Sacramento, CA 95818
916-731-4742
connie@cancerspirithealing.com
www.cancerspirithealing.com

FRED KOFMAN is the president and co-founder of Axialent, an international consulting company. He holds a doctorate in economics from the University of California, Berkeley. Kofman was a professor of management accounting and control systems at MIT's Sloan School of Management and senior researcher at Peter Senge's Organizational Learning Center. Fred focuses on leadership development, helping companies such as General Motors, Chrysler, EDS, Shell, Microsoft, Citibank, and Cisco in the United States, Europe, and Latin America. Fred teaches leadership programs at Notre Dame University, Naropa University, and Ken Wilber's Integral Institute.

Axialent is an international consulting company focused on the development of leadership, teamwork, and individual effectiveness. Axialent's work is based on Ken Wilber's integral model, which combines cognitive disciplines such as strategy and problem-solving with behavioral skills such as conflict resolution and performance feedback, and emotional competencies such as self-awareness and empathy.

Axialent
801 Brickell Ave., Suite 220, Miami, FL 33131
corporate@axialent.com
www.axialent.com

JACK KORNFIELD was trained as a Buddhist monk in Thailand, Burma, and India, and has taught around the world since 1974. He also holds a doctorate in clinical psychology. A co-founder of the Insight Meditation Society and of the Spirit Rock Center, he lives in Northern California with his wife and daughter.

Spirit Rock Meditation Center is dedicated to the teachings of the Buddha as presented in the Vipassana tradition. The practice of mindful awareness, called insight or Vipassana meditation, is at the heart of all the activities at Spirit Rock. The center hosts a full program of ongoing classes, daylong retreats, and residential retreats.

Spirit Rock Meditation Center
P.O. Box 169, Woodacre, CA 94973
415-488-0164
www.spiritrock.org

JOE KRESSE is a volunteer at the Foundation for Global Community, where he writes for its publication, *Timeline*, and coordinates its Business and Sustainability Group. He is a former partner of an international public accounting firm and received a bachelor's in economics and an MBA from Stanford.

The Foundation for Global Community is a nonprofit educational organization dedicated to building a world that works for all life. Recognizing that natural, social, and economic systems are all parts of an interconnected whole, the foundation has been promoting cultural change, facilitating personal development, and strengthening community connections for over fifty years. The foundation's Business and Sustainability

Group educates companies about the principles of sustainable development and promotes a broader measurement of business success, the "Triple Bottom Line."

The Foundation for Global Community
222 High St., Palo Alto, CA 94301
650-328-7756, ext. 317
jkresse@globalcommunity.org
www.globalcommunity.org

STANLEY KRIPPNER is the Alan Watts Professor of Psychology at Saybrook Graduate School and Research Center in San Francisco, California. He works with students who are members of the "consciousness and spirituality" concentration at Saybrook. Saybrook Graduate School and Research Center is an accredited at-a-distance graduate institution that gives master's and doctoral degrees in psychology, human science, and organizational systems. Stanley Krippner teaches courses in consciousness studies and transpersonal psychology. The most popular course is "Personal Mythology and Dreamworking," which is taught online. Krippner also supervises master's theses and doctoral dissertations and directs research projects as Saybrook's Chair for the Study of Consciousness.

Stanley Krippner
450 Pacific Ave., San Francisco, CA 94133
415-394-5979
skrippner@saybrook.edu
www.stanleykrippner.com

LINDA LANTIERI has over thirty-five years of experience in the field of education as a classroom teacher, administrator, and university professor. Currently she serves as the director of Project Renewal, a project of the Tides Center. She is also the director of the New York Satellite Office of the Collaborative for Academic, Social, and Emotional Learning (CASEL).

Project Renewal serves New York City teachers, counselors, administrators, and others working with young people as they continue the recovery process after September 11. Their goal is to take care of the caregivers, both to strengthen their ability to thrive when faced with unprecedented circumstances and to renew their spirits and sense of purpose.

Project Renewal
40 Exchange Pl., Suite 1111, New York, NY 10011
212-509-0022, ext. 226
llantieri@worldnet.att.net
www.projectrenewal-tidescenter.org

GEORGE LEONARD has been called by *Newsweek* "the granddaddy of the consciousness movement." He has published many books and award-winning essays and formally served as a senior editor for *Look* magazine. Currently he is president emeritus of the Esalen Institute and co-founder of Integral Transformative Practice. Additionally, Leonard holds a fifth-degree black belt in aikido, is a talented jazz pianist, and has written a musical comedy, *Clothes*. Integral Transformative Practice (ITP) grew from a two-year experimental class in human transformation conducted by Leonard and Michael Murphy, beginning in 1992. Its goal is to integrate mind, body, heart, and soul, while facilitating positive change through practice.

www.ITP-life.com

BRUCE H. LIPTON, PhD, is a cellular biologist, author, and former associate professor at the University of Wisconsin's School of Medicine. His pioneering research on cloned human cells at the University of Wisconsin and at Stanford University School of Medicine presaged the field of epigenetics, the mechanism by which nurture controls nature.

2574 Pine Flat Rd., Santa Cruz, CA 95060

831-454-0606

bruce@brucelipton.com

www.brucelipton.com

PAUL LOWE has devoted himself to the study of human potential, meditation, and spiritual practice. He is a highly trained personal development coach and spiritual teacher. Paul tours Europe and North America each summer doing evening, daylong, weekend, and longer gatherings. At these events he helps the participants see themselves more clearly, creating the possibility for change in a supportive and fun atmosphere. He also maintains a Web site where one can download articles, order books and tapes, and see the schedule of upcoming events.

www.paullowe.org

GAY LUCE is a writer and teacher who founded the Nine Gates Mystery School. In addition to teaching at Nine Gates, she is working on the design of a mystery school for young people aged nine to twenty-two.

The Nine Gates Programs, Inc. offers intensive, multicultural spiritual experiences and training from the world's major wisdom streams, structured along the energy gates of the body so that each person can access and consciously use his or her subtle energy system. They envision people awakening to their essential nature, experiencing union with the Divine and fully embracing the mystery of life as it embraces and challenges them, calling forth their inner wisdom and individual gifts in the service of the world.

The Nine Gates Programs
437 Sausalito St., Corte Madera, CA 94925
415-927-1677 or 916-660-1962
gluce@ninegates.org
ww.ninegates.org

MARLENA LYONS. See Jett Psaris.

PETER AND ANEETA MAKENA are singers/songwriters and facilitate Heartdance and Voice seminars. Peter gives concerts where he shares his ecstatic poetry and songs. They have been doing this work for twenty-five years, all over the globe. Peter and Aneeta now live in Northern California and give workshops and concerts in Europe and the western states.

19560 Stonegate Rd., Middletown, CA 95461
707-987-8132
pmakena@earthlink.net
www.petermakena.com

MARY MANIN MORRISSEY founded and for twenty-three years served as senior minister of Living Enrichment Center in Portland, Oregon. Mary holds a master's degree in psychology, was ordained in 1975, and received an honorary doctorate of Humane Letters in 1999. Mary's global audience is a tribute to her clarity, dedicated service, and a universal approach. Co-founder of the Association for Global New Thought, Mary has twice spoken at the United Nations and co-convened conferences with His Holiness the Dalai Lama.

Mary Morrissey Ministries
16044 S.W. Wimbledon Ct., Tigard, OR 97224
503-799-2133
mmmorrissey@aol.com
www.marymorrisseyministries.com

BARBARA MARX HUBBARD, renaissance woman, evolutionary explorer, social innovator, and author, is president of the Foundation for Conscious Evolution. A tireless champion for the earth's future since the 1960s, pioneering the use of media for global peace, she made history in 1984 when her name was placed in nomination for the vice presidency at the Democratic National Convention.

The Foundation for Conscious Evolution was formed to educate and communicate the worldview of conscious evolution. Its website is a global community center for conscious evolution, designed to empower a critical mass of co-creators to shift humanity toward a future equal to our full potential. The Evolve "Living School" offers learning resources for personal and social transformation, and the Gateway to Conscious Evolution is the premier educational offering of the Living School. Through the Gateway process they have co-created an evolutionary learning community dedicated to learning what it means "to be the change" we wish to see and to apply that understanding in co-creative action for the healing and evolving of our world.

The Foundation for Conscious Evolution

P.O. Box 4698, Santa Barbara, CA 93140-4698

805-682-3222

fce@evolve.org

www.evolve.org

SHANTIMAYI is the first woman (let alone Westerner) to inherit a seat among the line of ancient Sacha Masters. Sacha exists for the purpose of universal enlightenment. "The Pathless Way," through heart wisdom and a wide-open mind, cultivates a transparent and insightful view into our essential nature. Ganesh Foundation in the United States and the Netherlands, and the Ganesh Society in Australia, are all founded by ShantiMayi. These organizations support ShantiMayi's satsangs, Sacha ashrams, and charitable work worldwide. ShantiMayi's website is a rich journal of spiritual food and offerings and lists ashram addresses as well as her travel schedule.

www.shantimayi.com

AMY MCCARREL has studied the movement of the spirit through the arts of yoga, poetry, dance, and scripture. She is committed to bringing the light from sacred arts and discipline into the daily lives of the individuals and communities she works with. Amy holds a bachelor's degree in poetry as well as dance from Naropa University. She is a longtime apprentice of both David Deida and Sofia Diaz, combining insight with embodiment throughout her studies. Amy has been leading an ongoing committed women's group in Boulder, Colorado, for several years, as well as teaching women's weekends throughout the world. When she's not traveling she teaches Hatha yoga for men and women and gives private sessions by phone and in person.

amy@womenstent.com

www.womenstent.com

CORINNE MCLAUGHLIN is co-author of *Spiritual Politics: Changing the World from the Inside Out* (foreword by the Dalai Lama) and *Builders of the Dawn*. She is co-founder with Gordon Davidson of the Center for Visionary Leadership, based in Washington, DC, and San Francisco. She is also co-founder of Sirius, a spiritual, ecological community in Massachusetts. She coordinated a national task force for President Clinton's Council on Sustainable Development and taught politics at American University. A Fellow of the World Business Academy and of the Findhorn Foundation in Scotland, Corinne provides training and consulting services to business, government, and nonprofit organizations. She writes regularly for the Center for Visionary Leadership's monthly e-newsletter, *Soul Light*, and has recorded several CDs entitled *Creative Meditation, Mastering Time, Money as a Spiritual Asset*, and *Being a Practical Visionary*.

The Center for Visionary Leadership
369 Third St., #563, San Rafael, CA 94901
415-472-2540
corinnemc@visionarylead.org
www.visionarylead.org

MITEN. See Deva Premal.

DR. RICHARD MOSS. Once a practitioner of traditional medicine, Dr. Richard Moss left his hospital practice in the late seventies. Catalyzed by a life-changing realization, he has since dedicated his life to helping people achieve a unique and fulfilling human wellness, using an integrative approach to healing that unites body, mind, and spirit.

Richard Moss has been recognized for the past twenty-seven years as one of the leading educators in the transformational self-realization movement, and his work has inspired changes of consciousness in students, health care, business, and teaching organizations throughout the world. Richard Moss Seminars organizes and coordinates the conferences, talks, and seminars taught by Dr. Moss, as well as producing all of his books and tapes, thus furthering his dedication to a global conscious awakening.

Richard Moss Seminars
P.O. Box 1379, Ojai, CA 93024
805-640-0632 or 800-647-0755
miracle2@sierratel.com
www.richardmoss.com

MICHAEL MURPHY is co-founder and chairman of the board of the Esalen Institute. Murphy was born in Salinas, California, graduated from Stanford University, and lived for a year at the Sri Aurobindo Ashram in Pondicherry, India. In 1980 he helped initiate Esalen's Soviet-American Exchange Program, which was a premier diplomacy vehicle for citizen-to-citizen relations, and which played a significant role in breaking down the barriers between the Russian and American peoples. During his forty-two-year involvement in the human potential movement, Murphy and his work have been profiled in *The New Yorker* and featured in many magazines and journals worldwide. Esalen, the world's most famous growth center, is also a groundbreaking research site. Preparatory work for his book *The Future of the Body* began in 1977 with the building of an archive of more than ten thousand studies of exceptional human functioning. The archive has been donated to the University of California at Santa Barbara.

www.esalen.org

SATYAM NADEEN resides in Atlanta and facilitates weekend satsang retreats at the Pura Vida resort in the Blue Ridge Mountains once a month. He also facilitates a weeklong retreat quarterly at the Pura Vida Spa in Costa Rica.

www.satyamnadeen.com

DAVID G. NEENAN is the chairman and CEO of the Neenan Company, which he founded in 1973. He has shared his expertise with others by conducting "Business & You" workshops around the world, as well as several other workshops and in-house training for numerous organizations over the course of many years. He is a prominent national and local speaker, seminar leader, and business consultant.

The Neenan Company develops, finances, designs, and constructs medical, office, commercial, and industrial buildings under a concept called Archistruction. This approach blends all disciplines into high-performance teams for seamless delivery of value for clients. Their approximate revenue in 2003 was $120 million.

The Neenan Company
2620 East Prospect Rd., Suite 100, Fort Collins, CO 80525
970-493-8747
david.neenan@neenan.com
www.neenan.com

JAMES O'DEA, president of the Institute of Noetic Sciences, was formerly director of the Washington, DC, office of Amnesty International and executive director of the Seva Foundation. He is passionate about applying IONS' research to personal and social healing in our challenging times.

The Institute of Noetic Sciences employs the rigor of science, balanced by personal and collective wisdom, to support a global shift in consciousness. They serve an emerging movement of globally conscious citizens dedicated to manifesting our highest capacities. They are a nonprofit membership organization.

The Institute of Noetic Sciences
101 San Antonio Rd., Petaluma, CA 94952
707-775-3500
membership@noetic.org
www.noetic.org

TERRY-ANNE PAQUETTE was introduced to Waldorf education when her son, Joshua, enrolled as a third grader at Mariposa Waldorf School in Grass Valley, California. The soul- and spirit-filled community touched a place in her heart that she had longed for but had not previously experienced. While training at Rudolf Steiner College in Fair Oaks, California, she began a home Waldorf-inspired preschool called Heavenly Days. Subsequently she has taught at the Portland Waldorf School and the Mariposa Waldorf School and in 1994 helped found the Yuba River Charter, the first public Waldorf-methods charter school in the country. They presently serve approximately 250 children, preschool to eighth grade. The school is a community of families and teachers using teaching methods that nourish and educate the child.

Yuba River Charter School
13026 Bitney Springs Rd., Building #3, Nevada City, CA 95959
530-272-8078
terryanne@theunion.net
www.yrcs.tresd.k12.ca.us

SANDFORD AND SUSANNA PERRETT are deepening in their lives in a brave, real-life inquiry into the heart of embodied spiritual freedom and love. This includes sexuality, intimate relationship, work, and community. In this work they are inspired by David Deida and his teachers.

Sandford and Susanna founded a living community that consists of men, women, and children residing at Eldtjärn Life Temple in Sweden. It is an environment deeply committed to exploring the creation of sacred, creative living and the practical support of each other in giving the deepest gifts in the intensity and simplicity of daily life. Zoe Life is an organization that works with individuals and companies to align themselves and develop the tools to operate in this world from that perspective. The Perretts are currently on an indefinite break from teaching and live in Adelaide, Australia.

Zoe Life
info@zoelife.nu
www.zoelife.nu

STEPHEN G. POST, PhD, is president of the Institute for Research on Unlimited Love — Altruism, Compassion, Service, which applies scientific methods to unlimited love in human moral and spiritual experience within the wider context of a dialogue between science and spirituality.

Their goal is to use the very best science in better understanding the human capacity for generous love, and the role of culture and religion/spirituality in extending this love to all humanity.

216-368-6205
sgp2@case.edu
www.unlimitedloveinstitute.org

DEVA PREMAL AND MITEN have released ten CDs since meeting in India in 1990, including the bestsellers *The Essence, Love Is Space, Embrace,* and *Songs for the Inner Lover.*

They have appeared in twenty-one countries, sold over three hundred thirty thousand CDs, and have played for His Holiness the Dalai Lama. Their first book, *More Than Music: The Deva Premal and Miten Story,* was published in May 2004.

Prabhu Music, Bells Associates
Dreikönigstr 6, 79102 Freiburg, Germany
· 49-761-881-4875
rajen@PrabhuMusic.net
www.devapremalmiten.com

JOHN PRENDERGAST, PhD, is an adjunct associate professor of psychology at the California Institute of Integral Studies, author, and psychotherapist in private practice in San Rafael, California. He studied for many years with the European sage Jean Klein and more recently with Adyashanti.

The Conference on Nondual Wisdom and Psychotherapy, sponsored by the Center for Timeless Wisdom and held annually since 1998, explores the interface of nondual wisdom traditions, from both East and West, with the practice of modern psychotherapy. The conference is designed for mental health professionals interested in investigating the impact of spiritual awakening — the seeing through of the separative sense of self — on both therapists and clients. Practitioners of other healing arts as well as the general public are welcome to participate.

900 5th Ave., Suite #203, San Rafael, CA 94901
415-453-8832
jjprendergast@earthlink.net

JETT PSARIS AND MARLENA LYONS are the co-founders of the Conscious Living Center, a counseling and workshop center in the San Francisco Bay Area. They have been leading seminars and retreats that guide couples and individuals to cultivate the capacity for undefended love — with oneself as well as with others — since 1990.

Through their work together, they have gone beyond researching the reasons that people have failed to create exceptional relationships and have developed a unique approach to accelerate personal and relationship development, allowing individuals to connect with themselves and each other in an undefended and open way.

The Conscious Living Center is a counseling and workshop center for the pursuit of sustainable intimacy with oneself and others.

The Conscious Living Center
13800 Skyline Blvd., Oakland, CA 94619
510-777-9998
jett@undefendedlove.com
www.undefendedlove.com

ROBERT RABBIN is a writer, speaker, and spiritual activist whose passion for radically engaged spiritual wisdom is expressed in his lectures, workshops, and column of social commentary. Robert has published numerous books and articles about mysticism and socially engaged spirituality; he is a frequent speaker at national conferences.

Since 1985 Robert has been lecturing and leading seminars and Truth Talks throughout the country, coaching corporate leaders, and designing spirit-based retreats for executive teams and organizations. In 2004 he created Radical Sages: An Evolution of Spiritual Action, a global movement seeking to promote the highest expression of our common humanity as the medicine to heal our troubled world.

info@radicalsages.com

www.radicalsages.com

PAUL H. RAY, PhD, is a sociologist who has taught and done social research for forty years in academia, the government, and business. He's been on a spiritual path for twenty-five years and has taught meditation and done spiritual counseling. Co-author of *The Cultural Creatives: How 50 Million People Are Changing the World*, Paul is currently writing several books on the prospects for a planetary Wisdom Civilization and on authenticity in business. Paul is a founding partner of Integral Partnerships, LLC, which helps businesses and nonprofits develop authentic and transformative relationships, both with their constituencies and markets and within their organizations. It is especially valuable for organizations whose clients are "cultural creatives" or who work on ecological sustainability and socially responsible business.

415-897-2894

paul@culturalcreatives.org or paul@integralpartnerships.com

www.culturalcreatives.org and www.integralpartnerships.com

PAUL JOHN ROACH is a native of Wales. A graduate of Jesus College, Oxford University, he has bachelor's and master's degrees in English and a postgraduate degree in education. Paul has been the minister at Unity Church of Fort Worth since 1988, after ordination from Unity Ministerial School in Kansas City, Missouri. He has traveled extensively throughout the world, including extended stays in India and Nepal. He is a writer, poet, and amateur actor and loves walking and hiking.

Unity Church of Fort Worth is dedicated to teaching and living the transformative message of Jesus Christ in a loving community that celebrates the Christ Spirit in all people. A nondenominational spiritual movement over one hundred years old, unity teaches that through a practical understanding and application of what Jesus taught, every person can realize and express his or her divine potential for a happier, fuller, and more successful life.

Unity Church of Fort Worth

5051 Trail Lake Dr., Fort Worth, TX 76133

817-423-2965

unityfw@dfw.net

UnityFortWorth.org

PETER RUSSELL, MA, DCS, is the author of ten books and the producer of two award-winning videos. His work integrates Eastern and Western understandings of the mind, exploring their relevance to the world today and to humanity's future. He has degrees in theoretical physics, experimental psychology, and computer science from Cambridge University. In India he studied meditation and Eastern philosophy, and on his return took up research into the psychophysiology of meditation at the University of Bristol.

Peter was one of the first people to introduce human potential seminars into the corporate field, and for twenty years worked with major corporations on creativity, learning methods, stress management, and personal development. His principal interest is the inner challenges of the times we are passing through. His books include *The Global Brain*, *Waking Up in Time*, and most recently *From Science to God*.

3020 Bridgeway, PMB 307, Sausalito, CA 94965

707-763-0480

petertl@peterussell.com

www.peterussell.com

ISAAC SHAPIRO loves to love and is passionate in this love affair. He enjoys meeting other lovers of Reality and exploring the intricacies and delicacies of this exquisite moment-by-moment dance of life. He travels worldwide and in his meetings invites all to live and embody this fire that consumes us and leaves only love. People who love his work invite him to hold meetings in various cities around the world. In these meetings the knowing of what is real is tangible and invites transformation. He also holds retreats in Europe and Australia.

Prashant, Grays Ln., Tyagarah, N.S.W. 2481 Australia

61-(0)266-847-519

namaskar@ozemail.com.au

www.isaacshapiro.de

LEONARD SHLAIN is a surgeon and professor of surgery in San Francisco who has written three national bestsellers. They cover such diverse subjects as the relationship between art and physics, the impact of alphabet literacy on gender relations and religion throughout history, and the evolutionary history of male-female relationships. He is currently working on a fourth entitled *Leonardo's Brain: The Roots of Creativity*.

Lshlain@aol.com

JACQUELYN SMALL is a pioneer in the field of spiritual psychology and human consciousness research. She has written seven books on these subjects and is the founding director of Eupsychia Institute. She lives in Austin, Texas.

Eupsychia Institute is a nonprofit service organization that certifies students in Soul-based Psychology and Integrative Breathwork under Jacquelyn's direction. Their workshop intensives are conducted throughout the United States. Jacquelyn is a popular national speaker and workshop presenter who consults with mental health and addiction programs throughout the United States.

Eupsychia Institute
950 Roadrunner Rd., Austin, TX 78746
512-327-2214
jacquie@austin.rr.com
www.eupsychia.com

GREG STELTENPOHL guided Odwalla from its inception in 1980 through 1998. He led the company through its transformation from a small start-up venture to a publicly held corporation with a growth rate exceeding 50 percent per year. In building the organization, he focused on putting into action the ideals of environmental awareness, employee empowerment, creative corporate culture, and community support. After leaving the company he began to work with Visa founder Dee Hock on establishing the Chaordic Alliance and the Chaordic Commons for the purpose of bringing the principles of dynamic natural systems into the world of networks, organizations, and enterprise. Greg's current work is to provide loving support to his family and to launch Interra, a membership-based citizen empowerment initiative with the mission of exercising economic democracy. Its design is based on the technology of loyalty platforms using the global electronic exchange system put to the new purpose of a world that works for all.

The Interra Project
322 Cumberland St., San Francisco, CA 94114
info@interraproject.org
www.interraproject.org

JOSEPH L. SUBBIONDO, president of California Institute for Integral Studies, is a historian of linguistics currently researching the relationship between consciousness and language. He has served in a number of faculty and administrative positions, and he contributes regularly to studies on higher education.

California Institute of Integral Studies (CIIS) is an accredited graduate school with a focus on the interaction of Eastern and Western perspectives, offering master's and doctoral degrees in humanities, psychology, and social sciences. In addition to its degree programs, CIIS offers a full range of lifelong learning programs.

The California Institute of Integral Studies
1453 Mission St., San Francisco, CA 94103
415-575-6105
jsubbiondo@ciis.edu
www.ciis.edu

LAMA SURYA DAS is one of the foremost Western lamas and Buddhist teachers, and founder of the Dzogchen Meditation Centers. He twice completed the traditional three-year, three-month, three-day Tibetan meditation retreats at his teacher's monastery cloister.

Lama Surya Das is the author of the bestselling *Awakening the Buddha Within* and five other books, as well as innumerable published essays. A poet and translator, he is a regular columnist on Beliefnet.com, leads retreats around the world, and is active in interfaith dialogue and charitable work in Asian countries. He lived in the Himalayas for fifteen years, and with His Holiness the Dalai Lama founded the Western Buddhist Teachers Conferences.

The Dzogchen Center conducts meditation retreats, workshops, classes, and other activities in the *dzogchen* tradition of Tibetan Buddhism, including a hundred-day annual retreat at the Dzogchen Retreat Center outside Austin, Texas. Founded by Lama Surya Das in 1991, it is dedicated to transmission and transformation via Buddhist ethics, wisdom practices, and compassionate action in a manner accessible to all.

The Dzogchen Center
P.O. Box 400734, Cambridge, MA 02140
617-628-1702
surya@dzogchen.org
www.dzogchen.org

RUSSELL TARG is a physicist and author, a pioneer in the development of the laser and laser applications, and co-founder of the Stanford Research Institute's investigation into psychic abilities in the 1970s and 1980s. His work in this new area, called remote viewing, has been widely published. During the 1970s and 1980s, Stanford Research Institute (SRI) carried out investigations of our ability to experience and describe distant events blocked from ordinary perception. The research was supported by the CIA and many other government organizations for gathering intelligence about worldwide activities during the Cold War. Targ teaches extrasensory perception, precognition, and intuitive diagnosis.

1010 Harriet St., Palo Alto, CA 94301
650-323-8550
russell@targ.com
www.espresearch.com

CHRISTOPHER TITMUS teaches spiritual awakening and insight meditation worldwide. A former Buddhist monk in Thailand and India, he is the director of the Dharma Facilitators Program and leads dharma gatherings and pilgrimages. Poet and author of fourteen books on spirituality, Christopher lives in Devon, England. He is co-founder of Gaia House in Devon, an international retreat center.

Christopher leads annual retreats in all parts of the world and offers programs for experienced dharma students to develop skills in deepening their understanding and for leadership training. As a member of the international advisory board of the Buddhist

Peace Fellowship, he engages in peace campaigns and global issues, including peace pilgrimages, conferences, and demonstrations.

Gaia House
West Ogwell, Newton Abbot, Devon, TQ12 6EN, England
(44) 1626-333613
christopher@insightmeditation.org
www.insightmeditation.org

ECKHART TOLLE is an inspiring spiritual teacher who is not aligned with any particular religion or tradition but does not exclude any. He is the author of *The Power of Now*, a *New York Times* bestseller that has been widely recognized as one of the most influential spiritual books of our time.

Eckhart Teachings organizes Eckhart Tolle's Talks, Intensives, and Retreats throughout the world. They also record, publish, license, and distribute tapes, CDs, videos, and DVDs of his teaching events.

Eckhart Teachings
P.O. Box 93661, Nelson Park RPO, Vancouver, BC V6E 4L7
604-893-8500
info@eckharttolle.com
www.eckharttolle.com

LYNNE TWIST is a fund-raiser, global activist, author, and teacher, as well as founder of the Soul of Money Institute and the Pachamama Alliance. She has devoted her life to service in support of global sustainability, human rights, economic integrity, and spiritual authenticity.

The Soul of Money Institute is an expression of Lynne's life commitment to transformation. The institute offers a wide range of opportunities to connect with the transformational possibilities inherent in our individual and institutional relationships with money. Through workshops, consultations, and keynote addresses, the institute enables individuals, businesses, and organizations to find peace, freedom, and sufficiency in their relationship with money and to generate an expanding flow of resources toward the affirmation of life and the common good.

The Soul of Money Institute
3 Fifth Ave., San Francisco, CA 94118
415-386-5599
info@soulofmoney.org
www.soulofmoney.org

ERIC UTNE is the founder of *Utne Reader* magazine, a digest of "the best of the alternative press," which began publishing in 1984. From 2000 to 2002 he was a seventh- and eighth-grade teacher at City of Lakes Waldorf School. In the fall of 2004 he launched *Cosmo Doogood's Urban Almanac*, an urban version of the old farmers' almanacs. He lives in Minneapolis, Minnesota, with his wife, Nina, and their four sons.

4025 Linden Hills Blvd., Minneapolis, MN 55410

cosmo@cosmosurbanalmanac.com

www.cosmosurbanalmanac.com

FRANCES VAUGHAN, PhD, is a psychologist practicing in Mill Valley, California, and author of several books integrating psychology and spirituality. She was formerly on the clinical faculty at the University of California, Irvine, and has served as president of the associations for transpersonal and humanistic psychology. She is a trustee of the Fetzer Institute.

10 Millwood St., Suite 3, Mill Valley, CA 94941-2066

415-383-2050

email@francesvaughan.com

www.francesvaughan.com

JOYCE AND BARRY VISSELL. Joyce, RN, MS, and Barry, MD, have been a couple committed to the sacred path of relationship since 1964. A nurse and medical doctor, respectively, their focus of service since 1972 has been counseling and teaching. As a result of the worldwide interest in their books, they travel internationally teaching about personal growth, relationship, parenting, and healing. Their model of relationship and deeply heart-oriented approach have had a unique impact on thousands of people's lives. They are the founders and directors of the Shared Heart Foundation, a nonprofit organization dedicated to bringing more love to all relationships.

Shared Heart Foundation

P.O. Box 2140, Aptos, CA 95001

800-766-0629 or 831-684-2299

barry@sharedheart.org

www.sharedheart.org

NEALE DONALD WALSCH has been a newspaper reporter and managing editor, a radio station program director, and a public information officer for one of the nation's largest public school systems, creator and owner of his own advertising and marketing firm, and a nationally syndicated radio talk show host. He has now "retired" from his career in communications arts to pursue his vision of a world in which people no longer live in fear of God or of each other.

He has written fifteen books, including five *New York Times* bestsellers. His latest title is *What God Wants*. Neale is the founder of Conversations with God Foundation, a nonprofit organization that sponsors lectures, workshops, and retreats around the world for people interested in personal growth and spiritual understanding. Neale has a home in southern Oregon.

Humanity's Team is a grassroots initiative that seeks to free people from the oppression of its beliefs about God, about life, and about themselves in order to create a different world.

Humanity's Team

1257 Siskiyou Blvd., PMB 1150, Ashland, OR 97520

541-482-8806

neale@nealedonaldwalsch.com

www.nealedonaldwalsch.com and www.cwg.org

PAMELA WILSON. As a child Pamela realized something was amiss in the world. The human condition of discord, dissatisfaction, and unhappiness was not appealing. TM, the Sedona Method, and sheer exhaustion dropped her at satsang's door. Grace liberated her from society's hypnosis, and peace remained.

Pamela accepts invitations from individuals and groups throughout the world to hold satsangs and retreats and give private sessions. Her vision is the nondualism brought into focus so luminously by the great Indian sage Ramana Maharshi. Her satsangs celebrate self-inquiry, clarity, and kindness. Fellowship of the Heart is the church that supports Pamela's work.

Fellowship of the Heart

P.O. Box 747, Tesuque, NM 87574

530-628-5783

tonyk@sonic.net

www.pamelasatsang.com

JOHN ZWERVER, MA (SWP), co-director of Global Family, has over three decades of experience in senior management, planning, training, and leadership development in Canada, the United States, and abroad. He has also been a consultant to social service agencies, government ministries, and a wide range of foundations and organizations.

For contact information, see Carolyn Anderson.

INDEX

art and creativity, 221–47; *American Beauty*, 236–39; Andy Desmond (Miten), 239–41, 242; the body as an instrument, 244–46; film, 233–39; humor as translucent art, 243–44; Iago-driven, 222–25; Leonard Cohen, 229–33, 234; life as, 243; N.A.M. (New Age Mush), 227–28; nudging into transcendence, 246–47; stepping aside (techniques), 241–43; translucent, through the artist, not from the artist, 221–22, 225–27, 228–47; what makes art great, 233–36

Art of Sexual Ecstasy (Anand), 170

AT&T, 311

awakening (radical awakening, consciousness shift, enlightenment), 5, 50, 52–53; collective, 40–41, 54, 80–84, 418–26; extreme experience and, 35; as fruit of practice, 33–34; gender transcendence, 176; identity shift, 74–84; impact of, 44–48; "impersonal enlightenment," 81–82; initiation into endless evolution, 47–48, 54, 100; living it, 3–6, 435–36; many portals to, 35–36, 39–41; meeting in Being and, 152–54; myths about, 74, 101, 126, 147, 171, 199, 200, 226, 259, 288–89, 327, 364, 411–12; oneness, realization of, 25–26; people experiencing, 1–2, 6–7, 25–26, 27, 32, 33–36; personal belief system

and, 45–46; phrase or word leading to, 34–35; as portal to translucent life, 7; provoking, 7, 34–40; reentry high, 46; self-inquiry and exercise, 36–38; total supreme enlightenment, 46–47; translucent psychotherapy following, 351–54; waking down, 44–45; Waking Down in Mutuality, 84–86; what occurs in moment of, 7, 26–27, 30, 31–36, 39–40, 101, 321, 364; when things fall apart and, 31–32

Axialent, 285

Ayurveda, 338–40

B

Bache, Chris, 399, 406, 431

Ball, Alan, 228, 234, 236–39

Barnett, Michael, 135, 145–46, 148, 380–81

Bayliss, Roger, 284

Beatles, 225

beliefs and belief systems: actions based on, 92–101; anatomy of, 94–97; dissolving, 116; on education, 251, 252–59; fundamentalism, 100–101, 116, 361–63, 373, 387, 396, 407, 414–15; healing and, 334–35; Katie's four questions and a "turnaround," 105–6; liquid, 115–16; mistaking thoughts for reality, 101; nudging to translucence, 117–20; parenting, 205, 217; psychotherapy and, 351; put your

ABOUT THE AUTHOR

Arjuna Ardagh is the founder of the Living Essence Foundation in Nevada City, California, a nonprofit church dedicated to the awakening of consciousness within the context of ordinary life. He is the author of *Relaxing into Clear Seeing, How About Now, The Last Laugh* (a novel), and the creator of the *Living Essence Tapes* series.

Ardagh was educated in England, at Kings School, Canterbury, and later at Cambridge University, where he earned a master's degree in literature. Since the age of fourteen he has had a passionate interest in spiritual awakening, and he began to practice meditation and yoga at that time. In his late teens he trained as a meditation teacher. After graduating from Cambridge, Ardagh devoted himself completely to the call he felt inside, and studied and lived with a number of great spiritual teachers, both in Asia and in the United States. In 1987 he founded the Alchemy Institute in Seattle, Washington, and trained several hundred people in a transpersonal approach to hypnotherapy.

In 1991 he returned to India for a period of prolonged meditation and met H. W. L. Poonjaji, a direct devotee of the great sage Ramana Maharshi, with whom he went through a radical shift of perspective. After returning to

Seattle, he began to share this awakened view with other people at Poonjaji's request. He has traveled extensively since then, facilitating a profound shift in awareness with thousands of people throughout the United States and Europe.

Ardagh has developed the Living Essence Training, which prepares people to be facilitators of this shift in consciousness and to cultivate translucence. He speaks at many international conferences and has appeared on TV, on the radio, and in print media in twelve countries. He also teaches the Deeper Love seminars with his Norwegian wife, Chameli Gad Ardagh. They live in Nevada City with his two sons. You may contact him at:

arjuna@translucents.org

www.translucents.org

1-888-VASTNESS

Royalties from this book go to the Living Essence Foundation and are used to promote various programs to facilitate awakening and translucence.